THE 13TH STEP

Thriving in Recovery

Do You Know Who You Am?

Bob Reese, PhD

authorHOUSE

AuthorHouse™
1663 Liberty Drive
Bloomington, IN 47403
www.authorhouse.com
Phone: 1 (800) 839-8640

© 2017 Bob Reese, PhD. All rights reserved.

No part of this book may be reproduced, stored in a retrieval system, or transmitted by any means without the written permission of the author.

Published by AuthorHouse 08/24/2017

ISBN: 978-1-5246-9771-6 (sc)
ISBN: 978-1-5246-9769-3 (hc)
ISBN: 978-1-5246-9770-9 (e)

Library of Congress Control Number: 2017910083

Print information available on the last page.

Any people depicted in stock imagery provided by Thinkstock are models, and such images are being used for illustrative purposes only.
Certain stock imagery © Thinkstock.

This book is printed on acid-free paper.

Because of the dynamic nature of the Internet, any web addresses or links contained in this book may have changed since publication and may no longer be valid. The views expressed in this work are solely those of the author and do not necessarily reflect the views of the publisher, and the publisher hereby disclaims any responsibility for them.

DEDICATION

For all the 'sick and suffering,' may you find your way to recovery.
For everyone who is in recovery, may you thrive and flourish.

For Joan
I could not have written this book without your support and our morning conversations of marriage. Together we are *Magis*!

CONTENTS

Dedication v
Praise for *The 13th Step* xi
Acknowledgements xiii
Foreword: Dr. Warren Bickel.. xv
Prologue... xix

Ch.

PART 1: THE DRINKING YEARS...1

1	Insanity 3
2	The Families 12
3	Changing Times 20
4	Teen Drinking 23
5	College... 31
6	Grief, Relief, and Social Inadequacy................36
7	Purdue ~ Year 2... 46
8	Purdue ~Year 3 53
9	Purdue ~ Year 4 1969 59
10	Boston College... 64
11	Buffalo 68
12	The Jets 79
13	Jets ~ Walt Michaels Era (1977-82) 91
14	The Beginning of an End 97
15	Jets ~ Joe Walton Era (1983-89) 109
16	Jets ~ Steinberg & Coslet Era (1990-93)....................... 126

PART 2: BEGINNINGS OF A SOBER LIFE..............139
- 17   Rehab 141
- 18   The Hard Work Begins 160
- 19   The Coslet Years..172
- 20   The Pete Carroll Year (1994) 185
- 21   The Kotite Debacle..197
- 22   Starting Over.. 208
- 23   Spread Thin...221
- 24   Nuclear Family & Dysfunction 229
- 25   Beginning A New Family – Striving Toward a Functional Dynamic..................................... 248
- 26   Know Who You AM! 258

PART 3: THE 13TH STEP – THRIVING 273
- 27   Fundamentals For Thriving............................275
- 28   Positive Emotions & Thriving........................294
- 29   Forgiveness..307
- 30   Relationships...325
- 31   Neuroplasticity..345
- 32   Wrapping Up 349

EPILOGUE: Help us help others 353

NOTES 357

BIBLIOGRAPHY...371

APPENDIXES
- A.   The 12 Steps of Alcoholics Anonymous 383
- B.   The Enneagram 385
- C.   P-E-A Affirmation 388
- D.   Letting Go...389
- E.   Visualization – Go to Your Room Exercise ..391
- F.   Part 1 Energy Management – The Paper Clip Experiment 393
- G.   Feelazation 399

H.	Savoring: Exercise & Reflection	401
I.	Gratitude Letter	403
J.	Autogenic Training Meditation	404
K.	Compassion and Loving Kindness Meditations	406
L.	Defense Mechanisms	409
M.	Fallacies	411

INDEX **415**

PRAISE FOR *THE 13TH STEP*

Bob has made the real issue of long term recovery clear. What does one do once they are free of the addiction? Just not drinking or using is not enough. You have to get the core and repair what is broken, what drove the addiction. By sharing his story and his journey to recovery and happiness, he gives the insight that is missing from most recovery programs. Dr. Reese then goes into current research and methods to get better.

As a fellow traveler in the world of recovery, I am well aware that treatment has not changed in 50 years and we need to update how we help people with addictions. The only problem I have with this book is I did not write it. If you, or a loved one suffers from an addiction get this book now....

William Horton, Psy.D. MCAP
World #1 Trainer of NLP and addictions expert
Author of *The Alcohol and Addiction Solution*

****

An inspiring account of one person's transition from struggling with addiction to thriving in recovery. Dr. Reese exemplifies that there is life after addiction and demonstrates how he found fulfillment in recovery.

Mikhail Koffarnus, PhD
Research Assistant Professor
Addiction Recovery Research Center
Virginia Tech Carilion Research Institute

ACKNOWLEDGEMENTS

Beyond my loving, supportive wife and partner, Joan, to whom this book is dedicated, I want to acknowledge everyone who contributed to my experiences – positive and negative – as an alcoholic and as a seeker in recovery. I live in gratitude for the lessons learned and the thriving life I now enjoy because of the journey I have trekked and the psychospiritual evolution I have undergone.

I want to especially thank Warren Bickel, director of the Addiction Recovery Research Center (ARRC) at Virginia Tech-Carilion Research Institute (VTCRI), for welcoming me into the research team of the International Quit & Recovery Registry (IQRR) and the Social Interactome Project. You have provided me with a wonderful way to contribute to the recovery community. I extend this thanks to all my young colleagues at ARRC and IQRR. Your enthusiasm, intelligence, industriousness, and tech-savvy not only keeps me on my toes, it also stretches my neuroplasticity and keeps me young.

Finally, I want to thank all my colleagues and in particular my students at Jefferson College of Health Sciences. Having the opportunity to teach at Jefferson contributes to my thriving on a regular basis!

FOREWORD: DR. WARREN BICKEL

In 2011, I met Bob Reese a faculty member at Jefferson School for Health Sciences. I had just moved to a new research institute at Virginia Tech to continue my research on addictions and to lead the Addiction Recovery Research Center. When I met with Bob, he told me that he was in recovery and was interested in getting involved in my research. When I heard this, I was excited. I told him that I had realized that in the field of addiction science that there has been very limited research on individuals in addiction recovery and I wanted to start a program of research. Specifically, I wanted to create a registry for individuals in recovery so that we can learn from success. I asked Bob to assist me on this project. To quote from the movie, Casablanca; "this was the beginning of a beautiful friendship".

As we developed the registry, Bob provided the wise capable voice and perspective that allowed us to understand and be more sensitive to those in recovery as we developed the registry. He also participated in the news conference that introduced the quit and recovery registry along with myself, and the Director of the National Institute on Drug Abuse, Dr. Nora Volkow. Indeed, Bob became a face of our website and what became the International Quit and Recovery Registry. Over the ensuing years, the IQRR has grown and now has over 7,000 registrants in all 50 states, 25 countries and 6 of the 7 continents. And we have been learning from those who have joined the registry, who we call Recovery Heroes. We call them recovery heroes because to move forward in recovery is a heroic effort. And Bob is my recovery hero!

In this memoir/guide, The 13th Step, we learn of about the important events that Bob experienced and what he has learned in his life to thrive in recovery. And what a life Bob has had. We learn about his formative years and the role of alcohol during these experiences such as drinking at age 15. We learn about the football years, when Bob was an AT working for the Buffalo Bills and the New York Jets. Bob tells us how he used to consume codeine to cope with his hangovers and do his job. We see how alcohol permeated some teams and the consequences that resulted. Most importantly, we see the formation of a Recovery Hero who had the courage to push off the bottom, admit his addiction, and move towards a new sober life. Lastly, Bob shares the lessons and approaches that supported him to not just survive, but thrive. I particularly like his "Shields Up" intervention that prevent stress being felt from being insulted or hurt by others. Along the way of Bob's 13th step we can see the human quest for recovery and can see how to overcome challenges in one's life.

As a scientist who studies addiction, I have often sought out those in recovery to hear their stories and learn their process for success. In the 13th Step by Bob Reese, we all have a chance to learn about the pathway into and out of addiction. Bob as a psychologist has also sought out, devised, and implemented a variety of techniques to allow himself not just to survive in recovery, but to thrive. This is a compelling story with a method as well as a message. Read this book and learn the ways of a Recovery Hero.

Warren Bickel, PhD

- Inaugural Holder, Virginia Tech Carilion Behavioral Health Research Professorship
- Director, Addiction Recovery Research Center
- Professor of Psychology, College of Science, Virginia Tech
- Professor of Psychiatry and Behavioral Medicine, Virginia Tech Carilion School of Medicine

Warren Bickel is a world-renowned addiction and recovery researcher. Before joining the Virginia Tech-Carilion Research Institute in Roanoke where he directs the Addiction Recovery Research Institute, Dr. Bickel was the Wilbur D. Mills Chair of Alcoholism and Drug Abuse Prevention and director of the Center for Addiction Research and the Center for the Study of Tobacco Addiction at the University of Arkansas for Medical Sciences.

PROLOGUE

The purpose of this book is to share my personal story to better understand how recovering alcoholics and addicts not only maintain recovery but go on to thrive in life. I call thriving in recovery the *13th Step*. The term 13th Step is inspired by my continued psychospiritual development after joining the 12-Step program of Alcoholics Anonymous. (*I am not saying that a 12-Step program is the only way to sobriety and recovery; it was the program that I used*.)

My research with the International Quit and Recovery Registry and other colleagues impressed on me the importance of telling my story. No one has ever asked those of us in recovery how we maintain it, much less how to thrive in recovery. Briefly for me, maintaining recovery and thriving required realizing the dysfunction that preceded my alcoholic years, that was present during them, that challenged my sobriety, and that threatened maintaining recovery, thriving, and psychospiritual growth. These realizations informed choices and healthy changes required for my maintaining recovery and thriving. My story is told in three parts.

Part 1: *The Drinking Years* lays the foundation for understanding how I became alcoholic and the roles that drinking played in my life. My early life was permeated with dysfunctional relationships rooted in family and cultural traditions. Children, teens, and young adults commonly accept family dysfunction as normal. Normal is not necessarily healthy. How are we to know what is dysfunctional if that is all we know? Dysfunction underlies the insidious nature of addiction. Learning to identify dysfunction is a necessary step in maintaining recovery.

The drinking culture I grew up in primed me for the heavy drinking lifestyle of the NFL. For over 20 years I used booze to celebrate wins, drown losses, work harder, play harder, and relax. As I relate these stories and my *drunkalog*, the reader should keep in mind that it is not my intent to blame my drinking on anyone or any circumstance. While both nature and nurture contributed to my alcoholism, all along the way I always had a choice: I could have stopped drinking. I chose to drink. As typical with addicts, I used people and situations as an excuse to drink, but it was my choice to drink – and unfortunately, I did it with gusto.

The insidiousness of the disease, however, finally caught up to me: my body said "enough" and I began to experience blackouts. After several failed attempts to control my drinking I found myself in the alcohol and addiction rehabilitation unit of South Oaks Psychiatric Hospital on Long Island – where this story begins.

Part 2: Beginnings of a Sober Life is the story of my early sobriety and some of the challenges it brought with the changes necessary to remain in recovery. To rephrase Bette Davis's view of aging for those in recovery: "Recovery is not for sissies!" For an alcoholic, no longer drinking changes *everything*! For instance, while in rehab one day it occurred to me that I didn't even know how to grill a hamburger without a beer in my hand! Without a doubt, getting sober was the hardest thing I have ever done.

While getting sober is extremely difficult, maintaining recovery has its own challenges. The first challenge is overcoming the compulsion to drink or drug. I was fortunate in that I lost the compulsion to drink in a little over a year. For many this compulsion lasts for years. I was also fortunate in that I continued to perform well in my job.

Being a curious fellow, I became interested in the process of recovery. I wanted to know why silly sayings like "one day at a time" and "take it easy" seemed to work? This interest expanded to sport psychology and performance enhancement. My curiosity led me to a Master's in Psychology in 1998 and a PhD in 2005.

In 1996, after five years in recovery, my world was rocked. I was arbitrarily fired from my job of 20 years as head athletic trainer of the New York Jets. Over the next several years my already dysfunctional marriage became even more dysfunctional and progressively toxic and finally ended in divorce.

The 12-Steps and the "Rooms" sustained me throughout my personal *dark night of the soul*. Fearlessly self-examining as required by 12-Step programs was essential to my making decisions and taking actions that define who I am today.

Part 3: The 13th Step – Thriving reflects the evolving positive progression of my journey – and my life just keeps getting better and better. In 12-Step programs there is a promise that in recovery your life will exceed your wildest dreams. For me, that has been the case – and I had some audacious dreams! Realizing this promise is the 13th Step.

I describe simple (not easy) techniques and interventions that have helped me move beyond just maintaining sobriety to thriving in recovery. These techniques helped me discover who I am. They enabled me to learn to respect myself and my own humanity – and that of others. This has not been easy. I have had to learn to set firm boundaries and to stand up for myself and speak out about my beliefs instead of keeping quiet so as not to rock the boat. In order not to be pulled back into the proverbial barrel of crabs, I have had to distance myself from friends and even family – actually friends and family distanced themselves from me as in recovery I grew healthier and I did not run after them! The good news is that I feel I am now a fully functioning, whole person. Because I took the 13th Step, I live in integrity and congruency and I am self-actualizing. I also live in constant gratitude for my recovery process.

These are not merely self-help techniques in the "this worked for me, it will work for you" genre. As an educator and researcher I include research that shows the efficacy of these techniques. Numerous techniques described have been researched in either the field of positive psychology or sport psychology and have been shown to be not only efficacious, but both reliable and valid. The few – like *Shield's Up!* – that have not been previously researched provide opportunity for future study. For readers in academia, please consider my story as a qualitative case study; and even though it is a self-report, it is academically rigorous and is both trustworthy and dependable.

Striving – Surviving – Thriving. During my time as a corporate educator and coach, I taught that victims needed to move from surviving to striving to thriving. These steps, however, are not necessarily linear. They can overlap and repeat. Reflecting on their movement in this book, I consider Part 1 as striving. Striving is a trait inherited from my Dad who also nurtured me to be the best that I could be, regardless of what I was doing. So I strove to be a professional success, a solid provider, and a good father and husband. Because I was striving so hard, I never stopped long enough to recognize that I was neglecting myself and that I was spiraling down into alcoholism.

During my early time in recovery and again in my trek through the dark night of the soul, I felt as if I were just surviving. Many times I described it as holding on by my fingernails. Fortunately, even during my darkest times, I never stopped striving. It was the striving – the belief that something better was ahead – that stimulated me to keep putting one foot in front of the other so I could move beyond just surviving. Striving inspired me to have the courage to self-examine – making a searching and fearless moral inventory of myself became a continual process, not a one-time event.

It wasn't until I took the 13th Step that I came to thrive. Whether or not you achieved sobriety through a 12-Step program you can take the 13th Step – you can thrive in your recovery. As I thrive today, I still continue to strive. Even at age 68 I have lofty dreams and goals. And, as I constantly tell my students, "When goal setting always leave room for *Magis* – even more!"

This book is in large part autobiographical. Many positive and negative experiences are not shared because they are not directly relevant to the topic and would make the book overwhelmingly long. The life experiences that I share are for the purpose of showing the insidious nature of alcoholism; the challenges faced by those seeking sobriety; the changes and challenges needed to stay in recovery; and the eventual ability to thrive in recovery. If alcohol is not your drug of choice, just substitute your addiction – narcotics, stimulants, downers, nicotine, sex, gambling, food, etc. for alcoholism*.

Epilogue. Finally, in the *Epilogue*, I describe some of my research with the Addiction Recovery Research Center (ARRC) and International Quit & Recovery Registry (IQRR), which is dedicated to learning from success in addiction recovery. It is my hope that information and understanding obtained from this Registry can help more of the "sick and suffering" to recover so that they not only maintain recovery, but they also learn to thrive. If you are in recovery from *any* addiction, please register at IQRR and take the surveys that will help inform us of what works to maintain recovery. Become a *Recovery Hero* by helping us help others. <https://quitandrecovery.org/>

*The term *alcoholism* is used to describe people who have such a compulsion to drink that they cannot stop for any length of time. That compulsion *is* the addiction. The reason people are referred to as alcoholics as opposed to alcohol addicts stems from the medical definition of addiction. This is based on the plasma life of the drug. For example, heroin remains in the bloodstream for 4-6 hours. Therefore, a heroin addict needs a fix every 4-6 hours. An ounce of alcohol is generally metabolized every hour. To become addicted to alcohol, you would need a fix every hour. While alcohol addiction does occur, it is usually confined to those sorry individuals who have progressed to the "wet brain" stage of alcoholism (Wernicke-Korsakoff syndrome, Korsakoff's psychosis, Wernicke's encephalopathy), and the damage is usually permanent. In other words, most alcoholics are never addicted to alcohol the way one is addicted, for example, to heroin, or cocaine, etc.

For the record, I subscribe to the concept that alcoholism is a disease. What makes a disease is its terminal end result. That is if left untreated a disease will kill you; a disorder will not. So, you might guess I am not a fan of the designation in the 2013 Diagnostic and Statistical Manual of Mental Disorders 51 (DSM-V) of Alcohol Use Disorder (AUD), although I do understand some of the logic behind the designation. Make no mistake, alcoholism, if left untreated, will kill you.

One positive outcome accompanying the AUD designation is the evidence and emerging acceptance that addiction of any kind is a *chronic* condition, whether or not it is classified a disease or a disorder. The chronic nature of addiction requires *ongoing* recovery just like diabetes and heart disease. The chronic nature of addiction and ongoing recovery are foci of this book.

Part I
THE DRINKING YEARS

Chapter 1

INSANITY

"You think you are in control of your life? Take a good look around. Have you noticed you are an in-patient in a mental hospital?" The words reverberated and burst through to my awareness. *FUCK! He is right!* His words became background noise as I looked around the walls of the wide room until I found the placard on the wall containing the 1st Step of Alcoholics Anonymous: "We admitted we were powerless over alcohol – that our lives had become unmanageable."

Well, Charlie Dumbfuck. I'm not so sure about part one of that statement, but you must admit this asshole at the front of the room is dead on about the second part. I am in a mental hospital. And, while they say I can leave anytime I choose, if I leave I will lose my job as Head Athletic Trainer of the New York Jets. As this realization began to sink in deeper and deeper an almost overwhelming sense of fear came over me. It would be years later before I could identify that particular fear as fear of truth. It was accompanied by a nauseating sense of dread that life was never ever going to be the same.

This horrific insight struck me in the middle of my second week of alcohol rehab at South Oaks Hospital on Long Island. Until then I had been marking time until my 30-day stint would be up and I would be free to go back to my life and just not drink – or at least be more mindful and controlling of what I did drink.

FUUUUUCK! I screamed again inside myself. *Maybe I am an alcoholic. Am I powerless over alcohol? Think about it, Reese: Are you powerless over alcohol? What happened and how did you come to be in the drug and alcohol rehabilitation wing of South Oaks Psychiatric Hospital?*

Flashback ...

Early in January of 1991, I drove up to Kutcher's Resort in the Catskills for the annual Eastern Athletic Trainers' Meeting. The meeting always began on Sunday evening so the athletic trainers (ATs) convention could secure a good rate. Because the resort was usually busy on the weekend, conventioneers could check in, but could not access their rooms until after 4:00 or 5:00 PM. Traditionally an ever increasing crowd would gather in the bar to watch the NFL playoff games while they waited to get into their rooms. It was also traditional that the NFL ATs from the Eagles, Giants, and Jets would foot most of the bill since we were the ones with liberal expense accounts. Both the Eagles and Giants were in the playoffs, so it would be up to the Jets ATs to pick up the tab this year.

I was purposefully late. I wanted to avoid the tradition for several reasons. First, I had just gone through the inaugural season with my third head coach at the Jets, Bruce Coslet. While I really liked Coslet personally and loved his coaching philosophy, it had been an extremely stressful season for me. The new General Manager, Dick Steinberg, had come into the Jets with the belief that the medical department was too powerful – that we had too much say especially in personnel decisions. After 13 years I was no longer allowed to talk to the media about injuries. While I understood the reasoning – control the message – I thought I was very good at doing that and enjoyed the opportunity to parry with the press and use these occasions to inform the public about sports medicine. And, as long as I'm being honest, my ego was bruised. I liked seeing my name in print and doing interviews on national TV.

The biggest stress, however, came from friction with the new strength coach. The previous strength coach, Jim Williams, and I worked as partners. He was educated in anatomy, physiology, and kinesiology. He understood how to work around injuries so that the players could maintain conditioning as injuries healed. The new guy was ... well, not that way.

His biggest fault was that he wanted to treat every player the same, regardless of their injury history, age, or position played. Players were complaining and asking me to protect them. Because I could not reason with him, I went to the head coach. Coslet had a meeting with both of us and told us – while looking directly at me – to get along or one of us would be gone. While still looking at me, he then reframed it: "Get along with him … got it?" Hence, a stressful season.

The next reason I did not want to entertain the masses at the convention is that I was loathe to listening to how great the Giants were over and over and over. If you are the fan of any team just think of the biggest rival your team has and how you hate for their fans to rub their good fortune in your face. We rarely played the Giants except in preseason, so the rivalry was not born there. It goes back to the old AFL-NFL antipathy and the New York media's treatment of the Jets as second class citizens even when we did well. Since the Giants were having a great year, and we were reminded about it daily in the papers and on talk radio, I really did not want to hear about it anymore.

In my mind those were all good excuses to avoid the tradition. But the real reason was that I knew that my drinking was becoming problematic. Recently I had begun having blackouts after only a couple of glasses of wine. (I should point out these glasses were large – usually about 10-12 ounces, but that had never been a problem before.) I rarely got drunk, but more than a few times I could not remember going to bed. After one of these incidents, I cautiously asked my wife, SG, if had fallen asleep in my chair and if she had locked up the house the night before. She told me that, after watching TV, I locked up as usual.

My concern was compounded with a more recent incident. One of the coaches had a post-season holiday party and I was going to make sure I watched my Ps & Qs – literally, watch my pints and quarts. I had told myself no more than two glasses of wine, and I stuck to that. It was extremely difficult and I had less than an enjoyable time. As SG and I left the party we agreed to meet another couple for a night cap at a local piano bar on the way home. I neither remembered the end of the evening nor the drive home. At work the next day I asked my colleague if I had gotten drunk and he said, "No man, you had two drinks – like the rest of us – and then drove home."

"So, I drove home?" I asked. "Yep," he replied, "I pulled out right behind you and you were fine. Why, was there a problem?" I lied, "No, things just got a little foggy."

My mental review of how I landed in rehab turned next to recounting how I had adjusted my drinking over time. I used to be a beer drinker who occasionally had a mixed drink or wine. I did not particularly like wine because you were supposed to "sip" it, and I was not a very good sipper. At some point in my 30s beer began to bloat me – both my gut and my weight. I was packing on pounds at an alarming rate and attributed it to the beer. Switching to Lite beer had not helped much, so Scotch became my drink of choice.

When I first started drinking Scotch, it would be with water. After several years it became Scotch with a "splash" of water. Then, of course, "Scotch, straight up." At some point I recognized that I was drinking a lot of Scotch, so I decided to stop – cold turkey. Not drinking, just Scotch.

I switched to bourbon. I didn't particularly like the taste of bourbon, so I reasoned I would drink less of it. That worked great for a while. Then, in 1988 I herniated a disc in my lower back and the pressure on the nerve caused me to develop a foot drop. After the second game of the season, I was sent home for bed rest. The sciatic pain was unrelenting and I had begun taking the prescribed Percodan (Oxycodone) like candy to little effect. I was worried about becoming addicted to the pain meds and began self-medicating with the bourbon. At the time numbing the pain with Jack Daniels seemed the smarter choice.

After two weeks at home (drinking almost a quart of Jack Daniels a day) I had back surgery. Following my back surgery, I cut back on the bourbon and switched to wine – again, since I did not really like it. While I now knew that, like the bourbon, I would eventually grow to like it, I reasoned that I would have a few years to work on alternative management strategies.

All this preceded the trip to Kutcher's Resort. In order to be late and not have to endure the check-in tradition with the ATs, I stopped at a small Italian restaurant near the hotel. I resolved to have only one glass of wine with my meal, but soon after the first glass I rationalized that two would be okay since that would equal less than one of my usual 12 ounce glasses at home. I arrived at the hotel during dinner. I checked into my room and read until it was time to go to the welcome keynote and seminar. So far, so good.

After the keynote and seminar, I said hello to dozens of friends and glad-handed dozens of colleagues. I inquired after my two assistant ATs and was told that one had headed to the bar with several friends. I ran into a young AT who was also a Purdue grad. As we headed to the bar she caught me up on the happenings at my alma mater. I was at the bar for about an hour. My assistant, Joe Patten (Joe P), had the tab running, so I was not bothered by too many colleagues. After two brandies I headed for my room.

The next thing I remember my head was splitting. It felt as if it would explode and implode simultaneously. I had severe cottonmouth and felt nauseous – all the classic signs of an enormous hangover. Even with all my heavy drinking, I rarely had more than a level 5 or 6 headache from a hangover. On a scale of 10, this headache was at least a 12. As I opened my eyes and got my bearings I gradually remembered where I was. I was confused by the hangover, since I remembered really moderating my intake. Gingerly, I sat up in the bed. My confusion worsened; I was still in my clothes and had been asleep on top of the covers. A slight panic set in as I struggled to no avail to make sense of my condition.

I checked my watch and realized I had missed most of the morning seminars, which worried me less than how I came to be in my current condition. I stumbled to the bathroom and found my shaving kit and managed to dig out a codeine tablet that I carried in case of back trouble. I then sat very still with my head in hands for about 20 minutes until the codeine kicked in. As my headache lessened, I showered, shaved, and almost wore out my toothbrush in an attempt to get the taste of mud out of my mouth.

Coffee, I needed coffee. It was not quite noon, so I would have wait until then to access the caffeine, as Kutcher's only served food at certain times. While I waited, I checked in with the Jets to see if anything was going on and to remind the head coach's secretary where we were if they needed us. Nothing was happening there.

Finally, noon arrived and I headed for the dining room. Several hundred ATs were finding tables and the din of the conversation began to bring back my headache. Before I could find the coffee, a slight acquaintance came up to me. In a much too friendly way, he put his arm around my shoulder and asked how I was doing. I said I was fine. He looked at me with what can only be described as a shit-eating grin and said, "You don't remember, do you?"

I was immediately embarrassed, but I did not know why. I could feel myself flush as I asked him, "What are you talking about?" He said, "Last night, at the bar. You punched that kid in the face."

I said, "What?!" He repeated his statement and went on to explain that I had been in the bar and had knocked back a number of brandies. This young student AT had made some comment about women not belonging in the training room and I took issue with him. It escalated and I punched the kid in the face.

The narrator then waved to someone and a stocky young man came up to us. He appeared to be in his early twenties. He was introduced to me and then he proceeded to apologize to me for starting the fight in which I apparently punched him. *Huh?*

Now, I would think that to a clear-headed individual this would have seemed surreal, so you might imagine how someone with a nightmarish hangover was processing this information. I apologized profusely to the young man, all the time wondering if I was being set up for a lawsuit.

My new best friend then regaled me with how he and two or three other guys broke up the fight and half escorted, half carried me back to my room. He said I had passed out, so the best they could do was dump me on the bed and take off my shoes.

I thanked him – sincerely. I told him I needed to make a call and excused myself from the dining room – still with no coffee and a hangover threatening to make a full comeback. It was all a blur. I had to find out what had happened. (To this day I don't remember the incident, the name of the kid, what school he was from, or who my "benefactor" was.)

I finally located my assistant, Joe Patten, who had been in the bar earlier the night before. He commented that I looked like shit. I told him I felt worse than that. Before I could ask, he said that he had heard some rumors that I punched out some kid last night in the bar. I relayed what I had just learned and that I had no memory of any of it. I told him the last thing I remembered was heading to my room.

He said that I came back to the bar about 15 minutes after I had left and ordered a brandy and some coffee. Joe told me that he had come down to my end of the bar to see if I wanted to put it on his tab and I told him I would just start my own. An hour or so later, he got tired and left. He said I seemed to be having a good time and so he waved and headed to his room.

After I processed this information, I decided not to hang around the convention. I was thoroughly embarrassed and certainly did not want to explain to anyone what had happened – especially since I could not remember what had happened. I headed back to Long Island. (And for those of you who have been in a similar state – yes, I finally got two coffees to go at a diner before I got on the highway.)

Busted!

Three days after returning from the convention, while preparing for the NFL Combine, I got a call from the General Manager, Dick Steinberg, to come to his office. When I arrived I noticed the team internist was in the room, but sitting off to the side. *Odd*, I thought. Dick began telling me how valuable he thought I was to the organization and that I did a better job of predicting how long players would be out and how well they could perform if they played hurt than any AT with whom he had worked. He then asked me if I had any problems up at the Eastern Athletic Trainers' meeting.

Busted! I thought. There is no way you can work for an NFL team and not have someone report bad behavior. Now I knew why doctor was there: *this was an intervention*. Being the AT for an NFL team meant you were the point man for drug and alcohol problems with the players. I had been through this scenario as one of the members in the room more than a few times as we gave players the ultimatum to go to rehab – or else go.

I knew the drill. Anything I might say in my defense would be considered denial. I took a deep breath and told Dick the story as I had pieced it together. I apologized for embarrassing the Jets and hoped that he and Mr. Hess (the owner) would not think less of me.

He reiterated how valuable he thought I was to the organization …. Then he came to the anticipated "but." But, I needed to go to South Oaks and be evaluated. The Jets would go with whatever they suggested – inpatient or outpatient treatment. And, I had an appointment in an hour to be evaluated.

I went back to my office and told my assistants, Pepper and Joe P, what was going on, and filled Pepper in on the Kutcher's saga. I then called my wife, SG, and told her that I would be late coming home and that, although it was extremely unlikely, I might not be coming home at all because I might have to go into rehab. Since I had not told her about the incident at Kutcher's I also explained to her what happened. As expected, she went ballistic and proceeded with a litany of my greatest failures, which mostly centered about my not being home enough. I assured her that outpatient treatment would probably be the outcome – and I truly believed that at the time.

Ooops! Wrong again! The evaluation team at South Oaks gave me until the following Monday to get my affairs in order and report for inpatient rehabilitation for alcoholism. I assumed for 28-30 days.

So, here I was 10 days after entering rehab listening to some guy I could not relate to telling me to look around and notice that I was in a mental hospital. As I stared at the placard with the 1st Step of Alcoholics Anonymous written on it and reflected on the above mental review of how I came to be in rehab, I recognized that not only was my life unmanageable and out of control, but also I was, in fact, powerless to control my drinking. I had tried all the tricks: switching types of booze, counting drinks, limiting drinks, and even quit drinking for 28 days several months earlier to prove to myself that I wasn't alcoholic. (I was supposed to quit for 30, but managed to rationalize my way out of the last two days because of some event.)

Admission … well, I *may* be … Okay, I *am*

*Okay, Bob, **maybe** you are an alcoholic!* I conceded the *maybe* as I looked around the room full of people and stared again at the 1st Step of Alcoholics Anonymous on the wall: "We admitted we had become powerless over alcohol – that our lives had become unmanageable."

After a few more minutes of reflection I asked myself who I was kidding. *Admit it, asshole: you are an alcoholic.* Then I said it the first time to myself: *My name is Bob, and I AM an alcoholic.* Then I said it a few more times to myself, hoping it would get easier; but it did not. I was overwhelmed at the concept of never ever having a drink of any kind of alcohol ever again.

The voice from the front of the room broke through again, and I heard, "… and you don't have to do this alone. In fact, you *can't* do it alone! This is what AA is for. This is what this rehab is for: to teach you a new way to live."

I recognized the truths in those words. First, this was going to be a whole new way of living. Next, I could not do it alone. With all this in mind I reasoned that I had to listen and understand what these people were saying. I made up my mind at that moment that I was an alcoholic and that I would not just be another recovering alcoholic, I would be the best fucking recovering alcoholic ever!

What? The meeting is over? Okay, time to begin the first day of real recovery. *Oh, shit! Do I have to start saying these stupid platitudes? 'One day at a time.' 'Take it easy.' … Fuck me, this is going to be harder than I imagined!*

Little did I realize then that those little platitudes would so spark my curiosity. They would not only help me become a successful recovering alcoholic, but they would also lead me into a meaningful life as a teacher of psychology.

Chapter 2

THE FAMILIES

The Drinking Culture

I knew little or nothing of the alcoholic history of my relatives, except that everybody drank – a lot. There was rarely obvious drunkenness among the adults in my family. That changed with my generation. For example, a younger sibling beat me into rehab by three months.

After my sibling and I were sober more than five years, we shared some of our respective stories with each other and our parents. Apparently our candidness touched our parents and they opened the closet and let the skeletons roll out. At the time we were in our 40s. Most of the night we just sat with our mouths open, exchanging looks of incredulity. We both wondered if knowing about this family history of alcoholism might have tempered our drinking in any way. Regardless, from both the hereditary standpoint (nature), and the models we grew up with (nurture), we had a lot of alcoholism and/or alcoholic drinking patterns on both sides of the family tree.

To summarize the skeletons that came out of the closet: I come from a heavy drinking culture. Both my grandfathers were binge drinkers, and it apparently affected one's job history. There were seven Reese siblings, and all but my Dad could be classified as at least heavy drinkers. Of the seven, there was one diagnosed cross-addicted alcoholic, one whose drinking affected his business, and one probable alcoholic. My father was not alcoholic. He was the only member of either side of my family that seemed to be able to stop drinking once they started.

On my mother's side there were eight siblings. One was an admitted alcoholic who was in and out of AA for 40 or more years. There was a closet alcoholic and at least one undiagnosed alcoholic. Two more were very heavy drinkers, and the remainder could be considered heavy drinkers – at least when family was around.

My large extended families had a tremendous impact on my youth and my drinking. Drinking was associated with every family gathering – large or small. I could not wait to grow up so I could be like the adults in my family.

My "Wonder Years" Childhood

As a famous comedian so aptly described it, "I started out as a child." Of course, I was an infant before that, but I have no real memory of infancy. I don't know if that was my first experience with a "blackout" or just standard infantile amnesia. Regardless, my infancy and toddlerhood were not memorable.

Around the age of four I remember being a kid. It was the 50s and all was well with the world, at least my world. We lived on Grandview Drive in a small Cape Cod style house that my Dad, Bobby, built. He was a heating and air-conditioning contractor working in the family business – C. H. Reese & Sons: Roofing, Sheet Metal, Heating & Air Conditioning. He was the first person in his family to graduate from college. His degree was in Engineering from Vanderbilt, compliments of the GI Bill post WWII.

My childhood was like *The Wonder Years*. We lived in a blue-collar, middle class neighborhood where all the men worked and the women stayed home. Other than my Grandma Reese dying when I was about eight or nine, I can remember no tragedies affecting the Reese family.

My mother's sister, Gert, and my mom seemed joined at the hip and our families did almost everything together. Gert and her husband, J. B. Hatley had two children, Jimmy (two years my elder) and Trudy (three months younger). They were like my brother and sister. In high school I also was very close with cousins Jimmy and Delia Reese – two of Mike and Mary Katherine Reese's seven children.

The only stressful events that I recall were when the phone rang at night and it was a "service call" for my Dad to go out to service a customers' furnace or air conditioner. Since he was the service department for C. H. Reese & Sons, very early in life my siblings and I learned to say, "I'm sorry, he's not here." My parents went through some real mental gymnastics trying to explain why we were not lying, because it sure was not what we were being taught in Catechism class. My mom rationalized that my Dad was just not here for *that particular person*. As kids we just accepted this, and we did as we were told. Being a good Catholic boy, however, I covered my bases by including the number of times I told callers "… he's not here" in the total of lies for my weekly confessional. This issue was further confused when, as a teenager, I got in big trouble with my mom when I used this logic to defend not telling her the *whole truth* about something I had done.

These early minor challenges about religious dogma did not negatively impact my growing up. Almost every day, I played with Baptist, Church of Christ, and Catholic neighbors (Mike, Kenny, and Martin) who were my age. We did all the things that kids did in the 50s: we climbed trees; built forts and tree houses; played cowboys and Indians and cops and robbers; rode bikes with balloons or playing cards in the spokes to sound like motorcycles; caught crawdads in the creek behind the house; and played little league and sandlot baseball, football, and basketball (Dad put up a great basketball goal in our back yard). For excitement we rolled 'mockoranges' under car wheels as they drove down my street – Grandview Drive – and ran away giggling when the drivers would hit the brakes thinking they had run over something that may have damaged their cars. And for a real treat, we went fishing with our Dads.

While I realize in hindsight the pervasive dysfunction of the heavy drinking culture in which I grew up, overall I functioned well within it. It was, after all, the only life that I knew. I have a profound appreciation for not only my parents and extended family, but also for the period – the 50s and 60s – in which I grew up. Until my teen years the positives far outweighed the negatives.

Religion's Role

I attended eight years of elementary school at Christ the King School (CKS) and four years of high school at Father Ryan, the only Catholic boys' high school in Nashville. I had a very Catholic upbringing, but lived in a not so Catholic area of town. My home on Grandview was down the street from David Lipscomb, which is a Church of Christ college and high school.

I learned early on that Catholics were a minority in the Bible-Belt; this was my earliest introduction to discrimination. My Dad often told me of the time when he played high school basketball against Lipscomb. The Lipscomb fans threw actual fish at the "Mackerel snappers" from Father Ryan. (*Because Catholics at that time could not eat meat on Fridays, fish was the common meal. "Mackerel snappers" was a derogatory term to describe Catholics.*) My Dad never got over some of those insults.

There were several things my Dad did to demonstrate our Catholicism to our neighbors, who were mostly Southern Baptists or Church of Christ with some other Protestant denominations mixed in. One was to have parties in our back yard where the alcohol was made obvious by a big tub of iced beer. Dad would go out of his way to invite our next door Church of Christ and Baptist neighbors over for a beer. Both families were teetotalers. Over time I understood that this was his way of "flipping them off" for the discrimination he experienced growing up. During our skeletons out of the closet night, I learned that the Church of Christ neighbor had more than a few times gone on a "drinking spree" and that my Dad was called in by his wife to try to keep him "reasonable". Dad even brought him over to our house to sober up so his kids would not see him drunk.

The other "flip off" my Dad employed was not quite as understandable. Every Christmas we would string up Christmas lights around the edge of the roof and dormers and the front windows and up, across, and down the iron lattice supporting the front porch awning. We would also drape the shrubs in lights. After a few years we added an almost life-size nativity scene made from Masonite cut-outs and highlighted by a spot light. I guess you could say we were an early version of the Griswalds. For some reason my Dad thought that this nativity display and the lights was somehow "Catholic," although our neighbors also hung lights around their doors or on their bushes.

Years later I asked him about his reasoning behind this tradition and he confirmed my suspicions about "flipping off" the neighbors. When I pointed out that Christmas is celebrated by all Christians, even Baptists and Church of Christ members, and that he was not really insulting them, he failed (or refused) to see the logic of my argument. I dropped it and just accepted this practice as one of the several endearing quirks engaged in by my otherwise straight-laced Dad.

Pulling Weeds

One summer when I was about seven years old my Dad gave me the chore of pulling out the weeds from 12-inch swath between the gravel driveway and the house. The swath was about 20-25 yards in length. This was hard work for a seven-year-old. After an hour or so on the first day I did not want to continue so I began to cry. My mom took pity on me and told me I could finish it the next day. When my Dad came home, he took me outside and explained that what I had done was unacceptable as there were still a lot of small weeds. He told me I had to complete the job even if it took all summer and that I couldn't play with my friends until I completed the job to his satisfaction.

He also used this time to lecture my mom on the need to be tough on me so I could learn how to persist in a task. He had two sayings in this regard that I heard over and over as I grew up: "If it's worth doing, it's worth doing right." And, "do it right the first time and you won't have to do it again."

I cried and pouted for two more days, pulling up a small portion of weeds each day. Finally, something sunk in and I pulled the rest of the weeds in about a half day. I was proud of myself. Dad used it as another teaching moment without a lot of lecturing or saying "I told you so."

I realize that I have modeled a lot of my father's attitudes and traits. I definitely try to see a project through until it's done. I think if something is worth doing, it's worth doing right. I believe hard work can overcome a lot of deficiencies. I also learned and believe that working harder doesn't always work. Sometimes you have to work smarter. I thank my Dad for instilling these values in me.

The Camp

When I was about eleven, Dad bought a lot on Old Hickory Lake outside of Nashville. While it seemed like an all day trip to get there, it was less than 30 miles from home. The family lake venture contributed to my *Wonder Years* childhood and early adolescence – even though I often got poison ivy!

The first year that we owned the lot we picnicked, fished, and explored the area. Dad bought a used 16' runabout with a 35 hp motor. We trailed it to the lake and launched it from our lot. This brought on all sorts of new responsibilities for me: cleaning the boat, learning boating safety, and wearing a life-jacket or belt. My Dad was very strict about everyone in or on the water wearing a life jacket until he thought you could swim well enough; then you could wear a ski belt. By the end of the first summer I learned to water ski after what seemed about a hundred attempts. Dad had the patience of Job and was very encouraging.

The next year, we built the boat dock. This started in the back yard on Grandview. Every evening after dinner (I had to have my homework done) we would go out and work on the dock. It was rough oak, so it was very hard to work with. We would turn on the spotlights that had been installed for shooting basketball after dark and go to work. Tom and Joe, my younger brothers, would come out for a little while, and I always admired my Dad's patience with them. I felt they were clearly a nuisance and was always happy when they went to bed. They were eight and seven years old at the time.

With much help from my uncles and cousins, we floated the dock that we built. Oh yeah, the adults were always drinking beer while working or playing at the lake. Nevertheless, my most vivid memories are about the many great adventures that I enjoyed. By the end of the summer I was skiing very well, and I was allowed to take the boat out with Tom and Joe, or with my cousins, Jimmy and Trudy. It was heady stuff!

The next year we began to build what Northeasterners would call a cottage. We referred to it as "the camp." Dad would awaken me around 5:00 or 5:30 in the morning. I would have my clothes laid out. We quickly and quietly slipped out without waking anyone, especially Jane, my sister who was still a baby at that time. We would drive to the shop (C. H. Reese & Sons) and pick up a truck that Dad had loaded the night before with the tools and supplies we needed; and off we would go. We would stop at a diner or Waffle House and have breakfast and sometimes pick up my uncle J. B. We would work on the camp until dark.

I learned a tremendous amount about my father, construction, and life during that time. He was then and is still my first and most enduring hero. I wanted to be very much like my Dad and have used him as a model in many aspects of my life.

At this time, I was also allowed to work at C. H. Reese & Sons. I earned 50 cents an hour. I first worked over holidays, counting sheet metal elbows and other items that needed inventory. One of my favorite jobs was moving vehicles up and down the alley. I grinded a lot of gears and put some major wear and tear on the clutches – all my cousins did it before me and my brothers did it after me. It was part of the Reese male's rite of passage. I was only in the 8th grade at the time. I also enhanced my driving skills at the lake where Dad would send me to the local store several miles away for Cokes or cigarettes. This was one of the happiest times of my life.

Corporal Punishment

Corporal punishment was the accepted method of discipline when I grew up. I never considered the spankings I received abusive; and in hindsight, I believe that they were well deserved. If anything was abusive, it was having to wait for the spanking. When I screwed up, Mom would say, "Wait 'til your father gets home," and she would send me to my room. Boy, I hated that. Sometimes my Dad would make me wait through dinner; and, of course, my brothers, Tom and Joe, would tease me the whole time that I was going to get a spanking. As they got older, I had plenty of occasions to return the favor.

The last spanking I received from my father was at age 13, but it was not the last time I had my butt whipped – literally. Paddling by instructors was de rigueur at Father Ryan High School. Discipline in the classroom was maintained by the threat and administration of paddling. Every instructor had their own paddle – some brought them to class and hung them in the front of the room. Many were personalized and several were custom-made two handed affairs that looked like wide broadswords. "Mr. Reese, meet me in the faculty room after school" was the high school version of "Wait 'til your father gets home!"

My first paddling in high school came my freshman year – courtesy of Father Maxwell for talking in Latin Class. I learned quickly and only received three more my freshman year and one as a sophomore. But, there were other forms of punishment. For example, Father Sullins often took a different approach. He would make you kneel in the front of the classroom, extend your arms, and then he placed a dictionary in each hand. If your arm tired and you dropped a book, he would literally kick you in the butt and then replace the book in your outstretched hand.

The priests used punishments to teach obedience and respect. What I learned was how to avoid punishment and build resentments. I guess that doing what is required to avoid punishment might look like obedience and respect to others. The reality is that the mentality is quite different from genuine obedience and respect. On a more positive note, I also learned that sometimes I had to put up with assholes to achieve my goals – said another way, you can be successful in spite of assholes.

I readily felt empathy for my Dad when I, as an adult, arrived home from work was greeted with the news that one of my children needed a spanking. My wife, SG, foisted most of the corporal punishment on me as she was determined to be friends with our children. Oh, yeah – I always had a beer before I administered the requested spanking.

I also modeled my father by always making a big production about a spanking and giving the accompanying lecture. While I may have been angry, I never hit either of my children in anger. (*Unfortunately, I did do a lot of yelling when angry. So did my children's mother and she was far better at it than me. I know now that verbal aggression may be as bad, or worse, than physical aggression.*) Neither of my two children received many spankings compared to the number I received. They were both mostly well-behaved children; and I was much more lenient than my parents had been.

Chapter 3

CHANGING TIMES

Sports

Sport has always been an integral part of my life, and also of my drinking. While I was named a parochial league football all-star in the 8th grade, somehow my mother and cousin, Jimmy Hatley, convinced me that not playing freshman football would have no impact on me trying to play varsity the next year. So I became a student trainer/manager for the varsity. I did a good job and was asked to be the trainer/manager for the basketball team also. The next year I went out for varsity football. I had recurrent dislocating patellae (kneecaps) and could not play because of the swelling and the pain. Fortunately, I was able to resume my position as a trainer/manager and worked at these positions throughout high school.

    Sport was another area also influenced by religion. Because Father Ryan was the only Catholic boys' high school in Nashville, it drew students from all over the city. While a small school (less than 500 students), we had great sports teams. In my day, we were part of the Big Four high schools that were always in contention for city and sometimes state championships, especially in football and basketball. The other three teams – Montgomery Bell Academy (MBA), Hillsboro, and West High – were our chief rivalries, but whether it was respect, jealousy, or those just "those damn Catholics," it seemed every team we played considered us a major rival.

When I was in high school the Catholic Church was much more active in the social justice movement than it is today. In the 60s this meant integration. Father Ryan had been integrated since the 50s, but Blacks were not allowed to play sports. We integrated our basketball team in the 1963-64 season and this led to the integration of the Nashville Interscholastic League (NIL). We were also the first "white" school to play a "Negro" school (Pearl High) in January 1965. These events were transformative for me and helped to chip away at the segregationist culture in which I grew up.

In the fall of 2013 I was invited to Nashville to celebrate the 50th anniversary of integrating the NIL and to retire Willie Brown's number 50 for all sports at Father Ryan. Willie was the first African-American player to participate in the NIL. During that visit I learned that not only was Ryan the first team in Nashville to integrate, but the first in the entire South. As a teen, I had no idea of the significance of this event. I just believed it was the right thing to do. It was a very powerful reunion. In January 2015, there was a 50-year celebration of the Ryan-Pearl game, which was the first game between an integrated team and an all African-American team. It was billed as "Remembering the Game that Changed the South!"

Vatican II

Another paradigm shift that occurred for me was in the aftermath of Vatican II. In the 50s while attending Christ the King I became an altar boy in the second grade and by the fourth grade was sure I had been "chosen" to be a priest. I spent hours on painful knees offering up my pain (which I mistakenly thought everyone endured) for the poor souls in purgatory. My parents bought me a set of vinyl vestments so I could say Mass at the altar I created in my room. I even had my Church of Christ neighbor, Mike, serving as altar boy and making the proper responses in Latin.

My vocation to the priesthood suffered a blow when I entered 8th grade. My model, the kind and generous Father Davis, was transferred and was replaced by an authoritarian bully. This coincided with a surge of my male hormones and the fact that the girls' breasts were becoming noticeable. Regardless, while the rate of my impure thoughts increased,

I was still a good Catholic boy, just one no longer interested in the priesthood.

After Vatican II (1962-65), the altar was turned around so the priest now faced the congregation. That made sense, so I accepted that. When they got rid of the Latin, however, I felt betrayed. For years the nuns had been telling us that one reason Catholicism was the "one universal Church" was because we used Latin at mass and therefore you could understand it no matter where you went in the world. So, I had a big problem with that.

The straw that broke my back was the fact that it was now okay to eat meat on Fridays. The actual eating of the meat was not the problem. It was the fact that the week before the ruling, if you ate meat on Friday, it was a mortal sin, and you would go to hell for doing it – now it was okay. This seemed to bother me more than it did my buddies, who were delighted that they could now have a hamburger when they went out on Friday night. This inconsistency, however, caused me to examine my faith for the first time. Over time, it caused me to become a "non-practicing" Catholic. Later, as I learned more of the history and hypocrisy of the Church, I walked away from Catholicism, and eventually all organized religion.

Chapter 4

TEEN DRINKING

First Drink

Many alcoholics can remember their first drink – I do not. I'm sure it was sometime between the age of six and eight, and could have been earlier. My parents would occasionally give us a sip of beer. I can remember once when my brothers Tom and Joe were about four and five, respectively, they were given a swallow of beer and pretended to be drunk. They also wobbled and hiccupped and fell down. Everybody thought it was a riot. So, of course, they carried on until they wore it out.

    I do not know where they got the idea to act like that. Perhaps TV? I can never remember either of my parents qualifying as "being drunk" while I grew up. One time, at Christmas, when I was about 8 or 9 years old, Dad was a little tipsy. He had been out to a Knights of Columbus function. It was a Fourth Degree affair, so he was in his tux, plumed hat, and sword (which I admired very much). Dad, one of my uncles, and another man came in while I was still up. They were singing and having a gay old time. My mom laughed at them and pretended to be mad by stomping her foot and demanding "what have you three been drinking?" Everyone laughed. They each had another beer or drink. While they were loud, everyone had a great time. I remember thinking, I can't wait to grow up and be like that.

    I remember occasions when I was 12 or 13 stealing a beer from the refrigerator (only when I was with my cousin, Jimmy Hatley). Drinking the beer had only a mild effect. I was doing it more for the adventure than for the drink. I also recall mornings after my parents' parties, I would often sniff and sip half-full glasses left over from the night before. Again, I did not experience any effect from the alcohol. I just wanted to grow up, so I could have fun like the adults.

"Real" Drinking

My "real" drinking probably started when I was about 15. Some of my friends had their driver's licenses; a couple of the guys had fake IDs. We all knew a few places where we could get beer without much trouble. Usually a group of us would pile in a car, go to some dead-end street, and drink one or two beers, or a quart of Pabst Blue Ribbon. We would get giddy and talk about girls. Somebody might get sick. Everyone would get pissed at me because I always had the earliest curfew. I would be grounded if I was the least bit late.

During the fall of my junior year I was the head trainer/manager for the football team. After the game on Friday nights we would go out and split a six-pack. We would do it again on Saturday night. There were usually about five of the guys and my cousin Trudy. She was "one of the boys" because she spent so much time at my house and I could not go out if she did not go with me. No one seemed to mind initially.

I did not have an unpleasant experience with alcohol until the spring of my junior year. At a high school dance, I got drunk for the first time. On that night each of my usual group bought a six-pack of Colt-45 Malt Liquor. At intervals during the dance we would go out to the park and guzzle one or two of the tiny cans. We left before the dance was over to ride around – to "cruise." After going by the local drive-ins, everyone was pretty drunk. Trudy drove (she had only one of my Colts). I didn't have a blackout, but I remember we all got sick at various intervals. I remember lying on the lawn of a church, alternately dry-heaving, sweating, having chills, and looking up at the steeple with the moon shining behind the cross on top – silhouetting it against the dark sky. I prayed to get well – or die. It was clearly the sickest I had ever been in my life.

By the time Trudy rounded everyone up and drove them home

(except for the car owner), I was late for curfew. My stomach was in spasms and I went directly up the stairs. I heard Trudy give this great story of how we had been to classmate's party and some guys from West High (an intense sports rival of Ryan's) were there and would not leave. A fight ensued and I got hit in the stomach with a baseball bat. Of course, my parents and Trudy's parents were not buying her story. They tormented Trudy by saying that I should probably be X-rayed. She was then her most creative coming up with reasons why I was going to be okay. My Dad came up stairs to find me fumbling for an aspirin and spilling them all over the floor. He took one look at me and said angrily, "You're drunk! I'll tend to you in the morning."

Boy, did he! He woke me about 6:00 AM and shouted everything to me. That was my first hangover and I'll never forget it. Dad made me work hard around the house: clean the basement, cut the yard, and other physical chores. That night after dinner he gave me a lecture on the evils of drinking. Whatever he said, I agreed with – I was still hurting.

Oh, I almost forgot, I was grounded for six weeks. At that time of life, six weeks seemed like an eternity. I was concerned that SG, my girlfriend at the time, would start dating someone else, but that did not happen.

Unfortunately, all that I really learned from this incident was that I should not drink malt liquor. That much stuck and I have never had one since. Too bad it wasn't beer in general, but I probably would have just blamed it on the brand. I became very good at that kind of rationalization over time.

For the remainder of my junior year and into the fall of my senior year I didn't have any other bad experiences with alcohol. Now, instead of going out with the guys, I began steadily dating SG. One of my closest friends was Rupert (psydonym), who lived near SG. He could almost always get a car. He would pick up SG and then come get me. Then we would get his date. Because I always had the earliest curfew, I would be dropped off first. Rupert had several girlfriends over time, but he, SG, and I were almost inseparable our last two years of high school.

Rupert was 6'4" and looked older, so he had no trouble buying beer. Our routine was that Rupert and SG would pick me up. We would go to a certain area of town where we knew they were lax checking IDs and Rupert would go in and buy two six-packs. The boys would have four, and the girls two each.

Why Drink?

As I reflect on why I started drinking, I guess it just seemed cool and adult. Our parents did it (by the way, we all smoked cigarettes, too). I did not drink to "belong" to a group of peers – I already "belonged." I was always popular. I had a solid core of friends from grammar school and we remained close throughout high school. I had girlfriends from the second grade on. As I grew older, I had friends, boys and girls, who confided in me and asked for my advice. I ran with the "in crowd." (At least we considered ourselves the in crowd!) This was all without booze.

My cousin Delia came from St. Ann's parish in West Nashville and Trudy came from Holy Rosary in South Nashville. They brought their friends into the mix. By the time we were juniors this loose knit group was referred to by some as the Apostles.

Father Ryan high school was segregated into three main classes according to academics: A, B, and C classes. I easily floated socially with A class, which I was part of, and with the B and C classes which were populated by friends. Accordingly, I got along with the *Crew* (the preppies) as well as the *Jocks* and the *Hoods*. Bottom line: I certainly did not *start* drinking because I needed a social group. As a senior, there was no one that I knew who did not drink at least a little.

Problems Drinking

After the Colt-45 episode, I did not have another bad incident drinking until mid-way through the basketball season of my senior year. Father Ryan's team and fans traveled to Oak Ridge for a basketball game. It was a big deal because Oak Ridge was one of the best teams in the State. We had gone to the state tournament the year before, so it was supposed to be a close game. It was for three quarters, and then they pulled away in the fourth.

Afterward, even though we lost, there was still a lot partying back at the motel. Rupert and I had not planned ahead so we had to go from room to room bumming beers. Someone sold me a half-pint of whiskey. After I had a couple of sips I somehow got into a drinking contest with another guy to see who could drink a whole half-pint the fastest. I won – but I lost.

That was my first blackout. I don't remember much after that, except I ran to make team curfew and knocked on the wrong door to get in just as Coach Derrick was coming out of a room. Because I was in the wrong room, I hid in the shower, but it was too late. The next thing I saw was Coach Derrick after he pulled open the shower curtain. He told me I was off the team!

I was devastated, humiliated, embarrassed, and angry – especially at myself. I was also very fearful of what my Dad was going to do to me. Because the Nashville Catholic community was very close knit, I feared that this would be embarrassing for the whole Reese family and that I had damaged Dad's reputation and standing in the community.

I rode home with Mary Jo, Delia's older sister, who was chaperoning the cheerleaders. I got a lot of sympathy from the cheerleaders, but it didn't help. I was suspended from school for a week. Although Mary Jo tried to intercede for me with Dad, he was too pissed off to talk. Mom was not, of course. She went into full-blown suffering martyr mode because of the thorn I "stuck in her side." I really felt like a piece of shit. I was grounded indefinitely

Since I was no longer trainer/manager of the basketball team, I immediately began to work for Reese & Sons after school. I also had to apologize to Coach Derrick; that took all the guts I had. He really squashed and degraded me and made dire predictions that I would amount to nothing in life. For a long time, I really resented him for that.

All my buddies rallied around me. They all felt I had been dealt an unfair blow and that Coach Derrick was a prick. I learned two things from the incident: humility and not to guzzle hard liquor.

Sanctioned Drinking

Some drinking was somewhat sanctioned by parents. Two of my CKS classmates' parents – the Hanley's (pseudonym) – had a large farm 20 miles outside of Nashville. The parents allowed friends of their daughters to come out to their farm and drink. They felt it was safer for us to drink out there than to be driving around town. I guess they just assumed – correctly – that we were going to drink anyway. So, sometimes there would just be a few of us, sometimes several carloads. On occasion there would be a gathering of a hundred or more students and recent grads from Father Ryan and St. Bernard (one of three Catholic girls' schools) at an old vacant house on the property known as the "Party House." As strict as my mother was, going out to Hanley's farm was always okay.

Other sanctioned occasions included our proms and graduation. Parents knew we were drinking. These were pleasant memories.

My drinking career continued without any further bad experiences, for a while. That spring Rupert and I routinely double dated. Every Sunday we would gather up our dates and go to Percy Warner Park with a case of beer. We grilled hot dogs and had a nice time. We did not get drunk, just loose enough to do a little "making out." By this time SG and I were inseparable.

Senior Trip

After high school graduation a group of us went to Daytona Beach for our "Senior Trip." We had been planning our senior trip since we were juniors. We wanted to buy a used hearse to drive and intended to put a sign on the back saying, "Don't laugh, your daughter may be inside!" *Okay – today that makes me gag, but, at seventeen, we thought it funny.* We never got the hearse because no parents would co-sign for it.

Daytona was as wild as we had heard – women and parties everywhere. We rented a room for three days; after that decided we didn't need one. Hell, most of us spent the night somewhere else or partying all night anyway. We ran into a group of Ryan grads (2 years older). Because they were friends of my cousin Jimmy Hatley, they let us crash with them.

One night someone gave me a fifth of Old Crow. I drank most or all of it. I woke up the next day with a splitting headache. Everyone was laughing at me and I couldn't see what was so funny. I looked in the mirror and saw I had a big strawberry on my forehead. They proceeded to tell me how I had been the life of the party, running around the motel, telling jokes, etc. It got late and the manager wanted us to calm down, so one of the guys hollered up to me. I was on the 2nd floor and I bent over the railing to hear what he was saying and just kept on going. Apparently I did a 1½ flip onto the asphalt.[2] Everyone applauded because I didn't break the whiskey bottle. Now that's what I call positive reinforcement. I was pretty mellow after that. I had a headache even a beer could not cure.

High Voltage

The summer after graduation I was running air-conditioning service calls for my Dad. It gave me a lot of freedom and pretty good money – especially in those days. I would work as much overtime as I could. Because I was running service, I kept the C. H. Reese & Sons truck all night. SG had no problems going on dates in the truck – even to the drive-in movie.

I remember one incident in which I had been out the night before playing poker with some older Ryan graduates. One night a week they used to play and I was always welcome, probably because I usually lost more money than I won. We played nickel-dime ante and I never took more than $10 and a six-pack. It was great camaraderie and very manly. That was "my night out." And, if I busted early, I'd just ride by SGs for an hour or two. Her parents liked me so I was always welcome.

The morning after one of my night's out, I awoke with a mild hangover. Because I was young and strong and because it was hot as hell outside, I knew I would sweat out the booze and be fine in an hour or two. (At that time hangovers were not unknown to me, but were not a regular occurrence.) So, I went on a service call.

While going through a check list of potential problems on an air conditioner, I determined it was electrical and began to systematically short out different controls to find the non-functioning one. I could not find the problem and became frustrated. For some still unknown reason, I shorted across the 220-volt terminal at the transformer with a big screwdriver.

POW! With an instantaneous flash, I was thrown into the wall behind me hard enough to knock the breath out of me. I was at the peak of my attention then! After the realization I could have been killed subsided, the thing that hurt the worst was that the blade of the screwdriver was melted across the terminals. It hurt because it had a special ratchet handle that I had bought with my own money. I carried that screwdriver, or what remained of it, around the rest of the summer to remind me not to take haphazard shortcuts. Once again I avoided the obvious connection to my drinking.

Another incident also got my attention that summer. One night I was driving my Dad's Plymouth station wagon loaded with friends. We met up with some other friends and decided to go out to Hanley's farm. To get there, we went out River Road, a twisting, turning, treacherous road at best. It was dark. We were following a recent Ryan grad driving a Jaguar. I decided to try and keep up with the Jag – FAT CHANCE!

I wasn't drunk, but I had been drinking. I almost lost control twice going around mountainous curves before I finally slowed down. The girls in the car didn't stop crying for a half an hour. Two weeks later the brakes failed on my Dad in downtown traffic and he rear-ended someone. When I heard what happened, I literally shuttered as I thought of what would have happened if they had failed that night on River Road. It was a sobering thought that stayed with me for a long time. As usual, I misinterpreted the message and made it about the car instead of the drinking.

Chapter 5

COLLEGE

Notre Dame ... It's Cold!

From the time I could remember, there was an expectation I would go to college. I never considered it pressure or a burden; it was just something I always knew I would do. During November of my junior year in high school, my parents, uncle J.B., aunt Gert, Jimmy, and I went to Notre Dame for a football game. It was every Father Ryan parents' wish that their sons go to Notre Dame; and I certainly wanted to check it out. No one ever suggested that was why we were going on this trip, but I was thinking about it. On the Friday night we arrived there was about three feet of snow on the ground. I did not like that!

Jimmy and I went to the pep rally in the Field House and although I'll never know how, we found Jude Lanahan, a former Ryan Grad, who was now a sophomore at Notre Dame. After the pep rally he showed us around some of the campus and I was super impressed. We had a ball. Later, we trudged back to the motel through the snow and were half frozen when we got there. We had a nice conversation with our parents. We were allowed to sleep in a room separate from them. Somehow Jimmy managed to get four beers from their cooler (I think he climbed across the balconies). We smoked cigs, drank the beers, and talked about what it would be like to go to Notre Dame. Jimmy didn't have the grades, but he knew I did.

Getting To Purdue

After October 15, 1965, of my senior year, I began applying to colleges. I wanted to be an engineer like my Dad – but not like my Dad. He was a mechanical engineer. I wanted to be in construction. I wanted to build things – big things like bridges and dams. At least that's what I thought at that time.

My Dad went to Indianapolis once a year for a meeting of dealers of Peerless furnaces and air conditioners. While there in 1965, a business associate told him about Purdue being a great engineering school. I remember him being very excited about Purdue, so I applied there. I also applied to Vanderbilt, my Dad's alma mater, out of respect for him and to prove I could get in – not many people from Father Ryan got accepted to Vandy. I had no intention of going there, however, as I was determined to *go away* to college so I could escape my mom and her stifling rules.

After the snow experience, I had pretty much ruled out Notre Dame. Furthermore, since I had begun to question my Catholic faith, I was not anxious to continue in a Catholic educational environment. I also applied to the University of Tennessee, but I had no desire to go there for a different reason. Too many of my friends were going there to party; I was *very* serious about college! Where I really wanted to go was Georgia Tech.

Around the middle of November, I received a letter of acceptance from Purdue. I was flabbergasted. We did not expect to hear from any schools until around May 1966. I learned that Purdue had rolling admissions: if you met their requirements, you were admitted. My Dad's chest swelled to record proportions. My mom just kept hugging me and telling me how proud they were of me. I was the first in my class to be admitted to any college. Before long everyone at Father Ryan knew where Purdue was, that it had a great athletic program, and that it was a great school. It was pretty heady stuff.

That spring Dad and I drove up to visit the Purdue campus in West Lafayette, Indiana. I was agog at the size of it; I had never seen anything that big. It had 35,000 undergrads back then. We checked out all the facilities and also went to meet the Head Athletic Trainer,

Pinky Newell. I had no idea who he was at the time, other than the Head AT. As it turned out Pinky was the Executive Director and one of the founders of the National Athletic Trainers' Association and one of the most respected ATs in the country. We sought him out because I had been a student trainer/manager in high school and knew I would have to work while at college. I thought working in the training room would be more fun than bussing tables in a dorm cafeteria.

While I looked around the Physical Therapy department, Pinky and my Dad chatted. When I came back, Pinky told me I could work in the training room for my work-study for a year but if at the end of that year I did not want to be an athletic trainer, I'd have to look for something else to earn money. I readily agreed knowing that I was going to be an engineer, but figuring one year in the training room was one year less bussing tables.

At that time – before Interstate Highways – it was about an eight to nine-hour drive from Nashville to Purdue. Dad and I had a great ride back and ate at a steak house in Louisville where you picked out your steak from a cooler. It was another new experience that I savored.

That spring, I was accepted everywhere I had applied except Georgia Tech, which had been my first choice. I was disappointed but figured it was their loss as I decided that I was going to be a Purdue Boilermaker!

Funny, I never realized until later that Purdue was only 90 miles from Notre Dame and had the same weather. I guess that does not say much for the geography portion of my elementary and secondary education. Regardless, it was the beginning of a journey that would keep me north of the Mason-Dixon until 2002.

Purdue ~ Year 1

In September 1966, my parents and uncle J. B. and aunt Gert drove me to Purdue. They were all so proud of me. My mom kept telling me how proud my Dad was of me, but she was about to bust a gut gushing over me. Dad and I gave her a tour of the campus. I could see her agitation increase as she realized how huge it was. Before they left, Dad took a picture of me in my freshman beanie. I'm still mortified at that snapshot.

I checked into Wiley Hall, one of the newer 'H-hall' dorms on Purdue's immense campus. I was very excited to be 'on my own'. The freshmen had a week of orientation before classes started – Thank God! I cannot imagine finding my way around campus in one day.

As per Pinky's directive, after the first week of classes I checked into the training room. The student athletic trainers were in full-swing taping ankles for football practice. I stood with my mouth open, not believing the swiftness of the taping and the organized chaos that was going on around me.

When things slowed down, I was shown to Pinky's office, and he welcomed me (I was afraid he might not remember me). He introduced me to three or four students and his assistant Pat Dyer. Pinky and Pat were to become very important people in my life. Pinky was my mentor and also became a father-figure. Pat was also a mentor, but acted like a big brother to me. I became his favorite as I got older and more experienced. By my junior year I got all the plumb assignments and best road trips because of my relationship with Pat.

After two or three weeks of being in the training room, I got to know several of the freshman football players from my dorm. (Purdue did not have 'Jock Dorms' which were very popular at other colleges at the time.) This gave me a new peer group and also some minor celebrity status around the engineering students that I was getting to know.

These freshman players were a rough-and-tumble group mainly from Chicago. They were characters, to say the least. They had little respect for anything, especially authority, unless that authority was a football coach. We used to play cards (penny-ante poker) on weekends. Mostly I watched because they could really get pissed off at each other and throw things or forearm shiver one another – blows that could have easily knocked me into the hall. One calm, good-looking guy used to ride herd on these thugs. He was Mike Phipps, the quarterback of the freshman team. We became good friends, along with Mike Webster, a safety, and Tim Foley, a cornerback. Foley and Phipps became captains our senior year. I maintained contact with both of them in the years following Purdue as we all landed in the NFL. Phipps played QB for Cleveland and Foley played cornerback for the Dolphins when they were in their undefeated era. I was an athletic trainer with the Buffalo Bills and later with the New York Jets.

I did not do much drinking the first semester at Purdue. There was lack of opportunity and no desire to drink coupled with a dedication to my studies. The dedication, however, did not help my grades much. I was busting my ass. I was taking 14 credit hours, including five hours of Math that did not even count towards my engineering degree but was necessary just to get me up to Purdue's standards. I had a four-hour Chemistry course that was killing me. By mid-term I was sporting nine hours of 'D' and the Engineering Orientation Counselor's words were ringing in my head. Sitting in a lecture hall of about 1500, he had said, "... one-third of you will flunk-out, one-third of you will change majors, and one-third of you will graduate the best engineers in America." I sure did not want to be in that first one-third, so I thought about changing majors.

I was doing great and really enjoying my time in the training room. I had learned to tape within a month or so and will never forget the day Bob Griese jumped on my table and told me to tape him. Since he was the star quarterback, All American, and in contention for the Heisman trophy, I asked him if he was sure. He yelled at Pinky, "Is the kid okay?" Pinky yelled "Yeah!" so I taped him. He got up, tested the tape; said it was a great tape job. Poof! Instant credibility! After that, I never had a shortage of players at my table and I began to really consider athletic training as a profession.

The first home game was against Notre Dame. Purdue was heavily favored as Notre Dame was starting two unknown sophomores at quarterback and wide receiver. Terry Hanratty and Jim Seymour lit up Purdue's stadium and Bob Griese suffered his only loss to Notre Dame. In spite of that, the Boilers had a great season. We were 8-2 and went to the Rose Bowl where we beat Southern Cal 14-13 when the Trojans went for two on an extra point and we stopped them.

When I went home for Thanksgiving all I talked about was the training room. I taped Jimmy Hatley's ankle with a family audience looking on. They were all amazed at my dexterity with the tape. I told my Dad I was having trouble with math and chemistry. He suggested getting some older guys to tutor me if I needed it. He assured me that I was smart and would do all right.

Chapter 6

GRIEF, RELIEF, AND SOCIAL INADEQUACY

Good-bye Ma-Maw

When I went home that Thanksgiving there was also sad news. My last surviving grandparent, Ma-Maw Bauer, was very ill. Additionally, my parents were also in the process of building a new home in the Hillwood area of West Nashville. They were making it big enough for Ma-Maw to move in with them. To help finance the new house, they had put the camp up for sale. These were all blows to me. While I had probably been informed about all this, the significance of each had not sunk in until then.

I understood the reasons behind building the new house and for selling the camp which I associated with so many good times. I also felt a loss of security moving out of the house I grew up in. Finally, I rationalized, "What the hell! I don't really live here anymore."

My grandmother's illness, however, was not something I could rationalize away. She had a particularly virulent form of acute leukemia that worsened rapidly. The extended family was called to come to Nashville. Shortly after Thanksgiving I, too, was called; and I came back to see her for what I thought would be the last time.

All of my mother's siblings, and their spouses, and children were in town. It was very somber. Before I went to the hospital to see Ma-Maw, I had to undergo the Bauer indoctrination. The Bauers always seem to complicate things regarding emotions and what they perceive other people's feelings to be or what they *should* be. They told me not to show shock or fear and gave me an idea of what she looked like. I was told only to be positive and not to mention death – as if that would make it go away.

Ma-Maw was really gaunt. I had seen my uncle, Charlie Reese, waste away from cancer, but this really hit home. As I bent over to kiss Ma-Maw, my aunt Gert broke down and mom bustled her out of the room. Tears welled up inside me and I wanted to cry, but aunt Dot gave me a stare and then made a gesture to show me that I should be smiling. I tried, but I am not sure how successful it was.

Ma-Maw held my hand and told me how happy she was to see me and how proud she was of me. She told me to always remember her and I told her there would be no need since she would be up in no time. She told me not to worry and that she was ready to go. That made me feel better. But, as soon as she said that, Dot hustled me out and scolded Ma-Maw not to talk that way. Outside the room my uncles Joe and Jim were berating Gert, telling her to "get a grip." Didn't she know what her sobbing did to Ma-Maw. They intimated that Gert was always so weak. I left the hospital with good feelings about Ma-Maw but very mixed feelings about everyone and everything else.

This was the first time I had seen the dynamics involved with the dying and I was confused – at a minimum. I thought it was pretty smart of my grandmother to know she was dying and feeling "ready" to go; and so stupid of everyone else to deny it. Granted, I knew it was not a subject to dwell on, but I did not understand the pretense – the woman was dying and she knew it.

Ma-Maw passed away the next spring in March 1967. I had seen her a few times over Christmas vacation. I remember she always enjoyed seeing me, and I her. I went home for her funeral and was glad Ma-Maw was out of her misery. The wake was like a family reunion and the funeral was kind of like a dream – like I was watching myself going through the motions at the funeral.

Changing Majors

While at home in November to see Ma-Maw, I decided to tell Dad about my decision to switch majors from Engineering to Health & Physical Education so I could pursue a career in athletic training. I had discussed it with SG and she encouraged me, but we worried because she had recently asked her father if she could switch to Art and was told flatly, "No way!" She had to do something that would enable her to support herself. Her dad told her that if she did not want to stay in the business courses she would have to drop out of school. I was scared that Dad might tell me something like that because a Physical Education Major was something even I thought was kind of a joke at that time.

Later that night most of the men were gathered in our kitchen. I sat there listening to my uncles and Dad talking about everything under the sun. I was going back to Purdue the next morning, so I finally got up enough nerve to ask Dad to come into the dining room because I needed to talk to him.

I rapidly told him of my desire to switch majors. I told him all the good things and over-explained everything in hopes of avoiding an argument. There was no argument. He put his hand on my shoulder and said that it was okay and that he was not surprised. I think I was still trying to argue my point when he told me he didn't care what I did (for a living), as long as I enjoyed it and would be the best I could be at it. With that he said, "Let's go tell the others!"

He asked me to announce my decision. My current relief suddenly turned to regret. Tom Jr. and Joe Bauer, both engineers, immediately began to attack me. They wanted to know how I thought I could make a living and that there was no prestige in "that kind of profession." I argued with them while Dad stood by smiling. This seemed to go on for an hour, but I'm sure it probably was only 10-15 minutes. Finally, J.B. spoke up and told them all to "go to hell!" He said that I was a smart kid and that I sure seemed to know what I wanted. That was the first and only time I ever saw J.B. take up for anybody or anything.

J.B. startled everyone. They all started laughing and said J.B. was right. If I wanted to be a trainer, then they were sure I would be the best goddamn trainer in the country. I felt pretty good then and went to bed satisfied and excited to have that off my chest. J.B. was always my favorite uncle – how could he not be – our families did everything together. That night he carved out an extra special niche in my heart. *Thanks, J.B.*

Dad later informed me he suspected since the inaugural trip to Purdue that I wanted to be an AT. I demanded that he explain why he let uncles Joe and Tom Jr. jump on me. He said he knew I could handle myself and thought I did a great job. I felt pretty proud then. *Thanks, Dad!*

After Christmas break, I finished my first semester at Purdue with 'Ds' in math and chemistry, an 'A' in English, and a 'B' in Speech. I was relieved, however, because I had completed the math requirements for my new major, Health and Physical Education which also had an easier chemistry requirement.

Purdue went into basketball season with a competitive team. Because freshman could not play varsity back then, everyone was waiting for another of my classmates, Rick Mount, to get through his freshman year so that Purdue would be great (which we were).

Social Inadequacy

In my freshman year I had my first real confrontation with socially inadequacy. Unlike grammar school and high school, I knew no one. I will never forget my uneasiness at the first freshman mixer. The boys outnumbered the girls 3 to1 at Purdue; and it seemed even more lopsided at the mixer. I loved to dance, but I was petrified to ask anyone. In high school girls asked me to dance. Now, I was really out of my comfort zone at Purdue. Also, I missed SG even though we agreed to date other people in college.

Fraternity Rush

That second semester I rushed fraternities with the other guys in the dorms. (Purdue did not allow freshmen to rush the first semester.) Bob Skinner (pseudonym) was a junior student trainer at the time. He belonged to Phi Kappa Psi; and he pretty much paved the way for me to be a Phi Psi. There was some beer drinking associated with rushing, but no drunkenness on my part.

Later that spring, I attended another rush party. I was fixed up with a blind date, and we did not get along from the start. Bob Skinner had a motel room for the night for him and his soon to be fiancé, so we started there. I had 2-3 beers and then we went to the frat house. Later my date asked me if I would mind her leaving. I said "No," and asked her if she wanted me to walk her back to the dorm. She declined and left. I drank some whiskey and a few more beers. A friend of mine from the dorm who was also rushing Phi Psi and I then headed back to the dorm. I was high, but certainly far from stumbling drunk.

We got to the dorm and several people were in my room exchanging stories from the evening, as a lot of them had gone to rush parties. My roommate was on the phone across the hall from our door and was talking long distance to his girl. (There was only one phone per floor in each wing of the dorm.) The person in the room next to us came out of his room several times complaining loudly for my roomie to get off the phone. He had transferred at the semester from the Air Force Academy. He had been dismissed as part of an honor code scandal earlier that year and was generally disliked by everyone.

After the third time he hassled my roomie, I told him to fuck himself and quit bothering everybody. He went into his room and came back brandishing a small pocket knife. He threatened everyone and told us to leave him alone. He was holding the knife to stab not to cut, so I went for him. I missed grabbing for his wrist and caught him at the elbow. I landed a solid right to his face. We went down on the floor. I put my knees on his arms and started banging his head on the floor. My buddies pulled me off and he ran away crying.

A few minutes later my roommate noticed the back of my shirt had become covered with blood. I was still feeling the effects of the adrenalin rush so I was not feeling the cut. They insisted I go to the infirmary, and I did. I told the infirmary staff that I had cut myself on some glass I was moving at the fraternity house and didn't realize it until later. They seemed to buy it. Two days later, however, I was called before the Dean of Men and told him my side of the fight story – carefully leaving out the drinking and the frat party. He said he was sorry but that I had to leave the dorms as fighting was forbidden. The other guy got kicked out too. I was pissed and afraid of what my Dad and Pinky would say.

While I knew I would not have gone after this clown if I had not been drinking, I also did not accept any blame for this situation. I felt I was the victim. This was accentuated by the fact that my roommate got a petition signed by practically everyone in the dorm to allow my reinstatement – which, of course, did not happen.

Bob Skinner let me move in with him at his grandmother's, which was right off campus. This turned out to be temporary housing. After Skinner talked to some of the brothers at Phi Psi, they decided I got a rotten deal and allowed me to move into the fraternity house "unofficially." It had to be unofficial because I was not allowed to live on campus per the Dean of Men. Because of the housing restriction, I could not officially pledge until the following fall. During this time all my Purdue mail was sent to Skinner's and he brought it to me at the training room.

I became kind of the fraternity house mascot and ended up with a room to myself. The older guys couldn't give me any shit because of my non-entity status and the new pledges did not live there yet. I made some good friends. So when I pledged the next fall, they took it easy on me.

I let my Dad know about the incident, after the fact, when I had everything under control. I had successfully dodged another alcohol related bullet.

Spring Break 1967

That spring a group of former dorm-mates and I planned a Spring Break trip to Ft. Lauderdale. We set our route through Nashville with the idea of staying at my parents' new home. My parents said it was okay, knowing it was the only chance they would have to see me. We went through Nashville and visited all my old hang-outs. We were in a pick-up truck with a camper on the back. We picked up SG, who was distant with me, and we had a fight.

The next morning, we were off to Ft. Lauderdale; it was mobbed.

There had been a minor riot the week before and cops were everywhere. Just stepping off the sidewalk got you smacked with a night-stick (literally). I got so sun-burned the first day that I didn't even drink that night. Another guy and I spent the night looking for sunburn medication. We finally found something that worked and went to sleep in the cab of the truck which we parked in a public parking lot at the beach. The other four guys got drunk and slept in the camper-back.

About 6:00AM on Easter Sunday I awoke to the roar of motorcycles. There must have been 50 motorcycle policemen driving into town in pairs. As the last pair was passing, one peeled off and came toward us. I pretended to be asleep. He tapped on the window with his night-stick, and I rolled it down. He proceeded to tell me there were $250.00 worth of fines against the red camper and we were parked illegally on the beach. He gave us 30 minutes to get out of Ft. Lauderdale or we would be taken to jail.

I just sat there with my mouth open. My buddy in the front seat couldn't believe it either. Some of the guys in the back were half awake when I started the truck. I did not stop to explain until we were safely out of Ft. Lauderdale. Everyone was bummed out thinking Spring Break was over. I quickly told them about Daytona, and off we went.

Sure enough, some of the Apostles were at the Safari, the motel in Daytona where I did the 1½ off the balcony a year before. They welcomed us with open arms and we began to party.

After a day or two, one of my high school buddies and I met some girls who invited us to a party in their room. We went at the appointed time. The place was packed to overflowing, and their mother, who was in the crowd outside the room, asked us if we might come back later. We shrugged and left. As we were walking through the parking lot considering our options, several squad cars and a police paddy wagon pulled in. Cops jumped out of the squad cars, pulled guns on us, and told us to get up against the paddy wagon. We obliged. They proceeded to arrest us and threw us in the back of the paddy wagon. We, of course, tried to explain that we had not even had a drink yet, but they weren't having any of it. We rode around for about two hours while they filled the paddy wagon.

When we finally got to the jail, they booked us, printed us, took mug shots – the works. We kept trying to explain our innocence but no one would listen. Hell, we didn't even know what we were charged with. Since I was under 21, I was told that in Florida I had to contact my parents with my one phone call. I called my Dad and woke him up. I tried to explain the situation to him and he did not believe me either. He told me when I got out of jail, I had better get my ass straight home – my vacation was over. I humbly agreed.

After my buddy told them he was 21, he called the Safari Motel but was not sure the guy he talked to on the phone understand the message because he sounded drunk. We spent the night in one large rowdy cell with a bunch of drunks and hippies. I was scared to death. My buddy later admitted that he was too. The next morning, we lined up for court. The big bull guard must have realized that we were totally out of our element because he was nice to us.

He told us that the charges were minor and that, if we pleaded innocent, we would have to come back in a month or two for a trial. I panicked. No way could I come back there. I was already afraid of being kicked out of school. The guard told us that we should probably plead guilty, pay the fine, and leave. Images of the parochial school "permanent record" flashed before me. (The nuns used to threaten us that anything we did wrong would end up on our "permanent record" and follow us for life.) I did not want to be a convict for the rest of my life, but at the time it seemed the lesser of two evils.

So, standing before the judge in my cutoff jeans and a "Martinique – Best Damn Bar in Town" denim shirt I pled guilty to "disorderly conduct: not leaving a party when asked." I wanted to yell, "What the hell kind of charge is that?" But, I kept my mouth shut and I pled guilty. Imagine my surprise when I saw two of my Father Ryan alums in court. They paid our fines, which were about $25, and we went back to the Safari.

We worked out a deal. Several of us would take my buddy's car back to Nashville and he would ride back with my college friends. Then I would get with them to go back to Purdue. To make it work, I had to promise to organize a party out at Hanley's farm.

I got back to town feeling real guilty and I was very quiet. I talked to SG several times, but I knew we were in trouble. At the Hanley's party we officially broke up. While the party sucked for me, everyone else thought it a great success. My college buddies were a big hit; they thought Nashville kids were really wild and crazy.

Back at school I busied myself with studies, spring football, and all the frat rites of spring. That included drinking beer, but, without any real effort, I stayed very much under control.

SG quit school about mid-semester and moved to Florida to live with her aunt and work. Viet Nam was escalating. Friends were threatening to drop college and marry to get married status deferments. Two Apostles dropped out of Middle Tennessee State and joined the navy to avoid the draft. Another friend, who was in the seminary, decided he was not meant to be a priest and joined the Marines. Nobody wanted to get drafted and go to Viet Nam – getting drafted seemed like a death sentence.

Summertime 1967

In the summer of 1967, I again worked for Reese & Sons running air-conditioning service. I played a lot of golf and dated a few different girls. I began to regularly date Trisha (a girl from St. Bernard's) who had broken up with her steady boyfriend. They had gone steady even longer than SG and me. We had a good time together and became good friends.

Near the end of the summer Dad, Tom, Joe and I were working in the front yard of the new house when SG and her father pulled up. SG got out – her father stayed in the car. In retrospect it could have been a scene from a movie. I dropped my rake and walked over to her – I wanted to hug her but did not because I was drenched in sweat. We talked for five minutes and the old fires were rekindled. I told her that I was seeing Trisha; she already knew that (*Nashville – big city, small town!*). I told her I would call her in a couple of days.

My mother was pissed. She didn't like SG. I suspected that she saw how much I loved SG and was afraid that we might have to get married and that I would drop out of college. *I later realized that although those suspicions may have had something to do with my mom's attitude, the main reason she disliked SG was because they were so much alike.*

I went out with Trisha that night. At the end of the date she said, "I hear SG is back in town." That confirmed that the Nashville grapevine was in good working order. We talked about it for a few minutes. She gave me back my class ring. She told me she knew I still loved SG just like she still loved her ex and she did not want to stand in my way. I felt rejected and elated at the same time. Trisha was a real class act. There has always been a soft spot in my heart for her. SG and I got back together and all seemed right with the world.

Chapter 7

PURDUE ~ YEAR 2

Back to Purdue

I left for Purdue early to work football training camp. During training camp, I roomed with Bob Skinner and we had a good two weeks. One weekend we went to the Phi Psi Fraternity house, which was empty. Skinner's fiancé fixed me up with what she described as a real nympho. That proved to be true. I got a non-specific urethritis to remind me of my guilt for "cheating" on SG. I told her to explain why we could not have sex when she came to visit a month later. She was angry for a while and then seemed to get over it. (*She may have forgiven, but she certainly did not forget. Anytime in the future she wanted to lay a guilt trip on me, she would bring up the incident.*)

That year flew by. I was comfortable in the training room and frat house. I was very busy and I now knew how to successfully negotiate both my work and studies. In order to make up for my "lost semester", I took 19-21 hours per semester to graduate on time. I knew my brother Tom was supposed to start college the year after I graduated and I did not want to be a financial burden by taking an extra semester although Dad never said anything about it.

Pinky's idea of a well-rounded athletic trainer required taking every physical education course so the AT would know what the athlete had to go through physically in each sport. Along with taking athletic training courses, we were required to take most of the health courses and pre-med sciences. AT students also had a schedule block on classes so we could work in the training room every afternoon. That meant I always had a lot of 7:30 AM classes with rarely an hour off during the day. One of my small claims to fame is that I graduated on time, never dropped a course, never flunked a course, and despite my 'Ds' the first semester, graduated with a 'C+' average.

Purdue Sports

In 1967 Purdue shocked the nation by beating Hanratty and Seymour *at* Notre Dame. I worked the game; it was an awesome experience. Mike Phipps at quarterback was near perfect. Leroy Keyes, who had been a defensive back only the year before, played both ways. He gained over 100 yards rushing on offense and also shut down Seymour while on defense.

By the end of the football season, Purdue completed a new basketball arena that seated 14,000. It also housed the locker room facilities for all sports. It was already called the "House that [Rick] Mount built" and the former Mr. Indiana Basketball had not played a varsity game yet.

Purdue opened the basketball season and the arena against the NCAA Champion UCLA Bruins with the great Lew Alcindor (later to be known as Kareem Abdul Jabbar) and coached by the legendary John Wooden, a Purdue grad. Mount had fractured the 5th metatarsal in his foot a few weeks earlier. Pinky had the Engineering Department make an aluminum foot-plate for his shoe to give him stability and support while remaining light. Mount was nothing short of spectacular, but we lost on a desperation shot by Bruins' Bill Sweek at the buzzer (his only points of the game). [The next year we finished the season by losing again to the Bruins in the finals of the NCAA tournament.] It was a great time for Purdue athletics.

I hitchhiked home and back again for the Holidays and semester break. My parents assumed I was taking the bus, but I had done that once and it took over 13 hours. Hitchhiking took about eight hours. While my mom would have freaked out had she known, I enjoyed the experience and nothing untoward happened.

That spring SG came up for a Phi Psi dance. We had a great time.

We were drinking, of course, but I no longer thought it was cool to be drunk. I thought I now had an adult drinking pattern: enjoying booze without getting fucked up.

That summer I went home and again worked for Reese & Sons. In June I traveled to Columbus, Ohio, for my first National Athletic Trainer's Association (NATA) convention. Pinky let me bunk on his couch in his suite, along with another student trainer from Indiana University who was a year older than me. (That student was Dean Kleinschmidt, who later became head athletic trainer for the New Orleans Saints. We have been friends for over 40 years.) We listened that night to Pinky and some other "founding fathers" make policy for the NATA. That was the first time I realized how powerful Pinky was. He is now referred to as the Father of Modern Athletic Training. I was beginning to understand why Pinky was so adamant about the Purdue ATs being the best. At that convention I found out in a hurry that when I told people I was from Purdue it got their attention.

Side note: Pinky was also an alcoholic. I did not know this while I was a student at Purdue. I had heard some stories about him on road trips, but everyone joked about it, so I thought it was okay. Sometimes after home games several of us would sit around with him in his office and have some bourbon in our coffee. I just thought that was the way things were done. Many years later, after he was in AA, he shared some his struggles with me. In hindsight, I am pretty sure he was trying to hold up a mirror for me to see myself.

Marriage

After my sophomore year I returned to Nashville to work at Reese & Sons. Over the summer, SG and I were rarely apart. While not sleeping together, we had a great summer. I proposed to her and she accepted. I did the proper thing: I asked her father for her hand. He gave me his permission.

My parents were not quite as receptive and were very concerned that I was going to drop out of school. We assured them that was not going to be the case. We said SG was going to work – my Dad let me know that he could not support both of us. We compromised that we would get married during Semester Break of my upcoming junior year – January 1969.

Almost immediately the bickering began. Mr. and Mrs. G argued over the size of the wedding and where the reception would be. Mrs. G wanted a large wedding. Mr. G had more frugal ideas as he considered his three other daughters. My mother was upset that *she* was not running the wedding. After about a month, SG and I started arguing about it.

I got so pissed off at all the fighting with no solutions that I took matters into my own hands. I called a friend of mine (a "little sister" from Phi Psi) and asked her if we could use her apartment for a couple of weeks until we could find one of our own. We would be at school two weeks before classes started due to training camp for football so I knew she wouldn't be there. She agreed. I called SG and asked her if she wanted to get away from all this craziness and get married next week. She immediately said yes, but thought I was joking. When I convinced her that I was not joking, she said we should talk about it. I convinced her that it was the smart thing to do – screw the parents! The wedding was for us. I also did not want her to have to put up with all that bullshit while I was gone for a semester.

After we agreed, we went to the St. Henry's Church and discussed it with Monsignor Duffy, my old pastor from Christ the King. He said he would waive the bans of marriage and compress them into one the very next Sunday, but that we could not get married in the church proper because something else was scheduled. We said the rectory would be fine as we decided to have just a small wedding.

We then told the Gs. They were not happy but they agreed. I suspected that they thought SG was pregnant. Mr. G asked if we were getting married in the Church. When we said no, he quit speaking to me for a week until somehow we corrected his misunderstanding. He thought we were going to have a civil ceremony instead of being married in the Catholic Church. He was okay with our getting married in the rectory.

Going to my parents was a different story. I called them and told them I had something very important to discuss. They either guessed it or the Nashville grapevine was working overtime, because my mom (the suffering martyr) was so distraught that she had taken to bed. I was prepared to be disowned and "cut off" from any money. I believed Pinky could keep me in school until I secured a government loan and that we could immediately claim residency and cut second semester tuition by more than half.

I went into my parents' bedroom to try and talk some sense into my mother. Unbeknownst to me, SG took Dad into the den. I was pleading my case to mom and was getting nowhere. She was hysterical – weeping and sobbing – and kept telling me I had "thrust a thorn" in her side, betrayed her, and really let my father down. I tried to convince her that SG was not pregnant, but I knew she didn't believe me. This experience dredged up my resentment for my mother and her super strict ways, her sarcasm, and her unreasonableness. At this point I did not care if I ever saw her again. I left the bedroom and was ready to do battle with my Dad.

When I walked into the kitchen he asked me to sit down. I told him I'd rather stand. He told me that he had a talk with SG, that he was opposed to us getting married now, and that he was prepared to cut me off. I could feel my face getting red and my knuckles were white as I gripped a chair back. I looked at SG; she had this strange smile on her face that threw me.

He then told me he knew that we were in love and that I was prepared to get married anyway. He said that he could not bless the marriage at this time, but he would not cut me off. Upon hearing that, my mother let out a death wail from the bedroom. Dad went on to lay out some financial conditions, but I was barely listening because I was stunned.

Because of a cancellation, we got married in the Church proper about two weeks later. All the G's showed up along with some of our close friends. My parents and Gert and J.B. showed up right as the ceremony started. I had not expected them, but was glad they came. Much later I found out that my mother had refused to come to the wedding and was holding firm until Dad said he was going anyway and both J.B. and Gert said they were going with him. Mom relented – although I'm sure it was another thorn in her side!

Afterwards we had a reception at the Gs. Mr. G sprang for about four cases of beer and it was quite a nice time. I did not get drunk.

SG and I went to a new hotel at the Nashville airport and stayed in the Bridal Suite – which was really just a big motel room. I almost injured her when 'popping the cork' of a champagne bottle. I had only seen this done in the movies. The cork just missed her head and then ricocheted off all four walls and the ceiling. Another near miss.

The next day after the wedding, we picked up a small U-Haul trailer and hitched it to the back of SGs' Fiat and prepared to head to Purdue. We went by both our parent's homes to load up the U-Hall with our clothes, useful wedding presents, and any items the parents were willing to donate.

At my parents' home, Dad helped us load some of my items. He gave me his old tool box with some selected tools he knew I would need. (I still have some of them.) He seemed okay with everything. He wasn't cheerful, but he was not sad or grouchy either. My mother, however, had once again taken to bed because she was so "devastated" about the wedding. No mention was made of the wedding and the fact that they showed up late. As we were beginning to leave my Dad told me to wait a minute. He went into the house and somehow got my mother out of bed. She came to the door and waved good-bye. It was a pathetic sight.

We were glad to get out of there and head over to the Gs. We got some of SG's clothes (we knew we would be back for Christmas break, if not for Thanksgiving, so we didn't take everything from either house). We left things like the silver, crystal, and china we received as wedding gifts at the G's.

We had only two items that were "ours." One was an old metal icebox that we had discovered at a junk shop for about $7.50. SG spent the summer stripping it – it must have had 7 coats of enamel paint on it. She painted it black and trimmed in gold (Purdue's colors), used contact paper on the insides, covered the doors in burlap. I had a couple of glass shelves made. It was our liquor cabinet. We got lots of compliments on it. Later, when we were in Boston, refinished wooden ice-boxes used for liquor cabinets became quite the rage; we thought we were at the vanguard of good taste.

The other item that we acquired that summer was a brass bed. I cannot remember how much it cost, but I thought it was too expensive. SG insisted it was a great buy. She argued that it had been painted with a plastic coating so that it wouldn't require polishing (polyurethane was new back then). She went on and on about it so much that her mother finally agreed to buy it for us as our wedding gift. (*This was the first real instance of a pattern that I wish I had recognized back then: SG's relentless nagging until she got what she wanted.*)

After everything was packed and secured in the U-Haul trailer, Mr. G loaded up any open spaces with Johnson's Wax products (he was a route salesman for them). I moved some of that Pledge many times over the years. Every time we went to Nashville we got restocked, whether we needed it or not.

Chapter 8

PURDUE ~YEAR 3

First Apartment

We soon found a small, partially furnished apartment conveniently situated almost in the middle of Purdue's campus. Our rent with electric and heat was $82.50 a month. I agreed to cut the grass and shovel snow for a $10 monthly reduction

Did I mention the apartment was small? The double bed took up most of the bedroom – just enough space to walk around three sides of it. There was a small hall with the only closet. The bathroom had a midget tub. If you opened one leaf on the dining table, you couldn't get back in the kitchen from the far side. If you stood in the middle of the kitchen floor, you could cook, wash dishes, and open the refrigerator without moving a step. You had to turn sideways in order to squeeze between the refrigerator and sink to access the back door. The living room had a small desk with a chair and a really uncomfortable vinyl couch. It was GREAT!

SG busied herself "setting up house" while I worked training camp for football. I was earning $72 every two weeks in the training room as work-study. One check covered the rent. But even at prices in 1968, we needed more than that to live.

So, SG found a good job – better than the job she had in Nashville. She became a general secretary for a company and worked under an office manager, who had apparently been there for years. Not only was she was making good money (more than minimum wage) but they were also amenable to giving her a couple of days off at Thanksgiving and over Christmas break. She loved it. The office manager gave her responsibility and often asked for her input and suggestions – that made the manager a "wonderful person!"

Everybody at her job was "so great." Everything was going great. We were enjoying married life. I was really enjoying my junior year.

Raided

In the fall of 1968 SG and I were in a night club in Lafayette when it was raided. SG and I were both under age and had fake IDs. The police quizzed everyone on their ID information. SG gave them the wrong birth date. She was arrested along with 15-20 others including some of my fraternity brothers and football players. There was almost a riot outside the jail. (Marching for any cause was in vogue back then.)

I called a lawyer associated with Phi Psi. While I do not recall what he told me to tell her to say, it worked. She was released and the charges were dropped after a night in the slammer. Her night in jail was an adventure she bragged about for years, while mine during the infamous spring break had been a nightmare for me.

Not Pregnant!

For any holiday we would jump into the Fiat and drive home to Nashville. There was now Interstate Highways from Franklin Kentucky (just north of the Tennessee border) all the way to Lafayette, Indiana. So the trip only took six hours. That was nothing for a young couple. I remember one time we decided to leave about 1:00 am after I had finished a paper. Most memorable was the first Thanksgiving back in Nashville. SG proudly displayed that she was not pregnant. Only after returning for the Christmas vacation that year was everyone now certain that we did not "have to" get married. Nevertheless, my mom was still bitchy.

Upon our return to Purdue, SG decided she should get pregnant. I wanted to wait until after graduation and after I had a job. SG argued, convincingly, that since she had been on birth control pills for several years it would probably be a year or more before she got pregnant. Because I had also heard that, I compromised with her getting off the pill around January of the next year – my senior year. I thought we were in agreement but, without informing me, she immediately stopped taking the pill.

Residency and Sour Notes

As soon as SG turned 21 in January of 1969, she registered to vote. We were eligible for Indiana residency and, thus, for tuition reduction of more than 50%. This was a huge savings for my Dad for my last three semesters. At my graduation, he thanked me for that. I knew he was not thanking me for just saving him money; he was thankful for the consideration. My mom never acknowledged it. Even years later whenever I mentioned it she would change the subject.

We did not go to Nashville for the winter semester break that year because we could not afford it. So for those two weeks I mixed and carried hod (cement) for a construction company. The week before I got paid we decided to have an intimate party for just us. I bounced a check to buy a fifth of Jim Beam. Walking into the apartment the sack broke and the bottle crashed onto the sidewalk. I quickly brought it into the kitchen and caught what I could into a bowl. I was so angry I kicked in the metal cabinet door under the sink, denting it. I tried straining the whiskey through bread, and had enough for three or four drinks, but we decided it was too risky to drink. So much for an intimate night! I learned to never trust a paper sack to carry booze!

After the semester break, SG began to sour on her job. She repeatedly complained that the once wonderful office manager had become a bitch and groused about a "personality conflict" between them. I asked her to hang in there until the semester was over and then quit as we left for the summer in Nashville. She bitched and complained so much that I finally told her to quit. She got a part time job for less money at Sears and we struggled financially through the remainder of the semester.

Now I'm Pregnant!

Near the end of my junior year and one morning after we had sex, SG informed me that she "got pregnant last night." I asked her how she knew. She said that she "bumped into a wall after getting out of bed" and she "just knew." I asked her how she could be pregnant if she were on the pill. She informed me that she had stopped taking the pill a month earlier. I was stunned and immediately went into total denial of her deceitfulness and breach of trust. I just hoped that she was wrong. I had two streams of thought: 1) If she was wrong, and she wasn't pregnant, then I intended to be celibate until the following January; and 2) I started figuring out how I was going to provide for a kid without taking any money from my parents. I knew that SG's parents had no money to help us.

She was pregnant. The summer of 1969 we lived at her parents' house. They had turned the attached two-car garage into a family room. The garage doors had been replaced with large windows that had no curtains. The room had a washer, dryer, second refrigerator, and a pool table. We slept on a twin bed that also doubled as a sofa. There was one bathroom for the six siblings and me. SG's sisters were anxious and curious about her pregnancy, constantly feeling her belly and asking question. There was no privacy.

Buffalo Bills ~ 1st Summer Camp

The summer of 1969 I worked for my Dad until July 5, when I left for training camp with the Buffalo Bills. Ed "Abe" Abramoski was the head AT for the Bills and a Purdue graduate. He had called Pinky to see if he had someone that could help him through the Bills' summer training camp. Pinky recommended me.

For two hours twice a day Abe and I taped every player's ankles for both practices – and there were over 120 players in camp! It was hot and constant work. And, I loved it!

The highlight of summer camp was the arrival of O. J. Simpson, the man who beat out Purdue's Leroy Keyes for the Heisman Trophy. He was Buffalo's first round pick – the first pick of the entire NFL draft. He had held out for a bigger contract and was coming into camp a few weeks late, so the vets were really giving him the business. I gave him his first tape job as a Buffalo Bill. In the middle of taping, the TV camera lights came on and I almost froze, but O. J., who was used to the attention, talked me through it.

I don't think I ever worked so hard for so long. We ate a quick breakfast at 6:30 AM and then taped for two straight hours. Practice was usually a three-hour marathon. As the assistant trainer my duties included being the water boy. We had no rolling automated water pumps to help supply their hydration needs – everything was done by hand. I helped injured players from the field to the training room, which was on the second floor of the gym at Niagara University. This was quite a chore as we had no golf carts to help move them. I also helped the equipment guys with any equipment breakdowns.

After lunch, we had about an hour break while players were in meetings. Then we did it all again. After dinner we had about another hour before players would start getting out of meetings and come to the training room for treatment of their injuries. We would give treatments until their curfew at 11:00 PM. Then we went to the coaches' meeting and gave the injury report.

We did this routine for four weeks straight with only an afternoon off on Sunday. I literally forgot what day of the week it was. Relief came only when we started playing pre-season games. Most games were on the road, so we would have a light practice in the morning and then fly to wherever we were playing. Pre-season games were usually at night; this allowed us at least a day to rest. After the games we loaded the equipment truck and headed to the airport. Upon arrival in Buffalo we actually helped the airport personnel unload the equipment onto another truck which we drove back to Niagara University. There we unloaded the truck, unpacked the bags, and put the dirty laundry in hampers for the cleaners. Fortunately, the day after the game, usually Sunday, was a day off for the players; and we didn't have treatments until early afternoon.

That summer SG and her parents visited relatives in Brooklyn. During that time, the Bills played the Jets in a pre-season game in New York. The players had the next day off and the following day a light workout was scheduled. Abe told me to stay over in New York and see my wife. SG's cousins gave us a 48-hour whirlwind tour of Brooklyn, Coney Island, and Manhattan that I will never forget. We barely slept. What a wild weekend! I came away with the firm conviction that "New Yawkers" were crazy and that I would never want to live there!

I learned a tremendous amount that summer. Abe was a great teacher. While he wanted to know about treatments regimes currently being used at Purdue, he taught me how to accomplish results without the latest equipment. Dr. Godfrey, the team physician and one of the pioneers in sports medicine, was patient and also a great teacher. He really knew how to break things down simply for the players (and for me). I was like a sponge and there was plenty for me to soak up.

By the end of that summer, I, however, concluded that I did not ever want to work pro football. It was not about the amount of work it was about respect – actually lack of respect. In my opinion, Abe did not get nearly as much respect from the coaches – especially the head coach – as the ATs in the college ranks. John Rauch, the head coach, was antagonistic and demeaning. He approached us as if we were the enemy and were working against him. When I queried Abe about how he was able to tolerate the abuse, he told me to ask Tony Marchetti, the gruff old equipment man. Marchetti said, "We seen assholes like him come, and we seen 'em go … mostly go." Abe then added that he would just keep his head down and do his job – and hope it didn't take too long before John Rauch was gone.

Chapter 9

PURDUE ~ YEAR 4 1969

Winning the Lottery?

Back at Purdue in the fall of 1969 we easily fell back into the routine. SG got a job at Burger Chef. When she had to quit at Thanksgiving because of the pregnancy, I took her job in addition to working in the training room. If everything went according to plan, the baby would be born at the end of January 1970 during semester break.

The only major occurrence the fall of my senior year had nothing to do with drinking. Viet Nam was at its peak and all deferments, including marriage and college, were cancelled. It was the first year of the draft lottery and my birthday, September 7, came up #8.

The only chance I had of escaping the draft was a medical discharge. I still had trouble with recurrent dislocating patellae, the condition that kept me from playing high school football. I called my mom and had her get a letter from the orthopedic surgeon in Nashville who had treated me for the problem in high school and who had recommended that I not play high school football. The letter was a disappointment as it did not say I could not serve, it just said I would have a lot of problems squatting or crawling.

On the appointed day, I boarded a busload of Purdue students headed to Indianapolis for draft physicals. It was a quiet ride. When it came time to do deep knee bends, I refused saying that I could go down, but that I would not be able to get back up. They pulled me out of line and sent me to an orthopedic doctor. He read my letter and examined my knees. He then wrote something down and told me to finish the rest of the exams.

I thought, "Oh shit." Because of my medical background as a student AT, I could picture myself there as a medic with a big red cross on my helmet as a great target for the Viet Cong. I was distraught. After what seemed like an interminable time, my classification came back as 1-Y. This translated as having a physical handicap, but that I could be recalled if necessary. We were greatly relieved that I never got called.

It's a Boy!

We went to Nashville for Christmas 1969. SG stayed there while I returned to Purdue to take final exams. After exams during semester break, I went back to Nashville to the news that the doctor thought it might be another month before the baby came. We were using the Vanderbilt Clinic so we could afford to pay for the baby – still determined not to take any extra money from my Dad.

I drove back to Purdue to start the second semester. As I was getting up for my first 7:30 AM class of the semester, I got a phone call from my mom who told me that SG's water had broken and that she had gone to the hospital to have the baby.

I jumped into the Fiat and headed south. I had to drive through a blizzard to get to Indianapolis. The wind was gusting 60-70 mph as it came across the Indiana plains and it would literally 'freeze the car.' I would be driving 40-50 mph – as fast as visibility would allow – when the temperature gauge would suddenly plummet, the car would lose power, and then stall out. I would have to sit there for about 10-15 minutes, start the car, let it warm up, start driving, and the whole process would begin again after about 10-15 minutes of driving. After the fourth or fifth time I noticed that the trucks coming the other way had covers over their grills to keep the cold air out. I reached in the back seat and ripped apart some note pads and placed the cardboard sheets in front of the radiator. Viola! It worked; the Fiat didn't stall out any more.

Still, it took me two and a half hours to make the 60-mile drive to Indianapolis. Although I was able to catch a flight to Nashville shortly after I got to the Indianapolis airport, I was sure I was going to miss the birth. We had been through the Lamaze classes and I was planning on being present for the birth. This was a relatively new concept back then, but I really wanted to be in there.

It turned out that I arrived in plenty of time. SG was in labor for three days before the doctor's finally decided to take the baby by C-section. SG looked and felt like hell after she gave birth to our beautiful son, Robert Cowan Reese, III. I was told that I looked worse than SG did, but I did not care. As I held my infant son, I had never before felt such great love! That emotion was also combined with pride and a sense of great responsibility.

A day later, I went back to Purdue. Two months later I returned to Nashville during Spring Break to bring SG and Robert back to Purdue.

I graduated that June and was ready to get on with fulfilling the American Dream. I had applied to Physical Therapy (PT) school at U. T. Memphis, the University of Iowa, and Columbia University, Pinky's PT alma mater. I was, surprisingly, accepted to Columbia. I decided there was no way I could afford Columbia. Still, it was nice to be accepted to an Ivy League School, even it was just for a certificate in physical therapy.

Buffalo Bills & Boston College

Even though I had said I did not want to work in the NFL, I went back to Buffalo in July 1970 for the Bills' summer camp without hesitation when Abe called. First, I needed the money and working for the Bills was more lucrative than running service for Reese & Sons. I also knew working for the Buffalo Bills looked a lot better on my AT resume than air conditioning service man.

That summer was the first NFL Players' strike; so no one reported to training camp. I sat alone in the dorm for two weeks. Although Abe told me I could go home and he would call me when the players reported, I could not afford to give up the $200 per week I was being paid. While sitting alone at Niagara University, Pat Dyer, the former Purdue assistant AT, called me and asked if I would be interested in working as his assistant trainer at Georgia Tech. At the end of my junior year, Pat left his assistant's position at Purdue for the head AT job at Georgia Tech. I told him that I would jump at the chance. He told me that there was an opening for head AT at Boston College (BC) and that he had recommended his assistant for that job. If his assistant took the BC position, he wanted me to come and work with him. (Pat had been the head AT at BC for several years after graduating from Purdue and before returning to Purdue as assistant AT in order to earn his Master's.) I was ecstatic.

A couple of days later Pat called and asked if I would be interested in the head AT position at BC because his assistant did not want to move to the Northeast. He said that he had talked to Pinky and that they both thought I could handle the head AT position. While I was initially disappointed about not getting to work with Pat again, I was certainly excited at the prospect to start my career as a head AT. Several days later I got a call from Bill Flynn, the Athletic Director (AD), and we arranged for an interview.

I was shocked at the smallness of BC's campus compared to Purdue. It had the reputation of a big college but it looked like a large high school. Still, Pat said it would be a great stepping-stone to a major college position, which is what I had decided I wanted. I met the football coach, Joe Yukica, and the basketball coach, Chuck Daly. (Yes, the Chuck Daly who later coached the Detroit Pistons to back to back NBA championships and who coached the 1992 Olympic Dream Team to Gold.) I also met the head AT, Fritz Massman, who was leaving BC for the ABA New York Nets. Later I met again with Bill Flynn and we talked salary. Pat had advised me to ask for $8,000; being bold, I asked for $8,500. He said that figure would fit their budget and that he would contact me within a week to let me know something.

Apparently they felt Pinky's and Pat's recommendations were enough because two days later, I got a call and was offered the job. I called Abe to let him know. He was as excited for me as I was. I called SG and told her to start packing; we were moving to Boston!

When I got back to Nashville, I had another acceptance letter for PT school. This time from the University of Iowa, which was affordable.

It wasn't much of a decision: Immediate prestigious employment made more sense at that time than indebtedness for further education. That was a decision I never regretted.

We were off on a new adventure! At 21 I became the youngest head AT in the country.

Chapter 10

BOSTON COLLEGE

Living in Boston

At BC I went immediately to work. The former AT, Fritz Massman, was a big help getting me started. We stayed at his house and semi-babysat their two older boys while he and his wife looked for a house on Long Island.

Our housing search netted a great apartment in Brighton, just down from BC. As it turned out, we were about two blocks from two bachelor football coaches. They were always having parties, and we were always invited. Two single girls living next door to them helped at the parties and they happily babysat for our son while we partied next door. We even took a playpen to their apartment. This pattern continued for two years. While I got drunk on several occasions there was never a *bad* incident. I did some silly things, but nothing violent or harmful to anyone or myself.

A couple from New Orleans moved in next door. We Southerners immediately bonded. They drank even more than we did. None of us ever thought that our drinking was a problem. Not even when after the "water heater incident" occurred.

One day I came home to find Pam (pseudonym) frantically shouting for Carl (pseudonym) to come out of the basement. We went to see what was going on. She informed us that Carl was drunk. Because he thought someone was in the basement he had gone down there with his gun. She asked me to go down and get him out of the basement. I called loudly to Carl as I made my way into the dark and filthy basement. He did not answer. Suddenly I heard a noise and then a gunshot. I screamed at Carl. He yelled that he "got the sumbitch" and he turned on a flashlight. He had shot the water heater when it had automatically come on. We all laughed and, of course, had a couple of beers to celebrate the "bagging" of the water heater. I'm still not sure what story he told the landlord about the water heater with a bullet hole in it.

Several years later we visited Pam and Carl after they moved back to New Orleans. We laughed again about the water heater shooting. Only in the writing of this does it impress upon me the danger and utter stupidity of the incident.

That being said, Pam and Carl showed us a fabulous time in New Orleans. After the first night, which did not start until about 11:00 pm and did not end until the sun was coming up over Jackson Square, Carl introduced me to his "sure fire" hangover cure: beer and oysters on the half shell. That was the first time I had some "hair of the dog that bit me" and it was a lesson well learned. I found the oysters were helpful, but not necessary. Because I knew that drinking in the morning was alcoholic drinking, I did not employ it often. I held it in reserve for the most monumental of hangovers and I never used it when I was working.

While in Boston, I usually did not drink during the work week. It was mostly on weekends and rare days off from work. Looking back, I realize that couples with whom we socialized the most and stayed in contact with after leaving Boston were our card playing and drinking buddies. I remember playing a lot of cards and drinking cheap wine. Two couples shared the cost of a half-gallon of Cribari wine which provided more than enough for four us when playing cards. Twenty years later I could easily drink a liter myself during a night of cards.

Notwithstanding the drinking, Sundays and the infrequent days off from work we explored Boston. We loved Beacon Hill and the rocky coast around Marblehead and thought we could live there forever. When we started looking at real estate we were shocked and disappointed to find out the only areas we could afford were West of Boston, the exact opposite direction from where we wanted to be.

Working at BC I was in constant motion and had to learn how to improvise. I had two student ATs and a part-time assistant who had no training beyond first aid. After Purdue, the budget at BC was also a major shock. At Purdue, if we needed something, we got it. At BC we needed everything and could afford nothing. I was constantly fighting for budget items and getting nowhere. Because I had been hired late in the fiscal year only a preliminary budget had been submitted. It was only enough to get through training camp and the first several weeks of the football season. The bean counters took it as the entire budget and were determined not to let me go over it. This finally came to the head coach's attention when I informed him about the third week of the football season I was running out of tape and they would not let me buy any more. He went to the AD and together they convinced the bean counters to let me order tape – but nothing else. Being creative, I worked out a deal with the local supplier to order the other supplies that I needed; then, he would figure out how many cases of tape would cover the cost of those needed supplies and charge them as tape.

They had a saying at BC, "the Jesuits take a vow of poverty and expect everyone else to do likewise!" That was also true in terms of salary. You may recall I started at $8,500 per year. After I was there for about three months, I received a $500 raise to $9,000. I was thrilled and thought this was because I was doing a super job! Later I found out that the prior AT had been making $9,000 and the $500 was going back into the general fund instead of into Athletics. So they gave it to me rather than lose it to the general fund.

When we started looking for houses and after I realized what I could afford, I had another realization: Since the prior AT was only making $9,000 after five years, I couldn't expect a lot more over the next five years. I fought tooth and nail with the AD for a $1000 raise the next year and settled for $500. The idea of BC as a stepping stone was starting to sound better and better so I plugged into the Purdue grapevine for available jobs. Pinky Newell was the Executive Director of the NATA and practically every job in the country came across his desk.

In 1971, I worked the pro game when the Bills played the Patriots in Boston. I had a long talk with Abe after the game about how frustrated I was and that I wanted out. He told me to hang in. He encouraged me by saying that BC was a great experience for me and that something would come across Pinky's desk sooner or later. Abe understood my situation as he had had a similar experience at the University of Detroit, another Jesuit school.

NATA Certification

In June 1971, I took the NATA Certification Exam in Baltimore. This was the first time the exam had been given nationally. Pinky, of course, had worked hard with a group to create the certification exam. He was certain that it would help the profession gain respect. As students at Purdue we had been quizzed and polled about what should be in it. Over the past year I had several heated conversations with Pinky about the rule requiring one year of practical experience before being eligible to take the exam. I complained that people working full time, like I was, would not have time to study for the exam. I went to Baltimore and took the exam cold – not one ounce of studying. Whether it was confidence or arrogance, I was not the least bit concerned about failing the exam. I was, however, very concerned that I would not score high on the exam and that one of "Pinky's guys" would not be among the best. I passed, of course, and later that year Pat Dyer informed me that Pinky was happy and I had not embarrassed Purdue ATs. Whew! That was a relief. (Several years later they abolished the rule about working for a year prior to taking the exam.)

Chapter 11

BUFFALO

Off to Buffalo

In the spring of 1972 Abe called me and asked if I would be interested in a full-time assistant athletic trainer position with the Bills. I was very apprehensive after my experience working under John Rauch. Abe assured me that Lou Saban, the new head coach, was the polar opposite of Rauch. He said Lou was coming from Denver where he had hired a full-time assistant trainer and that he planned on doing that at Buffalo. This was in response to the number of injury grievances that were being filed by the NFL Players Association.

This would be Saban's second tenure at the Bills. Because of my summers in Buffalo, I was familiar with the Saban stories about how he took Buffalo to AFL Championships in 1964 and 1965 and how they had missed going to the first Super Bowl the next year by losing to Kansas City in the AFL Championship game. (If you were a Buffalo Bills fan, you also believed that the Bills team would have beaten Lombardi's Packers because they matched up with them better than Kansas City.)

Abe's enthusiasm about Saban was contagious and eased my apprehension. I also reasoned that since Saban wanted to hire a full-time assistant athletic trainer, he must have thought the position valuable. SG was also very apprehensive about leaving Boston. She had really started feeling at home there. I assured her, however, that this would just be another stepping-stone and that since it was the pros it would be a lot more money.

I interviewed with the new Bills' coach, Lou Saban during spring football practice at BC. The plan was to fly to Buffalo in the morning and be back to Boston for afternoon practice. It did not go as planned. Saban had an urgent situation come up and put my interview off until the afternoon, since he thought I was there for the entire day. I scrambled to arrange for my student trainers at BC to cover for me because the head coach did not know I was gone. In those days if you interviewed for a job, it meant you did not want your present job. This was often considered disloyal and disloyalty could get you fired. I never actually knew anyone this happened to, but that was the prevailing mindset.

At lunch with Abe, my dreams of "Big Money" in the pros were shattered. Abe asked me how much I wanted for a salary. I replied that $15,000-$16,000 would be good. He broke out laughing and informed me that he was only making $14,000. This was 1972 and he had been there since 1960. I had to readjust my thinking and figured that the minimum I could come for and still be an improvement would be $12,000. That was the minimum salary for an NFL player at the time and that is exactly what Saban said the salary would be. He figured that the assistant AT was as important as the last man on the roster.

After two agonizing weeks and numerous phone calls, I got the job. I was to begin as soon as the school year was over. There were several farewell parties. BC gave me a "Boston Rocker" rocking chair with a BC emblem on the headrest. The coaches gave me a set of luggage – they said they knew I would need it.

1st House & New Neighbors

I borrowed $2,500 from my parents and the same from SG's parents for a down payment on our "starter" home. It was an L-shaped ranch with beamed cathedral ceilings in the living room which made it appear larger than it was. It cost $24,500 and was in an area called Depew, not far from the Buffalo airport. We were excited.

Because I was at training camp, SG assumed the lion's share of responsibility for settling us into our new home and was adept at it.

This would be a trend in coming years for another move in Buffalo and a move to New York. It was a happy, busy time for both of us. SG took great care of our son Rob and generally got excited when I came home from training camp at Niagara University.

Shortly after we settled into our home, a neighbor came by to meet SG. Her name was Jeannie (pseudonym). Like us, she and her husband, Gene (pseudonym), were not from Buffalo. She and SG hit it right off. Later that year I met Gene and we rapidly became great friends.

Buffalo can be a very dreary and lonely place. The snow and the cold are tolerable, but because the city is nestled between two of the Great Lakes, it experiences what is known as the "lake effect." This causes it to be overcast most of the time and that causes the dreariness. The natives, while friendly, are vey clannish. In the off-season without football and all the excitement and socializing that went along with it, Buffalo was just fucking miserable.

It was the first winter in Buffalo that we bonded with the neighbors, Gene and Jeanie. The four of us never did anything that I can recall without drinking. Usually one of us would get sloppy drunk. The next day the other three would laughingly remind them of what an asshole they had been.

Gene and Jeannie moved to Jamestown, NY in 1975. We were miserable without them. They seemed to make new friends easily and Gene was climbing the corporate ladder in a big oil company.

We visited them often. SG was jealous of Jeannie's new house and furniture. While working with the Bills gave me a celebrity status that she fed off of, she constantly reminded me of how well financially Gene was doing compared to me. This continued as they moved to Philadelphia, to Raleigh-Durham, to Houston, and finally to Gulf Shores, Alabama.

In spite of SG's jealousy of how well Gene and Jeanie were doing, we still got together whenever an opportunity presented itself. This is a pattern that held true from 1972 until 1991, when we cancelled our planned vacation with them because I entered rehab. Things changed significantly after that and eventually we drifted apart. In hindsight, it was a very dysfunctional co-dependent relationship.

Pregnancy & Regret

Two years after Rob was born we began to try for a second child. Nothing happened. Rob had been so easy to conceive that we could not figure out why the second was so difficult. After moving to Buffalo we exhausted the tests available at that time, scheduled sex around SG's basal temperature, etc. The only thing the "experts" could come up with was what they termed "one child syndrome." They thought that something in SG was killing the sperm. She had experienced several early miscarriages while we were in Boston, so we were beginning to think Rob might be an only child. We discussed adoption, but neither of us were too keen on the idea. (I'm not sure why.)

Finally, after several years, we decided not to worry about it any longer. A few months after we had accepted that we were not going to have another child, SG got pregnant. We were ecstatic. The due date was in February, 1975; the same month as Rob was born five years earlier.

This time we had medical insurance and did not have to utilize a clinic. We planned a C-section and the doctor promised to remove a lot of the scar tissue from SG's original C-section surgery. We had learned over time that the surgery in Nashville had been crude with a very ugly vertical scar as a result.

Rachel's birth went well – up to a point. When the doctor came out to inform me that I had a beautiful healthy daughter, he went on to say that because of all the scar tissue in SG's abdomen, if she got pregnant again "another C-section would kill her." No ifs, ands, or buts. She was too small to deliver naturally, and another C-section would kill her – these words rang in my ears. He wanted permission to tie her tubes while she was still on the table. I was terrified for her life and at the thought of losing her. We had two healthy children, a boy and a girl. So I gave my permission for him to perform the laparoscopy and tie her tubes.

It seemed like the only decision at the time. I was panicked and thought I had to make the decision then. I have regretted that decision many, many times since. It was not my decision to make unilaterally. I should have discussed it with SG. We should have gotten a second opinion. Later, I learned that there was no real hurry. I fucked up. Maybe for right reasons and understandable fears, but I still fucked up BIG TIME.

As years passed, SG constantly blamed me for our not having more kids and for not caring enough about her to ask her about her own body. It became a huge guilt trip for me and a club that SG could pull out and beat me with any time the mood struck her – which was generally any time she got drunk (so quite often). I had no defense.

It was only when she was post-menopausal that she got off that broken record. My sense is that once Rob was in college and Rachel in high school, she recognized that neither of us wanted another child. She knew that by that time we both felt we were too old to be taking care of younger children. Still, it was an easy wound to prick any time the subject of women's rights came up, or if she just wanted to let someone else know what an inconsiderate bastard I really was. I suppose I resented her resentment of me. I was never able to make it up to her; and I am quite sure now that she would have never let me. If there is one thing I could change in my life, it would be that decision.

The Bills

Working for the Buffalo Bills was easy because I already knew my primary working associates: Eddie "Abe" Abramoski, the head AT; Tony Marchetti, the equipment manager; and Dr. Joe Godfrey, the team physician. Abe, my mentor and fellow Purdue alumnus, was my immediate boss. Lou Saban, the head coach, had just returned to coach the Bills after a five-year hiatus as the head coach of the Denver Broncos.

Lou had hired a full time assistant AT at Denver the year before and considered it a necessity at Buffalo. I was at the vanguard of assistant ATs that were brought into the NFL to keep better medical records. At that time there were only about three or four teams that had full time assistant ATs. The National Football League Players Association (NFLPA) had won a number of injury grievances because of lack of adequate record keeping. The head ATs at the time only kept track of major surgeries on index cards, if they had time to do that.

Abe gave me free reign to set up my own record keeping system and also put me in charge of ordering supplies and maintaining an inventory. Abe always appreciated my enthusiasm and I always felt he respected my opinion. He loved to teach and I loved to learn. Some of his basic theories I incorporated permanently and passed on to my assistants and interns. Beyond sports medicine, they also have application to wellbeing:

- Find (and eliminate if possible) the cause of the problem – don't just treat the symptom.
- Doing a little bit often is more effective than doing a single bout of exercise, rehab routine, etc.
- Moderation in all things. (This one Abe and I both believed in but neither of us practiced in our personal lives – respectfully his tendency to overeat and my drinking).
- Keep an open mind. Use good judgment and common sense, but don't rule something out just because it's not 100% scientific or because it sounds "off the wall" – it might just work. Abe reasoned, and I agreed, that if you wait for science to prove things before you used them, you would end up years behind the competition. Indeed, Dr. Godfrey, and other pioneers in orthopedic sports medicine/surgery, was always experimenting on new and innovative techniques. In short, sports medicine was aggressive and creative.

Tony Marchetti was the equipment man. Tony was usually referred to by his last name or Marcio (Mar-ki-o). Marchetti was one of the true characters I have known over the years. He was short, about 5'5", and had a big beer belly. He had a deep voice and was hysterically funny. His method of communicating was usually by insulting you. He came on like onions, but after a while you learned he was an old softie with a heart of gold. He broke players' balls at every opportunity. The bigger the name, the more shit they got from Tony. He was a former bus driver and bartender and had worked with the Bills since the mid-'60s during Saban's first tour with Buffalo. Tony was old when he started and when he finally retired in the mid-'80s, players from all three decades showed up for the party. Tony was loved. One of the lessons Tony taught me was how to barter Bills gear for services, future favors, or merchandise. This proved to be invaluable over the years and is definitely an unwritten perquisite of working for an NFL team.

Dr. Joe Godfrey was the team physician. "Dr. G" may be one of the most honorable and up-front people I have ever met. One of the founders of sports medicine, he was a great surgeon and most of the treatment and rehab techniques that Abe embraced were originally Dr. G's. He was also a great teacher. He was always willing to take the time to explain what he was doing, how to diagnose, and the reasons behind his thinking. I was like a sponge soaking up the knowledge he communicated.

Joe Murder

My main drinking buddy, however, when I wasn't drinking with my neighbor, Gene, was Joe Murry. Joe was hired in 1973 as Buffalo's strength coach and assistant equipment man. Back then, the concept of strength coaches was new; so we created a job description to justify full-time employment. Because he pushed the players in workouts and lifting, the players nicknamed him "Joe Murder."

Joe and I were roommates on the road. We were the same age and had similar goals in life. When we were on the road, upon arriving in town the traveling secretary would have a rental car waiting for us while the team took busses to the hotel. Abe, Tony, Joe, and I would go to the stadium and set up for the game.

By 1974, Joe and I had a pretty good routine down. We told Abe and Tony they did not need to come to the stadium. We would do the pre-game set up ourselves with the help of the local clubhouse guys, who always had beer available. This arrangement gave us the rental car to use to explore the town after we finished setting up. If there was some place we wanted to actually see, we would get a map and a six-pack; otherwise we would ask the clubhouse guys where the local hotspots were and head for them. When we would finally get to our room, we always had a six-pack or a bottle of wine awaiting us – compliments of the traveling secretary.

Pre-season games were always dangerous because we came in a day early and the games were usually the following night. We could stay out drinking late and not have to worry about getting up the next morning. Because this was also during the training camp period, which was grueling with its 16 hour days, we felt we "deserved" a night out.

Probably the worst of these deserved nights out occurred during a trip to Green Bay. Joe and I went to the stadium to set up and had three or four beers each. Then we went to the hotel and split a six-pack. We got another six-pack and drove around town. We drove up and down a street that ran along the packing houses. Across the street from the packing companies there were about six to eight bars per block; this went on for 10 to 12 blocks. We kept trying to count the bars, but kept losing count as we got into the 70s. After exploring, we went to Lum's where we had big schooners of beer. We then bar-hopped for a while and ended up back at the hotel bar and drank some more with some of the coaches.

Unfortunately, the game the next day was in the afternoon instead of the evening, so I had to be up early. I woke up with a terrible hangover. I went to the pre-game meal where I also had to tape ankles. About the third guy I taped, I got a whiff of his smelly foot and sprinted to the john where I puked my guts out. I managed to tape the rest of the guys but was only able to eat some toast.

When we got to the stadium I was pale and shaky, but I managed to tape the rest of the players. As the team was going out for warm-ups, Dr. Godfrey asked me what was wrong. I told him I must have had some bad beer the night before. Joe also felt like shit. Since we had both drank that much before without these results, we decided that the beer was green or something like that. Dr. G suggested I take an Empirin with codeine #3. I did and laid down while the team was out for warm-up. Twenty minutes later when they came in, I was feeling like a human again. Thanks to Dr. G I had found a terrific cure for a hangover.

Learning about Empirin #3 was a blessing and a curse. From that time on I never traveled without a codeine tablet or two. I never took more than one for a hangover, and one was all it ever took. Over the years after that, I never suffered from a hangover for more than an hour. If a couple of aspirins and an Ornade didn't do the trick, I took the codeine. I am quite sure that knowing I had the "cure" with me allowed me not to ever worry about having a hangover – the blessing – and so that having a hangover was never a consideration for me when I drank – the curse.

Joe, Abe, Tony, and Dr. G. were my primary working associates and had a great impact on my life professionally and personally. I could write three volumes telling everything that happened in Buffalo from what I learned about sports medicine to the football stories. Some of it – especially some of the football stories – would sound so fantastical that you might be disinclined to believe them. Heavy drinking was the norm for most players and coaches – and for this assistant AT. Cocaine and steroids were just coming on the scene and were not an issue while I was at the Bills. That being said, it was the 70s so there was a lot of other recreational drug use.

I got my first – and only – DUI in 1974 after a night pre-season game in Buffalo. The game ended around midnight. SG and I had agreed to meet some players and their wives at a downtown disco. We did not arrive until after 1:00 AM. Because SG was pregnant and not drinking, we left after about an hour. Less than a mile from home I stopped at a red light at a major intersection. SG was complaining about getting home and there was no traffic, so I took the right on red – which was not legal at the time. The next thing I knew there were flashing lights in my rearview mirror. While I was busy explaining to the State Trooper why I was out so late and that I ran the light because the intersection was empty and my pregnant wife had to pee, the second Trooper shined a light in SGs face. She yelled at him to shut it off. Then she commanded me to tell the "damn cop" that I worked for the Bills and take her home! Needless to say the next stop was the Trooper Station. I blew 0.15 which was over the legal limit of 0.1. At the time, I blamed the ticket and the 30-day license suspension (except to drive to and from work) on SG's outburst. Once again the wrong lesson learned.

Buffalo Bills – in Sum

While in Buffalo SG and I were also close to several players, especially a small group of married players who had their wives in town during the season. We partied with them a lot.

From the football aspect, the Bills were *almost* a great team. Saban built an offense around O.J. Simpson. In 1973 the Bills set an NFL rushing record of 3,088 yards with O.J. tallying 2,003 yards, which broke Jim Brown's single season record of 1,863 yards. In 1974 the Bills made it to the Playoffs and lost to Pittsburgh on the way to their first Super Bowl. In 1975 we were poised to win the AFC-East, but a controversial call cost us the last game of the season to Miami and knocked us out of the playoffs.

After the 1975 season the NFL added two teams: Seattle and Tampa Bay. A lot of teams still did not have full-time assistants so I thought I had a pretty good shot at getting one of those head AT jobs. I wanted to go south, so I aimed for Tampa Bay but I came in second.

After missing out on the Tampa Bay job, I reasoned that with the lack of mobility in the head AT ranks in the NFL we would probably be in Buffalo a lot longer. With that in mind we decided to get out of the neighborhood we were in and buy a bigger house. We had a lot of fun looking and finally bought a cape in East Aurora, not too far from the stadium in Orchard Park. It was brick and resembled the house I grew up in. SG swore that's why I wanted it so badly. Actually, I thought it was the best buy for the money. It was very well constructed and had a great deep back yard that was fenced in and had trees and shrubs that provided privacy.

We moved in right before training camp. Once again SG set up house. We had a good time in the house and really liked the area. The people were friendlier than our last neighborhood. East Aurora had a nice "village" atmosphere. The Bill's assistant PR guy and his wife lived a few blocks away. They invited us into a "rotating dinner club" where one couple would host a meal with an ethnic theme and everyone would bring a dish. It was a nice and inexpensive way to have a night out and meet with couples our own age.

The 1976 season, however, was a disaster that saw Lou Saban quitting after four games and Jim Ringo, the Offensive Line coach, taking over. The Bills were 2-2 under Saban, and then did not win another game. If the dismal football season wasn't bad enough, Buffalo suffered record snowfalls in November and December, followed by the "Blizzard of '77" in January. I could describe it, but again, you probably wouldn't believe me. I will just say that Buffalo, a city that handles snow like mowing a lawn, came to a standstill for more than a week and more than 20 people died. Snow drifts reached 30'. It was so bad Jimmy Buffett referenced it in his *Son of a Sailor* album. (Google it if you're curious).

Chapter 12

THE JETS

Do you want the Job?

At the opposite end of the state, another New York team was also having a really bad year. Lou Holtz had started 1976 as the head coach of the New York Jets and resigned before the season was over. At the end of the season the head AT for 14 years resigned. Walt Michaels, a long-time Jets assistant in the Namath era, was returning as head coach. (Walt had been in Philadelphia as defensive coordinator.)

In late February or early March 1977, the Bills' equipment man, Tony Marchetti, got a phone call from Bill Hampton, the equipment manager of the Jets. He asked Tony if I would be interested in the head AT job at the Jets. Marchetti said "sure" but sent Joe Murry over to our office to get Abe. Abe went over to the equipment room for the phone call and in short order Joe Murry was back telling me to get over to Tony's office. When I came in, I got the universal "Shhh" sign (index finger over your lips) so I sat quietly trying to figure out what was going on. Marchetti mouthed "New York Jets" to me, but I had no clue what the call was about. I finally heard Abe tell whoever was on the other end that "Yes, I'll speak with coach Michaels."

There was a pause and Abe introduced himself to Walt Michaels, the new coach of the Jets. They chit-chatted about people and players they had worked with. Finally, I heard Abe tell him that "Yes, Bob would be interested in the job," and "yes, of course, he was qualified and beyond that he would make a great head trainer." At that point, Walt apparently asked to speak to me, but Abe told him it would be best to call Jim Ringo and ask for permission, even though I did not have a contract and for that reason did not actually come under the NFL tampering rules. Abe also hinted that it might be best if Ringo thought he was Walt's first contact about the position.

I had known that the Jets position was open and had not pursued it for several reasons. First, it was in New York City, which did not appeal to me. Second, I had just bought a new house in Buffalo, and we liked the area. Finally, since Walt Michaels was coming from Philadelphia, the buzz around the NFL was that Philadelphia's assistant AT had a lock on the job. Coach Michaels, however, informed Abe that the former Jets AT had recommended me. I had not been aware of that.

I was trying to get more information from Abe, but before my concerns could be sorted out Ringo's secretary called down and requested my presence in his office. We all smiled and Abe reminded me to play dumb so that Ringo's ego wouldn't get bent out of shape.

Ringo was very formal and asked if I was aware that the Jets head trainer job was available. I told him that I was, but I hadn't looked into it – that seemed to make him relax a bit. He informed me that Walt Michaels had requested permission to speak to me about the job and he had granted it. I could expect a call from Michaels today or tomorrow and that I was to keep him informed of what was going on and of my decision. He then went on to tell me why he thought he was a better coach than Michaels. I wasn't sure if this was to try to keep me in Buffalo, or just his ego – which was considerable.

I'll Take It!

I had a lot of trepidation as I went to New York for the interview. Primarily, it was the concept of living in New York City. Second, the Jets had a reputation for being cheap. And, regardless of how bad the Bills sucked, we were still better than the Jets.

Bill Hampton, the equipment man, picked me up at the airport and began the sales pitch. First he talked about Walt. I could tell right away that "Hamp" viewed him like Abe looked at Saban, which was with very high regard. Next, as we motored out of Queens and into Nassau County, the City seemed to dissipate; there was a lot of green – not at all what I had expected. At the time, the Jets had a facility on the campus of Hofstra University in Hempstead, Long Island. They not only practiced there but they also had training camp there to boot. The Jets did not "go away" to training camp – that was intriguing.

The football complex was small, and inadequate, but they had plans for expansion the next year. The interview with Walt was low key. He reminded me of Saban in the sense that everyone was on a first name basis and he said what was on his mind. He probed me on how I handled injured players and seemed to know a lot about me. After about 45 minutes he told me I was "Okay" with him, but now I had to pass the real test with the team physician, Jim Nicholas.

I knew "Nick the Knife" by reputation and had met him several times. He was great friends and colleagues with Dr. Godfrey, and I also knew from Dr. G (and many others) he had a huge ego. He made his reputation on Joe Namath's knees and was frequently quoted in the papers. Walt called Dr. Nicholas' office to tell him that I had passed his test and asked him if he wanted me to come to the City for an interview. Walt had him on speakerphone, so I heard him say, "Is that the kid from Buffalo? I talked to Joe Godfrey about him, he's okay. Tell him I'll see him after he moves here." Walt seemed shocked, but pleased. I felt great and thought maybe this was worth real consideration.

I asked about a company car; Walt said they had not planned on that. I told him that I had a car in Buffalo as an assistant, so not having one as a head trainer was a deal breaker. He got on the phone with the business manager and told him the new trainer was going to need a car, so find a way to do it. I was impressed. Next, we talked money. I asked for $25,000 (I was due to make $17,000 at the Bills). Walt countered at $20,000. I said I didn't think I could afford to come for that, so he made a call and came back with $20,500. "Cheap-ass Jets" started echoing in my head. I asked about a bridge loan so I could buy a house before selling in Buffalo; I knew I would have trouble selling after the Blizzard of '77. Walt said the GM, Al Ward, would have to handle that. He would also have to approve any raise over the $20,500. To make a long story short, I agreed to $21,500, the bridge loan, and, of course, the car. I was to get a $1,500 raise the next year, but if I had not repaid the bridge loan in a year, the raise would only be $500. This was memorialized in a letter, which was the closest thing to a contract I ever had in the NFL.

Déjà Vu

When I arrived at the Jets the attitude was similar to my first year at the Bills: there was a new day dawning and everyone was optimistic. There was, however, an undercurrent of displeasure and distrust between the administration and the coaching staff, but that was somewhat universal in the NFL. As usual, as the head AT I was right in the middle. I knew I had to be loyal to the coach and also keep communications open with administration. And, both groups kept talking about "this problem with the doctor." That one directly affected me and would be the cause of much frustration and stress over the years to come. (More on this later.)

Abe and I had already been compiling injury information on college seniors for the upcoming NFL draft. This was accomplished by calling the college ATs and asking for an injury history of the players. Both clubs agreed that it would be most efficient for us to continue to work together for the next month and share the information until I reported to the Jets. Everyone at the Bills was happy for me, except for Jim Ringo, who became a real prick and treated me like a traitor. I wasn't allowed on the third floor of the stadium complex, lest I might see the draft board and tell the Jets about it. He even made sure that I was not invited to the unveiling of the 1976 Highlight Film, which really hurt my feelings. But, then again, how many highlights could there be in a 2-12 season?

I left Buffalo in mid-April to report to the Jets. The recently purchased house in East Aurora was up for sale. While I helped with packing, SG absorbed the lion's share of the responsibility for the move. She didn't complain, however, as we were getting out of Buffalo. While it was not as far south as Tampa Bay, it was at least in the right direction, and I had been assured that the sun shone on Long Island during the winter, unlike Buffalo!

When I arrived on Long Island, the first week was spent de-briefing my injury information with the scouts in preparation for the draft. After that first week, someone had the bright idea to send me on the road to physically examine potential draftees. This was about two weeks before the draft. No one in the NFL had ever done anything like that before, so I was excited. We targeted colleges that either had players the Jets were very interested in as high draft picks or schools that had a lot of players. I started at Boston College, then proceeded to Alabama, Memphis State, Missouri, Nebraska, Colorado, USC, Cal Berkeley, and then went back to New York through Kansas. I even examined one guys' knees on a shoe shine stand in the St. Louis airport. I didn't know it then, but this was the beginning of a huge change not only for the Jets, but for the entire NFL.

Pre-Draft Physicals

The 1977 draft was foundational for my first 10 years at the Jets. We drafted future All-Pros Marvin Powell, Wesley Walker, and Joe Klecko. It was the first two, Powell and Walker, that led to changes in how the NFL operated pre-draft physicals. It's a long story that I love to tell, but I will condense it as much as possible. We drafted Marvin and Wesley on my okay. I examined them at USC and Berkeley, respectively. Marvin had a right knee that had suffered a 2-3° medial collateral ligament sprain. Both knees had medial laxity and the bad one was only slightly more lax. So I said he was okay, but needed more rehabilitation. The concern with Wesley was a lateral ligament tear of his knee, which I said had healed very well making the knee stable, but that he also needed rehab. We drafted them in the first and second rounds respectively.

Jim Nicholas, the team doctor who had said that I was okay with him, was less than enthused about the two players because of their injury history. Leon Hess had just become majority owner and was present for mini-camp physicals. Dr. Nicholas, better known as "Nick the Knife," was putting on a show for him by making predictions about how players would hold up. In those days, top players were signed as soon after the draft as possible, which was before they came to mini-camp. After an hour of the "Nick the Knife" show, Mr. Hess was getting bored and finally said, "Where are those two players we paid all this money to?"

I rounded up Marvin and upon examination Nick noted that Marvin was loose jointed and that, according to his theory[3], Marvin would be subject to more knee injuries like the one he had suffered at USC. Nick predicted that Marvin would have to be braced his entire career, which would slow him down. In short, this was a bad first-round pick. Mr. Hess even commented that he could see that one leg was smaller than the other. Marvin looked completely nonplussed as I tried to explain that we could get the size back in the leg with rehab. No one except Marvin was listening.

Next up was Wesley Walker. Even before he came into the room, "Nick" was telling Mr. Hess that lateral knee ligaments never healed well and it would definitely slow him down. Since he was supposed to be a speedy wide receiver, the Jets had made another bad pick. At that point, I felt like I might have the shortest tenure as a head AT in the history of the NFL. Fortunately, Wesley's knee was solid as a rock – the surgeon at Cal had done a great job. Whew! At worst, I was 1 for 2. A crisis averted.

About 20 minutes later one of the student trainers helping with the physicals knocked on the door and told me he had a wide receiver that could not see the eye chart out of one eye. I was horrified to learn it was Wesley Walker. It turns out he had a congenital cataract in one eye that made him a medical risk and, thus, he should not have passed our physical. It mattered little to Nick the Knife that Wesley was good enough to be drafted in the second round, notwithstanding the congenital cataract.

An immediate meeting was called that included the Mr. Hess, Nick the Knife, Dr. Cal Nicholas, Jim's brother and the team internist, Walt Michaels, the GM Al Ward, myself, and the only remaining scout, Jim Royer. Mike Holovak, who had been player personal director and had approved my going on the road, had taken the Houston Oilers General Manager job right after the draft, and all the scouts except Royer took other jobs. All eyes turned to me since I had okayed Walker's health. I pleaded ignorance of the eye problem and said I had no knowledge of it and no suspicion of it. I had interviewed both the head coach and the AT at Berkley and neither indicated there was a problem with Walker's eye.

The remaining scout, Jim Royer, spoke up and said that neither Holovak nor any of the scouts had any knowledge about Wesley's eye and that he knew that my directive was to check Walker's knee. From that moment I knew I could depend on Jim Royer – and I hoped he was going to stick around.

For the record the panic over Wesley's blind eye was short lived as he led the league in receptions his first two years. He went to the Pro Bowl twice and never had a problem with his knee (although he did have a myriad of minor injuries that prevented him from being consistently great). Marvin Powell played Right Tackle for 11 years and went to the Pro-Bowl six times. While he did wear a brace on his knee for his entire career, he proved to be very durable.

Combine Evolution

From that experience, Mr. Hess decided that we needed to have our doctors examine future draft picks *before* the draft. So, the next year my new assistant and I brought in 113 college seniors, helter-skelter, to New York for physicals. It consumed the off-season.

Those 113 players only lasted through four rounds of the 1978 draft. Our 5th round pick was a linebacker from Penn State who had "never missed a game" according to his AT when I called him on draft day. When we examined him, he had two of the sloppiest knees I had ever seen and by every measure that we used failed the physical. Jim Nicholas again got on his soap box about drafting healthy players. After that Mr. Hess said that the Jets could never draft another player unless they had been examined by one of our orthopedic doctors. We got really organized and the next year brought in 240 players to New York over three weekends. My assistant and I were still the main travel agents, contacting the players, arranging flights, etc. We had some help from the new traveling secretary who arranged for the buses, hotel, meals, per diem, and the cab fare for the college players.

We took over two floors of doctor's offices at Lenox Hill Hospital. We had medical interns doing thorough histories. X-rays were taken, leg strength was Cybex tested, and eyes and teeth were examined. Internists were on hand for anyone with any non-orthopedic medical history. All this was done before the players ever saw the orthopods.

Dr. Nicholas was in his glory in the meeting after the physicals where we ranked the players according to injury risk. He, of course, personally examined those who might be our top picks. I would translate the medical terminology to Mike Hickey, our new Director of Player Personnel. Over time, he and I devised our own plus and minus grades to go along with Dr. Nicholas' four levels of rankings. These factored in talent.

Much of the League was laughing at us for wasting money, but some clubs began doing what we did in 1978. All of this eventually evolved into what is now known as the NFL Combine. Much of the pre-screening protocols can be traced back to those early pre-draft physicals we initiated at the Jets. I am very proud to have been on the vanguard of something that has become accepted procedure. On the downside, there began a growing perception around the League that the medical department at the Jets had too much influence on personnel decisions.

First Long Island House

SG brought the kids to Long Island for 10 days over Easter. We stayed at the Holiday Inn in Westbury. House hunting was nerve-wracking. We needed to find something that trip because the Jets were only paying for one trip. We were concerned we would have trouble selling the house in Buffalo since everyone was fleeing town after the Blizzard of '77. Also, we wanted to make sure that any home purchased on Long Island could be sold fairly rapidly if the coaching staff got fired and the new coach brought in his own AT.

With about two days left we found a nice four-bedroom colonial in East Northport on Long Island. We felt like we got a reasonable deal. The house cost $56,000. With the Jets influence at the bank, our mortgage payment was not going to be much more than our mortgage in Buffalo. Whew!

We closed on the house during training camp. I rented the Buffalo house to a Bills player for the season. That meant that I would not have to pay two mortgages until January. Hopefully by then it would sell. SG drove down from Buffalo with the kids and her sister, CG, in what was rapidly becoming an old Toyota wagon. (Those Buffalo winters had taken their toll.) Her sister's help kept me from feeling totally guilty that I was doing little to set-up the house.

All of the rooms needed painting. SG did that quite well before unpacking everything. The living room and basement looked like warehouses with boxes stacked almost to the ceiling. Gradually the house began to take shape. I was always amazed when I managed to get home, how much was accomplished each week. I would usually make it home after the pre-season games. If it were a home game, I would get home about 1:00 AM. After some of the road games it made no sense to go home because I had to be in for morning treatments at 10:00 AM. On those occasions, I would go home after treatments for a few hours before heading back for personnel meetings later in the day. Training camp was a bitch for everyone!

The Jets Drinking Culture

When I reported in April, the Jets footed the bill for one month at the Holiday Inn Westbury. After using up my allotted time at the Holiday Inn, I did what about half the coaches did: I moved into the Jets complex while I was waiting to close on the house in July. Two coaches had rollaway cots stashed in the film room and four of us slept on the treatment tables in training room – like a dormitory. This turned out to be a great bonding opportunity for me with the coaches. They already had a well-established routine of hitting certain bars for happy hour and free food at the end of the day. Then we would head to one of several bars where we either drank for free or for half price. Once or twice a week Walt would take us all out to eat on the Jets. Just about everyone drank heavily; so, since I was not a "lightweight" when it came to capacity, I fit right in. My tolerance was better than some of the coaches. The night would end when they got tipsy. I don't recall ever getting drunk during that period.

The drinking culture at the Jets exceeded that at the Bills. Walt kept Scotch in his office; Hamp kept beer in the equipment room; and

I eventually kept beer in the training room office. At the end of the day, usually about 5:15 PM, it was not unusual to see people walking around the complex with a beer in hand. It was just the coaches, equipment men, two secretaries, the film director, my part-time assistant AT, and me working at the Hofstra complex. The administrative offices were in Manhattan.

This routine was pretty much continuous until training camp when we moved into the dorms on Hofstra's campus. Then, the days became much longer. They began at 6:30 AM and finished with the nightly personnel meeting around 11:00-11:30 PM. The same as Buffalo with the difference being that a big refrigerator filled with beer graced the meeting room. So, when I came into the meeting after injury treatments, I would grab a beer and wait for my turn to give my injury report.

During training camp, we moved into Hofstra's gym because they had several locker rooms and a larger training room. I had a small fridge in the training room office that was also stocked with beer. After the afternoon practice and before we went to dinner, it became a tradition to have a beer with my student trainers that worked during summer camp. They could ask questions about a particular injury that may have occurred, rehab techniques, or just football. I always enjoyed that half hour. When we moved back into the Jets complex after training camp ended the fridge was not as well stocked, and I did not drink (there) every night. If I had to work late, however, I had no problem popping the top on a beer.

During this time, I became very close to Dan Henning, the receivers coach. Dan did not live at the complex as he was one of two coaches held over from Lou Holtz's short-lived regime. He lived in Northport, which influenced my residential choice of East Northport. It was during that first training camp that Dan introduced me to Bill's Meadowbrook. It was a bar across the street from Hofstra's main entrance and had apparently been there for years. I had eaten burgers and had a few beers at Bill's while living at the complex, but I never made it known that I was with the Jets. Henning changed that.

I had assumed that Henning went home after the personnel meetings, but most nights he went to Bill's. I got introduced to the bartenders and found out early on that if you put a $10 bill on the bar you paid for the first drink and then no more. Eventually I went to Bill's a couple of times a week with and without Henning. The film director and the groundskeeper were also regulars, so there was always someone to talk to. When we all got together there was little football talk and major "philosophizing" that occurred. Those training camp nights at Bill's Meadowbrook continued until I entered rehab.

Front Office Changes

Just before that first training camp some changes occurred in the front office. Jim Kensil was named president of the Jets. He had been Commissioner Pete Rozelle's right hand man at the NFL for 15-16 years. Everyone was a little wary of having someone from the league office running the show because we were afraid he might be too straight an arrow (every team tried to skirt some rules to gain an edge). Turns out it was a great decision. Over the years Jim Kensil turned the Jets into a first class organization.

On a personal level, Jim Kensil earned my respect – and my loyalty. Following that first season he "renegotiated" my contract. He tore up the letter about the bridge loan repayment affecting my salary, told me to repay the Jets whenever I sold the house in Buffalo (which took until the following fall), and gave me a raise to $25,000. I was ecstatic!

Pepper

During that first training camp Jim Kensil and Al Ward, the General Manager, came to me about moving my assistant, Tim Davey, full time into the front office. I had inherited Tim as part-time assistant AT and his other duties were managing the Hofstra training complex. Tim had informed me when I interviewed that he was thinking about moving full-time into administration, so this was not a complete surprise. Since it was now August and we were already under way in the pre-season, they asked me if I would have a problem hiring an assistant.

Ordinarily, the timing would have been a problem, except I knew of a Purdue grad, Pepper Burruss, who would be graduating from Northwestern University's Physical Therapy Program in October.

Management agreed that Tim would continue to help me part time until Pepper arrived in mid-October. This worked out great for everyone involved.

My relationship with Pepper began when I was at BC in the spring of 1971. A football player at BC asked me if I would speak to a high school senior from his hometown about athletic training as a profession. I said, "Of course." A couple of weeks later a skinny kid came to see me. As he shadowed me the entire day, he never tired of the pace or of asking intelligent questions. At the end of the day we sat and talked about where he could go to school for athletic training. He said he did not have a lot of money so he wanted to go to a New York state school. He finally asked me where I went to school and how I got to be a head AT at such a young age. I told him about Purdue and Pinky Newell. I opined that Purdue may be the best place in the country for athletic training. I explained that many jobs came across Pinky's desk and that coaches and athletic directors regularly called him for recommendations. As a Purdue grad, we often had first crack at those jobs. I named the Bills and Cowboys in the NFL and the Pacers in the NBA as having Purdue ATs along with about eight major colleges right off the top of my head. He was duly impressed. He asked me about BC and I told him not to come to BC because we really did not have an athletic training program. My student-ATs were just doing it for the work-study money and it was all I could do to teach them first-aid and to tape ankles well enough to help me out.

That fall I got a note from Pinky saying that a young man named Pepper Burruss was enrolled at Purdue, wanted to be an AT, and had used me as a reference. I immediately called Pinky and told him the above story. I suggested that he accept Pepper in the program; and he did. I followed Pepper's career until it merged with mine in the summer of 1977 at the Jets. He worked with me for 16 years until he left for his current position as head AT for the Green Bay Packers.

Chapter 13

JETS ~ WALT MICHAELS ERA (1977-82)

Season #1 ~ 1977

The first season with Walt Michaels was a blur. The team would spend the night before the home games at the Holiday Inn Westbury. There would be a team "snack" at 10:00 PM that was mainly just to make sure all the players were in the hotel before curfew. Burgers, chicken, pasta, and beer were on the menu. Players would have a couple of beers and take a couple to their room to help them sleep. I would generally stick around and talk with coaches or other personnel, and then take a couple of beers with me to my room.

After the home games, the coaches met back at the Holiday Inn Westbury where Walt would have an open tab so we could eat and drink. The wives were invited to this – that was helpful. As long as SG was included, she never bitched about me not being home. Most of the time we were the last to leave.

There were also a number of formal affairs, some black-tie. The assistant coaches were rarely invited to these. I suspect it was because the Jets would have had to buy an extra table or two to include all of them. So after the top administrators and PR people were accounted for, there was only room for a few more people and it usually included the equipment manager, Bill Hampton, and his wife and SG and me. There were also several stag dinners; I generally teamed up with

Dan Henning, the receivers coach, to go to these. All in all, it was a whirlwind. I learned rapidly that New York's reputation as a fast paced place was not a myth.

5 O'clock Club

On the road there was the *5 O'clock Club* tradition that began in the AFL days. It was a party hosted by Frank Ramos, our PR Director, where the press, coaches, and traveling staff could mingle. There was an open bar and heavy hors d'œuvres that usually turned into the evening meal, allowing us to pocket our dinner per diem. Most of the coaches only stayed a short while because they did not want to be questioned by the press. After the coaches left, it was just the traveling staff. Unless I had family at the game, I would usually stay at the *5 O'clock Club* until time for the snack. Quite often, especially in later years, these would turn into very low stakes poker games, which were a lot of fun.

After road games we were bussed from the airport to the complex. Walt had the habit of waiting at the complex until the game film was developed, which took 3-4 hours. (This was pre-video.) He also had the habit of "inviting" me into his office ("Reese, come in here!") to talk about the injuries. He always poured me a scotch. There were nights I stayed in the training room because I knew I couldn't, or at least shouldn't, drive home.

After a couple of years of this, Pepper once asked me why I didn't just go out the back door so Walt would not see me. I convinced myself that by going in and drinking with Walt, I got to know what he was thinking: which players he was pissed off at and the tact he was going to take the upcoming week. (*I used to joke that Walt stayed at the complex because he didn't want to go home. After many years of not following Pepper's advice to duck out the back door I realized my own projection of not wanting to go home.*)

Henning & Led

During those first two seasons I shared a ride to work with Dan Henning, the receivers coach, three or four days a week. It was the time of the 1978 gas crisis, and we had a 24-mile commute one way. I had no money to spare; so sharing a ride made sense and I liked Dan a lot. He was smart, humorous, and fun to be around. He loved piano bars where after a few drinks he would sing "Danny Boy" and other Irish ballads. He introduced me to the bars that gave us free drinks because we were with the Jets.

Dan grew up in Queens; he was a New York guy. He sold me on the concept that in New York you work harder than anyone else and you need to play harder, too. It was not a hard sell. His wife, Sandy, got along with SG, another positive.

Bob Ledbetter, the running backs coach, and his wife, Lois, also lived in East Northport. Bob was a social magnet. He loved to bar-b-que in the off-season and often had parties at his house. We were always invited. SG, Lois, and Sandy became a triumvirate. They car pooled to games and got together when we were stuck in training camp or traveling to games.

Led was a cross between a Southern preacher and a great salesman. He had stories and anecdotes for every occasion, and he was always upbeat. He had coached at Grambling and several other traditionally Black colleges; he was somewhat a legend in that circle.

Both Led and Henning could drink me under the table, and I had a pretty large capacity for alcohol at that time. That made hanging out with them dangerous for me. One problem that I had when riding home with either of them is that they always stopped for an "end of the work-day" drink. Of course, it was never one drink. I would often be poured from the car half in the bag. SG would bitch about me coming home late, but her bitching did not penetrate because I would have another drink and tune her out.

One time when one of SG's sisters was visiting, Henning brought me home. He came to the door to make sure SG was not mad at me – she never got mad at Dan, he was too charming. When he was introduced to SGs sister, she said, "Henning? Your last name is Henning? I thought it was Fault. All I hear whenever Bob comes home late is that it's because of Dan Fault." That became a somewhat humorous excuse every time I did something that did not meet SG's approval, I would just say, "Hey, it's Dan's Fault!"

Humor aside, this attribution of my behavior to the influence of others is a theme in my family that goes back to my teen days with my cousin Jimmy Hatley and has followed me through adulthood. My mother considered me nothing more than an easily influenced sheep that would do whatever someone I admired suggested and so she also constantly harped on my choice of friends. Recognizing this attitude, many times in my life I diverted blame for my bad behavior onto others; however, I made the choices.

The Players

That first year I got close to several of the players whom I knew would be around the next year. I not only drank with the coaches; I also drank with the players. And, they really drank. There were several mottos that were part of the culture of the Jets players in the late 1970s through the late 1980s. A favorite was: "Anybody can play this game sober, it takes a real man to play it with a hangover." Another was: "We drink when we win (to celebrate). We drink when we lose (to mourn). Regardless, we drink!" Perhaps my favorite was: "We may lose a game but we never lose a party!" This is pretty much how it went for the next five years.

There was one major change in my attitude and behavior that began to occur during the 1978 season (my second year): I had begun to realize that I could not keep going at this pace and that, quite frankly, I wanted to be a good father to my kids. I recognized that I could not be a good father if I came home half in the bag three or four nights a week. I also realized I was behaving as a jerk, so I quit riding with Henning unless necessary. After the 1978 season Dan Henning left for the Dolphins. I looked at the departure of my primary drinking buddy as an opportunity to get home straightaway after work. This change, however, did not slow down SG's bitching at me for never being home. At the time I felt I deserved it, so I suffered in silence – and had a drink!

The 'Aints'

That first year, 1977, the Jets went 3-11. The next year the NFL went to the 16 game schedule. We went 8-8 in 1978 and 1979 and felt we were getting ready to take the next step to the playoffs. Then, in 1980, we suffered through a 4-12 season. The second to the last game of the year we lost to the infamous New Orleans "Aints" – their only win of the year.

The players were so embarrassed that they all ended up at *Footsie's*, a tiny bar near the Hofstra complex. It was the only place they could go that they knew people would not harass them. I stopped in and over many beers engaged in several heart to heart conversations with some of the team leaders about what went wrong. About the time I was ready to call it a night, the alcohol had gotten to some of the younger players who didn't quite grasp the humiliation we had just suffered. Marty Lyons and Mark Gastineau (6'4', 275 pounds and 6'5, 285 pounds respectfully) proceeded to flank me. Each took an arm and a leg, lifted me onto the bar and mixed an "upside-down Margarita" in my mouth. After I quit sputtering and everyone had a good laugh, they decided to do it again. When you have two behemoths manhandling you, protesting doesn't do much good. After the second episode, I got one of the team captains to run interference for me and got out of the place. I had already drunk a lot of beers, and the tequila really hit me hard. I remember struggling to keep the car on the road as I drove home – fortunately there was little traffic on the Northern State Parkway at 1:00 AM.

The next thing I remember is the crash – or immediately after the crash. Apparently I had passed out and crashed the car into the median on the highway. I was able to get the car off the right side shoulder. I remembered that I had two beers in the car and tossed them as far away from the car as I could. I assessed the damage to the car and realized I had been lucky to get it off the road as it would not start again. I then assessed the damage to me. I had a killer headache. I had slammed into the steering wheel which knocked out three of my front teeth. Even in the dark, I could see I was a mess. I felt my lip swelling. I had blood on the front of my shirt. I bit down on a handkerchief to stop the bleeding. The pain helped to sober me up. I searched for my teeth but soon gave up because it hurt too much to bend over.

I knew no one in their right mind would pick me up, so I walked about a mile to the closest pull off with pay phones. I called SG who was not happy. She, however, felt a little guilty because it was the first home game she missed and had she been there I would not have gone to *Footsie's*. She took the kids by the Ledbetter's before she picked me up.

I had told her that I had knocked out my front teeth but did not need to go to the emergency room. She called the team dentist and woke him up. She drove me to the dentist who put in a temporary bridge so I would not have nerve pain and develop a possible abscess.

My story to everyone – including SG – was that I had a couple of beers, that I was exhausted from the long day and losing to the Saints, and that I had just fallen asleep at the wheel. Most people seemed to buy it. Other than losing my front teeth and having a swollen lip for a week, there were no other repercussions. Insurance covered the car, which was declared totaled; and I got another car. There was only one week left in the season. The Jets finished the dismal year with a win in Miami. By the next year hardly anyone remembered I had the crash.

Chapter 14

THE BEGINNING OF AN END

The good, the bizarre, and the especially ugly

As the Jets entered the 1981 pre-season, the loss to the "Aints" the year before seemed to bind the team together. We opened the season, however, with three consecutive losses, which placed head coach, Walt Michaels, in jeopardy of being fired.

During the week after the third loss there was an impromptu meeting in my office with the four team captains. We discussed the impact of another loss: Walt would be fired and there was no telling who would take over. Two of the older captains talked about the horrors for players when coaches were fired during the season. I told them about my last season in Buffalo and the impact of that 2-12 season on players. I'm not sure how much it helped, but the team turned the losing streak around that week against Houston. The Jets then went on to win 10 straight. We lost the wild card game to Buffalo, but it was a great year. It was the birth of the *Sack Exchange* as Joe Klecko and Mark Gastineau competed with each other to see who would lead the NFL in quarterback sacks. Freeman McNeil emerged as a star running back, and Richard Todd throwing long to Wesley Walker was just fun to watch.

The next year, 1982, a player's strike was called after the second regular season game. My biggest concern during the strike was monitoring Joe Klecko's knee injury. During the second game he ruptured his patella tendon and had surgery to repair it. I kind of danced around some of the rules about contact with the players during the strike in order to make sure Joe was progressing properly. Jim Kensil called me on the carpet at least twice about undermining management's position, and I argued strongly that at some point the strike would be over and none of us wanted to see Klecko's career end because he was not rehabbed properly. I definitely got the sense that my "wrist smackings" were for show and that Kensil just did not want the press to get a hold of anything that would embarrass the club. Klecko and I kept a low profile. We met at the nearby New York Islanders facility for rehab sessions. Weekly I drove him to Lenox Hill Hospital in Manhattan to see the team doctors. Consistent with maintaining a low profile, we only shared a beer at his rental home or a small bar in Point Lookout where the press did not venture.

The strike lasted eight weeks; it was a pretty crazy time. I acted as an unofficial liaison – perhaps 'messenger' would be a more accurate description – between Jim Kensil, Walt, and the players. It was unofficial because everyone wanted "plausible deniability" – like in politics. Klecko was not the only player I was secretly rehabbing. Beyond rehabbing players off site, I frequently saw Marty Lyons, a defensive lineman and integral part of the *Sack Exchange*. Marty had become kind of a second in command behind Klecko as a defensive team leader. He lived near me; and his wife, Kelly, had become good friends with SG. We did a lot of partying with the Lyons. They threw several parties for "player unity" that we attended. These parties usually turned into all night affairs and I would wake up in one of Marty's beds or on a couch somewhere. Being the "messenger" was a great excuse to party hearty.

'Nick the Knife' Strikes

We finished the 1982 season at 6-3 and were in the expanded playoff format created because of the strike. With only one game left in the season, I went through one of the most bizarre months of my life.

Team physician, Jim Nicholas ("Nick the Knife") no longer performed any of the surgeries on the players, and he did not travel with the team. He only attended home games. There, he quite often created major problems pre-game by telling Walt that some player that the other orthopod and I cleared to play should not play. He would just as likely tell some player that we had ruled out for that week that they could play. He was, at a minimum, crazy-making. Fortunately, because of his previous long tenure with the Jets, Walt knew the personality and antics of Nick the Knife. This was another dysfunction that we had to manage.

Nick the Knife got away with his crazy-making because he was close personal friends with the owner, Leon Hess, who thought he was just terrific. He was the ultimate second-guesser, not only of medical decisions, but also of coaching decisions. He was, in short, a nightmare. (This was the "problem with the doctor" referred to earlier.)

The last week of the 1982 season, as it became almost certain that we would go to the playoffs, Nick the Knife showed up at the complex every day. His dysfunctional meddling went into high gear and became unmanageable. First, everything I had been doing was now wrong. The players needed more – and different – treatments for their injuries. If I had them on heat, he wanted them on ice, and vice versa. And everybody needed massage – make that ice massage. Now this was not the usual frozen cup of water being rubbed on the affected area that was popular at the time. Instead, this was an English ice bag full of ice being forcefully massaged into the area for 20 minutes. This required much more hands-on time by both Pepper and myself and we were already stretched thin. Deep ice massage is extremely uncomfortable. The players hated it. It was an unbelievable situation.

Beyond that, he drove everyone else crazy. He had no sense of boundaries and thought nothing of walking in the PR room in the middle of a press conference. He talked to reporters without conferring with Frank Ramos, our PR guy, who spent the week trying to put out Nick the Knife fires. He walked into Walt's office and Jim Kensil's office unannounced and uninvited just to talk.

Panic Attack

That last crazy week of the season, we lost in Kansas City, but made the playoffs. The Jets were to play Cincinnati the upcoming week and were not given much of a chance. No one on the team, however, seemed the least bit intimidated or worried. I was more concerned about Klecko's knee. He was scheduled to come back for limited duty against Cinci, which was a big boost for the team's morale. I was just hoping we were not rushing it.

Nick the Knife was back out at the complex on Monday to "save the day." For the duration of the Jets playoff run, we hired two local ATs to assist us so that we could do everything that Nick was demanding. Tim Davey, who had his hands full working with the traveling secretary, also pitched in for a couple of hours a day. Jim Kensil had decided he could afford Nick's interruptions the best and tried to keep him occupied in his office for hours at a time, letting him think he was actually engaged in policy making. (Short-term solution, long-term mistake).

Thursday of that week I had my first panic attack. I'm not kidding. As I was heading home I was pretty confident the worst was over for the week. About five minutes after I got on the Northern State Parkway, I felt like Klecko was reaching into my chest and squeezing my sternum and my heart. I couldn't breathe. I pulled to the side of the road and decided I must be having a heart attack. I absolutely, positively, and literally thought I was going to die – right there on the side of the road. After what seemed like 20 minutes, but was probably only four or five minutes, I began to breathe a little and the pain began to lessen. I focused on my breath and on breathing deeply. The panic began to fade as I realized, at least for the moment, that I was not going to die. To date, this is the scariest experience I have ever had (and, no, I had not had a drink; but I wanted one terribly).

By the time I got home I was feeling pretty normal. I did not tell SG about the incident. I knew that would only lead to her haranguing me about how I should be dealing with Jim Nicholas, the injuries, the coaches, and everything else. She had all the answers! I would have been fired multiple times had I acted as she instructed. Nevertheless, the more stress I was under, the more she intensified her opinions. Asking her to lay off only made it worse. So, I just headed to the liquor cabinet, poured a Scotch, and mentioned nothing.

The next day I discussed my experience with Cal Nicholas, who was our team internist and the sane brother of Nick the Knife. He diagnosed it immediately as an anxiety attack. He said they were often referred to as a panic attack and explained that term was used because the person "panics" thinking he will die – which was exactly accurate for my experience. He further explained that they usually accompany high stress environments. He asked me if I was experiencing any unusual stress. I told him the only new stress I was experiencing was his brother. He chuckled and said he wasn't surprised.

He offered me a prescription for Valium, but I declined. The last time I took Valium was at BC when I had back spasms. The Valium I took totally incapacitated me, so I did not want anything to do with that. He told me if it happened again – and that it probably would – just to focus on my breathing and remind myself that I was not going to die.

His explanations were seriously comforting. I now knew what it was and how to breathe to alleviate the panic. I experienced three or four more episodes. Each was less traumatic than the one before it. By focusing on my breath, the panic attacks dissipated rapidly. I have since learned that the likelihood of panic attacks is also increased by heavy drinking. Imagine that!

Money Now: Walt

Part of the players' demands during the 1982 strike included "Money Now," which was to compensate players for salary lost during the strike. "Money Now!" became the rallying slogan of the players on strike. Another money issue was playoff shares. As part of the strike settlement, total playoff shares per player would almost double. The first round of the playoffs was $7,500 for each player. The second round made a moderate jump to $10,000. The third round, or the Division Championship game, made a then astronomical leap to $34,000 per player. The Super Bowl share per player was $50,000 for the losing team and $75,000 for the winning team

On the Friday before the first playoff game against Cincinnati, Walt had the Leon Hess, the owner, "loan" him $7,500 cash in $20 twenty-dollar bills. During the team meeting Walt became animated – which was very unusual for him. He asked the players why they went on strike. Without hesitation, one of the team leaders (who coincidently had been in his office only moments before the meeting) yelled out "Money now!" Walt chimed in, "That's right, money now!!!" and proceeded to pull out this huge wad of twenties. The players gasped. Most of them had never seen that much cash at one time, and only two or three of them earned $7,500 a game in 1982. Michaels said, "You want some 'money now'? Well, all you have to do is win on Sunday and you'll have it!"

We crushed the Bengals in the first playoff game. Freeman McNeil, who was coming off a hamstring strain, had one of his best days rushing and even threw for a touchdown. Klecko made his comeback. He only played a few plays, but on one of them skated All-Pro tackle Anthony Munoz back and dumped him on QB Kenny Anderson. While he did not get credit for a sack, we all knew that Klecko's knee was okay.

The Raiders & Walt's Meltdown

The next week we geared up for the Raiders. The training room was overflowing with walking wounded, but everyone was determined to play. Walt added $10,000 to the wad of $7,500. He brought the money in a grocery bag. The players loved it.

I have to say the Jets-Raiders playoff game was the most exciting football game that I ever worked. It had everything. The score kept seesawing back and forth. There were big plays on both sides. By the end of the day, we had taken the swagger out of the vaunted Raiders.

But here's where the bizarre really begins. During half-time the clubhouse guy came to Walt and told him he had a phone call from Leon Hess, the owner. Mr. Hess never called the locker room – that was what Raiders' owner Al Davis was known for doing. Walt took the call and knew within seconds that it was a crank call. I don't recall ever seeing him so angry. Most of the players were unaware of the call, but Walt's demeanor made them all want to go kick someone's ass.

After the game, everyone was celebrating – except Walt. During the post-game interviews, the press wanted to know how we beat the Raiders and all Walt could talk about was the phone call and "that fucking Al Davis!" He was never known for being particularly coherent in press conferences – often starting in the middle of a sentence – but was even less coherent than usual. He did not praise any of our players.

He did not answer questions about injuries. He just went on a tirade about "that fucking Al Davis!"

Anyone who had been around the NFL for any length of time, and especially anyone familiar with history in the old AFL knew Al Davis' reputation of bending the rules by spying on other teams, stealing playbooks, and getting any advantage any way. "Just win, baby!" was his motto – and he really did not care how. To add to that, Walt had once been interviewed by Davis for the Raiders job and he was convinced that Al had not only "picked his brain" but copied his Jets playbook while he was being interviewed. The only person Walt hated more than Don Shula of the Dolphins was Al Davis. He was convinced that Al Davis had been behind the half-time crank call.

The flight back to New York took the usual 5-plus hours. The traveling secretary had made sure there was extra beer on the plane. When we arrived in New York, about half the team was feeling no pain. Walt got really drunk on the plane. This was not unusual on long flights as they had hard liquor in first class. The difference was there were a lot of people traveling with us that never did during the regular season, including wives of the executives and team doctors. Walt was oblivious to who was on board and to political overtones. When he called me up front to talk about the injuries for the upcoming game against Miami, the "fucks", "motherfuckers," and his favorite, "cocksuckers" were streaming out loud and clear.

By the Wednesday press conference, the Raiders phone call was forgotten – at least by us – and we were in high gear prepping for the championship game against Miami. "That fucking Al Davis" had rapidly been replaced with "that fucking Shula."

Then, during the press conference on Wednesday, Walt apparently "ran out of gas." At least that's how it was explained to me by Frank Ramos, our PR Director. He said Walt was doing fine but about 15 minutes into the press conference he just stopped – his head sinking to his chest. Frank said it was as if someone turned off his battery. He hustled Walt out of the press conference, took him next door into his office, and called me to meet him in the hall. He explained what happened and wanted me to try and contain it with the players as he was going back into the press room to do some damage control.

From my end it would be no problem. The players all knew Walt's behavior to be a little bizarre – they not only accepted it, they reveled in it. Most important, they knew Walt had their backs and most of them would have run through a wall for him. All I had to do was tell anyone that asked about Walt this fact: he had been up all night watching films – which he had. From the players' viewpoint, it was "us against the world" so you could add "fuck the press" to the list of people we didn't give a shit about.

Unfortunately, Nick the Knife was there. He witnessed the shutdown. I later learned from Ramos that Nick was interviewing some of the old-time reporters about Walt's history in press conferences. He did this openly in the press room. A witch hunt had begun.

Jim called his brother Cal and told him to get to the complex right away. He called me into my office and began interrogating me on any medications Walt was taking. I informed him that he would occasionally take a Percodan or Valium from my bag, but he would always leave me a note to that effect as he knew I had to keep track of the inventory for the NFL. I checked my bag and he had taken 1 Percodan and 1 Valium the night before – and there was the note. Nick began to rant demanding to know who prescribed them? After I calmed him down, I reminded him that he had prescribed them and had told me to give Walt a Percodan anytime his terribly arthritic neck was bothering him. His brother Cal had told me the same thing about Valium if Walt was having trouble sleeping. Nick then told me to do a drug inventory[4] – immediately. I told him it would have to wait until I got the players out to practice. He headed upstairs to see Jim Kensil.

When Cal Nicholas showed up and after I briefed him on what I knew, he, too, headed up to Jim Kensil's office. I was hoping he could put a leash on his brother. I got the players out to practice and told Pepper to cover for me on the practice field until I accomplished my new mission. I began a prescription drug inventory. I was constantly interrupted by phone calls from Kensil's office asking me questions about Walt; by Frank Ramos trying to stay informed; and just about anyone else who was not on the practice field wanting to know what the fuck was going on.

The first time through the inventory all the Valium was accounted for, but I was short 30 Percodan. Now, I always ordered Percodan, and any of the Schedule II drugs in batches of 30 from a local pharmacy, so I knew there was probably some type of accounting error. I went through it again, and once again came up 30 short. About that time practice was over and players were coming in needing treatment and, of course, wanting to know why I wasn't on the field and what was up with Walt. Apparently for the first half of practice he stood off to the side just looking grim and rocking back and forth. They weren't sure whether he was drunk or pissed. (They could have cared less if he was drunk, but if he was pissed they wanted to know what about. That was a matter of survival!)

Nick the Knife stormed into my office with Cal in tow and informed me that he had been on the phone to Mr. Hess and needed to know the results of my inventory. I told him that I was short 30 Percodan, but before I could explain that figure was too obvious to be anything other than an accounting error, he headed back out – this time two doors down to Walt's office. I immediately called Jim Kensil to try to do a little damage control of my own. I explained in detail that there no way Walt had taken 30 Percodan without my knowing it, that it had to be an accounting error, and that I just needed some time to find it. Jim listened patiently and then said something to the effect that the "damage was already done" and that he was heading home. He asked me to call him at home when I found the error.

An hour or so later, as the complex began to empty out, I heard an ominous bellow from down the hall: "Reeeeeese – get your ass up here!" Apparently Walt wanted to see me. I went down the hall wishing I knew what the Nicholas brothers had told him – or worse yet, accused him of.

When I came in he told me to shut the door – not a good sign as he was sitting at his desk banging his Super Bowl ring on the glass top of his desk (always an indication he was really pissed). He told me to sit down. After I did, he leaned across his desk and put his sausage-size finger about an inch from my nose and shouted at me, "You were disloyal to me with Henning[5], and now you've been disloyal with these fucking doctors and that skinny little cocksucker (Frank Ramos, the

PR Director)!" He promptly got up, walked to the door, threw it open and told me, "Get out! You're through!"

I was stunned. It took me a moment to filter in what had just happened. I stood up and began walking toward the door when something possessed me to turn around and face Walt. I said, "Are you firing me?" He just nodded. I then did one of the bravest, or stupidest, things of my life. I pointed my finger at him and said, "Well, if you're firing me then I have nothing to lose by telling you what the fuck has been going on." (At that point I thought he was literally going to hit me – which probably would have killed me.) "First off," I said, "I was never disloyal with you about Henning – but fuck that – this is now. I don't know what those fucking doctors told you, but I've been trying to cover your ass all afternoon. You know Jim Nicholas is crazy. I know he thinks you've been stealing Percodan from my bag, and I am short 30 Percs, but I also tried to explain to him that I knew it was an accounting error and I would find it, but he wouldn't fucking listen. I called Kensil and told him and he wants me to call him tonight when I find the error. I have never, ever been disloyal to you – and I would never, ever side with Jim Nicholas over you!"

He seemed to lose all his bluster after that; and so did I. He just went back and sat down behind his desk. He didn't look at me, so I left and headed down the hall to my office – which was only two doors down. When I got back to my office, Pepper was there and he looked terrified. He had heard the shouting and wanted to know what was going on and asked me if I had lost my mind yelling at Walt – nobody yelled at Walt. I told him that I had been fired and that I wasn't sure if I had been re-hired, but we were going to find those missing Percodans, even if it was my last act as head AT of the Jets. Pepper was a wreck thinking he might have to take over the next day – and was especially terrified that he might have to deal with Jim Nicholas on his own. He, however, got his focus and helped me with the inventory.

About two hours later we finally realized there was a double invoice for one script of Percodan. I called the pharmacy and he went through his records and confirmed that he had sent a duplicate because he thought the original had been lost. I breathed a long sigh of relief and made my calls to both Jim Kensil and to Walt at their respective homes.

Both of them thanked me, but I still wasn't sure I had a job. I came in the next day and went straight in to see Walt. I asked him if I was still the head trainer and he told me not unless I got my ass back to work. That was good enough for me.

The rest of the week was relatively calm. Walt brought a suitcase with $51,500 to the Friday meeting and told the players if they wanted to see what another $75,000 would look like, they would have to beat the fucking Dolphins! Unfortunately, we did not get to view the $75,000 addition because our playoff run ended in the legendary (at least in Jet lore) "Mud-Bowl" in Miami.[6]

Pro-Bowl Consolation

As a consolation, the losing staffs in the Championship Game coached their respective conference all-star teams in the Pro-Bowl in Hawaii the week after the Super Bowl. The AT and equipment staffs had to be there several days before the coaches. So I left as soon as possible. I took my family. We stayed over two days in San Francisco before heading to Honolulu.

Overall it was a fun experience. I met all the AFC All-Pros. My son, Rob, who was 12 at the time, got to work the practices and the game. Other than practice, I hardly saw the coaches because the ATs came early to practice and stayed late. By the time we got back to the hotel, the coaches and their wives had usually headed out for sightseeing. I saw Ledbetter about mid-week just long enough for him to tell me Walt was telling all of the coaches to start looking for jobs because he was going to be fired as soon as they got back to New York. I couldn't believe it. The Jets had just gone to the Championship Game and would be knocking on the door for the Super Bowl again next year. Firing Walt would be crazy.

Because I did more work than play at the Pro Bowl, I cleared it with Jim Kensil that I would stay an extra week in Hawaii with my family. A few days into the vacation week, just about the time I was winding down from the season, I was awakened by a call from Jim Royer, the Pro Player Personnel Director, informing me that Walt had resigned but, not to worry, I still had a job. He told me to go ahead and enjoy

Hawaii, there would be a lot of work to do when I got back. I literally fell out of the bed. A few minutes later I called Pepper, who had also stayed on in Hawaii. He had just gotten off the phone with Royer and was preparing to call me. We were in shock that Walt was gone from the Jets. I later learned that Walt was given the choice: go to alcohol rehab or resign. He did not believe that he had a problem so he resigned.

Later that day I had my last Scotch, a Johnny Walker Red. As I was drinking it on the balcony of the hotel room overlooking the surf on the North shore of Oahu, I surmised that if Walt could be forced to retire the same could happen to me. I resolved to reduce my drinking. If I wanted some hard liquor, I would have bourbon from now on because I did not care much for it and, thus, wouldn't drink much. While I still loved beer, I couldn't drink many before it bloated me. Wine was okay, but I never drank a lot of it anyway. So, I deduced that if I quit drinking Scotch and switched to bourbon then I would cut down my drinking significantly. This contrivance made sense at the time.

Chapter 15

JETS ~ JOE WALTON ERA (1983-89)

Big Changes

After Walt Michaels was forcibly "resigned," Joe Walton took over as head coach.[7] He had been the Jets offensive coordinator for the prior two years; and he had helped Richard Todd realize much of his potential as quarterback. Our offense had become as good as our defense and Walton deserved a lot of the credit. The players called him "J-Dub," an abbreviated J-W. The offensive players liked and respected him and that transferred to the defense. The team knew the offense could get us on the scoreboard and that the defense could protect the lead.

Some of the immediate changes that took place were three mainstay coaches and friends – Bob Fry, offensive line; Dan Sekanovich, defensive line, and my buddy and neighbor Bob Ledbetter, running backs – all resigned and quickly took other jobs. Dan Henning had just been named head coach at Atlanta and Fry and Sekanovich joined him there. Ledbetter went across town to the Giants. Owner Leon Hess ordered all couches removed from the complex because he did not want coaches sleeping overnight. The rumor was that he thought that if Walt had gone home each night instead of sleeping on his couch he would not have drank so much alcohol or taken so many pain pills. What really hurt is that alcohol was banned from the complex. Now that was going to take some getting used to!

One tool Walton used successfully as offensive coordinator was a large board with the 16 teams that we played listed in a column on the left side of the board. Running across the top of the board was a row of target goals for the Jets offense (e.g., yards rushing, yards passing, 1st downs, 3rd down conversions, penalties, etc.). Walton's theory was that if the offense achieved 10 of 15 goals we would *probably* win the game – his theory held mostly true. Years later I learned in sport psychology that Walton's approach is called *performance goal setting* and is the most effective way to achieve overall *outcome goals*, such as winning a game.

Unfortunately, when Walton became head coach he threw out his theory of performance goals. Wins and losses became the only currency. When we won, everything and everyone was great. When we lost, everything and everyone was awful. Monday after a loss the complex was like a funeral home. Anyone caught laughing or smiling was considered suspect to the cause and told "you don't want to win!"

J-Dub: Micro-manager

Walton was also a micro-manager. Each department head went from being expected to run his own department to having to justify every decision and keep records of everything, including phone calls to players. I thought maybe this would ease up after he learned all that was involved with being a head coach, but it got worse as time went on.

In addition to keeping our routine medical records, Walton demanded we record every time we contacted or tried to contact a player in a big notebook in his office. I finally convinced him that we would keep our own book downstairs in the training room because we could not do our jobs if we had to run up to his office and make an entry every time we had contact or tried to contact a player.

During the off-season, personnel meetings were interminable. We always started with the quarterbacks. We usually had only two quarterbacks – at most we had three – but we talked about them for half a day. This made sense early on so that all the new coaches could get to know the different players. It, however, never changed over the eight years that Walton was head coach.

As a result of his micromanaging, the climate around the complex changed dramatically. It went from "us against the world" and "we're all in this together" to "cover your ass." Making a mistake or not following the rules was tantamount to treason. If we won, all was okay – even mistakes. If we lost, it made no difference if you did your job well, it was not good enough. Over time players quit taking chances to make big plays, especially when we were behind in a game and needed a big play the most. From my end, there was little room for innovation as we were too busy chasing our tails and documenting every detail.

One positive of the increased paper work that my department had to generate, both for the NFL and Walton, was justification for hiring of a second full-time assistant. I created a written "needs assessment" and job description. While this does not seem like a big deal, in 1983-84 this was a first for me. Up until that time if I needed something, I verbally made my case to the head coach. If he okayed it, it was pretty much a done deal. Under Walton, we became more "corporate" – he had begun reading business leadership books.

Additionally, such corporate-style changes were occurring throughout the NFL as it transitioned from family run mom and pop shops to teams being run as corporations. For example, I was required to create job descriptions for Pepper and me.

Both Pepper and I listed everything each of us did. Those early job descriptions were voluminous; and we were amazed at all we actually did. Soon thereafter I created a job description in order to hire a second full-time assistant AT. That job description was used by at least a half dozen teams to justify the hiring of more full-time help. Of course, these exercises and others that followed served me well later in life. At the time, however, I chafed at the onerous paperwork.

During the eight years of the Walton era at the Jets, my drinking was much more controlled even though this was a stressful time for me. I got into Walton's routines and learned how he wanted things done. During the season I went home after every home game, except when we played on the West coast and got back at 4:00 AM and I had to open the training room at 8:00 AM. Those times I usually just slept in the training room. Since there was no longer booze on the plane or in my office, I woke up with just jet-lag and no hangover.

Pre-Draft Physicals Evolve

At the Jets we had streamlined pre-draft physicals to three weekends and were now bringing in over 240 players a year. Other clubs and scouting combines had started similar projects and the NCAA was starting to complain about all the time the draft eligible college seniors were missing during their final spring semester. In 1984 the NFL sponsored its first Combine Physicals. The first attempts held in Tampa and New Orleans were absolute zoos as no one was in charge. I will say, however, that having an expense account in New Orleans where I took the doctors out to eat at restaurants like Commander's Palace and then out for R&R on Bourbon Street was a plus!

The Jets continued to bring 200-plus players to New York; this was in addition to the Combine until it moved to Indianapolis in 1987. By that time the Combine had incorporated many of the things we felt were critical for efficiency and effectiveness into pre-draft physicals: medical and orthopedic histories were taken first; X-rays were taken from the histories so the doctors would have them when they examined the players; and the Jets Cybex (leg strength) testing protocols were adopted.

The Jets medical meetings following the pre-draft physicals became an arena for Mike Hickey, the player personnel director, to see how well he could manipulate Nick the Knife to pass players on their physicals. He played to Nick's ego while he pushed his own agenda to draft players he thought would make a difference. Our original four grades (High Pass, Pass, Pass w/ injury, and Fail) expanded by adding plusses and minuses to each category so that there were at least 16 levels. I went along with Hickey because I knew that just because players were injury free did not mean they could play football. Hickey picked his battles carefully. He knew if I sided with Nick about a particular player, then that player was a huge risk and should not be drafted.

Walton was the new guy whose questions were heard but whose opinions were basically irrelevant. Over time, Walton learned to talk the talk, but I do not think he ever realized the game within the game.

You're Never Home!

Under Walton there was less job-associated drinking. Over the next few years there was also less and less time off associated with the off-season. I began to call it the "non-season" as there was nothing "off" about it.

In addition to the time the pre-draft physicals consumed, the NFL increased the number of allowed mini-camps. Adding to that, Joe Walton had multiple "volunteer" mini-camps for quarterbacks, receivers, and defensive backs. Walton also sponsored several United Way camps for underprivileged kids and I had to work them, too. Free weekends became incredibly sparse. I worked harder and longer.

Under Joe Walton, the "you're never home!" drumbeat from SG that began in Buffalo intensified, become louder, and more constant. It was as if her complaint received an injection of steroids. The only way I could quell it was with booze. Even when I did have a weekend at home, SG bitched about me not being home other weekends.

Unfortunately, she brain-washed my kids that I was never home. I have often wondered that my kids might have thought better of me if SG had explained to them that when I was not home it was because of my job. Instead, she complained to them that I was never home. She preached that I loved my job more than them, and that my being gone so much proved that I did not care about them. Sadly, my daughter continued to use these complaints against me even after she moved out of the house and was in her late twenties, after SG lived with another man, after SG and I divorced, and after I remarried!

Good PR is worth a lot. My mother always told my siblings and me how hard our dad worked for us. If he had to go out on a service call at night or work on weekends, it was because he loved us and wanted to provide for us. She taught us to appreciate how hard he worked. In a similar fashion SGs' mother had convinced her family that her father was "the smartest man in the world." This was to explain his affinity for going into the living room away from everyone and reading on one subject at a time until he was satisfied that he knew everything about it. (My take is that was how he effectively escaped in a three-bedroom house full of six kids.) The G children always felt warmly toward their father, thought he was the smartest man in the world, and never complained about the minimal time spent with them.

Perhaps, however, Mr. G's reading all the time at home might be why I was not *allowed* to read at home. If I tried to read a book, SG would interrupt me every five minutes with some inane question just so I paid attention to her. The only way I found peace was to numb out on booze and TV. It was okay to drink and watch TV with her.

Boating

One positive effect of the "you're never home" drumbeat was I took up boating to try to create some quality time – and hoping to erase the "you're never home" tattoo. As a kid I loved my time on the lake, so I surmised that my kids would love boating and the water. Additionally, Long Island Sound was only a few miles from our home.

My first boat was just a little 16' fishing skiff with a 7 hp motor. I bought it from a neighbor for under $200 in 1979. The skiff was okay for Rob and me fishing around Northport harbor, but it proved totally inadequate for taking SG and Rachel with us. A bigger boat was in our future.

Also, by 1979, SG had become convinced Rachel could be a child model because so many people talked about how cute she was. It started slow with the usual expensive headshots and selective auditions. By the second year, however, Rachel had an agent and SG was trucking her into Manhattan for every "cattle call" audition available. I was supportive of this endeavor for several reasons. First, I, too, thought Rachel was cute. Second, if she landed a national commercial it could pay for her college expenses. Third, SG had less time and energy to bitch about me not being home because she was too busy and exhausted from hauling Rachel into NYC.

During this time, she met and befriended a fellow "stage mom," Merry (pseudonym). Merry was dating a guy named Hank (pseudonym) who owned a 42' Trawler. It was big and roomy and had teak decks. One spring weekend they cruised over to Northport harbor from Cos Cob, Connecticut, and picked us up. We cruised around to Oyster Bay where Hank rafted up with several other boats. The kids jumped from boat to boat, swam, and played. The adults drank and drank. The thing I liked best was no one gave a shit that I worked for the Jets. They all thought it was interesting, but they wanted to talk about the latest LORAN technology (predecessor to GPS), whether or not they needed radar, what the weather report was for next weekend, and where they should meet next weekend. I hadn't been so relaxed in years. I thought: I've really got to look into this boating thing.

We went out with Hank and Merry several more times. Each time was just as pleasant as the last. Rachel and Merry's daughter were the same age and enjoyed playing together.

So, I began researching boats. I thought it would be a great way to spend quality time with the family, since quantity time was harder and harder to come by. I shopped around and found myself at Gudziks Marine in Port Jefferson. I got into a conversation with one of the owners, who happened to be from Nashville, we became fast friends. He sold me a 24' Bayliner with a cuddy cabin.

That spring we began to meet Hank and Merry on weekends, even sleeping overnight on the boat several times. It was cramped, but it was also fun. Hank began to teach me the basics of boating on the ocean (versus a big lake). I was an eager student. I found an escape from the pressures of work and SG was off my ass as she and Merry plotted how to make the girls superstars.

Hank spoke poetically about going to Menemsha on Martha's Vineyard every 4th of July, where he essentially spent the rest of the summer living on his boat. As half owner of a family wholesale jewelry business, he commuted to his sales region for two or three days a week and then returned to Menemsha for R&R. I thought that sounded great, but I was not comfortable taking my "little" 24' Bayliner out across the high seas – or even the low seas. Only one thing to do: boat-up!

By the next spring I traded in my 24-footer for a 28' Bayliner with a cabin, tiny galley, a tiny head that also doubled as a shower, and a fly bridge. It would sleep six (if you were very close friends). I named it the *Chimera*, at Rob's suggestion. The *Chimera* was an ugly mythical beast, but a secondary definition meant any impossible fantasy. And, that's what the boat became for me: my fantastic refuge. Pagers and cell phones had not yet infiltrated our lives so I could really escape football for a while.

In general, the boaters I met did not give a rat's ass about football. That was great for me as I no longer had to defend bonehead moves by coaches and personnel directors. Even when we did not go anywhere, it was nice to go sit on the boat at its mooring in Northport harbor. I felt like I had a condo on the water. Of course, SG and I drank constantly, but there seemed to be fewer arguments when on the boat. The second summer, after taking a Coast Guard course on piloting, doing a lot of planning on charts, and programming and re-programming my LORAN, we cruised to Menemsha for the 4th of July. The whole experience was great!

While I drank constantly when boating, I had only one alcohol related incident. On the way to Menemsha one year, we met Hank and Merry in Mattituck, on the north shore of Long Island to spend the night. We grilled some steaks in the picnic area and had wine. After dinner Hank and I drank Amaretto with our coffee. After dark I went back to the boat to get something. I forgot the tide had gone out. I stepped off the seawall and onto the dock, which was now about 7' lower than it had been when we started eating. I was knocked unconscious as I did a face plant on the dock. The next morning Hank, Merry, and SG had a good laugh at my bruised forehead, my hellish hangover (which could have been my third concussion), and their description of how it took all three of them to get me on the boat and into bed. For some reason, I didn't think it was funny. It took a codeine and some hair of the dog to kill the headache. I'm not sure if the lack of memory of the actual fall was a blackout or post-concussive.

Beginning The New House Saga

In 1985 and 1986 the Jets had the best years under Walton. In 1985 we made it as a Wildcard into the playoffs. In 1986 we advanced to the Division Championship. At that time there was every reason to believe we would continue to improve.

Also, I had averaged a 10% raise each year since being hired by the Jets and there was no reason to think that would change. Jim Kensil, with whom I negotiated my salary raises, was very aware of how much time and effort "above and beyond the call of duty" I gave to the Jets – including having to deal with Nick the Knife.

Coinciding with the above good fortune, SG added an addendum to her "you're never home" repertoire. Because I was never home, she wanted to move to a better neighborhood, either closer in to Hempstead so my commute would not be as long or into Northport proper which had a higher social reputation than East Northport. Either choice would result in more than I wanted to spend on housing. The 1980s real-estate boom on Long Island escalated the value of my home, which had cost $56,000 in 1977 to an excess of $225,000 by 1987. Of course, all that profit – and more – would have to go into a new house.

After looking for more than a year, I determined it might be cheaper to build a house in Northport than to buy an existing one, if I could find an empty piece of land. I finally found a vacant lot in Northport Village that began a saga that added a huge amount of stress to my life and ended in my financial ruin less than a decade later.

My Aching Back

In the spring of 1988, I sold the house in East Northport for $240,000 and rented a furnished house on nearby Makamaw Beach. We packed up the house and moved everything but clothing into a large commercial storage container. By the 1988 summer training camp, I was exhausted. In the second week of camp my usual sciatica started up. A couple of times as I helped players from the field, I also felt a sharp twinge in my back. I began experiencing more back spasms than normal. I took Motrin (prescription strength Advil) regularly and on bad days a codeine to get through practice. I received physical therapy at every chance, worked on my flexibility, and tried a variety of different back braces and lifting belts. I kept thinking I would work through it like I had in the past – but it did not happen. I then told myself that when we broke camp and went to one practice a day where I would not be on my feet all day, that it would get better. That didn't happen, either.

Remarkably, after we broke camp and my workload decreased, my back got increasingly worse. The sciatica was non-stop and the back spasms were only relieved when I was sitting or lying down. During training camp, I had been X-rayed and examined several times by Dr. Hershman, our team orthopod.

I was drinking more heavily at home to kill the pain. At work I graduated from codeine to Percocet to make it through the day. By the first week of the regular season I was in constant misery. By the second game of the season I needed eight Percocet to get through the game. Pepper told me the next day that I was so spaced out by the fourth quarter that players were laughing at me on the sidelines. By that time. I recognized I had a bigger problem with my back than I had been willing to admit. Dr. Hershman examined me again and found I had developed a foot-drop in my left foot, the leg with the sciatic pain. An MRI showed a bulging disc at the L3-4 level and a herniated disc at the L4-5 segment. Complete bed rest was ordered.

I reluctantly agreed to go home for two weeks of bed rest. I had NEVER missed a day of work for any reason during the season; so this was a huge deal for me. After a week at home the foot drop had worsened. Because the doctors did not believe me when I told them I only got out of bed to go to the bathroom, they put me in the hospital. The foot drop continued to worsen. After a week in the hospital I had surgery. I missed a total of six weeks before I returned to work. After the surgery I realized how much I had been drinking and really cut back.

I told Dr. Pellman, the team's internist (he was hired following Dr. Cal Nicholas' retirement) that I was concerned about my drinking. Prior to the surgery for the herniated disc, I was drinking bourbon like it was beer. The plan I devised in Hawaii after Walt Michaels was forced to resign had failed to curtail my drinking. That was the plan to switch from scotch to bourbon because I did not like bourbon and therefore would not drink much of it. This was preceded by switching to scotch from beer which bloated me – beer had been my favorite drink for a long time and I drank a lot of it. So, now I resolved to quit drinking bourbon altogether. I decided to switch to wine, knowing from my experience with bourbon that I would eventually begin to like it; but I was not ready to think of life without booze at this point.

Dr. Pellman told me a good test to see if I was alcoholic was to quit drinking for 30 days and if I could do that I probably was not alcoholic.

I made it 28 days. There was a function – a wedding I think – that I attended and decided to break my abstinence. I reasoned that 30 days was arbitrary – it was a month. February had only 28 days and it was a month. So what could two days matter? There's nothing like a good rationalization to make you feel positive about failure.

The House Saga Continues

Construction on the new house in Northport Village began during football season. It was exciting to see it take shape. It had an open floor plan with lots of space. By spring 1988 it was nearing completion, and it looked like it would be finished by Memorial Day – which was when I had to vacate the rental house.

About that time, I was informed by letter that the mortgage I had locked-in for the house at 8.5% had been lost because I failed to return a renewal form that I never received. I went to bank and alternately bitched, begged, threatened, and finally pleaded that they respect the earlier mortgage commitment; they would not. Mortgages were now almost double what I had locked-in, and the best I could do was 14%. My payments on a $260,000 mortgage were going to be astronomical. I was also figuring property taxes at about $1000 per month.

In a panic, I met with Steve Gutman, the former accountant who succeeded Jim Kensil as president of the Jets, and asked him if I could afford this. He crunched the numbers and told me that the first year or two with my then salary would be really tough, but after that with anticipated raises I should be okay.

Because the mortgage would not be approved by Memorial Day, I was forced to find another rental home. I found a nice partially furnished two-bedroom ranch style house on Eatons Neck with a two-car garage that opened into a full basement the length of the house. It was cheaper than the previous rental, but added another 15-20 minutes to my commute. None of this went smoothly and, of course, SG was haranguing me constantly about getting into *her* new house.

PFATS

In June 1988, I was scheduled to go to the Professional Football Athletic Trainers' Society (PFATS) meetings two days prior to the National Athletic Trainers' Association (NATA) convention. I was in the second year of my first term as president of PFATS, and elections were to be held. I called the other officers and told them I could not make the meetings because of all the chaos occurring in my life (the house debacle mentioned above). Knowing my colleagues in PFATS very well, I knew there was an almost certainty I would be re-elected president even if I was not there. I told Pepper to make sure that did not happen. I knew the next year was going to be stressful and I did not want the added stress of having to run PFATS.

This decision was a hard pill to swallow. As the assistant at Buffalo, I had been in the small group that morphed the NFL Athletic Trainer's Society into PFATS, and I had been directly involved in PFATS since then. I knew that, in reality, I could have returned as president and been able to do a good job. Deep down, I was hoping SG would appreciate me giving up something I loved doing to have more time to "be home."

True to form, the brotherhood of PFATS tried to have me re-elected. Pepper protested, telling them over and over that I said I could not do it. As I recall it took Abe, my old boss from Buffalo, to speak up and tell everyone to give me a break and respect my wishes. I became past president of PFATS and that news was met with contempt from SG. She played both sides almost simultaneously: on one hand, it was a stupid organization that meant nothing; on the other hand, I must not have been very well respected if they didn't re-elect me. I drank even more heavily to suppress my anger and stuff my ever growing resentment of her.

I was beginning to think we might be better off staying in the rental long-term and selling the house that we were building because of the mortgage debacle. It was still a sellers' market and we might even make money if we sold it. I was not looking forward to paying that gigantic monthly nut that was awaiting me.

Additionally, my financial obligations had increased with Rob's acceptance to Boston College. While still in the old house, I had managed to salt away what turned out to be first year tuition, room and board; but knew I would have to take out loans for the remainder. I rationalized by convincing myself we might have a shot at playoff money that year. I had to keep my thoughts about future finance from looking too far into the future because it was overwhelming. Anytime this occurred, I turned to find relief with my Tennessee homeboy, Jack Daniels, or my new French friend, Pinot Noir.

When I broached the topic of staying in the rental and selling the house, SG went ballistic. She screamed that Printinghouse Circle (the address of the new home) was *hers*, and she deserved it because of all the time she had put up with the fucking Jets and my not being home. I corrected her by saying that if we moved into Printinghouse Circle, the house was *ours*. She responded with one of her regular malapropisms, "Yes, you're right. What's yours is mine, and what's mine is mine." She had been saying this for years and always said it with a giggle so it would sound like a joke. It was only years later that I recognized that she meant every word of it – literally.

Tensions grew as training camp got closer. The afternoon I was leaving to move into the Hofstra dorms, she started drinking early and we had a huge fight. It culminated in her standing on the balcony eight feet above the driveway. She raised a 10" potted plant over her head and hurled it onto the hood of the company car as I was getting in. It exploded and of course dented the hood. Rachel was standing next to her, aghast, as she continued to hurl expletives my way. I was stunned, and then, of course, angry. I just bit my lip, climbed in the car, and left. I stopped before I got off Eaton's Neck to clean the pot shards and remaining potting soil off the hood. I surveyed the damage, which was not as bad as it could have been, but still something I was going to have to explain. The rest of the drive in I was busy trying to come up with some explanation of what had caused the dent and surrounding scratches. I finally decided a tree limb had fallen on the car. That explanation must have seemed plausible, as the Jets had the damage repaired with no further questions asked.

After I left for training camp SG had an almost a daily problem with landlord. She complained he was always leering at her, especially when she tried to lie out in the hammock to get sun. She said he would cut the grass whether it needed cutting or not, just so he could stare at her. She had taken to carrying a baseball bat to protect herself. I suggested that she should sun herself on the chaise lounge on the wraparound deck that was about 20' above the back yard. She, however, insisted she had a *right* to lie in the hammock. (She was always very big on what her *rights* were!)

When we first moved in, the landlord had told me he was a pilot for American Airlines, and worked 3-4 days on, then 3-4 days off. I knew he could not be there every day she complained about his disturbing her tanning. On top of that, she was a redhead, burned more than she tanned, and covered up any time she was in the sun. And, she had never laid out in the hammock at any prior address or at the beach. In fact, she had told me she felt like it was a waste of time to lay there and do nothing.

She was relentless in her efforts to convince me how much eminent danger she was in. She insisted she needed a gun to protect herself. I reminded her of the incident a few years earlier where she had been arrested for pointing a starters' pistol at a cable repairman and ordering him off the property.

Back-off Boogaloo

The story of SGs pointing a starters' pistol at a cable repairman goes back to the early 1980s. I bought the pistol at the suggestion of several cops who hung around the Jets complex. At that time there was a rash of home break-ins on Long Island.

One summer while I was away at training camp a cable guy knocked on the house door to tell SG that he working be working on the telephone pole in the back corner of our lot. My cousin Jimmy Hatley's daughter, Tiffany, who was spending the summer with us to escape Nashville, answered the door. SG had been drinking and demanded to see the guy's I.D. He said it was in the truck, which plainly displayed the cable companies' logo. He also told her that he really didn't need her permission because he could access the pole through an open yard and he was just trying to be courteous. She threatened to call the cops.

The cable guy told her to go ahead and that he was going around to the pole to do his job.

SG got the starter's pistol and went into the backyard. As the cable guy began to ascend the pole she pointed it at him and told him to get off her property or she would shoot him. According to Tiffany, he was really shocked. He tried to explain that the pole was not actually on her property and he had a legal right to climb it to do his job. She screamed, "Back off boogaloo, or I'll shoot you dead!" The cable guy climbed down the pole and went to a neighbors' house where he called the cops on the crazy lady. They came and arrested her about 20 minutes later. She vehemently complained about her rights, persistently told them that her father was a lawyer, and threatened that she was going to sue them for false arrest – and, oh yes, my husband is the head trainer for the New York Jets.

Fortunately, when they found out the gun was a starter's pistol they reduced the charges from assault with a deadly weapon to simple assault. At the station, she used her one phone call to call the wife of a football player, who bailed her out of jail. The cable company decided not to press charges and the whole thing went away without going to court. The police kept the starter's pistol and I did not replace it. Tiffany went back to Nashville the next week, apparently thinking Nashville was not such a crazy place after all.

Back on Eatons Neck

So, with that history, I responded to her request for the gun to protect herself from the landlord by first having a few drinks and then by dismantling the hammock in the backyard. I told her to use some common sense. If, in fact, the guy was potentially dangerous, (which I really did not believe he was), why provoke him. Just stay the fuck away from him – just be smart. She knew I was in training camp and I could not be there to watch over her. I told her that if she really felt unsafe, she could go to her family in Nashville or to her sister in Atlanta for the remaining few weeks of training camp.

Of course she went crazy, screaming that I had to get her out of there and into *her* house on Printinghouse Circle. I left and went back to camp to spend the night. Fortunately, this time she found nothing heavier than curses to throw down on the car; I would have had a hard time explaining another tree limb denting the car.

By the time training camp ended, the new mortgage had finally been approved. Now I had the problem of closing costs. I went back to Gutman and requested a salary advance to cover the closing costs, which I estimated would be $8,000 plus or minus. He said he would talk to Mr. Hess and see what he could do. The next week he called me to his office and said that Mr. Hess would not consent to giving me an advance on my salary. Then he presented me with a personal check for $20,000 signed by Mr. Hess. He said it was a gift – not a loan – and that all Mr. Hess asked is that I use it to alleviate the financial burden I was under so I could concentrate on the season and my job. I was speechless! I finally stuttered out some thank you. Gutman told me how much Mr. Hess had appreciated my work and loyalty over the years and felt this was well disserved.

SG was happy, too. We closed around the first of October and began moving into the new house. While we broke our lease on the rental house, I think that our landlord was glad to be rid of us.

Working Harder Didn't Work

Working for Joe Walton truly meant being on call 24-7; he could have been the poster-child for micro-managers. Very often I had messages waiting for me when I got home to call him. Each time that happened it set off a new round of "you're never home!" I had to tell Walton where I could be reached even when on vacation. I thought I was safe on the boat since I never informed him about ship-to-shore radio, but, nonetheless, he managed to spoil one of my vacations.

One early July I arrived on the *Chimera* in Menemsha pond on Martha's Vineyard and radioed the Harbor Master requesting a slip. When I identified myself he asked me if I worked for the Jets, which I thought was very odd. I told him yes, and he said, "Well, after you get docked, come around to my office and call some guy named Walton from the Jets. His secretary has called five times over the past two days and you're supposed to call him immediately!"

When I called in, Maureen, his secretary and my good friend, was super apologetic for having to call me. When I spoke to Walton he told me it was about the physical condition of some free-agent player we were thinking about picking up and that since he could not get in touch with me, he had Pepper contact Dr. Hershman who examined him and said there was no danger in signing him. I told him that even if there was a problem we could always flunk him on the physical at training camp, so there was really no need to get the doctor involved (*or call me while I'm on my boat in Massachusetts!*). He ignored that, asked how long I would be available at Menemsha number, and then told me to enjoy my vacation. Of course, SG spent the next several days telling anyone who would listen how I couldn't get away from my job and how I was never home.

Joe Walton was very organized, but he had trouble adjusting to changes in circumstances. For example, when the NFL imposed the 80-man training camp roster limit in 1988, he could not adjust. In training camp, he continued to conduct practices as long and hard as if he had 120+ players. When the veterans we were counting on started to drop from injuries because they were taking so many extra reps, I begged him to shorten practice and lighten up on the hitting. He said "Okay" and then grudgingly took five minutes off a three-hour practice. We went into the season hobbling. His inability to change contributed to his downfall.

The other thing that hurt Walton was his motto: "If things aren't working, work harder." We had two very good seasons under him: 1985 (11-5) and 1986 (10-6). In the 1986 season we won the first game, lost the second, and then went on a 9-game winning streak. When we lost game 11, we were pretty beat up, but he decided the team needed to work harder. We did, and we lost. We worked harder still, and we lost again – five straight. Get the picture? He didn't!

That was our MO for the next two years. Between the unrelenting training camps and the "work harder when it's not working" attitude, the Jets were so bruised and battered by November that we couldn't win. The chants of "Joe Must Go!" would have been deafening if the Meadowlands stadium had been more than half full. The players began to play to protect themselves; a team cannot win when that happens. Everything pointed to Walton's inevitable dismissal. With the hiring of a new General Manager the last week of the 1989 season, everyone knew Walton was gone.

Chapter 16

JETS ~ STEINBERG & COSLET ERA (1990-93)

Dick Steinberg

Dick Steinberg came to the Jets as General Manager in mid-December 1989. He had success with the Rams and the Patriots and was one of the most respected player personnel people in the League. He was the first General Manager the Jets had hired since the firing of a general manager in the spring of 1977. From 1977 through 1989, the Jets were run by a committee that included the president, the head coach, the college player personnel director, and the pro personnel director. Leon Hess, who became majority owner in 1976 and sole owner by 1984, was essentially a hands-off owner. The rule by committee was a good business model but it did not translate to success on the football field.

Just before the season's end I was summoned to Dick Steinberg's office to discuss players' injuries. He seemed less concerned in the specifics of treatment and rehab than with who made the decisions and who talked to the media. I was not sure what he was really asking, but I answered his queries as best and fully as I could. After a while I sensed the purpose of his questioning. He made a comment that "around the League" it was thought that the team doctor (Jim Nicholas) and the AT (me) for the Jets had too much influence on football decisions.

I was astonished that anyone other than team physicians and fellow ATs knew who I was. I told him that while Jim Nicholas could be a pain in the ass, both former head coaches knew how to humor him; and in my opinion he had much less influence than he thought he did. I gave him a condensed version of the history of our pre-draft physicals and explained that taking only healthy players was Mr. Hess' edict, not the medical departments'. I told him I always worked closely with the coaches trying to let them know the plusses and minuses of having a player play when hurt. He quizzed me about certain players and their injuries and then dismissed me.

The only thing that bothered me about the meeting was the lack of feedback. I had no idea whether I gave Steinberg what he was looking for or not, nor did I have any idea of his expectations of me. I was used to a give and take and discussing potential scenarios. I learned over time Steinberg's trademark: all information goes in, little, if anything, comes out. It was frustrating. I intuited that the status quo was going to change. I hoped that I would be there for the changes.

While Steinberg refused to initially say Walton was a goner, we all knew the "Joe Must Go!" chants from the fans at the Meadowlands were about to become reality. Two days after Christmas it became official. When I got the call from Jim Royer that Walton and all the assistants were fired, I drove into the complex and I went to Walton's office and thanked him for the opportunity to work with him and wished him well. We hugged, and then he thanked me for all my hard work and loyalty – and I had been loyal.

Loyalty is definitely a big part of who I am. Loyalty to my wife and family; to team, organization, and League; to the head coach; to the doctors. I am a loyal guy – probably to a fault. And certainly, at times, to my detriment!

Loyalty & Super Fan

In fact, my loyalty caused one of the few rifts I ever had with my Dad. Over the years my Dad became a rabid Jets fan and began to take their losses personally. It became somewhat of a ritual for him to call me on Monday nights after the Sunday games to talk about the games. In 1987, as the Jets endured a 6-10 season, those phone calls became increasingly onerous – and I dreaded them. My Dad would go on a rant about Walton's stupid play-calling and I would calmly try to defend my boss, even though I absolutely agreed with my father.

During one of these calls, I stopped my Dad mid-rant and told him to *please* (with heavy emphasis) quit bitching at me about Walton. I went on to explain to him that this was my job and because it was my job I had to be loyal and defend the head coach. I also had to deal with this shit every day; and his complaining about it was not helpful. In fact, it was making me dread his phone calls. I told him he needed to "back-off" being super fan and consider my position. He took this as a personal affront and did not speak to me for almost a year. I finally took the first step and apologized to him. He, in turn, apologized to me and for the next several months would always preface any football question with: "Is it okay to ask you a football question?" I finally had a reasonable discussion with him and told him it was always okay to ask me football questions, just remember the position I was in and go easy on the ranting because I could not change the way Walton did things.

This is an example of another family dynamic. The only time my parents ever called me, other than a family emergency or a death in the family, was during the football season. Otherwise, it was up to me to keep in touch; which I did usually once or twice a month. During the time my Dad was not speaking to me, it became almost comical as he would talk to my mother and she would ask questions or pass along anything he wanted to say. It was historically the other way around: my mom talking in the background to my Dad while he and I tried to have a conversation. I often asked why she did not pick up an extension and just talk, but apparently she enjoyed speaking through my Dad.

This criticism of Walton and his play calling, of course, was not limited to my father. Everyone who knew I was associated with the Jets – whether at restaurants, at liquor stores, at the hardware store, etc. – had the same complaints. I taught Rob and Rachel that the best way to handle the Jets inevitable season-end collapse was just to agree with anyone who said, "Hey, the Jets really suck!" It deflates the argument and they tend to go away. From a PR standpoint, I did not have that luxury.

Job Security ... NOT!

After Walton was fired, my driving into the Jets complex was not totally altruistic. Jim Royer told me that all the coaches were fired; that Mike Hickey, the player personnel director resigned; that Steve Gutman was still president; and that he was still in his position as Pro Personnel Director, but was not sure for how long. He also said that as far as he knew, I still had a job. I wanted to confirm that. So, after seeing Walton, I went to see Steve Gutman, who informed me that according to Steinberg the Jets were not in the market for a new head AT, but it would be up to the next head coach. Like everyone else, including Steinberg, Gutman had no idea who that would be.

Historically, head ATs had little mobility in the NFL. Unlike coaches for whom the number of times being fired seems to add to their experience and value, a fired head AT had little chance of working in the NFL again. Since I had been in the league it only happened once when the Miami head AT quit in 1973 (versus being fired) and returned two years later when his replacement quit. Assistant ATs might move up or to another team, as I had from the Bills to the Jets; but when head ATs were out, there were few options. This was also weighing heavy on my mind as the Jets' search for a new head coach plodded on.

As January dragged on, my assistants, Pepper and Joe P, were becoming more and more ill at ease. The lack of knowing whether or not we would have jobs the next month wore on them, too, and began to interfere with our work. We could not have a conversation without it turning into who might be the head coach and would they bring in their own head trainer and assistants. We were making calls to colleagues to see if they heard anything; rumors abounded. Every time we called a player to check on how they were recuperating from end of season bumps and bruises, the same conversation occurred. As usual on the home front, the more pressure I was under at work the more pressure SG put on me. She wanted answers! Not only that, she *deserved* answers! Of course, I had no answers – so once again, it was my fault. It probably comes as no surprise that, as usual, I reverted to my old friend Jack Daniels to help me find that "click" in my head that would shut her out. I say "out" as nothing shut her up. It was not a fun time.

About the third week of January, just before the Super Bowl, I finally went up to see Steinberg about the impact on moral. I told him that we were trying to prepare for the Combine Physicals, but this uncertainty hanging over our heads had Pepper and Joe P wondering whether or not they might be better off looking for jobs. (Of course, I had the same misgivings.) Steinberg told me that he was telling candidates that the Jets were not looking to replace our training staff, but after the first year if I didn't get along with the head coach I would be replaced. Since this was a close as I ever got to a secure position, I was relieved. Pepper and Joe P were overjoyed.

Bruce Coslet

After a false start with a prominent college coach, Steinberg announced the hiring of well-respected Offensive Coordinator of the Cincinnati Bengals, Bruce Coslet. A day or two after all the press conferences and hoopla surrounding his hiring, Coslet called me to his office.

He seemed very friendly and said he was not looking for a new AT. He told me he had heard good things about me, but, if we did not work well together, next year he would have to bring someone else in. I told him that sounded fair enough and that I would help him every way I could to be successful. We talked in general and he told me to just keep doing what I normally did this time of year. He was going to be tied up the next several weeks hiring assistants and then after that he wanted me in the coaches' personnel meetings as we prepared for mini-camps.

To describe Bruce Coslet as a breath of fresh air would be a huge understatement. We went from being tightly micromanaged under Walton to a relaxed, "don't sweat the small stuff; just don't let it turn into big stuff" organization. It took us a while to adjust.

Perhaps the best example of the change in management styles was when Coslet was preparing the playbook for training camp. He called me into his office to go over the training room rules. He had no problem with the intent of most of them and we condensed them into about three or four general rules. After that we chatted a while about how we would run water/Gatorade breaks, how much time I needed to tape the players, and other logistical concerns. As we were wrapping up, he flipped to the front of the playbook and said, "By the way, what the fuck are all these rules?" He was referring to the four or five pages of player rules that Joe Walton had. It was a NFL rule that all player rules had to be read out loud to the players, and Coslet figured this must take about 15-20 minutes. I told him it was usually closer to 30 minutes and assistant coaches took turns reading the pages. He just kept shaking his head as he read some of the rules out loud, especially the more ludicrous ones like "Players must be in the airport waiting area 45 minutes prior to the scheduled departure time."

I explained that many of the rules were known as "Gastineau rules." To keep themselves occupied during the reading of the rules, players used to count the number of the rules created because of Mark Gastineau. For example, "be in the airport waiting area 45 minutes prior to the scheduled departure time" originally read "be in the airport 30 minutes prior to departure." After Gastineau dodged the fine by saying he was in the airport, Walton changed the rule to "be in the waiting area 30 minutes prior to departure." Then, twice he dodged the fine for being late, because the plane was late departing the gate, hence the "scheduled" departure time was changed. I informed Coslet that at last count 60-70 of the 100 plus rules were Gastineau rules. While they were mostly about time issues, they extended into dress code and appearance, and even into how long after the game you had to get on the bus at away games. Gastineau was always one of the last in the showers and would often proceed to shave his entire body, leaving everyone waiting on the bus for 10-15 minutes for him. That was an eternity after a loss and Walton would chew his cigar to a nub with the frustration.

Coslet declared he had one major rule: Be on time and be prepared. A second rule was: Don't embarrass the team. He said that in his experience everything pretty much fell under these two rules, and that was all that was necessary. He then repeated his unwritten rule: "Don't sweat the small stuff; just don't let it turn into big stuff." I really, really liked this man!

Coslet was an optimist with a ready smile, and he genuinely enjoyed life. He made it clear that football was not the end-all be-all and that everyone needed time off to recharge their batteries. He ordered a

Lay-z-Boy chair for his office so he could power nap. He let everyone know that he believed in Paul Brown's theory that if you didn't have it done by 8:00 PM, you were not very good at your job.

Pete Carroll

As Coslet began hiring his assistants, they all seemed to embrace his work ethic. One of his first hires was his defensive coordinator, Pete Carroll, who had been a defensive back coach at Buffalo and Minnesota. I got an immediate call from Abe at Buffalo telling me that Pete was the real deal – which meant that not only was he a good coach, but also he could be trusted.

As it turned out, Pete was – and is – indeed the real deal. He is a great coach and trustworthy. We share similar interests in performance issues: for example, why some players get the most out of their abilities and others do not.

The staff hired by Coslet were good people. Everyone seemed enthusiastic. I had not felt that much optimism since I came to the Jets in 1977. A "breath of fresh air" permeated the complex.

Sport Psych

One interesting thing Coslet did after hiring his coaching staff was to bring in sport psychologist Ken Ravizza, PhD, from Cal State Fullerton. Ken and Coslet had been roommates at University of Pacific, which was also Pete Carroll's alma mater.

When Ravizza showed up at the Jets mini-camp, he met several times a day with the coaches. When I finally learned who he was – a sport psychologist – I thought it another way my role was being limited. Steinberg had already made it clear that I was not to talk to the press, now Coslet had hired a sport psychologist. Nick the Knife commented that he thought my position was being undermined and my lack of input added to my insecurity.

It turns out Ravizza was there to work on team building with the coaching staff. Because Coslet was hired late, he had to hustle to find assistants and none of his hires had worked together before – hence, the need for team building.

Ravizza came to Hofstra a couple of days a week during training camp. Because I was always curious about what made players – and others – tick, I quizzed him at every opportunity about sport psychology. One day while questioning him about sport psychology he told me, "Reese, you do this stuff all day long." I asked him, "What *stuff*?" He replied "sport psychology." I pondered that a few minutes; then I asked him, "What was I was doing that was sport psychology?"

He informed me that he had watched me working with players. He noted that every day when rehabbing players, I used two basic sport psychology techniques: goal setting and visualization. Not only did we set goals for each rehab session, but I also had players seeing themselves back in action – sometimes even by watching old game film. He also said I did a great job with stress management, another building block of sport psychology. Ravizza commented on how I coached and coaxed players back on the field after a major surgery, allaying their fears and assuring them they would be alright. Therefore, I did this sport psych stuff all day long!

Ken Ravizza was a very significant mentor for me as I moved formally into the world of sport psychology and mental skills training for enhanced performance. He recommended the first books and articles that got me started. He was exceedingly patient as I peppered him with questions every time he was on the practice field. I also incorporated his favorite motto: *Attitude is a decision!* Ken had this phrase printed on little triangular stickers that he surreptitiously placed all over the Jets complex – on windows, office and classroom doors, even on some mirrors and stall doors in the bathrooms. I also liked that when asked about them, he smiled and pretended he had no idea how they got there.

Danger, Danger

There was one problem with the new staff: the strength coach. He was Steinberg's hire as Coslet had no one in mind for the job. He talked a good game, but it took me about 10 minutes to know this guy was going to be trouble. While I never saw his resume, I knew that what he knew about strength and conditioning was self-taught. While there's nothing wrong with that, the downside is that self-taught strength gurus tend to think everyone benefits from the same exercises and the only way to get strong is to push through pain: that is, "no pain, no gain." Now, that's insane. Realistically, there is nothing that can fuck up a player quicker than that philosophy.

By 1990 strength coaches had become part of every college and pro staff. Most of them were certified by the National Strength & Conditioning Association and were used to working with ATs. That meant they knew how to work around injuries and not overdo rehabilitation regimens. They also were very astute in measuring the progress of individuals. The new strength coach for the Jets did none of that.

He built a sand pit and had players semi-wrestling in it. Within days I had a half-dozen players with strained calf muscles and shin splints. I tried explaining to him the problems with his ideas and that he needed to take into consideration some of the injuries the veterans had and the need to work around them. He nodded in agreement and then did what he wanted anyway. Every time I turned around he had some new gimmick that was going to make players bigger, faster, and stronger. None of his gimmicks were based in science or experience; they had no correlation to playing football.

The Jets had picked up Bill Pickel as a free agent to give us some depth in the defensive line. Pickel had nine years with the Raiders and had a laundry list of old injuries including an old torn calf muscle, disc surgery in his back, and a ruptured pectoralis in his chest, which meant he had some limitations on certain lifts like the bench press. "Pick" came to me one day and said, "Reese, you've got to save me. This fucking strength coach has me pushing an SUV around the parking lot. My good pect is about to explode from doing all the work and my Achilles is getting hot. If you can't get me out of this shit, I'll have to retire."

Now I knew Pickel not only from reputation around the league, but also because George Anderson, the Raiders' AT, had called me after we signed him and told me what a great guy and tough s.o.b. he was. As a side note, there is a persistent public misconception that in the NFL the players have to be made to play or coerced or threatened into playing. I have rarely found this to be true. In my experience, the only players who tried to nurse an injury were those that knew they would be cut as soon as they were well enough to play. I always spent more time holding players back than trying to push them onto the field.

So, here we had a proven tough guy complaining about off-season workouts, and threatening to retire if he had to push any more trucks around the parking lot. I went out into the weight room and called the strength coach a stupid fuck and proceeded to tell him how he was hurting players instead of helping them. I told him if he couldn't understand it from an injury standpoint, to look at it from an investment standpoint. We had paid players like Pickel a nice bonus to sign, and if he retired, we would lose the money!

Power Structure

It is incidences like this that tell you more about the power structure of an organization than anything on an org chart. About 30 minutes after I blew my gasket at the strength coach, Coslet was in my office. I found out later that the strength coach had run straight up to Steinberg and then the shit started flowing downhill. Steinberg went to Coslet, and Coslet came to see me.

He asked me what the fuck was going on and I gave him my version. He said, "We cannot have this shit happening." He pursed his lips, let out a deep breath, stuck his head out my door into the training room and told one of my assistants to go get the strength coach and tell him the head coach wants him in Reese's office – NOW!

He came in, somewhat sheepishly and Coslet told him to sit down. Coslet placed himself in a chair so he could look at both of us. He gave us a little pep talk about how we were all in this together and he could not have us fighting with each other. Then he laid it out. If I said a player was hurt, the player worked with me. When I cleared him for full work, he would work with the strength coach. He asked if there were any questions. I asked him what about a player rehabbing his knee – did he work with the strength coach for upper body strength? No, came the answer. If he was injured at all or in rehab, he worked with me and my staff. If healthy, he worked with the strength coach. I nodded thinking that was not going to give the strength coach very many players to work with, but decided not to voice that. When both the strength coach and I nodded assent, Coslet looked directly at me and made sure we had eye contact. He then said, "If you two can't get along, one of you will not be here next year." I got that message loud and clear – the strength coach was Steinberg's guy and I better toe the line. The strength coach's grin did not look so sheepish now; it was more like the Cheshire Cat.

This was a different power structure. Every coach that I had worked for to date – Saban, Michaels, and Walton – pretty much had the final say, or at least veto power on decisions regardless how the org chart was set up. Now, the GM was definitely in charge. While this was somewhat unsettling, it was also good to know.

After Coslet and the strength coach left the office, I called Pepper and Joe P in and told them the deal. We would essentially be strength coaches for anyone with any injury. They needed to be healthy before we turned them over to the strength coach. Joe P stated the obvious that after the second game of the season the strength coach could go on vacation because no one except the scout team would be healthy enough to work with him. I cautioned them both to tread lightly and to not make waves. My job was on the line and there was no guarantee one of them would inherit it if I got fired. (That was really for Joe P as Pepper had been around long enough to understand the dynamics.)

Overall the summer went well. Word had gotten out about the new strength coach, so there were not many players working out at the complex – which translated to few new run-ins with him. Coslet was great about time off. After mini-camps he and his coaches were off until two weeks before training camp. They drew straws to make sure one of them was around the complex every week. He said he did not care which of ATs was in the training room as long as it was open every weekday when players were working out. I worked it out with Pepper and Joe P that I had off four consecutive weeks to spend on the boat. This arrangement also had me returning to cover the last several weeks before training camp so I could make sure everything was ready to go.

The Coslet coaching staff was much more social than Walton's staff. Coslet was inclusive of families. Several of the coaches settled on the

North Shore of Long Island in the Huntington area, which was not far from my home in Northport. After several get-togethers with coaches and their wives for dinner in Huntington, even SG was enjoying the atmosphere. The "you're never home" mantra slowed – until I left for training camp.

There should not have been a lot of pressure the first year of a new regime because expectations of winning are not that high. Problems with the strength coach, and Coslet's direct threat that I would be the one gone if we could not work together, kept me under a lot of stress. The vets learned in a hurry that they only needed some small injury to keep them from working out under "Krazy-man" as he was called. I just called him "dangerous" under my breath. He had no concept that a football season was underway; I think he thought he was getting the players ready for some fitness contest. It was maddening.

On the home front, SG was no help at all. If I complained about the strength coach, she would say something stupid like, "Just have him fired." She was semi-enjoying being part of the Jets for the first time in a while and she was not going to let my concerns spoil it for her. True to form, the more I felt pressure at work, the more she added to it home. I spent a lot time feeling sorry for myself with my buddies Jack Daniels and Pinot Noir, the latter which I was now purchasing by the case.

The Jets went 8-8 in Coslet's first season. It should have been more fun, but I had this sword of Damocles hanging over me and struggled to maintain control. I coped by drinking. That brings me back to Chapter 1: "You think you are in control of your life? Take a good look around. Have you noticed you are an in-patient in a mental hospital?"

Part 2
BEGINNINGS OF A SOBER LIFE

If you had asked me what kind of life I had experienced prior to 1991, I would have told you categorically that I had lived a charmed life. Since leaving college I had nurtured a prestigious career and was respected by my peers. I had a high profile job and I was making great money. This was actually true.

I also thought I had created a secure and ideal life that included a loving wife, two bright, healthy and loving children, and a nice home for my family. Little did I know this façade would crumble as I became sober and began to see the many dysfunctions in my life. My alcoholism was a symptom of an unhealthy and toxic reality. My alcoholism had masked the insidiousness of the many dysfunctions in my life.

Chapter 17

REHAB

I Am an Alcoholic

So, here I am in rehab for alcoholism. I had come to the conclusion that I had been assessed correctly, that is I am an alcoholic. I practiced hundreds of times in my head before I ever said out loud at a meeting: *Hi. I'm Bob. And I'm an alcoholic.* Because I had focused only on making that statement, I had not prepared anything else to share. So, after an uncomfortable silence, I finally said that I had nothing to share and that I just wanted to experience what it felt like to say out loud, "I am an alcoholic". I got a few laughs and several people applauded. The meeting moderator congratulated me and told me that making that admission took courage and demonstrated that I knew what I had to do: "Don't drink, and go to meetings."

That was the first time I experienced anyone calling me courageous for anything. While I felt trepidation about admitting that I am an alcoholic, I had not considered it a courageous act. In hindsight, I know it was courageous.

The next year of my life took all the courage I could muster. I know now that anyone who can get sober and remain in recovery is a brave and courageous soul. My journey in recovery, while often difficult and sometimes overwhelming, has resulted in a life beyond my wildest dreams, which is one of the promises of the 12 Steps of AA. The rewards are great, but you have to move from surviving into thriving. And, as the saying goes: "It's simple, but it's not easy."

Rehab: Rumor Control

When I reported to South Oaks Rehabilitation Center for evaluation I was relatively certain that, after assessment, I would begin an outpatient treatment regime. My interpretation was the result of multiple interventions with players who were, in my opinion, much worse off than I was. I was astonished when told to report the following Monday for in-patient treatment.

SG was pissed! She wanted to know why I did not lie better. She argued I should have known what they were looking for because I had been in many interventions with players. Actually, I thought I had softened the truth quite a bit about how much I drank. Consequently, I suspected that the decision had been made beforehand; the assessment was probably a formality.

That Monday I had to drive myself to South Oaks as I could not awaken SG to drive me; she had spent most of the night drinking and calling me names. I called into the Jets and told the operations assistant that I needed one of the clubhouse guys to come to South Oaks to pick up my car. Because of her experiences with players at the Jets entering rehab, she knew the routine. She did hesitate, however, and said, "*your* car?" After telling her that it was indeed *my* car, she confirmed the routine: tell no one anything about who was entering rehab.

During my time in the NFL I learned that rumors were worse than truth. If you wanted to keep something quiet, the absolute worst thing was to try to keep it a secret. I knew first-hand that if anyone tried to hide or dance around the truth the rumors would end up being worse than the reality. In the realm of alcohol/drug rehab I also knew that within days the bean counters would be getting a call or letter approving treatment – if they hadn't already. The accountants were not bound by medical confidentiality; and because of the way the NFL reports injuries to the media there is little in the way medical confidentiality in the League.

Experience had taught me that the best way to keep something quiet was to announce it. If everyone thought everyone else already knew, no one would bother to talk about it. With that in mind, I informed the operations assistant that I was entering rehab and that it was *NOT* a secret. I had already told my assistants. Management and the head coach also knew. So, I told her to tell anyone who asked that I was in rehab and to give the same directive to her two sisters who also worked at the Jets. One sister was the head coach's secretary, and the other worked in the ticket office. If something was going on in the Jets complex, at least one of the sisters would know about it. I did not want rumors starting because they were trying to protect my reputation. So, I also told her that I was neither ashamed nor embarrassed (even though I was both at that time).

Similarly, I headed off league-wide rumors. Because my four week stay in rehab would overlap the annual NFL Combine Physicals in Indianapolis, I wrote to my old friend Dean Kleinschmidt who was the Saint's head AT and the president of PFATS at the time. I asked him to read my letter to the membership at the PFATS meeting that preceded the Combine. In the letter, I told everyone I was in rehab for alcoholism and that I intended to overcome the problem and could use their support.

This was fortuitous because Pepper and Joe P, my assistants, had created some complex and convoluted story as to why I was not attending the Combine. They told me later that they were relieved I removed that burden from them. Also, some coaches on other teams began to "inform" their ATs that something was going on with the Jets' trainer. While some reports were accurate, others had me in DUI car crashes, drunk and disorderly in a Manhattan bar fight, and one even suggested I was arrested for dealing steroids. Fortunately, my PFATS brothers were able to quash the rumors before they got completely out of control.

Interestingly, but not surprising, because there were no secrets when I returned to work after rehab hardly anyone even asked me where I had been. Several of the younger assistant coaches just assumed I had been on vacation. Also upon return to work, I had many letters of support from my PFATS brothers waiting for me. That turned out to be hugely important as time went on. As I grew and matured in recovery, my early decisions about disclosing rehab provided a powerful example of how important having "No Secrets" is to recovery. This learning further elucidates the power of those words: "I'm Bob and I am an alcoholic."

Rehab: Engagement

Rehab is a very structured environment. Breakfast was at 7:00 AM, an educational class from 8:00-9:00 AM, followed by a short break and a group therapy session that ran until lunch. After lunch there was about an hour's free time. Then back to classes or individual therapy or counseling sessions in the afternoon. After dinner there was another break until the nightly AA meeting at 8:00 PM which was followed by free time until lights out at 11:00 PM.

My rehab environment had many restrictions. There was no outside contact the first two weeks. Then, limited use of the phone and a restricted number of visitors were allowed. Also, leaving the campus was a breach that led to being dismissed. Bottom line: rehab is not a vacation

After my realization and public admission at the meeting that I was an alcoholic, I began to approach my stay at South Oaks differently. Instead of just marking time, I began listening to what was being said. At the time, I was a full blown cynic and skeptical about nearly everything. I was – and always had been – curious about how and why things work. I also knew that science, reason, and logic did not explain everything.

During educational meetings and daily group therapy I began to question and challenge just about everything. I thought *Okay, if you want me to change my life you're going to have to convince me this is the way to do it.* Initially the group counselor, Paul, was a little flummoxed at my newfound engagement. After a few days, however, he realized I was serious and not just trying to be a pain in the ass.

Grill a Burger?

One of the first startling wake-up calls about how different life was going to be without alcohol occurred in the third week of rehab. I was in a men's group that consisted of most of the male inmates at the rehab center. The idea was to discuss male issues. Most of the sharing was about how they were going to get laid – or introduce themselves to a woman – without booze. I semi-tuned out and began my own mental review about what was going to be different in my life. After about five minutes I let out (quite loudly) an "aw fuck!" Realizing I had verbalized this out loud, I looked up to see everyone staring at me. I felt my cheeks flush as one of the counselor's asked me to share. I said I had just realized that I did not even know how to grill a fucking hamburger without a beer in my hand. There were gasps and a lot of "aw shits!" and other expletives as everyone started to realize, like I had, how much alcohol had been a part of their lives. This realization of the pervasiveness was almost overwhelming. It did, however, cement the necessity of the viewpoint: one day at a time!

Spirituality vs. Religion

Another of my early challenges in rehab centered on the difference between spirituality and religion. According to the 12-Steps I needed a "spiritual awakening" to achieve sobriety. I saw this as a major stumbling block because by this time I had little use for organized religion. While I still identified as Catholic, I would always preface myself as a "non-practicing" Catholic. I did believe in God, but not the "old man sitting in the clouds directing traffic" God. In 1977, I had adopted the concept of God as the universal life Force, similar to what is described in the first *Star Wars* movie. I did not explore it; it just felt right. Until I was in rehab I had no reason to plumb the mysteries of faith; nor had I ever dwelled on the BIG question: "Why are we here?" Unless, of course, I had been drinking a lot! And then, while I may have solved that mystery, I usually remembered little of the discussion the next day.

Being raised Catholic my assumption was that spirituality and religion were synonymous. Since I was not about to go back to church, I did not know how I would become spiritual and without spirituality how could I get and stay sober. This discussion took up at least three days of group sessions. All but one person in our group was fed up with me, but she had exactly the same questions and problems as I did. Paul seemed to enjoy the dialog, but at times I could tell he knew we needed to address other topics or he was going to lose the group altogether.

After three or four days of discussions in and outside of group, the light bulb switched on. I got it! Simply put, I learned that spirituality is a connectedness with community, nature, and/or the cosmos – like the Force in Star Wars. Much of religion's job is to help one become more spiritual, but religious and spiritual are not synonymous. I could be spiritual without being religious. Furthermore, one can be religious without being spiritual or one can be both religious and spiritual. The Force, religion, spirituality, or a support group can be the "Higher Power" in the 12-Steps.

Bottom line was I had to have a "Higher Power" to help me get sober and maintain recovery. I could not do it alone – which most alcoholics want to do. I did not have to believe in God or practice religion, I just had to believe that I needed the help of someone or something that was more than me. When Paul finally said that my local AA group could be my higher power, the light bulb really came on.

For me, this was huge! It seems obvious in hindsight, but it was a real challenge for me. Like so many other things in recovery, however, once I "got it," it smoothed the road for other insights. I could now focus on staying sober, and I could look into the mysteries of the cosmos later. I had several other important experiences and revelations while in rehab.

SGs 1st Visit

SGs first visit to rehab came in third week. We had had limited phone contact, about once or twice a week for 10 minutes. The visit was to be only for 30 minutes, so I was determined to make the exchange worthwhile. I prepared by doing a lot of reflection and worked with my counselor, Paul, on what I needed to say and how best to say it.

I could tell when she entered the room she was pissed. I assumed erroneously it was for my past transgressions. I began by apologizing to her. I told her how sorry I was for "never being home" and for not considering her enough. My statements were heartfelt. I was emotional and tears rolled down my cheeks. She told me to "shut-up and quit crying!" She said she didn't want to hear any of this AA bullshit and went on to tell me I needed to do or say whatever it took to get out of there so I could get back home and we could get back to normal. Oh, and furthermore, she did not think I was alcoholic anyway. I am not sure what response I expected, but it was not that.

I then discovered that she was pissed that "assholes" from South Oaks had insisted on interviewing her and Rachel to see how much my alcoholism had affected them. She had agreed to it only because she thought it might get me out quicker. That interview resulted in inpatient treatment being recommended for both SG and Rachel: SG for alcohol and Rachel for an eating disorder.

She ranted about the intrusion into her life. She fumed that she did not have a fucking drinking problem and that the only reason they wanted to put them both in rehab was because we had good insurance. Not wanting further confrontation, I avoided the fact that I thought rehab was indicated for her, but I did tell her I thought it could not hurt Rachel to go into rehab. Rachel had become obese over the past several years and our preaching about her weight seemed to have a negative effect. SG retorted that it was most likely my fault because I was never there – not because of my drinking or hers, but because I was never home.

She again ordered me to say or do whatever it took to get out of there so I could come home as soon as possible and to tell these South Oaks "assholes" to stay out of our family's life. It was bad enough they were in my life – stay out of hers. All of this took less than 15 minutes. Then she said she had had enough of this bullshit and she left. I was nonplussed, to say the least. After that meeting I never shared another personal emotion with her. I had opened myself up and had been vulnerable but she had stomped on my feelings. I would not ever give her that opportunity again.

Psychiatrist: Humor – and Other Pearls

In addition to meeting with a counselor one-on-one a couple of times a week, I also met with a psychiatrist once a week while at South Oaks. After reviewing my history, he wanted to know if I needed any meds – valium or sleeping pills – to help me with my withdrawal. I informed him that I was not experiencing withdrawal. This led to a discussion about my drug use; that is what other drugs did I take.

I was honest and told him about the occasional codeine to ward off hangovers and about the Percocet I had taken a few years earlier for my back problems. I informed him that because of my job with the NFL I gave all illegal drugs a wide birth. I told him I had smoked marijuana in college and taken a few tokes off a joint or two to be sociable but not even that since 1978. He informed me that I was a member of a vanishing breed, people who were "just" alcoholics. Most people he encountered were poly-drug abusers and it was often difficult to determine their drug of choice. Because of my NFL education, I was familiar with this concept.

The most important thing I learned from the psychiatrist occurred during my third or fourth session. He told me that he recognized that I had a good sense of humor and to never lose it. He said that recovery did not have to be a miserable experience and that it would not be for me if I continued to look for the humor in situations. I have followed this advice. While my sense of humor has changed over time, I have never lost it. I can find humor in almost any situation, especially those displaying my ignorance or stupidity!

Later on he informed me that I only knew intellectually that I was an alcoholic and that until I learned it here (pointing to his heart) I would not be able to remain sober. I thought to myself that this was another one of those spirituality versus religion things – and I was right. It took me quite a while to learn it emotionally, but when I did it really made a positive difference. Coming from a family that generally discouraged feeling emotions, I had to give myself permission to feel emotions. I had stuffed them and drowned them with booze for so long that I had to learn about getting in touch with my emotions. This began with anger which I discuss below.

Another significant concept that he brought to my attention was my need to help people – especially my family. He said that was admirable but that I seemed to be doing it at my own expense. He pointed out that, while I cared for everyone else – my family, the Jets players, etc. – I wasn't caring for myself. He told me I needed to think of myself first. He said that if I did not take care of me, especially my sobriety, I would not be able or available to take care of others. While I immediately got this intellectually, it took me some time to understand emotionally that taking care of myself first was not a selfish attitude. I had to overcome years of Catholic, family, and cultural programming. One analogy that I used to get this is the instruction given at the beginning of flights: when in an emergency while on an airplane you must place the oxygen mask on yourself first, then on the child next to you.

The final important direction I received from the psychiatrist was to continue to question everything. He told me it was good to be skeptical, but I needed to work on my cynicism, sarcasm, and anger. I'm quite sure I said something sarcastic under my breath. It would take me years to finally "get it" regarding cynicism and sarcasm, especially how they related to my anger.

Dan: Dump Truck Full of Cocaine

Another startling revelation that made me extremely grateful that I was "just" an alcoholic occurred in a regular group session. This group usually consisted of about 8-10 people (male and female) and we met daily. The membership was consistent except when someone "graduated" or a newbie came in. An elder was someone who had been there three or more weeks. Our group was facilitated by my personal counselor, Paul.

Around the time of our discussions about spirituality and religion the New York Lottery ballooned to very large number – one of the highest ever at that time. Everyone in South Oaks was trying to figure out how to get someone on the outside to buy them a ticket. Paul used it as a topic for discussion in group: What would you do if you won this lottery?

As the question went around the room, the usual answers surfaced: pay off my bills; quit my job; buy a house on the beach; travel; etc. I was semi-listening as I asked myself what I would do. I had often played Lotto and had a game plan that usually centered about buying a big boat and moving to the Florida Keys – where I could drink in peace. So, I was thinking about whether I would quit drinking if I actually won the Lotto.

I was shaken from my reverie when Dan (pseudonym), one of the elders in the group, began to share. This was his third try at rehab and his drug of choice was cocaine. He was pretty wide open about his life and certainly knew how to "talk the talk" of 12-Steps. He and I had become friends; we had shared a lot about our lives during meals and other free-time. Because he was so open and honest, I always paid attention to him when he shared.

Without hesitation he said, "I would buy an island in the Caribbean. Then I would buy a dump truck full of cocaine and dump it on the island. Then I would snort that coke until my heart exploded!" He finished by spreading his open hands apart like an explosion and saying "POW!"

After his statement he sat back in his chair with a look that could only be described as ultimate satisfaction. The rest of us were aghast. Paul was speechless. Paul eventually regained his composure and asked us what we thought of Dan's scenario. Some people said that surely Dan was joking. He assured them he was not, but since he was not playing Lotto he could not win and so the scenario could not occur.

I told him he scared the shit out of me and I was glad I was "just" an alcoholic because cocaine seemed a lot tougher to give up. I also expressed my concern that he was kidding himself if he thought just because he was not playing Lotto that he did not have a real problem he needed to address before he graduated the next week. I could see by the look on Paul's face that he was in agreement. Everyone chimed in and recommended he stay in rehab longer and not graduate the next week. Dan sloughed it off and said everyone was taking it too seriously. I realized at that moment the power that addiction exerted. I became determined not to ever take addiction – any addiction – lightly.

About six months later I learned that Dan had overdosed on cocaine and died of a heart attack. I was – and am – extremely grateful that I am "just" an alcoholic.

Rehab: Anger

At the beginning my fourth week in rehab, I began to look forward to graduation. Through a friend of a friend I had found a sponsor in Northport who had agreed to shepherd me to local AA meetings. I had filled two composition notebooks with my drunkalog (much of the first half of this book comes from that effort). I felt ready to enter the world as a sober, recovering alcoholic.

As the old saying goes: "Men plan, the gods laugh!" When I had my counseling session with Paul, he informed me that I would not be graduating the upcoming weekend because they felt there were some issues I still needed to address. He said the Jets were on board with the decision that I could stay as long as South Oaks deemed necessary. I could, of course, leave, but it would cost me my job. At first I was shocked. I had done everything they had asked of me, and I felt I was certainly more prepared to be successful in recovery than some people who had graduated before me. I couldn't believe it.

Then I got pissed. After ranting a few minutes about the unfairness of the situation, what it was going to cost me and how it might wreck my marriage, I finally asked what it was they thought I needed to work on. He smiled and said it was my anger. He went on to say that all the counselors and the psychiatrist felt I had anger issues that I needed to get in touch with. I exploded, missing the point entirely.

I told Paul that it was normal for me to be angry with their making me stay in fucking rehab another week. He stopped me and said that it might be more than a week; they were going to keep me in rehab until I came to terms with my anger. I told him this was like some Catch-22: you tell me something sure to piss me off, then you say, "See, you're angry." Then you make me do the thing (stay in rehab) that is making me angry, and it feeds on itself. I told him I was beginning to agree with SG that the only reason they were keeping me in rehab was because I had good insurance.

He admitted that it might appear that way, but the Jets had agreed to pay out of pocket if insurance did not cover it as they also thought it was that important. He also told me that he understood why I would be upset at not graduating but that particular upset was not the anger problem. There was something else that made me angry at a deeper level and I needed to admit it, understand it, and come to terms with it.

When I asked him what it was, he smiled sheepishly and said he could not tell me. I had to discover it for myself. He added that at some point in the future I would look back at this situation and think it humorous. I was so pissed off I told him that I doubted that very seriously.

The phone call to SG informing her of the extension of my stay and the uncertainty of my release had the expected results: she went ballistic. It was all my fault! What had I done wrong to make them keep me longer. Rachel was being admitted to the eating disorder unit the next day. Rob was away at school. She was now going to be all alone. And, what the fuck did I have to be angry about? I was on vacation in rehab while she was doing everything. The vacation remark pushed one of my buttons. I screamed at her that if she thought rehab was such a vacation she should try it and the sooner the better!

For the next two weeks I was truly an angry individual. When I shared at meetings or in group, I introduced myself as, "Hi, I'm Bob, and I am one pissed off alcoholic!" I put up walls to counselors and fellow inmates. I did, however, begin a process of relentless self-examination: "What is it that pisses me off!"

Number one on the list had been Joe Walton, the previous head coach. His micro-managing made me crazy. But he was gone, so he could not be a cause of my ongoing anger.

Next was Jim Nicholas, the team physician. He thrived on crazy-making. Coping with his erratic moods and his undermining my decisions had provided me with a great excuse to drink. But, with the new regime, he had been all but neutered. Dick Steinberg barely humored him and Coslet gave him little access, so he was no longer a major source of aggravation. Granted, he was still around, but I didn't see him as the source of my anger.

The strength coach came to mind next. He was a problem and would continue to be. I had learned to work around him – when he was out of sight, he was out of mind. Although he could still cause me problems, his antics did not account for the anger that was keeping me in rehab.

It was in the sixth week that Paul, after reading my journals, asked me why there was little mention of SG in them. I told him that I did not want to put anything in them that she might find insulting or put her in a bad light because it would piss her off. He asked me why she would be reading my personal journals. I stammered, hemmed, and hawed. I finally replied that if she thought there was anything about her in them she would feel she had a right to look at them. To be truthful, I felt sure she would snoop into the journals, so I refrained from mentioning her in them. He smiled, and said, "So, let me know when you figure out what it is that's making you so angry." I just stared at him blankly.

Talk about denial! It took another whole day for it to sink in: SG was what was keeping me angry. I told him in the next session – without ever mentioning her name – that "I finally got it." He asked me if I was sure, and, if so, what was I going to do about it? I told him that I was not sure what I was going to do about it in the long run, but now that I knew what it was, it would not be something that would make me take a drink. While I knew that's what he wanted to hear, I also meant it to my core. He just smiled and said for the umpteenth time, some day you'll look back on this and laugh about it.

[*Paul, for the record, I still can't laugh about it. I do get a smile on my face, but that's as far as I can go because thinking about it is so painful. I will say that it took more than a decade for me to truly come to terms with my anger and release it.*]

Control – or Lack Thereof

I remained in rehab for a total of eight weeks. When I found out I was not being released after the usual four weeks, I talked to Elliot Pellman, the Jets internist, about the Jets role in this. I told him that I wanted to know for sure if I had a job waiting for me when I got out. I was not making a demand, but if they were going to fire me I wanted to be able to work on that during my remaining time in rehab. He made a special visit two days later and assured me that I would have a job as long as I abided by whatever South Oaks prescribed. That was a huge relief.

During the fifth and sixth weeks there was a lot of growth on several levels. Beyond finally recognizing I had anger issues and the major underlying cause of them, I had to come to terms with my lack of control of my current situation. This was also a hard lesson and the last two weeks imprinted on me the absolute lack of control I had in the decision to extend my time in rehab. My wants, desires, good behavior, hard work, and sheer force of will – all things that had served me well in the past – made no difference in this situation. By the end of the eighth week I was resolved that if they decided to keep me in another week or two, I would just accept it.

During those last two weeks, I rationalized that South Oaks needed me to be successful in recovery, maybe even more than the Jets needed this result. After all, I was the Employee Assistance Professional (EAP) for the Jets. I led the interventions for the players in trouble, so how would it look if I did not stay sober. They wanted the business and the prestige of being the provider for an NFL team, so I determined that the extra month in rehab was the closest they could come to an insurance policy that I would be okay. Then an awakening occurred: *cynical* Bob did not give a rat's ass about South Oaks; but *sober* Bob was going to stay sober for Bob and it was okay if my sobriety also helped South Oaks. This was also consistent with what the psychiatrist had said about taking care of yourself first puts you in a place to help others.

Rehab: Melanie comes to South Oaks

The final instance of import during my stay in rehab was a close relative of SGs', Melanie (pseudonym), visiting me at South Oaks. At this time, she had been sober for more than eight years. She had married a man, who was also in recovery.

She came with SG who had reached out to her family for someone to share the burden of her being alone – she hated being alone. (Rachel was in eating disorder unit; I was in limbo, not knowing when I would be released; and Rob was away at college). Together, Melanie, SG, and I attended a Sunday family therapy session. While family sessions were held every Sunday afternoon, I had never participated in one because SG had refused. Apparently Melanie gave her no option.

SG and I had had little contact with Melanie for years. She had lived with us for a time in Boston after she graduated high school. I was not really close to her, but we always got along.

Melanie had begun experimenting with drugs while in high school, By the 1970s she had embraced the hippie life-style – drugs and all. Soon after her stay with us in Boston, she returned to Nashville and took up with a like-minded hippie; they built a cabin in the woods outside

Nashville. By the early 1980s she had two daughters and decided her lifestyle was not conducive to raising them. She was one of the first individuals whom I knew that went into rehab.

After she was released from rehab, Melanie was going to stay at the G's house. I remember being in Nashville at that time. Everyone was concerned about how she would react to the constant beer drinking. SGs' mother demanded that all of the beer be taken out of the house and put in coolers in the garden shed out back. I recall making some sarcastic remarks about being inconvenienced at the interruption of standard procedure. I also remember I had no empathy and little sympathy for Melanie at that time.

Now she was with SG and me in a family therapy session attended by 35-40 people. Everyone had their spouse or significant other by their side. There were a few teenage children and a couple of infants. I recognized most of the inmates. I also recognized that most of them were newbies who had been in rehab only one to two weeks. There were two counselors; the session started slowly with no one seemingly wanting to share. Finally, a couple of the spouses spoke up with some questions about what their partners were actually doing in rehab. The conversation drifted to why people enter rehab. There was a lot of soft-peddling of the reasons.

I could feel Melanie getting anxious sitting next to me. Finally, she spoke up. "Well, I don't know why all you came into rehab, but I'll tell you why I did. I was afraid I was going to die! Literally die!" She went on to say that she recognized that if she kept going the way she was and taking the amount of drugs and drinking as much as she had been that it would have killed her. She knew she had to change. She had two small daughters. If she died, then what would become of them. She was terrified.

She slowly looked around the room holding everyone's gaze for a moment. Then, she told us that we were kidding ourselves if we did not think whatever shit we were drinking or taking was not killing us. She challenged everyone in there to really dig deep and look at the reality of their situation. She emphasized that rehab was no joke and that she had lost many friends. She added that some did not try to get straight, some went into rehab and then relapsed, and some died. She warned us that if we did not take advantage of this opportunity, we might not get another.

The room went silent. What Melanie shared I had heard before at many AA meetings, but this time I "got it" emotionally. Melanie had shared from deep in her heart about her experience. This was not someone saying what they were supposed to say: "Talking the talk." There was no room to doubt that this was real. When she talked about her fear it was palpable. I stole a glance at SG; even she was squirming.

Melanie finished by saying that she was not going to say anymore and that she was visiting from out of town to support me. She said that she was not a spouse, so probably should not have spoken up, but that not facing the facts about what you were up against [addiction] would not only wreck your life, it could kill you. She said she lived in gratitude every day for the gift AA had given her. Both counselors thanked her repeatedly for sharing and probably half the participants, both spouses and inmates, came over afterwards to personally thank her for her words.

I realized that alcohol would kill me if I continued to drink. In AA I learned about "think through the drink" and imagine what life would become like if I took another drink – and another, and another. As they say in the rooms of AA, one is too many and two (or 10, or 20) is never enough. While I was determined to remain sober, I helped myself by reframing how I thought of alcohol: in my mind it was now *literally* poison. From that point on I looked at every alcoholic beverage as cyanide, arsenic, or Drano.

After the group session we went outside. Even though it was late February, it was a warm, sunny day. Melanie told SG that she wanted to talk to me alone. Although SG seemed miffed, Melanie and I strolled around the South Oaks campus without her. She asked me if I understood what she had said in the meeting; I responded that I did. She reminded me that I had an opportunity to make my life better than ever. She warned me not to blow it. Here was someone much younger giving me advice, and I was listening with both ears.

We talked about AA and my time in rehab. We compared experiences. We talked about Rachel and her challenge with food in the present and in the future. I apologized to her for my lack of compassion and empathy when she was first getting sober. She told me that she had not noticed. She said that she was in such a fog early on that she could only focus on herself. She recognized that no one at that time realized how truly difficult getting sober is. She reminded me that the real work would begin when I went home. She said I should be grateful for the extra time in rehab because it was going to get a lot harder when I went home.

That brought the conversation around to SG. I shared with Melanie my concern that SG was alcoholic and needed rehab as badly as me. She agreed. She said that SG wasn't ready yet and that, until she was, I could not do much about it. Melanie's concern was for me. She warned me not to allow SG to pull me back into alcoholism. SG had told her numerous times since she had come to Long Island that I was not an alcoholic. Melanie had told her that obviously I was alcoholic and that she needed to support me. While SG had agreed, Melanie did not know how long that would last and that I might have to make some tough decisions down the line. I assumed she was talking about drinking or not drinking. Later I understood it was also about relationship.

We concluded the walk with a powerful hug. I did not want to let go of her because I could feel the strength of her conviction, confidence, self-esteem, compassion, and courage. I wanted some of that! When SG asked what we talked about, Melanie told her, "Just AA stuff." She added, "If you want to know about it, you'll have to join." That ended SG's line of questioning. A couple of weeks later I graduated from rehab. I was about to experience what Melanie had warned me about: the real work was about to begin. The next year would be the toughest of my life.

Compulsive Overeating

As mentioned above, Rachel was in the eating disorder unit on the South Oaks Campus. Her admission occurred after several rancorous discussions with SG. Rachel had just turned 15 and had been packing on weight over the past three or four years. When she was a girl, she and SG were inseparable. Since she had become a teen, they could barely stand to be in the same room together. I suggested to SG that time apart could be beneficial for both of them and that a 12-Step program would be helpful to Rachel.

She was in the eating disorder unit at South Oaks for about three months. During her first several weeks in rehab, I was still in South Oaks and attended her evening 12-Step meetings once or twice a week. I hoped we would be better able to understand each other. I knew Rachel would have a very tough row to hoe, especially since her mother thought it was all bullshit.

There was a young woman in the alcohol and drug addiction unit who had also been anorexic. She gave me a lot of information about eating disorders and drove home the fact that eating disorders were much tougher and required more change than drug and alcohol addiction. She pointed out that you can live without booze, you can live without coke, marijuana, uppers, or downers but you cannot live without food. So, if you have a food addiction, you cannot quit it; you have to learn to manage it.

He's There for Me

For me, one of the most positive experiences to come out of Rachel's stay in the eating disorder unit occurred after I was out of rehab and during Rob's college spring break. He agreed to attend a family group session scheduled at the eating disorder unit. At that session several parents were criticized about their parenting by the teens in the unit. A couple of parents broke down and admitted to verbal and even physical abuse. As the sharing moved around the big circle I was anticipating the "My dad is never home" refrain coming from Rachel; I was not disappointed. SG, of course, piled on. All eyes were on me for my response. I apologized for "not being home" as often as I would have liked to be there. I, however, did not explain that my "not being home" was about my mandatory work schedule and obligations as an NFL AT. I simply said that it was not by choice that I spent so much time at work.

Rob leaned over and asked if he was allowed to speak; I told him yes. He proceeded to tell the group that this was his first meeting of this sort and that it seemed to him that the purpose was to beat up on the parents. He went on to say that, while my job caused me to be away from home a lot, I was there for him if he ever needed anything. He added that neither he nor Rachel were ever neglected or abused by me, that he knew I was always trying to do what was best for them, and that he knew I loved them. Then he re-emphasized that he knew he could count on me to be there for him for anything important in his life.

The room fell silent. A tear or two rolled out of my eyes. I silently admitted to myself that Rob was right. I had always done what I thought was best for my family and I was there when things counted. I realized that I had been relentlessly beating up myself for years for "never being home." SG had convinced not only herself, but also Rachel and me – but not Rob. I felt so proud of my son for speaking the truth and such deep love and gratitude that I thought my heart would burst. His statement helped to boost my self-esteem enough to start realizing the truth. It would take me almost two decades, however, to really internalize how he accurately described my conduct as a father and man and to refute the lie that I was never home. After several minutes, one of the counselors spoke and tried to get the session back on track: beating up the parents.

Chapter 18

THE HARD WORK BEGINS

Back to Work

After two months of rehab, where I only had to be concerned about myself, returning to the real world was culture shock. At work I was playing catch-up on the status of Jets players and their injury rehabilitation and on the upcoming college draft. Fortunately, Pepper and Joe P had stayed on top of everything. Coslet was easy going, so he made few demands on them. When I met with him, he welcomed me back and shared that a couple of his friends had gone through rehab. He advised me to keep my priorities straight and to do what I needed to do to stay sober. He said that my sobriety status was my business and that he would not be asking me about it.

Dick Steinberg was also supportive. Like Coslet, he told me that I needed to keep my priorities straight. He reminded me that he thought a lot of me and my abilities as an AT and that I should be appreciative of the investment the Jets had made in me. I assured him that I was and that I would continue to work hard and do my best for the team. We then discussed my role in the draft. Like last year, I was not needed in personnel meetings but I had to be available to answer questions about players.

Next I met with Steve Gutman. Having been the bean counter for a mental health organization once upon a time, he was much more inquisitive about my stay in rehab and how I was doing mentally and emotionally. He was particularly interested in how much I thought the extra month in rehab helped. I told him weeks five and six were very valuable and that I experienced a lot of personal growth. I also shared that in weeks seven and eight I learned about control, or more accurately, lack of control; but for the most part I just marked time. He informed me that Mr. Hess was very interested in my recovery and had insisted that the Jets pick up any costs associated with my extra month in rehab.

While I never learned how much out of pocket my rehab actually cost the Jets (if anything) the reality was they had invested two months of my salary and services. I was not there. I was extremely grateful to be on the Jets payroll during that period. While these were important incentives to stay sober, I knew that I had to stay sober for myself or it was not going to work.

Back Home

At home things did not go as smoothly. SG had kept her word to Melanie to support me by getting all the alcohol out of the house (or at least hide it where I would not see it). Financially, while she had paid the mortgage, most of the other bills had not been paid and late fees were now attached. She tried to act happy that I was home, but any questions that I asked about whether something had been done were responded to with anger or sarcasm and with the goal of making me feel guilty for "never being home," especially over the last two months.

Once a week, on Sundays, we went back to South Oaks to visit Rachel. She seemed to be doing well in rehab and was beginning to talk the talk. She had made a few friends. She actually seemed happy.

The first week home my sponsor, Bobby M., picked me up just about every night and we went to an AA meeting. Who knew there were so many people in recovery just in the Northport area? There were at least four meetings a week in Northport proper, one in Centerport, and a couple in East Northport. There were dozens more in Huntington and Smithtown on either side of Northport.

By the second week, SG had already grown tired of my going out almost every night to an AA meeting. She complained that I might as well be back in rehab. While I agreed with her, I was still determined to be the best recovering alcoholic ever, which meant in my mind, I had to make 90 meetings in 90 days as recommended by AA.

Additionally, I was also expected to attend outpatient therapy at South Oaks. I met once a week with Bob Cahill, the Assistant Director of South Oaks. After several one-on-one sessions he suggested I join a weekly group session and just see him monthly for individual sessions. During the second week I told him of my quest to make the 90 in 90 and the strain it was putting on my already strained marriage. He laughed out loud.

When he had composed himself, he informed me that the 90 in 90 was the recommendation created by AA long before they had rehabs. He asked me how long I was in rehab and I told him two months. He said, "Do the math." I had already attended a minimum of 60 meetings in 60 days. He clarified the requirement; a lot of people considered therapy, especially group therapy as a meeting, so I had probably already made 90 in 90. He suggested that I lighten up; after all I would not get a medal for making 90 in 90. He explained sober was sober and I would not be *more* sober by attending more meetings. The idea was for the meetings to help me in life, not for my life to be about meetings.

After that I settled in to Bobby M's home group in Northport and declared it my home group. It met one night a week for a regular meeting and had an open meeting Sunday night. I also attended another group's Saturday morning meeting. I could make that meeting and be back at home by 10:00 AM before SG was out of bed; which cut down on the "you're never home" grousing. I made the Saturday meeting about twice a month. I also liked the Centerport meeting – which was really big – and attended it sporadically on Friday nights. I found a lunch time meeting in Westbury, near the Jets complex, and managed to make it three or four times a week. While I knew this was still a lot of meetings, I looked at it like a squirrel putting away nuts for the winter. I knew once training camp opened and the season started my ability to attend meetings would be severely compromised.

I also recognized that I could not let SG's bitching deter me from attending meetings. While I had not yet begun to formally study psychology, I knew that if I caved in and did not go to meetings to avoid the bitch-fest it would only reinforce the fact that her bitching would keep me at home and that after a while I would have to quit them altogether. I knew that I could not allow that to happen. Quite often I would head out to a meeting with SG haranguing me all the way to the car. I learned to ignore it.

Another Catch 22

Over time I also learned that going to a meeting was a great excuse to leave the house to avoid the nagging. Once or twice a month when SG started in on me for something I had no control over, I would just say I had to go to a meeting and leave. There was always a meeting somewhere in the area; so I never lied and I always went to a meeting. I hoped that after a while she would learn that if she bitched I would leave and that similar to Pavlov's dog she would quit bitching. So much for classical conditioning. What she learned was that if she wanted a drink, she would start bitching and I would leave. Then she had an excuse to drink because, once again, I was never home.

So, SG created another Catch 22. Either way I was screwed. If I stayed, I had to put up with her bitching about something that I could not change but was somehow my fault. If I left, I escaped the bitching for a while but came home to a drunk who was much more vicious than the nag that sent me out the door. Because I no longer had my coping device – booze – I occasionally exploded in a verbal rage. Unfortunately, this insanity went on for years.

What Would Bobby Say?

My sponsor was the perfect fit for me. I had dreaded having a mother hen or drill sergeant sponsor who would constantly be on my back and refer to me as his little pigeon (that I assumed he was going to train to come home on command). Bobby M. was the polar opposite of these types of sponsors. Even though he was about 10 years younger than me, it was easy for me to respect him and listen to him. I had met him before AA on a few social occasions. On those social occasions I had been drinking and never even noticed that he was not. Now, on reflection, I thought it was cool that he could go to parties and not preach about the evil of drinking.

When he came to South Oaks to meet me as a fellow alcoholic, he shared a brief version of his story. Turns out that, like me, he was a relatively high-bottom drunk. He told me that he was low key as a sponsor and would not chase after me. My sobriety was up to me. He was neither my keeper nor my baby-sitter. He said that he considered himself my temporary sponsor and that any time I felt he was not right for me or if I connected with someone else I should just let him know. He would not be offended. There was nothing he said that I did not like.

He picked me up for meetings during my first week home. Then he said it was up to me to go to meetings. He gave me his phone number at home and work. He explained that he would often not be available while at work, but he would get back to me as soon as possible. He advised me that in an emergency (i.e., I felt like I was going to drink), I was to get my ass to a meeting. Otherwise, just ask myself, "What would Bobby say?"

This worked out well for me. I only called him twice; he was unavailable both times. I asked myself, "What would Bobby say?" and came up with a reasonable answer. When he called back, I went over the question with him and he gave the answer I imagined he would. After that, I did not need to call him, I would just ask: "What would Bobby say?"

The second week I was home, I met Bobby at the Northport home group meeting and afterwards we walked down to the pier. He told me he liked this group because there was a lot of "good sobriety" in there. I was not sure what that meant. I asked myself, "Was there 'bad' sobriety?" Bobby went on to say that in AA, like any organization, there were hard core members who lived for AA and there were members, like him, who used AA to help them live. He told me it was my choice: I could live for AA or I could let AA help me live. I chose the latter. He repeated that there was a lot of "good sobriety" in this group.

Bobby explained that no matter which group I attended I would hear all the rules regarding the 12-Steps and the different ways to go through them. He told me, "Take what you need and leave the rest behind." I looked at him quizzically. He smiled and told me that, if I tried to do everything everyone told me to do, it would make me crazy – or worse make me drink. He cautioned me to just listen and take in only what applied to me. If it did not apply, let it go and do not be concerned about it. So, "take what you need, and leave the rest behind" became a mantra that has served me well over the years; not only in AA, but also in life.

Probably Bobby's most important suggestion came when he asked me how I was doing working the Steps. I told him I was up to number 4 and should be able to get to the others soon. He laughed and told me to "take a breath." He pointed out that completing the 12-Steps was not a race, so there was no hurry. Living the 12-Steps is going to be my life: the rest of my life. His words helped me to understand that I needed to learn to "live" the Steps, not just "do" the Steps. He told me to do myself a favor: for the first year just concentrate on the 1st Step: *We admitted we were powerless over alcohol, that our lives had become unmanageable.* He said the first year was going to be tough enough and I did not need to make it tougher by trying to do too much. I heard the echo of Bob Cahill's message about making 90 in 90. One of those silly AA sayings popped into my head, "Take it easy." *Okay*, I told myself, *I'll do "one day at a time."*

Over time I learned what Bobby meant by "good sobriety" at the Northport meetings. Few of the attendees ever pontificated or chastised someone and most gave suggestions rather than advice. Also, a lot of different experiences were represented as the attendees were a wide range of "drunks" of all ages, all socio-economic backgrounds, and often almost as many women as men. So, no matter what your problem, someone usually had experienced it, or something like it.

The First Test

Four or five weeks after I returned to work I had my first real test about being around alcohol and people drinking it. The Jets Highlight film was premiered to the media each spring and was always a great party. It would generally start off at a big name restaurant or hotel in Manhattan. There would be an open bar and plenty of food. The head coach and one or two of the top players would make some comments and then everyone would watch the film. Afterwards, the press would interview some players and coaches. Then the PR Director would invite a bunch of the staff out for a night on the town on his expense account. I was usually a very willing participant and would often pour myself off the train in East Northport during the wee hours of the early morning or get a ride to the Jets complex and sleep it off on a training table.

This time I drove into Manhattan so I could leave when I wanted. To say I was nervous as I went to the upstairs room at Gallagher's Steakhouse would have been a gross understatement. I was literally sweating as I sat at a table watching everyone get their drinks. None of the players knew I had been in rehab. Several of them kept offering to get me a beer or a drink and looked perplexed when I told them I did not want one. They kept asking me if I was okay.

After about 30 minutes of sheer torture, I decided to get something to make it look like I had a drink so that people would quit asking me if I wanted one. I made my way to the bar and asked for a club soda with a lime. The bartender did not bat an eye and poured me what I ordered. I am not sure what I expected – maybe for him to make fun of me – but I thought, well, that was easy enough. What happened after that was close to a miracle.

As soon as I put the glass in my hand, my craving for alcohol diminished almost completely. I learned two things that evening. First, when I put a glass (or 12 oz. can) in my hand, the need for a drink dissipated rapidly. This was sort of the inverse of Pavlov's classical conditioning. Instead of the bell ringing and my beginning to salivate, a glass in my hand stopped my salivating for booze. What a relief!

The second thing I learned as the evening went on was how few of the attendees drank anywhere close to the amount I thought everyone drank. Except for a few of the players and my main drinking buddies on the staff, everyone else seemed very controlled and they all seemed to have a good time. It occurred to me that I really did drink a LOT more than most people.

Third Generation Graduation

In June of 1991 Rob graduated from Boston College. He had taken college seriously. I was very proud of him and I bragged on him a lot. I now knew why my Dad had bragged on me. My parents met us in Boston for the graduation, and my Dad was almost as proud of Rob as I was. By paying Rob's way through college, I also felt as if I had paid forward the debt I owed my father who had paid my way through Purdue (even though I now had at a college loan debt in excess of $65,000). I have this great snapshot of the three of us at the graduation – three generations of college grads. The only thing weird about the picture is that both my arms are in heavy splints. Now, that's another story.

Carpal Tunnel

That spring during mini-camps my hands began cramping severely every time I taped more than two or three players' ankles. The sensation was not new as I had been experiencing it for several years – but previously only in training camp and usually only by the afternoon practice. The year before I had spoken to my old boss in Buffalo, Abe, who was complaining of the same problem. We determined it was probably carpal tunnel syndrome due to the Purdue method of taping ankles – using an underhanded pull of the tape so we did not have to change hands with each strip of tape. Because it was more efficient, it made the Purdue ATs speedier tapers than most of our colleagues. Now all that repetitive motion had caught up with me and was causing a problem.

The Jets orthopedic surgeon and hand surgeon both confirmed the diagnosis of carpal tunnel syndrome. The hand surgeon suggested that to avoid the cramping and the numbness in my fingers that I was also experiencing, I could wear wrist braces for several months and that might alleviate the symptoms. I told him that was not an option since I had to be able to tape by mid-July for training camp. He said the only other option was surgery. He could schedule me for one wrist the next week, and the other one in six weeks. Again, I reminded him that time-line really was not an option. I wanted to do them both at the same time. He reminded me that I would be in splints for at least four weeks and the problems I would have with both hands and wrists in splints – for example, wiping my ass. I convinced him I could handle it and stressed that I needed to be ready for training camp.

This was the one of several personal medical decisions I made that were in the Jets best interest but not necessarily in mine. Beyond the football mentality of "playing in pain" that surrounded me, I also felt indebted to the Jets for my two months in rehab and the $20,000 *gift* from Mr. Hess. I could not imagine asking them to hire an additional person to help tape because there was something else wrong with me. No one at the Jets, not even the doctors, blinked an eye when I told them I was having both wrists operated on at the same time.

As you might guess by now, SG was not of the same opinion. She yelled and screamed that I was stupid and an asshole for putting *her* through this – and that I always put the Jets first. I told her I was the one having the surgery. She acknowledged that was true but complained that *she* was going to have to take care of me. She declared that she would not, under any circumstance, wipe my ass!

The Ring is Cut

While I had arranged to have someone from the Jets take me into Lenox Hill Hospital for the surgery, at the last minute SG insisted on taking me in herself. While I drove in, the whole way I was her whipping boy for her anger. Not only was she pissed that I was having both wrists operated on, she was also pissed I needed the surgery at all. It was all because of those fucking Jets. I wished I had a drink so I could shut her out. I smiled once to myself as I thought of my counselor Paul saying that someday I would think about the source of my anger and I would think it funny. But my smile was for the irony, not because it was funny.

As I was being prepped for surgery, the nurse told me I would have to remove my wedding ring. I told her that I could not get it off. The reason I could not get it off was that I had packed on a lot of weight. When I came to the Jets, I had been hovering around 200 pounds. At 5'9" that qualified me as "heavy" – at least that's how I described it. I wore 36" waist pants and large shirts. During the Joe Walton regime, I added another 25-30 pounds and had gone up to a tight fitting 38" waist and X-L shirts. Since I had gotten out of rehab, I had begun eating desserts to replace after dinner drinks and had packed on some more weight; I was hovering around 230-235 pounds.

Because of the increase in my weight there was no way the ring would come off my sausage of a finger. The nurses tried all their little tricks to get the ring off but nothing worked. They told me they were going to have to cut it off. I tried to argue with them but they said I coulet not keep it on because my hands would swell from the surgery and they would have to amputate my finger if I left it on. Seems like a no brainer, right?

I had a bad feeling about cutting the ring off. While I had not begun to study about the energetic universe, I knew in my gut – in my heart – that something was being broken and my marriage was on a downhill progression. I felt that cutting off that ring symbolized the beginning of the end of my marriage. Even with all the bitching, complaining, second-guessing, and entitlements, at that time I could not imagine life without SG. I shed a few tears as they cut it off. The nurses thought it was because they were hurting me physically, but I felt a pain in a place I could not identify.

That's the backstory to being at my son's graduation with both hands and wrists in splints. By training camp, I was able to tape at full speed. And while it was difficult, no one other than me had to wipe my ass.

1st Year Sober

The remainder of my first year of sobriety passed slowly. My fear of "how do I grill a hamburger without a beer" resurfaced with just about everything I did outside of work and a few things at work. My intake of coffee increased dramatically. I began purchasing cans of club soda by the case. This was slightly more expensive than buying it in big liter bottles, but the ability to hold the can was more important than the price.

That summer I was able to take almost a month's vacation. I had feared that my time in rehab would be counted as my vacation, but Coslet told me to get the hell out of there so I could get my mind right for training camp. SG, Rachel and I took a number of short boat trips around Long Island Sound. We docked the boat in Greenport for several weeks. I took the train in to Northport to attend some AA meetings and Rachel went to some of her meetings which were much fewer and further between than mine. Rob was home and working for the summer. SG seemed content. The compulsion to drink was ever present but overall it was a nice month.

When training camp opened I was glad for the routine. Coslet had moved training camp from Hofstra's gym into the Jets main complex. The complex was air-conditioned and the lack of beer after the afternoon practice was not missed that much. I had no drinking buddies among the coaches. The other staff members, who were regulars at Bill's Meadowbrook, carried on without me.

Interestingly without a hangover I was in much better humor when taping ankles for the morning practice! Several old timers accused me of going soft because I was not regularly cutting down the rookies with my biting sarcasm. I told them it was part of Coslet's edict that rookies be treated like team members and not torn down, but I knew that it was really because I felt human as opposed to miserable. While I was a high functioning, high bottom drunk, I was amazed at how much more I could accomplish during the day without having to spend the morning crawling out of a lingering stupor.

I still had problems with the strength coach, but I managed that without too much anxiety. On the road, one of the players who was in recovery and I would have our own little AA meeting after the evening snack before curfew. Things were tolerable and life was looking up.

At some point during the season I attended a formal function. On the small place cards with your name on it there were famous quotes or sayings. Mine was perfect for me: *Action Relieves Anxiety*. This became a mantra to remind me to keep busy.

Around January or February 1992 – about a year after rehab – I lost the compulsion to drink. What that means for the uninitiated is that the thought of having a drink that drives you to want a drink was gone. It is like when you feel hungry you want something to eat and so that is pretty much all you can think about until you eat something.

The compulsion to drink nags at you constantly. It took a while before I recognized that the compulsion was gone.

I was fortunate to lose the compulsion to drink after only a year; I will always be grateful. For some addicts and alcoholics, it takes many years. Some apparently never lose it. With more than 25 years sober and with contemplative hindsight, I hold these insights with great conviction: The first year of sobriety was the toughest time of my life. Overcoming the compulsion to drink makes "one day at a time" the most important mantra of 12-Steps. These insights are essential to surviving and overcoming the compulsion to drink or to drug.

Chapter 19

THE COSLET YEARS

Back to Football

In the second year of the Coslet era the Jets began to shed the oppressive mood of the micro-managed Joe Walton years. The team took on a more optimistic and – dare I say – joyous attitude. Football was fun again. Coslet's philosophy was that you need to be serious when doing your job – in this case practicing or playing football – and lighten up when not on the job. And, "off" meant off. Coslet understood the necessity of stress management, although he never referred to it in those terms.

By the second season the players had learned that relaxing and having fun did not mean they did not care about the team's winning or losing. They were taking on Coslet's personality. It was like a breath of fresh air had blown a big dark cloud away from the Jets complex.

There were, however, a couple of Coslet policies that took some getting used to. First, he wanted players as close to 100% healthy as possible. This meant that if a player with a minor injury could improve with a week off, then he should sit out a week so that he would be closer to 100% the next week. He believed this 100% policy cut down re-injury and/or injuring some other body part. This was a logical concept. The problem was that it was contrary to the common practice in the NFL: If a player could line up, he played. Everyone knew the injury would take longer to heal, but injured players played anyway.

Another Coslet policy was that players who did not practice did not play. It was consistent with his 100% policy. The way he explained it to me was that the NFL had become so specialized and the talent was so competitive that every player needed to be as healthy as he could be to compete. If resting a week meant a player would be better the next week, they rested a week, regardless of who they were. And, those who could not practice did not play, period. Coslet believed that not only did players need to practice to perform their best but they also needed to rest when injured. Many other coaches had this no practice, no play rule to motivate players to practice, even if they were injured, or risk not playing. Coslet's policy, however, was not punishment meant to get players to practice just so they could play.

Players begged me to plead their case for playing with minor injuries. I would argue to Coslet: "You mean a back-up player at 100% is as good as the starter at 90%?" His counter would be: "No, but if the starter plays how many weeks will he be at just 90%? With a week off, he'll be closer to 100%. But, if he continues to play hurt how long will it be before he's playing at 80%?" This was a major paradigm shift for the players, the ATs, and even the doctors.

In 1990, Coslet's first season, the Jets finished with a 6-10 record, which was an improvement of Walton's 4-12 record the year before. In 1991, we went 8-8 and landed a Wild-Card spot in the Playoffs against Houston. We lost that game 17-10.

On a side note: Without really consulting Jim Nicholas (Nick the Knife), Dick Steinberg named him Team Physician Emeritus – which gave him no say in anything. Elliott Hershman, the orthopedic surgeon and my confidant and trusted friend, turned down the offer to become Team Physician. Elliot Pellman, the Internist and one of Jim Nicholas' harshest critics, readily accepted the position. Unfortunately, after several years, his ego grew to dwarf Nick the Knife's.

1992 – A Big Year for Change – On & Off the Field

Spring and summer 1992 was relatively uneventful. I was getting more comfortable in my sobriety and was attending a couple of AA meetings a week. SG was working towards a Bachelor of Fine Art at the State University of New York (SUNY) at Old Westbury. She was doing well in school and her drinking was less frequent. She abstained most of the time with occasional binges while working late at night in the studio that I had built for her in the basement of the new house.

Rachel continued to monitor her food, but her attendance at 12-Step meetings had dropped because of the distance from Northport and the fact that she was not old enough to drive (in NY driving age is 17). Only much later did I learn that SG had been suggesting to her that she did not need to attend those "bullshit" meetings because she knew how to monitor her food. She had dropped about 30 pounds, looked great, and was really proud of herself.

After months in rehab Rachel felt out of place at Northport High School. Because she appeared to be serious about going to college, we enrolled her in the Academy of the Holy Family, a private girls' boarding school in Baltic, Connecticut, in the fall of 1992. Rachel, SG, and I believed that the structured program at the boarding school could help her improve her grades and enhance her chances to attend a higher ranking college than her current academic record allowed.

Rob had been living at home since graduating college. I had finished the basement, building an extra bedroom, bathroom, and a large studio work area for SG to do her art. So, he essentially had his own apartment in the basement. From my perspective he had matured well while in college. I liked my son and was beginning to relate to him as an adult – again emulating my father's relationship with me. Shortly after he returned home he was accepted into an internship at Improv Olympics in Chicago which did not start until the next fall. He decided that if he did not land a comedy writing job in New York before then, he would take it.

SG Intervention

Near the end of the Jets training camp in 1992, Rob was preparing move to Chicago and Rachel was preparing to go to boarding school in Connecticut. Both expressed concern to me about SG's increased drinking that they observed while I was in training camp. We planned an intervention. The three of us discussed what each of us would say and how we would express our concern about her drinking and the impact it was having on each of us.

We gathered on the deck of our home. After each of us told her how we felt, she just said that was our problem. She had the right to drink and we did not have the right to tell her what to do. She pointed out that nothing she was doing was illegal and that she had not been arrested, or totaled her car or anything like that. Then she just turned around and went back into her studio.

We were dumbfounded even though SG's response was consistent with her long-time attitude about her rights and her insistence that she did not have a problem. I observed Rob looking at Rachel; either they read each other's mind or had discussed her possible response before the intervention because they grinned knowingly. Rob turned to me and said that he was sorry mom did not listen, but it was my problem because in a couple of weeks they would both be gone.

In hindsight, it was a poor attempt at an intervention with a hard core alcoholic in denial of her addiction. The problem was we did not have a professional with us and all the threats were "soft." For example, "If you keep this up, I *might* leave you." This type of statement is ineffective because it has no real teeth.

I thanked Rachel and Rob for their efforts and honesty with their mother and for their dubious best wishes about my handling SG's drinking problem in the future. I was already bracing for the future. It was about that time that I decided not to do anything drastic (like divorce) until I had five years' sobriety. I had heard a number of times in the rooms of AA that it took five years to get your brain back if you had been drinking for any length of time. With that in mind I determined that unless things got a lot worse I would give it another four years before I made any decisions regarding my marriage.

Home Games With SG

Prior to Coslet wives were not allowed at the team hotel the night before the home games. Coslet had no such rules. Instead, he encouraged having family around. Heck, he even had his daughter keeping his headset cord straight on the sidelines. How cool is that?

With Rob and Rachel out of the house, SG began to stay at the hotel with me the night before home games. After the Saturday morning practice, I would pick her up and we would go into Manhattan and just kick around. We would then have dinner at a little Italian restaurant near the hotel in New Jersey. It was very pleasant.

The problem was after the games. A group of tail-gating super-fans who had been mainstays at Shea Stadium in Queens moved over to the Meadowlands Stadium in New Jersey when the Jets moved there in 1984. Somehow they always bribed their way into the players/staff parking lot. One of them brought a Winnebago and they would set up shop with plenty of beer, booze, and food for players who stopped by after the games. Over the years, as players came and went, I became the constant. I told new players about the group and encouraged the stars to stop by after the game. In return SG had a place to hang out after the games until I finished working – usually an hour and a half after the game was over. One thing I could be sure of was that by the time I showed up she was drunk. The best I could hope for was that she would sleep for the two-plus hour drive back to Long Island. If she did not, it made a very long day much, much longer. SG continued this pattern after home games throughout my tenure at the Jets.

Al Toon

Coslet's third season, 1992, was a tough year on the field. We went 4-12. Of greater significance two dramatic injuries occurred that year on the field that had far reaching impact. The first happened in Denver in Week 10 of the season. Al Toon, our great wide receiver, caught a ball close to the ground and cradled it into his belly as he slid on the grass in a modified fetal position. The Broncos defender could have really punished him but he went to his knees and sort of slid into Al, his knee hitting Al's helmet.

Now, this was nowhere near a vicious blow. In fact, the video shows it as almost inconsequential, except for the fact that Al did not get up. Pepper and I went onto the field. It was obvious that Al was concussed. He was conscious but he could barely sit up. He was extremely dizzy, complained of photophobia (sensitivity to light), and felt as if his head was going to split open. He was transported from the field directly to the locker room. Later Pepper called on the walkie-talkie informing me that there was no way Al would be returning to the game. The doctors, however, did not think it was serious and thought he might even be ready the next week. That was prognosis was off as Al never played another down of football.

Al suffered severe post-concussion syndrome for about three years. Even after it subsided he suffered what he called "spells" where he had to close himself in a dark room for two or three days until the headaches and photophobia subsided. Al's injury in 1992 was one of the catalysts for concussions finally becoming a primary concern of the NFL.

As memory serves me, Al had suffered about seven reportable concussions: that is a concussion that caused him to miss more than three days of practice or one game. He also had non-reported concussions and continued to play like most NFL players of the time. He counted a total of 11 concussions. Interestingly in the late '80s – separated by several years – he twice received brutal hits that laid him out, unconscious, on the field. For at least those two he was taken off the field on a stretcher. Remarkably, after a few days he recovered from those rapidly and played within a week or two. That's why this seemingly light hit he received in Denver was so perplexing.

At that time the treatment for concussions was to let the player rest at home. Usually within a week or two, they were chomping at the bit to get back in action, even if they had a lingering headache. By the third week Al had not improved at all. His wife, Jane, came to see me and told me bluntly that we had to do something because "Al was no longer Al."

I asked her what she meant. She told me that he was mean and yelled at her and their son all the time and that he was just miserable. Plus, he had a constant migraine type headache. I knew that the behavior was not normal for Al even with migraines.

The Al Toon I knew was a consummate gentleman. He was a class act. He was bright, clever, and just an all-around nice guy. He was so smart that he was our disaster quarterback, not because he could throw the football, but because he knew what every player on every play on offense did. Also, he could read defenses as well as the quarterbacks. He was like having an extra coach on the field. Now he was uncharacteristically acting like a jerk and suffering chronic headaches. I agreed with Jane, something had to be done.

I began to push the internist, Elliot Pellman to "do something." He said the only treatment was rest and I insisted that was not good enough. If for no other reason than PR we needed at a minimum to appear to be doing something. This finally got his attention. So, we scheduled Al for an MRI, some other brain scans, and a neuropsychology evaluation. The neuropsychology eval only told us what we already knew: Al was suffering from post-concussion syndrome. Bottom line, we just had to wait it out.

Al officially retired later that season. Hoping that he might get better and want to play again, I encouraged him to wait a year. He told me that even if he healed he could never risk going through this much pain and misery again. Al Toon's experience stayed on my mind. Over the next several years I became very proactive in how both the Jets and the NFL handled concussions. The NFL asked me to help coordinate a new committee on concussions. I was named secretary: I recommended Elliot Pellman as Chair. [*For this last recommendation, I sincerely apologize to my fellow NFL ATs and players. You know why.*]

Dennis Byrd

(some of the following is directly from *Develop the Winner's Mentality*[8])

The second major event of the 1992 season involved Dennis Byrd. Dennis was a second-round draft pick as a defensive lineman. His career was cut short by a catastrophic neck injury suffered in a collision with teammate Scott Mersereau while playing against the Kansas City Chiefs on November 29. Byrd and Mersereau, both defensive ends, were rushing the passer, Chiefs QB David Krieg, and were about to make a QB sandwich of him. Krieg, however, stepped up out of harm's way. Byrd, who had already launched himself to sack Krieg, crashed into Mesereau's chest, snapping his head down.

When my staff and I came to Dennis on the field, he told us he was paralyzed. I immediately stabilized his head and neck while he was examined by the doctors. Our training allowed us to safely "board" him and transport him off the field without making the injury any worse. He was rushed to the hospital where he was diagnosed quadriplegic. He had fractures in his cervical spine at C-5, C-6, and C-7 and a subluxation (partial dislocation) of the vertebrae. Several days later surgery was performed to stabilize his spine.

After the surgery, the prognosis was grim. The doctors predicted that, at best, *maybe* Dennis would be able to get around on crutches or a walker in two or three years and that *maybe* he could learn to feed and care for himself enough not to need 24-hour care. This was the "best case" scenario.

Dennis, however, never bought into this gloomy forecast. He believed that there was a purpose to his injury. He was certain that his recovery would serve as testament for himself and others of the power of his Christian faith.

Dennis defined his dream. He created his vision and set his goal: he would *walk* out of the hospital. He did not give up hope and did not succumb to the negative prospects that others believed about his future. He also did not suffer from the depression that the physicians and the caregivers predicted that he would have as soon as "he *realizes* he'll never walk again." The rest of the story is history. Several months after his surgery Dennis Byrd walked out of the hospital! His story is memorialized in *Rise and Walk: The Trial and Triumph of Dennis Byrd*[9], and in a TV movie of the same name.

A lot went into Dennis Byrd walking out of the hospital. Medically there was the proper initial care and transport from the field, followed by a massive dose of corticosteroids early on to reduce the swelling of the spinal cord, and then superb surgery by gifted surgeons. This initial care was followed by experimental medications and excellent aftercare and rehabilitation, and local and national prayer groups. Unknown to Dennis, one of the coaches also coordinated an international group of energy healers to simultaneously send healing energy to Dennis.

That all these actions combined to support Dennis Byrd's determination to "rise and walk" cannot be denied. From my perspective the key to this miracle was his positive attitude, his positive vision, his ability to block out the negativity, and his giving *purpose* to his life though this accident. Without Dennis' proactive belief, he may have been crippled for life, notwithstanding all the other actions.

Dennis serves as one of my greatest inspirations. He also provided a model of goal setting for me years later when I wrote my first book, *Develop the Winner's Mentality*. In my mind Dennis is the ultimate goal setter. If goal setting can be so powerful that it enables a paralyzed man to walk again, think about how it can positively impact your life. What I have learned is that effective goal setting combined with a sense of purpose and vision will allow you to *cause* your own future and to create your own miracle!

Dennis Byrd died in a car accident in Oklahoma on October 15, 2016. He was only 50 years old. I keep a picture displayed in my office of Dennis and me laughing together on his first visit to Jets Training Camp after his broken neck. It serves as a reminder of the power of goalsetting – and now it is also a reminder of how transitory life can be.

1993 – More Changes: Pepper Leaves

Like all losing seasons, 1992 was a very stressful season. Fortunately, I neither had any compulsion to drink nor to use alcohol to cope with stress (alcohol had been my main method for coping with stress). I maintained a pretty good routine attending two or three AA meetings a week and avoiding some old triggers.

The first big change for me in 1993 was Pepper, my assistant since 1977, left to become the head AT for Green Bay. Before Ron Wolf took over as GM for Green Bay in 1992, Ron spent a year as a scout with the Jets. He called me and asked my permission to talk to Pepper about the head AT job in Green Bay. I told him that he would have to talk to Steinberg and Coslet. Because I knew that he knew that, I asked why he was calling me. He said that he did not want to go over my head; and if I said "No," then he would not ask Steinberg. Instead, he would start looking elsewhere. (*Does this sound reminiscent of how I was "recruited" from Buffalo to New York? Even though the NFL was more corporate these days, some things didn't change.*)

I told him of course he had my permission. Things moved rapidly from there. Within several weeks it was a done deal and Pepper was the new Head AT for Green Bay. I summarily promoted Joe P to first assistant; and with no hesitation we both agreed that Darryl Conway would be number two if he wanted the job, and we had no doubt that he would want it.

Pepper had "discovered" Darryl several years before. He had worked for us for three summers. He was bright, hard-working, and easy going. We all loved him. In fact, that was the only restraint I put on Pepper: I told him I would give him permission to talk to Green Bay as long as he agreed not to try and hire Darryl away from me. He laughed and said that it was a good thing I told him because Darryl would have been his first choice for an assistant. That's pretty much the way it works in the NFL. Decisions like that are often made with the assumption the person will take the job. There is rarely any advertising for jobs – it is word of mouth and who knows who. All I knew was that Darryl was a keeper!

Hypnosis

Early in 1993, I saw a sign for a stress reduction workshop in a New Age Nutrition store in Huntington. I reasoned that it could not hurt since I no longer had my old coping mechanism, booze. Besides, the workshop was free.

During a guided visualization I became profoundly relaxed. I had a couple of full body tremors that occur when the body releases pent up stress. It was a wonderful experience.

After the moderator finished the guided visualization he explained that, essentially, we had been hypnotized. I thought, *No way!* I was conscious of everything he said; I even heard conversations in the hall. I also thought hypnosis was some type of mind control exerted by a third party. These ideas stemmed from movies but my experience was debunking them. The moderator explained hypnosis so well that I hung around after everyone left to ask him some questions.

Without letting on I worked at the Jets, I questioned him about hypnosis, first from my personal interest, stress reduction, and then what I really wanted to know: could hypnosis be used for pain relief?

He said yes and if I wanted to learn more I could take his course and become a certified hypnotherapist.

The next week I told Steve Gutman – now president of the Jets – what I had learned and experienced. I asked for tuition for the hypnosis course. It was a short course of about 20 hours: four hours on Friday evening and then eight hours each on Saturday and Sunday. Gutman approved.

I took the course and learned several things. First, hypnosis is not some mysterious state where someone can control another's thoughts and minds. Hypnosis is naturally focused state of attention. In other words, it is a common brain-wave state that we go in and out of every day. An example of hypnosis is correctly driving to work and appropriately responding to external events but not remembering the drive.

I also learned that only 20 hours of education did not make me a competent hypnotist, even though I had a certificate saying that I was. I was, however, enthused. I immediately made a relaxation tape for myself and began working with a couple of Jets staffers who wanted to quit smoking. During mini-camps I got my first taste of the fear of hypnotism due to misconceptions held by some of the veteran ball players whom I told about my new found skill. After that, I took a more low-key approach.

That spring I convinced Gutman that the hypnosis was something useful and received tuition for a week-long Eriksonian Hypnosis course at the Omega Institute near Woodstock, New York. At the time, I had no idea what Eriksonian hypnosis was and how it might differ from other hypnosis programs. I just knew I needed more education and training.

The course proved fruitful. I learned that Milton Erikson was a psychiatrist who utilized hypnosis to shorten therapy time for his patients. He developed the use of what he called therapeutic metaphor, creating long narratives and painting wonderful vivid pictures for his patients. His work provided a foundation for neurolinguistic programming (NLP).

Eriksonian Hypnosis was a more indirect approach than I had learned. I came to understand that while suggestions to the subconscious need to be specific, the route to get there can be circuitous. For me that meant I did not have to read or memorize hypnosis scripts as long as I knew what I wanted to say and could guide my client into trance state. After taking this course, I was much more confident working with people in hypnosis.

I also was beginning to learn some of the limitations of hypnosis which fueled my curiosity to learn more. I began seeing the connections to some of the areas I had read about in the sport psychology books that Ken Ravizza had recommended. Hypnosis would prove to be a valuable tool for me both personally and professionally.

Over the next several years at the Jets I used hypnosis to help many players manage pain, heal quicker, and enhance their performance. (*Pain management techniques were always employed in concert with and the full permission and knowledge of the team physicians.*) When Jim Sweeny, the Jets Center, suffered a herniated disc in his neck and it looked like his football career was over, hypnotic pain management allowed him another 10 years in the League. It helped the great Ronnie Lott heal a pinched nerve in his neck weeks earlier than the doctors predicted. It helped Cornerback Aaron Glenn overcome a slump and regain his confidence in his second year. And, most famously, using hypnosis, Rob Moore healed a fractured scaphoid bone in his wrist in half the expected time. Rob Moore's case study was published in *Athletic Therapy Today*.[10]

Hypnosis has been an integral part of my sobriety. More specifically, the self-hypnosis skills that I learned have been an essential part of my ability to thrive in the world. All hypnosis is really self-hypnosis and everyone can learn these skills. (*The role of hypnosis will be discussed further in Part 3.*)

1993 – Free Agency For Real

After surviving the 4-12 season, conventional wisdom said that the Jets needed at least a winning season in '93 for Coslet to keep his job. We had lost an All-Pro in Al Toon and a dependable defensive lineman in Dennis Byrd. We also needed a quarterback. Fortunately for Coslet, a new NFL Collective Bargaining Agreement had been signed and this was the first year of true free agency since 1976.

Mr. Hess let it be known through Dick Steinberg that we were going to be competitive and go after some top free agents. The great Reggie White, All-Pro defensive end for the Eagles topped the list of free agents. The Jets went after him in a big way and thought we had him. After a month or so, every other team had dropped out of the running; and it came down to Reggie choosing the Jets or Green Bay. The offers were about the same, and we thought we had offered a lot more perqs than the Packers. Ron Wolf in Green Bay, however, seemed to know where our limit was and added another million to the package. We blinked, and Reggie White became a Green Bay Packer. Over the next six years he helped lead the Packers to two Super Bowls, winning one of them. In hindsight that extra million dollars looked pretty paltry.

Licking our wounds over losing Reggie White to Green Bay, we then overpaid Leonard Marshall, a defensive lineman from the Giants who was at the tail-end of his career. On the bright side, we signed future Hall of Famer Ronnie Lott, DL Bill Pickel, DB Lonnie Young, and RB Johnny Johnson; all who played well for us. We also traded for Boomer Esiason, the Super Bowl quarterback for the Cincinnati Bengals, and Coslet's protégé.

We got off to a slow start (2-6) but seemed to find our legs with a five game winning streak. Then it got bumpy again. The Jets finished 8-8 and were out of the playoffs. Coslet was fired.

Chapter 20

THE PETE CARROLL YEAR (1994)

Bob's Great Adventure

One reason Coslet was fired was because Steinberg wanted him to hire an offensive coordinator. Steinberg felt Coslet's role as offensive coordinator in addition to being head coach took too much of his attention and, consequently, he was not on top of the defense and special teams. Coslet's refusal to give up being offensive coordinator cost him his job.

While I hated to see Coslet go, I was happy with the new head coach: Pete Carroll, the defensive coordinator. Pete is one of my favorite people on planet earth. In addition to being football smart, he has real world intelligence. He is the consummate optimist without being a Pollyanna, has a great sense of humor, and is a cut-up. Above all that, I consider Pete a friend.

Shortly after the Combine Physicals were over in February 1994, Pete called me to his office to talk about performance enhancement. This was an extension of discussions we had for several years about why some people maximized their talents and others just coast. Pete asked me "to see what's out there" in the world of performance enhancement. He had heard that West Point was doing some interesting things and wanted me to check it out. He had names of some other possible "experts" in the field, but gave me the freedom to network and come up with suggestions for any techniques or interventions that could enhance individual or team performance.

I asked why he had not just called on Ken Ravizza, the sport psychologist that kindled my interest in performance enhancement. He replied that he had talked to Ken, but he wanted to explore beyond the conventional. He told me to take a week or so to do some research and then "hit the road." He gave me permissions to check out anyone even if they sounded weird. He did not want to waste any money or time bringing people into NY if I did not think they were worthwhile. I was supposed to narrow it down to two or three that could have the most immediate impact on the team. I was about to begin an adventure that was not only the most fun I ever had doing my job, but also the most informative and growth producing both personally and professionally. I met people who would inform, influence, and positively impact me for the rest of my life. Below are three of the most important that I met on this quest.

West Point CEP

My first trip was to West Point. I met with Nate Zinsser, PhD, the civilian director of the Center for Enhanced Performance (CEP) and Brad Scott, the Army Major in charge of the CEP. Nate invited me to spend a day with him; and I began my odyssey into the world of performance enhancement and mental skills training that took some of the information in the books that Ken Ravizza had recommended out of theory and into application.

When I arrived at West Point, Nate gave me a tour and a brief history of the CEP. It began with Colonel Louis Csoka in 1989. He instituted some mental skills training and worked mainly with the football team. This approach paid off immediately as the always undersized Army football team posted a 9-3 record and went to the Sun Bowl where they lost to Alabama by only a point. The next several years they posted winning records. This convinced the Army brass that, if mental skills training could help the football team, it could probably enhance performance in other areas, as Csoka had promoted that it could.

Before long the CEP had an entire floor in one of the buildings on a campus that seemed to be bursting at the seams with no room for growth. Under the umbrella of the CEP the sport psychology mental skills trainers and the academic skills group joined forces. They began using the same techniques to train a student for a Chemistry exam as they did an athlete to run a race in track. The mental skills training had application for all aspects of cadet life.

Being Army, they were efficient in their application. This was crucial as West Point Cadets are extremely time challenged. Coming to the CEP was totally voluntary and had to be squeezed into their already hectic schedule. The CEP administered services in under 30 minutes.

Initially the cadets filled out an intake and had a brief session with Nate or one of the military mental skills trainers. In their next visit they sat in a big egg-shaped Alpha Chair where music they had chosen was pumped in. They were also hooked up to biofeedback that measured skin temperature and pulse-rate so they could learn to control their stress response. A mental skills trainer provided a guided visualization of successful completion of the sports event, training exercise, or academic exam. This was recorded and the cadet left with an audio tape to use to reinforce whatever performance area they were working on.

I readily saw how I had been on target, if slightly naive, with what I was doing with Jets players with hypnosis for performance enhancement. Additionally, I developed a professional relationship with Nate Zinsser. This relationship would become very important as I pursued my Master's' degree and as I transitioned from the NFL and began to apply mental skills training to my life.

Diana McNab – The "Ski Lady"

A colleague who heard about my quest suggested I contact Diana McNab, MEd in Sport Psychology. She worked part-time with the Seton Hall basketball team mainly doing mental skills training. She also worked privately with a variety of high school and amateur athletes and with a few New Jersey Devils' players. Diana had been a downhill skier for the Canadian Olympic Team for eight years. She had high energy and diverse experience. At that time, she was married to Peter

McNab, a star NHL player, so she was neither intimidated nor in awe about working with professional athletes.

Lou Tice and The Pacific Institute

One of our scouts, Marv Sunderland, heard about the performance enhancement quest and told Pete about Lou Tice of the Pacific Institute in Seattle. Lou did corporate performance education. Pete told me to check him out.

I went out to The Pacific Institute office in Seattle and met with Lou for an hour. He was charming and intelligent. Additionally, I noticed he was interviewing me as much as I was interviewing him. I liked that he was not going to just agree to do something with the Jets just because it was the NFL. After the meeting he invited me to attend a half day seminar he was giving in Detroit the next week. I agreed. I called Pete and told him I thought Lou Tice had something to offer and I was going to his seminar the next week in Detroit.

I met Lou in Detroit and attended his four-hour seminar: *Investment in Excellence*, the foundation of his corporate program. I was like a sponge. He used many of the cognitive-behavioral concepts of sport psychology and packaged them into in systematic self-improvement program. After the seminar I told Lou how excited I was about his program. He told me that was a good thing because Pete had called him after our meeting in Seattle and their discussion resulted in Pete deciding to send several Jets coaches to Lou's next upcoming seminar in Pittsburgh and I was to go with Lou and act as intermediary. When I confirmed this arrangement with Pete, he shared his agreement with my assessment: Lou Tice had something that our coaches and players needed.

On our way to the airport Lou asked me how much one or two wins a year would mean to a head coach. I said, depending on the season, it could mean everything. If Coslet had two more wins the year before, he would still be the head coach. Lou looked very thoughtful and said he thought if the Jets incorporated his program we could add two wins a year to Pete's record. I warned him that there were a lot of uncontrollable variables involved in an NFL season that affected games. No one had control over injuries, illnesses, bad bounces, bad calls by the officials, bad weather, etc. I told him I liked him a lot and I thought that he had a lot of good things to bring to the table, but if he were smart he would not say that out loud. He grinned and winked at me and said conspiratorially, "Okay, we'll just keep between us, but I still believe I can deliver two wins!" I smiled, shook my head, and thought *if it were only that easy*.

The dinner that night with the coaches went well. Most of them were not sure why they were there – Pete had left it up to me to explain it to them. With Lou's help, I think we got across to them the nature of the program and their purpose to evaluate the program for how it could help the improve the Jets.

The next day we all attended the program – I got even more out of it the second time. All coaches, except one, liked the information, but they were unsure about how it could be used with the players. I told them that if they were positive about the program they did not have to worry about the delivery. I had confidence Lou had a method for delivery.

About a month later Lou came to New York. At the Jets complex he gave a two-hour mini-seminar to coaches who had not been at the Detroit meeting and to most of the administrative staff. I was shocked at their negativity both before and after. The people on the administrative staff were not even willing to consider change, much less change their attitudes or way of approaching their jobs. Their resistant to Pete's efforts to improve the team combined with their knowledge of the team's history stirred up anger in me. It was now 1994 and the closest the Jets had been to the Super Bowl since Namath was the "Mud Bowl" in Miami in 1982. We were not a laughingstock in the NFL, but we were middle tier, at best. I often think of this event whenever someone says, "Change is hard."

On a positive note, Pete and Lou bonded. Their relationship lasted until Lou's death in April 2012. In Lou, I found both a friend and mentor who helped me through some of the toughest times I had yet to encounter. (These times are discussed chronologically in later sections of this book.)

The Performance Enhancement Adventure Results

For every one of the positive encounters I had on my great adventure, there was at least five others that were hapless, guru wannabes, or just plain charlatans. I met with and interviewed fire-walkers and over-broken glass walkers. There were people with machines that knew their product would work, if only we gave them a chance to experiment on our million dollar athletes. And there were the teambuilding and leadership camps that were lawsuits waiting to happen if anyone got hurt.

Pete and I determined that as a group the Jets were not ready for Lou Tice's work. West Point served as a great model, but there was no way we could actually model it because we did not have the personnel. We decided the first step would be to bring in Diana McNab as a consultant. Her background and experience made her credible in everyone's eyes and she had demonstrated her competence working with Seton Hall basketball players (Pete had spoken to their coach, P. J. Carlesimo). Pete and I also appreciated that she was energetic and positive.

That season Diana came over one or two afternoons a week to work with players individually. Not only was she professional, but she also generously shared her techniques with me. While I did not know it at the time, she provided a model for making a living as a sport psychology consultant.

Pursuing A Master's Degree

My adventure into the world of performance enhancement was not the only thing that kept me busy that non-season. Coslet's firing reminded me of how tenuous working in the NFL had become. When I started working at Buffalo in 1972, Abe had told me that while an AT did not make as much money as a coach we had job security: ATs never got fired.

This changed in 1992 when three long-time ATs were summarily fired. In each case their club owner had died and the son who took over fired the AT. Only one of the three clubs gave the AT the option of moving into a managerial position. The other two were out with only a month's severance. Leon Hess, owner of the Jets, was 79 at the time. I was on friendly terms with his son John, but the enduring rumors were that Mr. Hess would not pass the team on to John; instead it would be sold. So, with these circumstances and my memorable insecurity at the time of Dick Steinberg's hiring, I asked myself: *What will I do if I get fired from the Jets?* Since I had been in the NFL, there had been only one case of an AT getting back in the League after leaving or getting fired; so the probability of getting a job with another team was slim to none. I needed a back-up plan.

Next I had to ask myself: *What am I qualified to do?* Colleges and universities now had so many ATs on staff that they almost always hired from within if someone left. Also, more and more head ATs in colleges had master's degrees, which were necessary to teach at that level. The only job outside of a sports team that I was qualified for was working in a sports medicine clinic; and unless I owned the clinic, I would have to work under a physical therapist. Not only would the money be nominal but I would also be doing my least favorite part of being an AT: giving physical therapy treatments. It quite literally made me shudder to think about it.

Then, I contemplated: *What would I like to do?* I had been enjoying the reading and learning about sport psychology. I had also expanded my hypnosis work with the players to include performance enhancement and had enjoyed success. During my recent expedition in search of performance enhancement for Pete, I was really impressed with Nate Zinsser and Brad Scott and their work at West Point. Meeting Diana McNab let me know that there was a living that could be made with a Master's in Sport Psychology. I saw a need for sport psychology and mental skills training in the NFL. I began my search for a program that would work for me.

Regis University

In 1994, I found no accredited distance programs in sport psychology. I enrolled in the accredited Master of Arts in Liberal Studies: Psychology at Regis University in Denver. Since this program allowed students to design their upper level courses, I could focus my upper level courses on sport psychology. Also, the residential requirements (mandatory time on campus) best fit my schedule at the Jets. In the fall of 1994, at the age of 45, I became a college student once again.

Another advantage of attending Regis was that I could chose the professor to be my course consultant for each course. For my first course I settled on Paul Haber, PhD; there was something in his bio that resonated for me. Although we got off to a rocky start because I had no clue what was expected of me, Paul ended up being my faculty advisor and course consultant for all my coursework. I had found someone who understood me, had a great sense of humor, held me to high standards, and challenged me to think way beyond sport and performance psychology. We remained close until his passing in 2003.

After I graduated, Paul shared with me that he was once called before the Psychology Department Chair to explain why he was the only course consultant working with me. The implication was that favoritism was, or could become, an issue. Paul immediately went to his office and grabbed a couple of my papers and brought them back to the Chair for him to examine. Paul told him that if he did not think this was 'A' work then he would not act as my Course Consultant for any further courses. This apparently quieted the Chair's objections, so Paul continued as my Course Consultant. The Chair must have been somewhat impressed because he invited me to join the faculty as a Course Consultant (adjunct instructor) shortly after I graduated. I agreed, went to Denver, and took an intensive on how to facilitate as a course consultant. That was the beginning of my involvement with online teaching.

Ouch! My Back – Again!

As mentioned earlier, in 1988 I suffered my first serious back injury at the Jets which resulted in surgery. In the 1994 pre-season, the Jets had a scrimmage with the Eagles at our Hofstra training site. It was during this scrimmage that my back was injured for the second time. I was standing between two drills conversing with Otho Davis, AT of the Eagles, as we watched for potential injuries. On one side was 1-on-1 pass blocking drills between the offensive and defensive linemen.

About five yards away 7-on-7 (passing game) drills were being run. At some point Perry Williams, the former Giants cornerback who was at the end of his career, got beat on a sideline pattern and headed directly toward Otho and me. While we saw him coming, neither of us moved because he had plenty of room to avoid us. But, he just kept coming. By the time I realized that he was not going to stop or make one easy step to the right to avoid us, it was too late. He hit me full force and I went into the air and landed on the small of my back. I felt this sickly squishy feeling in my low back and knew that was not a good sign. After I regained my breath, Otho checked me over and then helped me up. While I was unsettled and felt tightness in my back, I thought I would be okay. I finished covering practice.

Later that night at the personnel meeting when I gave my injury report, I told Pete that he needed to cut Perry Williams. Several of the coaches laughed and told me not to take his running me over personally. I responded that I was not taking it personally but that any DB who could not change directions in 15 feet was not agile enough to play in the NFL. At the first cut-down date Perry was released; it was rumored among the players that I had him cut. I did nothing to change anyone's opinion. The erroneous perception that I could have someone cut, however, gave me a certain status of power, especially to the new players.

The next day I knew something serious had happened to my back. I could barely move and I had mild sciatic pain reminiscent of the pain that led to my back surgery in 1988. That coupled with the "squishy" feeling I felt in my back had me terrified that I was in line for surgery again. An MRI confirmed I now had three herniated discs. The good news was that none of the herniations seemed to be pressing directly on the nerve root as had been the case previously. While I had severe back pain, I was not experiencing the horrific sciatica that resulted in my foot drop and ultimate surgery with the first injury.

I was not as incapacitated this time around. I eventually had two epidural cortisone injections. Those coupled with chiropractic care and acupuncture allowed me to work through the pain and disability. By the start of the season I was able to manage, but I was – and am still – very careful about lifting and twisting.[11] For traveling to away games I purchased a carry-on suitcase with wheels. Back then, all the players mocked me for being a wus. Little did I realize I was being a trendsetter as almost everyone uses them now.

1994 – The Season

The Jets began the 1994 season with high hopes – which is usually the attitude of every team in the NFL. Pete hired a new offensive coordinator, Ray Sherman. Sherman had risen rapidly through the ranks as a coach and was the receivers coach for the 49ers when Pete hired him. Pete also elevated defensive line coach, Greg Robinson, to defensive coordinator. As head coach, Pete gave them the autonomy that he enjoyed as a coordinator – this would prove to be a grave error as neither were ready for prime time.

One of the challenges of a new head coach is that you don't know what you don't know. Every top assistant dreams of being a head coach – and I am sure they play through scenarios of how they would handle situations. The problem is they do not understand all the administrative responsibilities that go along with the position of head coach. In the NFL I had only worked with one head coach who had prior head coaching experience – Lou Saban. I saw Walt Michaels, Joe Walton, and Bruce Coslet go through this very steep learning curve when they became head coach. Pete endured the same challenge. He was totally surprised at some of the decisions he had to make that did not directly apply to footballs' Xs and 0s[12] or personnel. On one hand he was the leader and public face of the team. On the other hand, with every decision he made, or wanted to make, he was told of potential ramifications that could ripple into tsunamis if things did not go as planned. Fortunately, he had a few people he could depend on to help him get through his rookie year as head coach.

The actual season started great with two wins in a row, then we dropped three in a row. Next we won a couple and then we see-sawed: win – loss – win – loss. By the end of November, we were 6-6. There is a lot to say for parity in the NFL, because even with that record we were heading into a showdown with Miami for a share of the AFC East lead. We absolutely outplayed the Dolphins for three quarters and were up 24-6. Then Dan Marino found his groove and led the Dolphins back to make the score 24-21. On the last drive of the game, Marino had the Dolphins at the Jets five-yard line. With 30 seconds left and out of time-outs, and with no huddle, Marino motioned that he was going to spike the ball to stop the clock. This would give Miami time to kick the field goal and send the game into overtime. But, instead of spiking the ball, Marino took the snap, and with most players on both teams just standing there waiting for the spike, he whipped it into the end-zone to Mark Ingram for the touchdown and the win. We never seemed to recover from "The Spike," as it soon became known in Jets lore. We lost the last four games finishing the season at 6-10. While the season finished badly, no one expected Pete to be fired.

Are You Sitting Down?

A week or two after the season ended, I headed to the Florida Keys for some R&R before the madness started again. About my third or fourth day in the Keys, I once again received a phone call from Jim Royer. I knew immediately that someone had been fired. I assumed – or hoped – that maybe it was the offensive coordinator, whom I thought was totally ineffective. Royer told me to sit down and then announced that Pete had been fired. I was speechless.

Royer asked me a second time if I was sitting, and I reported that I now was. He said, "Good, because they hired Rich Kotite" (Joe Walton's former offensive coordinator). He went on to inform me that it was Mr. Hess's decision.[13] I got a sick feeling in my stomach.

When I walked out onto the boat dock where we were staying, I must have looked awful because SG gasped and said, "Oh no! They didn't fire Pete, did they?" I replied, "Yeah, and it gets worse, they've hired Kotite." She grabbed her stomach and I thought she was going to puke (like I almost did).

SGs sick stomach lasted only moments before it transformed into anger. She had softened toward the Jets during Coslets' tenure, and she had positively enjoyed herself with Pete and his staff. Many of the coaches lived around Huntington. We often met some of them for dinner and enjoyed casually seeing them around town. Pete and his wife Glenna were socially inclusive. SG had lightened up considerably on my "never being home" because she felt a part of the team for the first time since the early days of Walt Michaels. She knew, like I knew, that Kotite would return to the gloom and doom of the Walton era – and she was pissed.

Because she could not take out her anger on Leon Hess, Steve Gutman, or Dick Steinberg, it was directed at me. She cursed that she could not believe she let herself get involved again, and swore at me that she was through with the Jets! While I had similar feelings, I knew on a deeper level that I was not about to walk away from a job that I loved and a salary of over $140,000.

Chapter 21

THE KOTITE DEBACLE

Kotite Takes Over

I did not dislike Rich Kotite as a person. I simply thought he had been incompetent as the Jets offensive coordinator and assistant head coach. From my perspective, he was, at best, a decent receivers coach. He was, however, an adept political climber. When Joe Walton was named head coach in 1983, he hired Kotite as a receivers coach. By 1985 he was named offensive coordinator and eventually assistant head coach.

One thing that Kotite and I shared was the knowledge that whoever spoke to Walton last at the end of a day would likely be the most influential. Walton would listen to what we had to say or recommend and then go home and sleep on it. The next day that recommendation would be presented as his idea. The last several years of Walton's tenure Kotite always hung around long enough for me to give my injury report and recommendations to Walton and then he would make sure to see Walton before he left for the night.

I later learned that that his political astuteness did not stop with Walton. For years he sat in the coaches' box as Joe Walton's offensive coordinator. Apparently Leon Hess, the owner, frequented the coaches' box to avoid the distractions that accompanied the entertaining required in the owner's suite. Kotite used this time to establish a personal relationship with Hess. Now in 1995, he used this relationship to become the Jet's head coach.

On hindsight, he also returned to the Jets with a historical grudge against me that led to my firing. The grudge stemmed from his perception that, when Walton's staff was fired after the 1989 season, I should have been fired with the coaches because I had so much input into decisions. His history shows he did not let a grudge or an opportunity to advance go unused.

After being fired from the Jets in 1989, Kotite went to the Eagles as offensive coordinator in 1990 and worked under head coach Buddy Ryan. He took over as head coach in 1991 after the controversial Ryan was fired. Otho Davis, the long-time head AT for the Eagles complained bitterly to me about Kotite's undermining Ryan to the owner and positioning himself for the head coaching job. Because Davis was one of the few ATs with a long-term contract, Kotite could not fire him, although he tried. Their relationship became so strained that the long-time assistant AT, David Price, began delivering the injury reports to Kotite – and their relationship prospered.

Kotite inherited a very talented roster from Ryan. In 1991, the Eagles had a good year going 10-6. The next year they went 11-5 in the regular season and then lost to Dallas in the NFC Division playoff. Things, however, began to unravel in 1993 as their defense was hit hard by free agency and they went 8-8. In 1994 the Eagles went 7-9 and Kotite was fired.

So why all this focus on Kotite and the Eagles one may ask? Because it all serves as a background for my last year with the Jets. During training camp of 1994, Kotite arranged for the Eagles to scrimmage the Jets at our Hofstra complex. It was like old home week for many players and a few coaches, including my old friend strength coach Jim Williams. I complained to Williams about my problems with our current strength coach and he complained about the dysfunction in Philly with the new owner. He said that unless the Eagles went to the Super Bowl the coaching staff would all be looking for a job.

Interestingly, during the day of the scrimmage, Kotite sought me out and pumped me about Pete Carroll. When I began to sing Pete's praises, he openly derided the basketball goal Pete had installed in the parking lot where he and his assistants would play for exercise and a mental break. I learned later he did this with any of the old Jet personnel he encountered. He was already positioning himself for Pete's job. So, now you can see why I became sick to my stomach when I heard Kotite had been hired.

1995 Season

Upon his arrival, Kotite wanted to make sure everyone knew he was in charge. One of the first moves he made was to force the retirement of my good friend and confidant, Jim Royer. Royer's role had been diminished considerably under Steinberg, but he maintained his title of Pro Personnel Director. Kotite delivered the coup de gráce, all the while making it seem like he was doing Royer a favor. It was the first of many classless personnel transactions that peppered Kotite's brief tenure. About the only good thing that happened when Kotite returned was that the Jets now had a strength coach that was not only good at his job, but one I could work with, Jim Williams.

Training camp progressed reasonably well, but I began to notice that few coaches asked me questions about players and their injuries – at least in nightly meetings. After my nightly injury report, I was excused from the meetings. I started to feel that I was being marginalized. This intuition became reality when, after we broke camp, I was told by Kotite not to attend the daily morning team meetings. When I later asked Kotite why, he told me that they were only for players and coaches and that he would tell me what I needed to know. I tried to explain to him that my being at those meetings helped me understand his message or theme for a given week and that I could reinforce it in the training room. He told me that was not necessary as the players would understand him perfectly well without my help.

Even with the injury report, Kotite seemed to not hear me regarding certain player's injury status and whether they would be able to play – or play well – the next week. I was rarely consulted on game day regarding who should be inactive. Jim Williams told me this was what he did at Philly. I now better understood Otho Davis' (Philly's AT) total disdain for the man.

Kotite seemed to respect the doctors. Elliot Pellman, the general medicine practitioner, had replaced Jim Nicholas (Nick the Knife) as team physician. He practically lived in Kotite's office and became what he had hated about Jim Nicholas: someone with no football experience having input into team decisions. Whereas I had formerly been the one informing the medical staff of what the coach and administration were thinking, this now became Pellman's role. And he reveled in it, doling out bits of information hoping we would beg for more. I called him on this several times, comparing him to Jim Nicholas on steroids. While I could tell he resented the comparison, I thought he needed to hear it. It did not, however, dampen his fervor as he knew what all arrogant manipulative people know: knowledge is power.

Fortunately, I still had Elliott Hershman, the orthopod, whom I could trust. When he came out on Wednesdays, after examining the injured players, I made sure he went with me to report to Kotite. That way I knew Kotite would listen to the options. I also had Hershman tell Pellman exactly what was going on, so that there would be no, or at least less, confusion on game day.

Game days were sometimes chaotic because players were never sure who was playing or even dressing. Several times I bumped heads with Pellman on game day because he would tell me "Richie [Kotite] wants so and so to play." I would remind him that we had all agreed that so and so should not play and that he would be close to worthless if he did play. On those occasions I reminded him that his job was not to please the head coach. His job was to provide the head coach with honest information so he could make a decision who should play; and sometimes it was necessary for the medical team to override the head coach's wishes about who should play. Regarding injuries, our responsibility was first to protect the player; then to the Jets so they would not be sued by an injured player; and lastly to the head coach.

The season itself was a disaster. We went 3-13 as Kotite bungled calls and made personnel decisions that made players whisper that he was trying to lose. By mid-season players were already suggesting that he was trying to make sure we got the first pick of the draft by finishing with the worst record in the NFL. After several weeks into the season I could not even pretend to be in mourning on Mondays as we had under Joe Walton and as was now expected under Kotite. I was indirectly accused several times of not wanting to win. Pellman imparted this information "directly from the head coach" as a warning.

Kotite was not openly hostile towards me, just cold and removed. But he was always that way. Occasionally during practice, he would sidle up next to me and start a conversation about something other than football like we were old friends. I never antagonized him or challenged him directly. On several occasions I did buck him – and Pellman – on whether or not someone should play, but I always did it with respect, reason, and logic (at least I thought so).

Kotite's lack of communication skills was only outweighed by his deficiency in organizational skills. He would change practice times and not tell the ATs or the equipment men. He would change venues for practice at the last minute. For example, if it were raining, he might decide we should practice in Hofstra's gym. The first time he did this with only 15 minute's notice. The equipment staff was supposed to fit everyone with sneakers but they did not have enough to go around (we had not practiced in the gym since Joe Walton left). Kotite also overlooked the fact that Hofstra had Phys Ed classes in the gym or that a Hofstra team was practicing there. Examples like this were commonplace and were reflected in the Jets losing record.

This was the worst season I had experienced since my last year in Buffalo when we went 2-12. The good thing was that I was sober now and could go to AA meetings. They kept me grounded and gave me perspective about my job in the NFL. Regardless how bad it was at the Jets, I recognized that in the big picture I had it pretty good. I managed to find gratitude in this dismal time. For example, as things became more and more demoralizing I could be thankful that I was sober; that I had a great paying job that I loved (most of the time); that I was working on my master's degree; and that I had come to recognize that life was about more than football.

We finished the season with four straight losses. I could not wait until the season was over. The players were absolutely playing not to get hurt – and I could not blame them. I did not know how Kotite could ever right this sinking ship.

It's Over

When the season finally ended, I decided that we should stick around town instead of taking our usual R&R break. I felt changes would be made. While I hoped it would be Kotite, I doubted that since Mr. Hess was the one that hired him. I presumed that the offensive or defensive coordinator – or both of them – might be offered up as the reasons why we were so terrible.

The week of the Super Bowl SGs grandmother passed away and we went to Nashville for the funeral. Upon arriving at my in-laws' house, I was told that Steve Gutman, president of the Jets, had called and I was to call him back immediately. SG practically shouted with joy, "I hope they fired Kotite!" I went into the bedroom and made the call.

With no preamble, Gutman told me that I worked at the pleasure of the head coach and that I was being let go. I was speechless. Whatever he said next was just noise. I finally digested what he said and asked him to repeat it – which he did. He told me to take my time with the family tragedy and we would discuss my severance upon my return to New York. When I became more cognitively aware, I asked him if Kotite was hiring David Price from the Eagles. He drew a deep breath and said yes. He went on to explain that he hated to intrude on this time of family grief, but he did not want me to read it in the paper. I asked him about my assistants, Joe Patten and Darryl Conway. He said that Joe P was also being let go, but Darryl was being kept on to help with the transition. As we hung up, I may have thanked him out of habit of being well-mannered but I sure did not feel very thankful.

When I went back into the den, Mr. G said I looked pale. SG demanded to know who got fired and I said, "Me." SG was the only one in the room who did not believe me. When I finally convinced her I was not joking, she went through the stages of grief rapidly – and ended up caught between anger at the Jets and blaming me, because I *must* have done something wrong.

The next few days were a blur. Family members from both sides were offering condolences to SG for her grandmother and to me for my loss of my job of the past 19 seasons. It was not until I returned to

New York that I began to think somewhat more clearly and to weigh my options.

Upon returning to New York, I was still in shock that I had been fired. On one hand I was trying to be objective and look at what my opportunities might be. On the other hand, I was devastated and in a significant funk. This depressed state interfered with my ability to think rationally and concentrate for any length of time.

When I went to the Jets complex to meet with Gutman, it was odd that many of the staff had no idea I had been fired. The people who did know avoided me like I had the plague in fear that whatever I had that contributed to my firing might rub off on them.

I went to my office and found Joe P and Darrell there. Joe P was also in a daze and his anger was bubbling over. I told them that this had totally blind-sided me and had to be personal and not professional because we did our jobs as good as any AT staff in the NFL. In my opinion we did our jobs better than most in the NFL.

I called upstairs and went to see Gutman. He again repeated the company line that I worked at the pleasure of the head coach and the head coach had decided I needed replacing. I asked him if Mr. Hess was aware of this and he said, "of course," that a decision like that could not be made without Mr. Hess's approval. I asked if there was a reason beyond him wanting to hire David Price. He told me that I would have to discuss that with Kotite and that he was waiting for me in his office. He told me he would discuss my severance with me after my meeting with Kotite.

I went to Kotite's office and told Maureen, the head coach's administrative assistant, that I was supposed to see the head coach and she let him know I was there. He made me wait a good 10 minutes even though there was no one in the office with him. Maureen was as uncomfortable as I was and finally broke the ice by saying "I can't believe they're letting you go." In my best gallows humor, I chucked that "they're not letting me go; they're booting my ass out!" She had a tear trickle down her cheek. I found myself in the odd position of consoling her about me being fired. We were good friends and colleagues who had shared a lot of common interests over the years.

I got a lump in my throat and then thought: *I cannot go into Kotite's office like this!* So, I immediately used my anger to gain control of my emotions. This was a trick I had learned during my drinking years to maintain an attentive state. When I had too much to drink and needed to drive home – or away from home – I would let my resentment of the way SG treated me come to the surface and I would use that anger to focus my attention enough to drive where I needed to go. By the time Kotite called me in, I was in a righteously pissed-off mood. Now I had to tamp it down so I would not do or say anything stupid.

Kotite busied himself at his desk as he told me to take a seat. I could see he was uncomfortable and I was not about to make it easy for him. I just sat there waiting. He finally looked up, glancing at me before looking beyond me. He said, "You no longer seem to have urgency needed to do your job, so I am replacing you." I questioned him about what he meant by "urgency"? Did he mean I did not run out on the field fast enough when someone was injured? I told him that I knew I was not as fast as I used to be but I had three herniated discs from when his Philly team scrimmaged us two years before. I made a semi-joke that if I was moving slower it gave TV more time to go to a commercial and gave him more time to consider his options on the sidelines. He obviously had not thought his reason through and so just he repeated it.

I repeated that I did not understand what he meant. I inquired that if it was so important that I "move with urgency" why hadn't he warned me about it earlier? He mumbled something like "he did not have to explain it." By this time my anger was bubbling over and I told him, "Richie, this is bullshit and you know it! Why don't you just be a man and tell me what this is really about!"

Well, that got his full attention. He stood up, puffed up, and began yelling at me. He told me that I was fired, that he did not have to explain himself to me, and that he was the head coach! He was really angry and an interesting thought entered my head, *Reese, if he hits you, you will own him!* So I stood up and glared at him. I put my hands on his desk and leaned toward him hoping he would punch me.

He was fuming and screamed at me to get out of his office or he would call security. I almost laughed since our security guard was a long retired cop who was about 5'6" and was almost as round as he was tall. But, I decided nothing more could be gained so I turned and walked out the far door in his office – slamming it open like an irate teenager. He continued to yell and curse me as I made my way back to Gutman's office.

Severance

When I got to Gutman's office, his wife, Carol, whom I knew socially, was there and she seemed a little nonplussed as how to greet me knowing I had just been fired. Gutman asked how the meeting went and I just looked at him quizzically wondering how to answer such a stupid question. He apparently understood my look and immediately asked me if I would go down the hall and wait for him in an empty office. On my way out the door, he asked me how I was doing? I again looked at him quizzically, and he said, "You know ... with your condition." I said, "Steve, what are you asking? Are you asking if I'm going to go out and start drinking again? If that's what's concerning you, the answer is NO, I'm not!" Carol looked startled, but he was visibly relieved and said "that's good" and that he would see me in a few minutes.

While I waited for Gutman I wondered what he would have said or done if I had told him that as soon as I left the complex I was going to go on a three-day bender. I came to the conclusion that would not have helped anyone and that no way a punk like Richie Kotite was going to cause me to drink again; or, even get credit for making me drink again.

I was offered the usual 12-month severance that was traditional for non-contract employees at the Jets. Prior to this meeting I had spoken to two labor attorneys who both said the same thing: New York is a "right to work" state and they do not have to give you anything. They both also said that in a long-term middle management position such as mine a month's severance for every year served was somewhat traditional.

So I asked for 19 months' severance. Gutman seemed shocked that I had talked to an attorney and immediately put on his corporate face. In the end, I took the 12 month's severance. I negotiated the use of the company car for six months which gave me some sense of satisfaction.

Knowing that I would now get $147,500 over the next 12 months helped crystallize my financial reality. I felt I could stretch it over two years if I could sell my house in a hurry. I had already broached the subject of selling with SG who was not happy about it. I knew the real estate market was down, but I also knew that I would continue to hemorrhage money if I did not unload the house.

The severance package from the Jets had two "conditions" attached to it. First, I could not say anything negative about the Jets in the media for a year. They knew that after a year, no one would care – it would be old news. So when the flurry of calls from the newspaper reporters came in, I simply told them that I could not talk about it. The result was – as you might expect – little to no mention that I had been replaced.

The second condition was that I help David Price with the transition. The first several days were uncomfortable, but bearable. David seemed as uncomfortable as I was, and I did not see any reason for me to try to make him feel comfortable, especially since I had learned from his old boss, Otho Davis, that he had been lobbying for the position since Kotite took over. By the second week the situation had become really depressing. I had cleaned out the office of all my "stuff" and had shown David everything from the combination to the drug safe to the way the computer programs operated. I gave him all the contact information about the doctors and explained how, with the exception of Elliot Pellman, the internist, the rest were located in Manhattan. Because he had been in the NFL for 10 years, I did not have to explain the job to him or expound on any NFL rules.

I finally asked David if he thought he needed me around on a daily basis. He said no and he would call me if he needed something. I then went to Steve Gutman and told him that my presence was making everyone uncomfortable, that Price could call me if he needed anything, and that I could really use the time to try and find a new job. He agreed that it was no longer necessary for me to come in as long as I would make myself available if needed. He also informed me in a magnanimous gesture that the Jets were going to cover my expenses to the NFL Combine in Indianapolis. He knew coaches used it as a job fair and reasoned I could also.

The NFL Combine

I had less than a week to prepare for the NFL Combine so I had to scramble to focus my approach. I decided to promote myself in the area of performance enhancement and try to convince whoever would listen that I could be a bridge between the sports medicine team and the strength coach by using my new sport psychology knowledge to enhance the work of both.

The experience was bizarre. My AT colleagues readily commiserated with me about how I had been screwed over, but most were not convinced about the new position I wanted to create. I could tell most of them thought it threatening to their positions. I spoke to a number of assistant coaches; again, a lot of commiseration and little in real support. Most said they would talk to their head coach and get back to me. I never heard from any of them.

The closest thing I had to a real meeting was about five minutes with Bobby Bethard, the GM for the San Diego Chargers and one of Dick Steinberg's closest friends. He at least listened to my proposal with some interest. He invited me to come by that evening to one of the suites where he and his coaches were interviewing college players. When I arrived, the room was chaotic with several coaches and scouts huddled around some college players interviewing them. I got Bethard's attention and he brought me in and introduced me to Bobby Ross, the head coach. Ross quizzed me about some of the coaches and players we each had in common, but nothing about performance enhancement. He then handed me back to Bethard, who said he would be in touch. There was no follow-up. I was not surprised.

To say I was depressed after the Combine would be an understatement. I, however, learned two fundamentals at the Combine: First, I needed to better articulate the position I wanted to create. Second, I had to look beyond the NFL. This second realization was terrifying as the past 24 years of my life had been spent in the rarified world of the NFL.

Chapter 22

STARTING OVER

Goal Setting: What I Do NOT Want?

As I started to look outside the NFL, I did an early round of goal setting. I was not sure what I wanted to do, so I began identifying what I did not want to do. While working within the NFL made the most sense because I knew the business, I knew I did not want to take anyone's job as head AT; but if there was an opening I would go for it. The same went for the NBA and the NHL – although the likelihood of getting a foot in those doors was slim to none. Major League Baseball was out for two reasons: One, they employed a farm system and their ATs moved up through the ranks. Two, I did not like baseball enough to work in it full time.

I knew I did not want to work in a sports medicine clinic. As an AT, I would have to work under the auspices of a physical therapist (PT), which did not make sense because of all my training and experience. Also, the part of my job that I had come to like the least was giving physical therapy treatments. Applying hot or cold packs or administering ultrasound treatments did not appeal to me at all and the pay was insulting. I enjoyed assessing injuries, prognosticating the time to return to the field, creating special taping techniques and protective pads, and occasionally supervising rehab.

Resume: Focusing My Abilities & Experience

A close friend suggested I meet her friend who was a "head hunter". The friend helped potential clients polish their resumes. That was the first time I had heard the term "head hunter" in the context of job placement! (The head hunters I knew were either linebackers or strong safeties.)

Meeting with a head hunter was invaluable as I learned how much I actually did and the breadth of responsibilities I had as a head AT. The first meeting we discussed what I did at the Jets in terms of administration. The responsibilities were really quite enormous. While I had created a job description at the Jets, I had never articulated the details of what I did into business administrative categories. Also, I had never created a resume.

After I spent a couple of weeks listing and defining all the different administrative jobs I performed and responsibilities I held, I returned for more coaching. We grouped the duties under corporate headings. She then told me to compress my new five-page resume into one page – two pages at most – and to highlight certain aspects for certain positions. Therefore, I would need more than one resume.

First, these reductions of information were hurtful because I wanted everyone to know all that I had done and was capable of doing. Second, having different resumes was costly. In 1996 it was not acceptable to print a resume from your computer; you had to pay for professional printing on high grade paper. In time I got over my resistance and developed resumes highlighting my qualifications for positions that I was seeking. I also created a Curriculum Vita, which is needed for academia.

Networking

Networking is the best way to promote your services to individuals, groups, and businesses. Basically, I am an introvert and "working the room" is difficult for me. Unless I am with a group of people I know, I prefer a corner of the room to observe what is going on.

That being said, I knew if I wanted to create my own business I would have to reach out to others. Initially this was also embarrassing for me because everyone I contacted wanted to know about the situation with the Jets and they knew that I needed some sort of favor. I had to swallow my pride and ask for help.

Housing Issues

I also knew that I had to sell my house to get out from under its $2800 a month mortgage. In 1996 the real estate market was on another downturn on Long Island. The house finally sold that fall. I lost every penny of equity in it. I was depressed thinking I would probably never own a home again, but I was relieved when it finally sold. From 1996 to 2002, I would move nine times to lower rents and/or to take advantage of business opportunities.

Hypnosis Practice

One way I thought I could make a living was through the practice of hypnosis. I had experienced success at the Jets with accelerated healing and rehabilitation, with pain management, and with using hypnosis as an adjunct to performance enhancement. I had worked with several people outside the Jets and also had success. I expanded my networking to professional organizations including the National Guild of Hypnotists (NGH) where I had been a member since 1994.

Since I did not have training camp for the first time since 1967, I attended my first NGH convention in August of 1996 to broaden my hypnosis skills. The NGH was approximately 15% the size of the National Athletic Trainers' Association (NATA) annual convention. Nevertheless, it was very crowded as it was held in a small venue and 10-12 sessions ran simultaneously. It was a unique and somewhat overwhelming experience. There seemed to be three main groups of people in attendance: some dentists, medical doctors, PhD psychologists, and chaplains; lay hypnotists (the category I came under); and stage hypnotists. It was quite an eye-opener and I learned a lot that proved useful.

Hypnosis became a big part of my toolbox – both personally and professionally – as I began to recreate myself. I used it as a method of behavior change and as an adjunct to performance enhancement and executive coaching. As stated earlier, all hypnosis is really self-hypnosis and everyone can learn these skills. Self-hypnosis can be used for improvement in any area of life. It has been an integral part of my sobriety, my psychospiritual development, and my thriving in recovery.

1996 – West Point Externship

The main avenue I pursued, however, was performance enhancement. I contacted Nate Zinsser, the civilian Director of the West Point Center for Enhanced Performance (CEP). He arranged for me to spend a couple of weeks with him as an apprentice to their hands-on approach for working with athletes. This "externship" was invaluable to me. I learned more about the delivery of mental skills training and I cemented a relationship with Nate and Brad Scott, the military Director of the CEP. Thanks to their generosity and willingness to share, I gained more confidence in my training abilities and techniques to enhance mental skills that helped me move forward more confidently with my professional goals.

1997 – Cybex & a Different AA

An athletic training colleague who contributed to my professional development was John Bruno. John had formerly worked for Cybex, once the leading company in iso-kinetic testing for muscle strength. Iso-kinetic testing was used by most NFL teams to compare the strength of an injured leg to that of a non-injured leg to help determine readiness to return play. Dr. Nicholas's Institute of Sports Medicine and Athletic Trauma (NISMAT) had been an early proponent of Cybex testing and the Jets became a beta test site for all their new machines. The Jets had instituted Cybex protocols for pre-draft physicals and insisted that they become part of the NFL Combine physical protocols.

After I was fired, John contacted me and asked me if I wanted to do some Cybex testing for his fledgling company INRTEK. I confessed that I had not actually performed a Cybex test in years as my assistants had done that. I also informed him that I had no desire to work in a clinic. He laughed and said relearning the Cybex protocol was like riding a bicycle – I could relearn it in about a 20-minute review session. He went on to explain that this testing was for American Airlines as part of their pre-employment screening process, so there was no clinical work involved. American Airlines would contact me and tell me they had one or several people to test and arrange a time for me to meet them at their offices at JFK airport where I would do the screening. I did not even have to grade the tests, as they were sent to his office in Ohio for consistency. I asked him what it paid, and I recall it was around $30 per test. The clincher, however, was that I would be considered an American Airlines employee and could fly stand-by on any American flight with paying only the taxes for the flight.

While I never particularly liked doing Cybex testing and quite often complained about being stuck in traffic on the Belt Parkway, the perq of almost free air travel served me well over the next several years as I expanded the reach of my business. I will always be grateful to John Bruno for thinking of me.

Neurofeedback: The Pergamon Institute & Lexicor

When Pete Carroll sent me on the quest for peak performance methods in 1994, I investigated a group called the Pergamon Institute (pseudonym) north of Manhattan. It was run by a psychiatrist, Dr. Archer (pseudonym), and her partner, retired Major-General Arthur Brummagen (pseudonym). They were using neurofeedback mainly to help stroke victims and other brain damaged individuals to regain both physical and cognitive function. I was intrigued by their claims of using neurobiofeedback for enhancing performance and was impressed with the potential for helping brain damaged patients regain cognitive function. (Since then neurobiofeedback has been shortened to neurofeedback.)

I had established a working relationship with the Pergamon Institute in 1995 when Jets quarterback Boomer Esiason suffered a significant concussion. After my experience with Al Toon's concussion, I did not want to just sit and wait as we had with Al, so I cleared it with the Jets doctors and took Boomer to the Pergamon Institute. They performed a quantitative electroencephalogram (QEEG) and gave me a crash course on how to install and use the neurofeedback program on my computer. I figured a worse-case scenario: it would not help but it also would not hurt and would give Boomer a way to be pro-active in his recovery.

Boomer missed the next five weeks. He returned on November 19 against the Bills. Boomer had a great game in a losing effort (28-26) and told me afterward that he was in the zone for most of the game. We both wondered if the neurofeedback had anything to do with that.

Now in 1996, as part of my networking, I contacted Arthur Brummagen at the Pergamon Institute. I was convinced they had something worthwhile to offer with the neurofeedback. I was looking at it not only as a partial solution to the growing concern about concussions in the NFL, but also I wanted to learn how it could be used for performance enhancement. Bert suggested that I let them fully train me as a neurofeedback technician. I readily agreed.

I began driving up to Hastings-on-Hudson three to four days a week. Beyond the technical issues of wiring someone up for an EEG, I reviewed brain anatomy and learned about the plasticity of the brain and the holographic nature of its two hemispheres. That is, if one side of the brain could no longer function because of injury or stroke, the other side could be taught that function. I found the entire process fascinating. This peaked my interest in applied neuroscience – an interest which I have maintained.

After three months of working as an intern I was certified by the Pergamon Institute as a neurofeedback technician. I also took an exam and became certified by the Biofeedback Certification International Alliance (BCIA). After my internship, Bert and I began to confer on how we could best leverage my NFL connections so I assumed the position of Sports Performance Liaison for the Pergamon Institute. Of course, this was a non-paying position that held the promise of a future payoff.

Bert introduced me to Michael Hickey from Lexicor Medical Technologies, the company that made the Quantitative EEG (QEEG) products utilized at the Pergamon Institute. I told him that beyond peak performance I thought neurofeedback offered tremendous promise in the area of concussion management. While time consuming, a baseline EEG could be established for players that could then be used for comparison post-concussion. He was excited at the prospect and invited me to Boulder, Colorado, where I toured the facility and took a two-day intensive to become an Advanced EEG Biofeedback Technician. I was then named Lexicor's Sport and Performance Liaison (another non-paying position with future potential).

I assisted Michael at several venues where he was trying to establish a foothold for further research at several universities. It was my job to explain how neurofeedback worked for peak performance and concussion management. This was the beginning of my education as to how corporations and institutions of higher education could work together.

Dennis Vaske

In late November of 1996 I was surprised to get a call from Dr. Elliot Pellman. Since my firing, Pellman had used his position as Jets Team Physician and as Chair of the NFL Concussion Committee to become the Team Physician to the NY Islanders. In this role, he contacted me about using neurofeedback with Islander defenseman, Dennis Vaske. Dennis had suffered a concussion the season before and had missed most of that season. He had returned for the 1996-97 season and was doing well, but suffered a second concussion in November. His post-concussion syndrome was hanging on and Pellman wanted to give the neurofeedback a shot. I set up an appointment with the Pergamon Institute to evaluate Dennis. Because of my working relationship with Lexicor, I was furnished the hardware and software needed to serve as the technician for Dennis' therapy. We negotiated an agreement based on what Pergamon would charge and I was actually paid for the neurofeedback sessions. This looked like the beginning of the partnership that Arthur Brummagen and I had been discussing.

I worked with Dennis from mid-December 1996 until early March 1997 under the supervision of Dr. Archer and kept in contact with Pellman and the AT of the Islanders. In one of the sunrooms of the house that I was renting, I set up my treatment center. Dennis came by

3-4 days a week for neurofeedback treatments. While it took months, Dennis returned to a "normal" that he reported as being better than he felt when he took the ice earlier that year in training camp. He returned to play at the end of the 1997 season. Everyone was happy.

Don't Yell at Me!

As 1997 progressed I began to get some local publicity for my peak performance business. Any opportunity I had I mentioned the Pergamon Institute and the exciting promise of neurofeedback. One newspaper interview mentioned Arthur Brummagen and Dr. Archer by name. On my next visit to the Pergamon Institute, Arthur asked me to come with him to Dr. Archer's office. As we entered, she immediately began screaming at me for mentioning her relationship with Arthur since he was divorced in a different state and those laws did not work in their favor. (If the reader is confused, so was I!)

I stated that their running the Institute was public knowledge. I explained that I knew nothing of their relationship beyond that and had no knowledge about Arthur's former marriage or divorce. These facts just seemed to incense her more as she continued to scream at me so loudly that I thought she might stroke out.

I looked over at Arthur; this former Major General in the Army was just standing there with a sheepish look on his face. Dr. Archer abruptly stopped yelling and dismissed me from her office. Arthur accompanied me out. I was shocked and asked him, "What the hell was that about?" He mumbled something about the divorce laws in the other state and about the possibility that his ex-wife could demand more support money, blah, blah, blah. I could not really focus on what he was saying as I was emotionally somewhere between embarrassed and outraged. He kept telling me he hoped this would not impact our proposed partnership. I am not sure how I replied.

On the ride back to Long Island I replayed the scene. It occurred to me that only three other people had ever yelled at me like that: SG, Walt Michaels, and Jim Nicholas, the Jets team physician for years. I resented SG for the yelling and put-downs. With Walt it was only once when he fired me, and then when I challenged him, that was over and done with. I had endured Jim Nicholas' rants partially out of respect for his age and his credentials, and partially out of self-preservation – wanting to keep my job. It occurred to me that if I became partners with Arthur and Dr. Archer, I was just inviting more of the same. I gave it a couple of days before I called Arthur and told him there would be no partnership. He tried to talk me out of it and apologized for Dr. Archer. I explained that I had put up with that kind of treatment from a doctor for years, and I was not about to do it again.

This was the first in a long line of promising business and personal relationships that I terminated after the other party acted out in an outrageous fashion. Later I learned the wisdom of terminating abusive relationships as tolerating abuse only invites more abuse. At the time, however, I did not fully appreciate the significance of my resolve to be in healthy relationships and my commitment to healthy self-respect.

While my relationship with the Pergamon Institute disintegrated, my relationship with Lexicor, the software company that made the neurofeedback possible, was growing stronger. Michael Hickey told me not to be concerned about Pergamon because he had physicians and technicians across the country. My personal challenge was while I enjoyed the neurofeedback work I determined I did not want to spend most of my time tied to an office working as a technician.

Master's in Psychology: The Winner's Mentality

I had started my Master's in Psychology at Regis University in Denver, Colorado in 1994. When I was fired in January1996 my master's work came to a halt and I applied for "incompletes" for six hours of coursework. Finding or creating a new job became my priority. In the fall of 1996, I was notified that if I did not complete the coursework I would lose those credit hours and would jeopardize my continued matriculation. I decided a master's degree was important for credibility in the area that I wanted to work: performance enhancement. I added graduate coursework back into my already stressful workload.

I worked diligently to complete the coursework that was prerequisite to beginning my master's project. For one self-designed course I compared popular sport psychology programs to see what they had in common.

These included the programs of Mark Anshel[14], Linda Bunker[15], Jim Loehr[16], Rainer Martens[17], Shane Murphy[18], Bob Nideffer[19], Terry Orlick[20], Ken Ravizza and Tom Hanson[21], Bob Rotella[22], and Nate Zinsser and Brad Scott[23] at West Point.

For another course, I compared popular self-help programs. That reading list started with Norman Vincent Peale's *Power of Positive Thinking*[24] and included books by Anthony Robbins[25], Stephen Covey[26], M. Scott Peck[27], and Zig Zigglar[28]. I also included Lou Tice's recent book, *Smart Talk For Achieving Your Potential*[29], along with his audio and video programs[30, 31] from The Pacific Institute.

For my master's project I decided to design my own performance enhancement program to use with athletes by combining and distilling sport psychology and self-help programs. Using the above mentioned comparisons, I began to develop what became my *five essential mental skills*: goal setting, visualization, stress management, effective thinking, and mental toughness.

But, before I could begin my Master's Project I needed one more course. Paul Haber, my course consultant at Regis suggested I choose anything in psychology that interested me – that it did not have to be about sports or performance. I returned to my roots in sports medicine and decided to create a course on the psychology of healing.

By this time, I had studied and used hypnosis since 1990. As early as the late 1970s, I had explored the mind-body connection, aromatherapy, and acupuncture (including a non-invasive electrical probe to acupuncture points). I had also investigated magnets to speed healing. I had been blessed to work with Abe at the Buffalo Bills who had taught me not to scoff at anything that might help.

Additionally, I had established a relationship with a local chiropractor, Lenny Izzo, who had several Jet players as clients. Not only did I learn a lot from Lenny about the needs of players that were helped by chiropractic treatments, but he also helped me with my back problems. Later he *attuned* me to Johrei, a Japanese energy healing modality similar to Reiki.

Lenny gave me a copy of Richard Gerber's *Vibrational Medicine*[32] to help me better understand the concept of energy healing. Reading that book aided my course design. I included books by Gerber, Deepak

Chopra[33, 34], Barbara Brennan[35], and Carolyn Myss[36]. I also added Dan Millman's *Way of the Peaceful Warrior*[37] because of its sports theme.

Creating my course of the psychology of healing required distilling the commonalities among all of the above mentions modalities and resources. All of this led me to the most important component for my own program: the role of energy.

The final product of all of the above learnings, trainings, and experiences culminated in my master's project: a certification course for mental skills trainers[38]. This project has served me very well personally and professionally. I used this material to develop executive coaching and corporate training programs. It is fundamental to the Sports Hypnosis Certification Course that I taught annually at the International Convention of the National Guild of Hypnotists. It eventually became the basis for my first book *Develop the Winner's Mentality: 5 Essential Mental Skills for Enduring Success*[39]. (As I will detail later, these five essential mental skills are also foundational for thriving in recovery.)

Performance Enhancement Consultant

One trickle of income came from working with NFL players for performance enhancement. Pat Kirwan (PK), a Long Island native who had worked his way up from a high school coach to Assistant General Manager with the Jets – and someone I trusted implicitly – hooked me up with several players' agents to work with performance enhancement for some of the players they represented. This led to some satisfying, but sporadic work. I also developed several programs for the NFL and interviewed with a couple of head coaches and General Managers. I was especially proud of a program I developed to shorten the learning curve for rookies so they could contribute sooner and avoid the "rookie slump"[40].

As I deepened my education and broadened my experience, I perceived a real need for a performance enhancement specialist on NFL teams. I developed a job description for a peak performance coordinator to not only work one-on-one with players but also to facilitate coordination of the sports medicine staff (ATs, physicians, PTs, etc.), strength coach, and all the ancillary collaborators (nutritionist, chiropractor, etc.). This concept was before its time; it did not open doors for me in the NFL. I, however, used it to further evolve my Winner's Mentality Program.

Years later for my doctoral research I conducted a program evaluation of the Winner's Mentality Program with a Division I Volleyball team. This research yielded an 84.69% positive program evaluation rating. That evaluation showed enhanced individual performance, enhanced individual mental toughness, and enhanced team chemistry[41].

The Dot-Com Boom and Bust

A dot-com boom began in 1997. New York, especially Wall Street, was in a frenzy as it seemed every week there were new millionaires created by going public with an internet company. PK connected me with several people trying to get sports information websites going.

During that time, I became the *Jock Doc* writing a weekly column about sports medicine and sport psychology for *SportsFan-on-Line*. I wrote about common injuries like shin-splints and tennis elbow and about how to treat and rehab them. Part of my duties as the *Jock Doc* was to answer e-mail questions from readers. Here, I would incorporate information about using basic mental skills such as goal setting, visualization, and positive self-talk.

That led to a stint as a contributor to *The War Room* which was a football e-zine dedicated to scouting player personnel through free-agency and the draft. My job was to tell the public what I had traditionally reported to coaches and general managers about how injuries might affect the short term and/or long term careers of certain players. The problem was that I had extremely little inside information about players' injuries. Because I no longer participated in the NFL Combine physicals, my input was limited to what I considered the obvious: what was in the papers. Nevertheless, there was interest in my postings.

I invested time in several other dot-com ventures. My challenge with these ventures was everything was on the "if come." That is, I would receive an equity share that would have some value if and when the venture company was sold. None of my equity shares paid off. These experiences did, however, help me improve my skills as a writer and for delivering succinct presentations to groups.

In hindsight, the single most productive networking contact I had was PK. Beyond having the ability to not piss off anyone, he is one of those guys who maintains and cultivates relationships. He stayed in contact with Bruce Coslet, Pete Carroll and all the assistant coaches and scouts that came through the Jets. He was a Long Island native and had coached at a local high school and at Hofstra University. PK went out of his way to find me work, and, over time, proved to be a pivotal catalyst in my future successes. In terms of degrees of separation, PK was one degree away from a number of people that helped me.

Chapter 23

SPREAD THIN

It's Just a Goal!

To say that I was scattered and spread thin throughout the remainder of 1996 and well into 1997 would be an understatement. I would jump at any opportunity that looked like I could make a buck – short term or long term. Since I was still exploring what I wanted to do, I looked at everything. I spent a lot of time networking and trying to position myself for the future. I learned rapidly that my Jets credentials could open doors but that was all.

As I was completing my master's degree and formalizing my *Winner's Mentality* program, the reality that my severance would soon run out was an ever growing specter. I was still hustling for Lexicor, but nothing substantial came from it. I was coaching several athletes for performance enhancement, including some NFL players. I was working with several dot.com start-ups and consulting with several more. I was also practicing hypnosis.

I decided I needed some help and contacted Lou Tice at the Pacific Institute. Lou said if I could get to Seattle he would sit with me and go over my options. I took advantage of my American Airlines relationship and met with Lou two days later in Seattle.

Lou listened to me as I explained all I was doing and then said the obvious: it is too much and I was spread too thin to be effective. He suggested I model the military chain of command where no one is responsible for more than five people. He told me to pick the five areas at which I was best – or that I liked doing the best – and focus on them. We spent the next half hour laying it out on paper. I was extremely relieved as I now had a plan. Lou said he had to go meet with some Japanese businessmen. I thanked him earnestly. As he was going out the door he turned and said, "Remember, Bob, these are just goals, not promises." And he was gone.

I was nonplussed. What did he mean "just goals?" I hurried out into the hall, but he was engaged with the group from Japan. So I was left to sort it out for myself. I almost felt betrayed His words seemed to contradict my understanding of the combined value of goal setting with the power of positive thinking and the *Law of Attraction*: If you envision an end-result goal clearly enough and add the energy provided by belief, you engage the *Law of Attraction* and make your future.

I ruminated over Lou's piece of advice and my subsequent realizations for weeks. One day while perusing a sport psychology book, I noticed a reference to goals as tools to get you to your goal: to your desired end result. It then crystallized for me what Lou had meant by "they are just goals." Goals can change and be modified. This made such sense: life is dynamic and that dynamism is change which requires adjusting and modifying. Because of this insight I re-wrote the chapter on goal setting in my master's project and began making necessary adjustments in my own life. I was taking my first step toward realizing that you cannot *make* things happen.

The above is stated in the goal setting literature. So, why do so many of us not get that life is change and change requires adjusting and modifying while persisting in movement toward desired end results? Why do we tend to overlook that our goals may also change with life's adjustments and modifications? One reason is scotomas.

Scotoma is another favorite term that Lou Tice used. It means blind spot. When we have a scotoma we cannot see what may be obvious to others. I had multiple blind spots as I was trying to *make* things happen. Recognizing scotomas is easier said than done; just as trying to *make* things happen is not an easy habit to modify. Having a scotoma can lead to a version of the definition of insanity popular in 12-Step programs:

doing the same thing over and over and expecting different results. In Part 3, *The 13th Step*, I discuss how I met these challenges.

Executive Coaching

Soon after my visit with Lou Tice I came across the term executive coach. I read about an executive coach who was making big bucks doing what I wanted to do: enhance mental skills and improve mental toughness. The difference was she was doing it with executives and I had been focused on athletes. I realized that my experiences and expertise were transferable to executive coaching. I decided to find out more about it and looked it up on the internet. In 1998 my internet search produced three executive coaches. At this writing there are over 110,000,000 hits for executive coach on Google.

I sent an e-mail to the three executive coaches requesting information about executive coaching. Only one, Colle Davis, responded. We traded several e-mails and he offered me an apprenticeship at his usual coaching rates. This was an important concept for me to incorporate in my practice because I needed to learn the value of my coaching services and be comfortable charging for them. A more profound understanding was that if I wanted to be paid for coaching I had to value coaching enough to be willing to pay another coach for services rendered to me. (After years of working in the NFL I was used to either the club paying for me or people giving me services just because of my affiliation.)

I agreed to be coached in order to learn how to coach and began having hour-long telephone sessions once a week for about nine months with Colle who had been trained by Thomas Leonard, founder of Coach University. He was one Leonard's first students. He introduced me to its concepts and assessments. After about three months Colle suggested that he would coach me as I coached a client. It was a valuable educational experience.

McD

As I worked with my executive coaching mentor, I told PK that I was looking for executive coaching clients. He immediately referred his cousin, John McDermott (McD). McD was an out of work sales executive. He was out of work because he refused to move with his former company to the mid-west. He and his wife were from Long Island and wanted to stay there. He wanted to get involved in the new internet business but was struggling to find a position. And, like most, his biggest challenge was handling the stress associated with being out of work.

He was the perfect candidate for me. He was smart and aggressive. As a former college soccer player he enjoyed my sport psych approach. I worked with him for several months. I took my questions or concerns to my mentor, Colle Davis. Apparently I had a pretty good handle on things because little correction was needed.

McD landed a job as a sales manager for a cable optics company. His sales team was a mix of old veteran sales executives and some young and hungry ones. The problem for them was that they were selling broadband, a new concept, instead of a tangible product. Said another way, they were selling intangible space on broadband – and at the time no one knew what that was.

McD brought me in to work with his sales team. I began getting paid for coaching and making good money! After a while, I was spending three or four days a week coaching 17 sales executives. The HR department was talking to me about doing group trainings. My mental skills coaching of athletes and hypnosis practice was now secondary to my executive coaching practice.

Corporate Takeover

Eight months into this great coaching gig, a large telecom company absorbed the cable optic company. Unfortunately, my position was deemed unnecessary. As an independent contractor, I had no job security, no severance pay – nothing!

I had quit marketing myself. I had only a few clients outside the corporate world. I learned a very hard lesson about the need for continuous marketing when you are an independent contractor or entrepreneur.

Most of McD's sales teams were also out. Fortunately for McD, he was retained and was soon elevated to regional sales manager. As he assumed his new role, he was able to bring me in to work with another new sales group. I got to sit in on what he referred to as "Sales 101" meetings as he brought them up to speed. He informed me from the start that this coaching gig would only be for a short while.

McD and I have remained friends over the years. I later worked with him again as he transitioned to another company. I will always be grateful to him for the opportunity and the education he provided. I am also grateful to PK for introducing me to McD and for all his support and friendship.

The Pacific Institute & Joe Pace

As my corporate coaching job in New York unraveled, a position opened at The Pacific Institute (TPI), Lou Tice's company. I did not know enough to realize I was not qualified, so I applied. Upon receiving my application, I was contacted by the president of TPI, who informed me that while I was not what they were looking for that position, Lou would like to meet with me about the possibility of becoming a Project Director for TPI. Of course, I was interested. I was asked to meet Lou at a presentation he was giving in Louisville, Kentucky, where I met Joe Pace, the Director of the Education Initiative.

Once again I took advantage of my American Airlines connection and headed to Louisville. I attended Lou's talk and afterwards had dinner with him and Joe Pace. Joe and I hit it off and Lou invited me to become a project director. This involved going to Seattle for a two-week training. If I liked TPI – and vice versa – then I would be working mainly with Joe.

Several weeks later in November, 1998, I was on my way to Seattle. Here I learned the art of facilitation as a teaching method. I was well schooled in lecturing, but facilitation as a teaching method was new to me. It became another irreplaceable and valuable tool for me. Presently, it serves me well as a college professor.

I also learned that as a project director I would not only be facilitating the TPI curriculum but I would also be selling TPI programs to organizations and companies. Because I had been impressed with Lou's curriculum since 1994, I assumed it would be an easy sell. So I was all in.

Joe Pace turned out to be another great mentor who provided me with much more than I could have imagined. His doctoral work on resilience helped to make us a natural fit. He had been the president of five proprietary colleges in Florida. Joe's main concern was how to keep students from "coming in the front door and then walking straight out the back door." He wanted to keep them in school. For these purposes, he modified Lou's curriculum and geared it toward students. And, he found it helped significantly.

Another area in which Joe was a visionary was seeing the promise of distance learning on the future of higher education. Because I earned my master's through distance learning, I shared his enthusiasm. He included me in a project with National American University to put the Pacific Institute curriculum online. It was through this experience that I learned the essentials of online teaching and the use of learning platforms like WebCT and Blackboard.

Additionally, Joe arranged for me to work with Waunda Thomas. Waunda, another former proprietary college president and close friend to Joe, guided me through the actual on-ground facilitation process as we instructed several proprietary colleges in the TPI curriculum. The way it worked was we would show a 20-minute video of Lou teaching a topic like goal setting. Then we facilitated the group to make sure they understood the message.

A typical contract with a proprietary college included our facilitating the faculty, administration, and staff of the school with their learning the Pacific Institute curriculum. Then we worked closely with selected individuals who would be teaching the course to students – usually as a college success course or sometimes as an introductory psychology course.

As time went on Waunda turned more and more of the facilitation process over to me. She told Joe and every other Project Director (PD) at TPI that I was not only ready to be on my own but also that I was very good. This led to several other PDs hiring me to facilitate the curriculum for some of their clients. My corporate background now came into play as I also began to facilitate corporate education.

The most beneficial thing Waunda did for me, however, was to ask me to help her facilitate the program for the faculty, staff, and administration at the Katherine Gibbs Schools in the New York area. The schools were so large that I did multiple three-day trainings. One day I mentioned to the Director of Academics for the Manhattan campus that I would be interested in teaching the course to the students. I wanted to see how it actually rolled out with students. No one at TPI had done this, and I thought it would give me valuable insight as to its efficacy with the students. Since I had my Master's in Psychology by this time, she thought it was a great idea. The next quarter I was teaching the course one night a week. It was different than corporate facilitating, but I loved it when I saw the students' eyes light up when they "got it".

While I had anticipated only teaching it once, I ended up teaching the course about 10 more times. During this period, they also asked me to teach their Introduction to Psychology course several times, which I did. I did similar adjunct work for other colleges in New York.

My love for facilitation and teaching were ignited and rapidly growing! It was easy and joyful for me. I had not felt this at home at a job since leaving the training room. Executive coaching was fun and I was good at it, but facilitation of groups was much better. I worked with the Pacific Institute from 1999-2002, where I continued honing in my skills as a facilitator, along with being deeply indoctrinated with Lou's positive messages over and over again. Accordingly, cognitive psychology concepts such as the Reticular Activating System, Self-Talk Cycle, and End-Result Thinking espoused by Lou became integral components of the *Winner's Mentality System*. From Lou I also learned the value of demonstrating the applications of these concepts with personal stories. Now I have my own stories that embody the same positive messages and techniques. As a college professor of psychology, I teach more theory than I did when facilitating TPI curricula, but I always remember that theory is useless without application. I strive to get that across to my students.

Lou Tice transitioned in 2012. He had been a friend and mentor. My association with him, and everyone at The Pacific Institute, was more than an education, it provided me with a firm foundation for the direction that I took in life. One of Lou's favorite sayings was, "We all have the freedom to choose. We always have. Choose to make a positive difference every day." I do, Lou – thank you.

5x7 Notebook

One of the interventions that my executive coaching mentor, Colle Davis, taught me proved to be critical to improving my decision-making at the time. This intervention required filling three pages of a 5"x7" spiral notebook every day. On the first page every sentence must begin with "I feel ...." On the next page, "I want ...." On the third page write whatever comes to mind. Each page had to be filled each day – even if filled with repetitions.

There is something about writing that eventually brings out what it is you really want. After a while you quit writing about how you think you should feel and you begin discerning the emotions you are actually feeling. After a while you quit writing about what you think you want or think you should want, and you get down to what it is you really want. After a while you write something that is truly meaningful in the context of your life. The next challenge and opportunity is to pay attention to what you feel, what you want, and what is truly meaningful and then to act on it.

This intervention helped me immensely in 1998 and again in 2001 when I came to another crossroad in my life. As part of this process in 2001 I decided to review what I had journaled in 1998 and 1999. The answers to my questions were all there. They had been there all along – I had just looked past them.

Chapter 24

NUCLEAR FAMILY & DYSFUNCTION

Dysfunction is the Norm

> As 96 percent of all families are to some degree emotionally impaired, the unhealthy rules we're living by are handed down from one generation to another and ultimately to society at large. Our society is sick because our families are sick. And our families are sick because we are living by inherited rules we never wrote. – John Bradshaw[42]

When you grow up in a dysfunctional environment that becomes your normal. There is an old saying that "you can't fix something unless you know it is broken." So the problem is being unable to recognize dysfunction that has been your normal and, thus, not understanding its pervasiveness and actions needed to be healthy.

I share my stories not to blame, belittle, or demean anyone. I share them because experience and observation have informed me that dysfunctions of this nature are common, but for most are difficult to recognize. I have also learned that to be healthy we must acknowledge the dysfunctions, for example in AA admitting, "I'm Bob and I'm an alcoholic."

Until I stepped back, recognized, and evaluated the dysfunction of family members and our interactions, I accepted their behaviors and dynamics as normal. I made excuses for their deceptions and rejections. Accepting dysfunctional behaviors as normal caused me to build deep resentments. I would stuff the anger with these resentments until they accumulated and I finally exploded with rage. The expression of this rage would be a verbal assault (never physical) against whoever piled on the "final straw" – usually SG. Afterwards I always felt guilty and beat myself up for verbally ranting. This provided family members with another club to guilt me and emotionally beat me up. It was also the crux of the anger issue I was asked to address while I was in rehab.

So, I begin this section with a forewarning: My experience, observation, and research indicate that the more you change the more push-back you will receive from dysfunctional family members. While everyone said they were happy that I was in recovery, family members pushed-back when I changed by setting boundaries and requesting they respect my humanity and that of my wife. It seemed the healthier I became, the harder they pushed-back trying to keep me as I was. This push-back eventually resulted in their telling me to stay out of their lives.

Crumbling Home Front

Dysfunction and addiction impact everyone in the family. Parental dysfunction and addiction can be replicated by children. Dysfunction and addiction are insidious.

My daughter, Rachel, graduated high school in 1995 and decided to live at home while in college. She enrolled at SUNY Old Westbury. Since she was not sure what she wanted to "do" in life, I suggested she get foundational courses out of the way the first two years, show she could do college work, and then transfer into the college of her choice to pursue her major. I offered her the same deal as I had with Rob: graduate even if it takes longer than five years, and upon graduation I would buy her a car – most likely a used one as I had done with Rob.

She, however, needed a car immediately for her commute to college from home. Because I was not paying for college room and board, I co-signed a lease for a new small car that had very manageable monthly payment.

She then reneged on her part of the deal by flunking out of college the first semester. Her mother and I were shocked. Either she intercepted her mid-term report or the college did not inform the parents because of FERPA. Regardless, we did not know she had flunked out until she informed us she could not register for the spring semester. Throughout the fall semester, when asked about how things were going, she lied and told us "great! The school was great and she was doing well!" She later confessed she had been going to the campus, cutting classes, and just hanging out. She said she was just tired of school.

I was angrier about her lying and her deception than her flunking out of college. I gave her a couple of months to find a job and take on her car payments – possibly pay us rent if she continued to live at home. I later found out SG told her not to worry about the rent; and, if I required her to pay rent, she would refund it to her. This was typical of SGs duplicity and her intentional undermining Rachel's assuming responsibility and my parental authority. All of this was all happening as Kotite's first season was coming to a dismal close – just before I was fired in February, 1996.

So, by fall 1996, we had sold the house and were living in a rental. Rachel had flunked out of school and was still living at home. SGs drinking was getting worse and so was her screaming at me. In alcohol fueled fits of rage she pounded on my bedroom door, cursing loudly in the middle of the night. I decided that Rachel needed to be out of the line of fire. Also, she had been working for an insurance company that downsized by closing the Long Island office, and she had lost her job. She worked for several months at the home office in Manhattan; then they downsized and she was let go. I suggested that she move to Nashville and stay with some family member until she found a job and could afford her own place. She liked the idea, and so did SG.

SG discussed with her sister, CG, Rachel's challenge of keeping jobs with the insurance companies that were downsizing. CG, who lived in Lakeland, Florida, said there was an abundance of insurance companies in Lakeland and many were hiring. Rachel moved to Lakeland and lived with her aunt.

Over the next 18 months she worked for several insurance companies approximately three or four months each until each downsized. Eventually the job market in Lakeland dried up completely and she was jobless. She was very demoralized. After a month of not being able to find a job, her aunt began to get on her case – especially when she was drinking heavily. According to Rachel, this happened every weekend. (I come back to her job challenges latter.)

Separation & Divorce

While I was scrambling to create a new business and new life, SG's conduct worsened. I had often thought of divorce and had consulted a divorce lawyer in 1988. Nevertheless, after rehab I was determined to hang in there at least five more years and try to make the marriage work. I had heard enough times that in sobriety "you don't get your brain back for five years." So, I thought it wise not to do anything I might regret until I was sure I had my full faculties in working order.

In the spring 1997, while I was working at the computer, SG burst into the room. Out of the blue, she began berating me and shouting that I needed to "get off my lazy ass and get a job!" I was stunned. I had been working 14-16 hour days, seven days a week – training camp mode – ever since I was fired from the Jets. I was doing everything I knew possible to create a performance consulting business and/or get a full time job with a pro team or a corporation. Plus, I was completing my master's degree since Regis told me if I took anymore time off I would lose those credits for which I had taken an Incomplete. SG knew all of this!

After a few days of mulling it over, I decided "Fuck it!" I could not continually try to make SG feel secure and convince her everything would be alright. I was already putting up with her drunken verbal abuse once or twice a week. We had been sleeping in separate bedrooms for several months. I had to keep my door locked because she would get so incensed when drunk that she pounded on the door and cursed me for never being there and for fucking up my job with the Jets (which she so hated when I had it)! She could go on for hours. (This was another reason for my suggesting Rachel needed to move – as mentioned above.)

More Wake the F*ck Up

Around this time, I had been re-listening to audio tapes by Carolyn Myss[43] as part of my master's research. One segment of a tape caught my attention shortly after SGs' outburst about getting a job. Paraphrasing Myss: sometimes marriages are not meant to last forever. When you have learned all you can from the relationship, it is time to move on. She continued with a warning: staying in a bad relationship can be toxic to your soul. I played that segment over and over and over because it touched something deep within me.

During the next several weeks, I deeply contemplated my marriage. As I decided to quit working on saving my marriage, I realized rapidly that I had been the only one who cared enough to work on it. A light bulb went off that I had over five years of sobriety, so I should have all my "brain back." I began to think once again in terms of separation and divorce.

Over the next two months I asked myself questions like: *Do I really love her?* And, *Love, or not, is this relationship healthy?* At that time, the answer to the first question was, *I'm not sure.* The answer to the second question was a definitive *No!* Not only was it unhealthy, I became more and more convinced that it was toxic: that it was actually killing my soul. I decided that I had to get out of the marriage.

When I made that decision, I felt as if a huge weight was lifted off me. This decision was the first time I deeply felt the positive resonance of a healthy decision. I had been exploring energy medicine and, in turn, energy work. So, in addition to the logical decision to divorce, I had the felt sense of resonance in my gut and in my heart. It would be several years before I would really understand what a "felt sense" was, but that is the best way to describe it.

It took me several more months to work up the courage to broach the topic with SG. I imagined and replayed scenarios in an attempt to be prepared. I could see her crying, becoming depressed, and then drinking herself into oblivion. Or, I could easily imagine her screaming and throwing things at me, and then drinking and getting even angrier.

Imagine my shock when, after one of her outbursts, I finally told her, "You know, we can't keep going on like this. I think we need to separate." She paused, and then said with a flat affect, "Okay." I said, "Okay?" "Yeah, okay. I just need to stay here while I finish acupuncture school and then I'll move out." Then, she shrugged her shoulders and left the room. Once again, I was left nonplussed.

From then on the atmosphere was much calmer around the house. Within several weeks she had worked out an arrangement with her sister, MG, that after she graduated acupuncture school – in about six months – she would move in with her sister, who lived in another state. Once there, she would open up an acupuncture practice. Once established, she would get a place of her own. She believed that she could easily earn $80,000.00 a year.

I was hit with another reality. She expected to walk out the door, hang up her acupuncture shingle, and begin making $80,000 a year for her alone. *We* had not been struggling financially. *I* was the one struggling. SG never once asked what she could do to help.

In hindsight, this should not have surprised me because of her history. When we were at Purdue she had a nice job that she initially loved. After about six months, the people she worked with began to turn into "assholes and bitches." By the seventh month the conditions were "intolerable," so she had to quit – never mind the burden that put on us financially. After getting her BA in Art, she worked for a while as a costumer. I supplemented her expenses for costumes that she made because she could not stay within the budget she was given. I hoped she would be successful at this job as she initially reveled in what a "creative environment" it was and everyone was so "wonderful" to work with. She, however, quit less than nine months later as everyone that she thought was so great before turned into an asshole. After that she never tried to get even a part time job in order to lighten the load. I had assumed she started acupuncture school so that she could contribute to "us" as a couple when she graduated. Wow, was I mistaken!

Over the years, she had regularly said, "What's yours is mine and what's mine is mine." This was followed by a giggle at the mis-phrasing as if it were a joke. Like so many of the things she said, I learned this was not a joke. She wanted no part of having to support me or us in any way. Yet, out of some sense of guilt or duty that I still do not understand, I agreed to continue to support her until she graduated acupuncture school. That was not enough for her. As we moved toward divorce, she consistently asked me to assume all our debts and then I could file for bankruptcy, leaving her totally debt free.

Guilt

Guilt was one of several dysfunctional residuals of my childhood that I carried into adulthood. I had become conditioned to feel guilty about anything that I thought was my responsibility or in my capacity to control – and for some reason I thought I could control a lot more than I realistically could. This began with the Catholic Church and was reinforced by both my mother and SG. For them, deftly using guilt to manipulate me, or a situation, seemed to be second nature. To say that I was guilt-ridden about moving toward divorce was an understatement. Not only did I feel guilty, I felt like a failure. Fortunately, my NFL background had conditioned me to accept losses, fair or not. I knew how to pick up the pieces and move on, but I did not know how to alleviate the guilt.

Like Mother Like Daughter

While networking with one of my old Father Ryan High School classmates who had a successful advertising agency in Nashville, I told him about Rachel's woes in the insurance business. He said that she sounded pretty competent; and if she came to Nashville he could offer her a paid internship for six months. It was not a lot of money, but, assuming she did a good job, she could get her foot in the workforce door with a recommendation from his company.

I informed Rachel about the potential internship with the advertising agency. I also told her she could probably stay with one of my siblings until she got on her feet. At this time, I also informed her that her mother and I were separating. She did not seem surprised and asked me, "What took so long?"

A few days later Rachel made her decision to move to Nashville. She arranged with my brother Joe to stay at his house for three months. She also pursued the intern position with the advertising agency and was hired. I was impressed with her initiative and grateful that I was not in the loop. I did not have any "co-signer" responsibility to either my family or to my old Father Ryan classmate. She did very well at the advertising agency and loved the job. After three months she moved out of my brother's house and found her own apartment. She was doing well.

The advertising agency liked her so much that they helped place her in a nice job with one of their clients. After about six months, however, she began to sour on the new job. She sounded just like SG: At first she loved the job, the environment, and the people, but somehow *all* those people became assholes.

I was still coaching her occasionally. During one coaching session she committed to stay with the job for a least a year after I pointed out that her resume looked like she could not hold a job and after she realized that she needed to show some stability. She made it the year and quit just before she was going to get fired. Thereafter, this became a regular pattern.

Change of Venue

About a month after SG agreed to separation, I began to notice that I was having trouble concentrating after 4:00 or 5:00 PM. By the next week, I began to lose my focus around 2:00 PM. Over the next several weeks my focus continued to lessen so that by 10:00 AM I was dull and could not concentrate. As I examined my symptoms I realized I was stressed out.

In trying to take care of everyone else and regain financial stability, I had been ignoring my own health and well-being. I had been pushing and pushing to make things happen for more than a year. I was mentally and emotionally exhausted. I had ignored the advice given by the psychiatrist in rehab that I need to take care of myself first, so I can take care of others. While I had been studying stress management and looking for methods to include in my program, I was now smacked in the face with the reality that I had better practice what I was going to teach.

I needed time off. I felt the need to go somewhere that I would not have to think. I remembered a Yoga retreat in the Bahamas that

I had read about. It was inexpensive and also regimented. I reserved a bunk and flew down on American Airlines. SG was pissed that I did not invite her, but she was in acupuncture school and could not go anyway. Besides, we had agreed to separate and she had not disputed my statement that "our relationship is toxic." This was the first time since we were married that I went on a non-business trip without her. There was a little guilt, but I overcame it.

The structure of the schedule at the retreat was great. After three days I began to get my brain back. I knew I needed more time, so I flew over to the Florida Keys and found a cheap motel on the beach. For another three days I sat on the beach reading mystery novels and took long walks for exercise – something I had not done since being fired. When I returned to New York, I felt refreshed and able to once again be productive.

I have never forgotten that situation and the need to pay attention to my stress levels. Today, when I start getting dull cognitively, I tell my wife, Joan, it's time for a change of venue. Then, we go out to a movie or take a walk or a drive in the country.

I Want Your Body

After SG graduated with her Associates degree in acupuncture in the spring of 1998, we separated. Basically she took the lion's share of our personal property – 30 years of accumulated stuff. I kept only what I considered necessities: my computer, stereo, clothes, a mattress, a large projection screen TV, a small breakfast table and two stools, and just enough kitchen utensils and equipment to not have to clean the dishes after every meal. I also took responsibility for Delta, our aging bulldog.

Finalizing the divorce dragged on until late 2001. In 1998, we had agreed to come to a settlement as we realized the need to avoid court and the cost of lawyers. Every time I proposed a settlement, SG would agree and then renege. We would start all over. This went on for years. On hindsight, her reneging is consistent with her constant threat during our marriage that if we ever split, she would "take me to the cleaners."

There was one incident that excruciatingly sums up SGs' overreaching demands. I will never forget it. I was in Nashville working on some TPI projects. As I was heading into downtown Nashville on I-40, SG called on my cell and informed me she would agree to accept the latest settlement offer on the condition that when I died she would have the right to direct my funeral. I could not believe my ears. Fortunately, there was a wide shoulder on the side of the road. I pulled over. I was speechless. She repeated her demand. First, I asked her if she was serious? She assured me she was. I then posed the question that if I died 10 or 20 years after our divorce and I was married to another would she still be in charge of my funeral? "Absolutely!" She added that I owed her that "for 30 years of never being there!" I informed her that no amount of time with her meant that she owned my body. In my best locker room language, I told her what she could do with that proposal and that I would just see her in court.

Eventually, after more time and more rancor we finally got divorced.

No Good News About Change

When we change, others react to our changes. Even positive changes can be met with negativity. My family was no exception to this dynamic. My increasing health, happiness, and success was met with resistance and hostility.

In 2002, I moved to Roanoke in January and married Joan in May. After my marriage the calls from Rachel increased both in frequency and in length. She couched the calls as a need for coaching. By 2004, she was calling me every time she had a problem no matter how insignificant and anytime she was experiencing dissonance about something no matter how minor. I slowly came to realize that she was really just using me to dump her frustrations and whine about life. She counted on the fact that I always tried to build her up and would always be supportive – and I was. From this dynamic with Rachel and others I have learned that that bending over backwards to help another and making yourself available at a cost to yourself is not a virtue. It only reinforces the negative behavior of the one you are trying to help.

Her calling became more and more demanding of my time. One Saturday Joan left the house to run errands to take some pressure off me and to give me needed time to work on my PhD. After she left Rachel called needing a coaching session. This session lasted three hours – the time I needed to work on my PhD and the time Joan needed to run my errands. Later Joan pointed out to me that all my coaching sessions with clients had time boundaries and that there was no point in her running my errands if I did not use the time to my advantage. I recognized Rachel was demanding more and more time that I did not have. I had never been very good at setting boundaries with her. When I tried she would accuse me of being a workaholic and, like her mother, remind me that I was never home. I was carrying guilt for "never being home" and trying to make up for it by being available any time she called me and for as long as she wanted.

Eventually, Joan asked what constituted "never being home" and suggested I "do the math." The accusations of my never being home were about job related responsibilities that included training camps, travel to away games, Combine physicals, and weekends in the non-season. Joan then asked me if I was mad at her for out-of-state travel for her graduate studies and research which totaled more time away from me than my work related travel time with the Jets. Of course, I was neither mad at her nor accused her of never being home. I was stunned that I had ever bought into the guilt trip prompted by "never being home" – a blatantly false statement.

Soon after that marathon call with Rachel, I received a call from Rachel while she was on break from her job. It was a Friday afternoon as Joan and I were heading out to a dinner and a movie. She started complaining about one of her girlfriends who had said something that hurt her feelings. I told her I did not have time for this high school bullshit and instructed her not to call me on Friday afternoons. I explained that I had set aside Friday afternoons to be with Joan; it was our sacred time away from work and from our doctoral programs. It was the first firm boundary I ever really set with Rachel. She was then 29 years old!

Her response was a nasty e-mail reminding me that I was never there for her as a child, and now was not there for her when she needed me. This began an e-mail exchange in which I laid out my expectations of her behavior toward me and set some hard boundaries. I told her that I was no longer going to coach her, that after four years of coaching she had the necessary tools, and that she needed to use them. Several times she belittled my marriage and made insulting remarks about Joan. She just concocted crap. She avoided contact with Joan and getting to know her. Somewhere along the way I also told her to "stay out of my marriage" and to "grow the fuck up!" I also suggested she "do the math" regarding my never being home and supplied the data.

After that we had little contact for several months. Then, on Mother's Day, 2004, she called and left a message on my voicemail. She was screaming into the phone (it sounded and felt like she had an audience). She was trying to guilt me into apologizing to her in essence for my trying to set healthy boundaries. She screamed that she was "tired of all my psychobable," (i.e., for the coaching sessions she had demanded). She pronounced that she going to be a great success and that she was not going to share her success with me. She warned me that I would be sorry. She told me in no uncertain terms to get out of her life. I have honored her request.

Blessings in Disguise

Rachel's ultimatum to stay out of her life has been a blessing. The amount of dysfunction and anxiety that I was relieved of was astounding. I cannot begin to calculate the amount of actual time and emotional energy spent in dealing with her whining and addressing the same problems over and over and over and with her tirades when she does not get what she wants. It was insanity.

In hindsight, I should have expected that her insults and dismissals of me would be extended to Joan when we married. After we married, Joan and I visited Nashville so I could introduce her to my family. Several invitations were given to Rachel to meet Joan, to join us as I showed Joan around Nashville, and to have dinner with us. She established this pattern: accept the invitation, not show up at the designated time, then call after some time lapsed to make a lame excuse for not showing up. Notwithstanding her conduct, Joan and I enjoyed Nashville and visiting with my family of origin.

My brother, Joe, and his wife Margie turned their regular Sunday afternoon dinner with their four children and their spouses, their grandchildren, and my parents into a reception for Joan and me. They extended an invitation to Rachel, my other siblings and their spouses.

Joan and I shared our wedding experience in Las Vegas including a video of the ceremony. The video ended with "Congratulations to Mr. and Mrs. Reese." In front of the family, Rachel turned around and loudly exclaimed, "You're not Mrs. Reese!" There was stunned silence. I am thoroughly embarrassed that I said nothing and neither did anyone else. Joan broke the strained silence by asking Rachel what she meant. Rachel mumbled something about she assumed Joan would not take the Reese name. No one said anything else about Rachel's outburst, which was a common family dynamic: sweep it under the rug and pretend that it never happened.

Rachel's unwarranted insults to Joan and me continued thereafter. Probably the most obnoxious put down of me, however, came when the family was gathered at my parents' house after my father had passed away in December 2004. Minutes after Rachel joined the family, her cell phone rang. It was my ex-wife, SG, who apparently asked Rachel to tell the family that she was, at great expense and personal sacrifice, flying back from Utah for the service. As Rachel relayed this to everyone, I told her to tell her mother that she did not need to come. Rachel angrily screamed at me: "It's not just about you, Dad!"

I was so shocked and enraged that I shut down. (Later in this book I use the Enneagram Type Nine to explain this propensity.) Rachel's behavior not only enraged me but also triggered my anger and resentments toward SG and everyone else who had dismissed me over the years. These emotions welled up within me as I was in a very raw emotional state of grief over my Dad's death. I knew that if I said anything I would explode and lash out cruelly at Rachel. So I shut down. I bit my lip and sat on my hands and felt as if steam was coming out of my ears. I could feel others in the room judging me for tolerating her yelling at me like that, but I also knew if I opened my mouth, my reaction could be an overreaction. Joan asked me to go for a walk -- so we could both breathe.

In hindsight, I realize the Catch-22 dysfunction that I bought into with members of my family of origin, my children, adult offspring, and my ex-spouse. My emotional needs were not considered by them while they demanded that I meet all of theirs at any cost to me. So, I either closed down and gave them their way to keep peace or I erupted in a verbal rant and then shut down taking my guilt with me.

These are just some of the egregious incidents that make up a long-term pattern of Rachel's disrespect and disregard for me – and of her emulating her mother. Since her phone call telling me to get out of her life, she tried a few times to re-establish communication. Each time she has ignored my request for a true apology without qualifiers and my guidelines for reestablishing communication and an adult relationship. She also tried to come in the back door by having friends contact me. She posted a video photo collage showing our father-daughter relationship when she was a little girl. When she was 28 or 29 years old she told me that she wanted her "Da-Di" back to take care of her – now, that I believe.

She has in writing what she needs to do if she wants to have a mutually respectful adult relationship with me. She has not done any of what I asked. She is now in her 40s.

Deterioration of a Relationship

In fall 1991 Rob moved to Chicago to attend classes at Improv Olympics. For several years I visited him after the NFL Combine Physicals in Indianapolis. I stayed at his apartment where I slept on a futon for one or two nights. We used the time to catch up and go out to dinner and brunch. He seemed to enjoy these times and the good meals. If I was lucky, I got to see him perform at Improv Olympics. I was interested in his work and asked him to explain improvisational comedy to me. I appreciated and learned from his explanations in spite of his persistently patronizing manner.

On one visit, after I was comfortably indoctrinated in The Pacific Institute program, we did some long-term goal setting. We discussed the importance of his self-talk – especially regarding his budding comedic career. I was concerned that he might be sabotaging his desired success by his insistence that commercial success was a sell-out to his art.

After two years in Chicago and having graduated from the Improv Olympics' training program, Rob returned to New York. He stayed with his mother and me until he found an apartment he could afford in Manhattan. He wanted to be in Manhattan so he would be close to opportunities to audition for acting, writing, and/or directing positions.

He finally found a three story walk-up he could afford – what most of us would describe as a dump. But he was still young enough and had a starving artist's attitude that it was okay with him. When he first moved there I helped him convert the one bedroom into two tiny bedrooms so he could get a roommate to help with the rent. Together, we also constructed a platform bed with storage beneath it. He and I seemed to have a pleasant, mutually respectful, adult relationship.

When working in Manhattan, I often met Rob for a cup of coffee or dinner. One day when I was bitching about his mother and my latest attempt to negotiate a divorce settlement, he asked me to take him out of the loop and quit complaining about his mother. I apologized to him and was careful in future meetings to talk about things other than the relationship with his mother and the divorce.

I, however, explained to him that one reason I divulged such matters was so that there would be no secrets that could create more problems. I had learned in 12-Steps the insidious nature of keeping "family secrets." Moreover, SG already demonstrated a history of talking about me behind my back and of sabotaging my parental instructions to Rob and Rachel. I was well aware of the innuendos, half-truths, and manipulative rumors at which SG, my mother, and Rachel were experts.

I was determined that everyone know everything. He said he understood, but said he still did not want to hear my version of what was going on. I conceded with the caveat that if he heard that I had said or done something questionable, he would ask me directly about it instead of assuming its truthfulness. This seemed to work for several years.

Over time I learned a bitter truth: my children did not have comparable concern for my well-being as I had for theirs. A painful incident highlighted Rob's lack of compassion for me. During a snowstorm I was stuck at Penn Station and called Rob to see if I could crash at his apartment in Manhattan, which I had done once or twice before after I had given him prior notice. He later told me that he had turned his cell phone off because he was in rehearsal. Hotels around Penn Station were filled, or asking $500 for the night, so I spent the night in a chair at Penn Station along with 100s of other stranded commuters.

Later that week I asked Rob for a key to his apartment, just in case I was in a similar emergency situation while he was in rehearsal or out of town. I assured him I would always call first and never "pop-in" on him, and that I would only use the key in case of an emergency. He said, "Sure, Dad." I reminded him twice over the next month when he was on Long Island, and each time he said he forgot the extra key. I asked one more time when I was in Manhattan, and he had some other lame excuse. I quit asking, and he never offered me a key.

I have never quite understood this. I grew up in a family where we had access to each other's homes. If you did not have a key, you knew where one was hidden. Rob always had a key to the houses where his mother and I lived even after he left home; and he knew where I kept a spare key at my apartment after I separated from his mother. Nevertheless, I excused him for not growing up in my family in Tennessee!

His snub, however, hurt me deeply. I thought I had a good relationship with Rob as a child, a teen, and as a young adult. I did not – and still do not – understand why he would not trust me with a key to his apartment. All I wanted was the opportunity to crash on his futon if I was forced in an emergency to stay over in Manhattan.

Trying to Build Family

In 2002 Joan and I invited Rob and Rachel for our first Thanksgiving after we were married. Rachel canceled at the last minute. Rob came – I paid the airfare.

Rob had recently returned from a trip to Kuala Lumpur, Malaysia. For two and one-half days he regaled us with stories about his trip. He gave us a tour through all the photos he had taken.

The night before he was to leave, we showed him our wedding video and talked about experiences in Las Vegas. Joan recalled an interesting time at a craps table. She remarked that a writer could get inspiration from the dynamics that develop and play out among the diverse people at the table. Rob verbally pounced on her, declaring that he did not want any suggestions from her. In a hostile condescending tone, he informed her that his friends knew not to give him suggestions about what to write because it would taint his originality. I had been on the receiving end of this ridiculous demand before, so it was not new to me. I knew it was a power play and just BS because he reads extensively to get ideas for writing.

Joan, however, was shocked for several reasons. One, she wasn't telling him what to write and wasn't even making any suggestions. She was sharing an experience that she had had in Las Vegas. As she patiently and kindly explained that, Rob sat up tall on the couch and became more verbally aggressive. He belligerently and accusatorily, demanded: "What are you trying to do here?"

At that point, Joan understood his game. She calmly and firmly stated that Rob had certainly changed the energy in the room and that she was going upstairs as she refused to be verbally abused. I, however, once again to my great shame, said nothing. I went into my shell and completely shut down (to be further explained with the Enneagram discussion in Part 3). In relative silence, I took Rob to the airport the next morning.

After several days of reflection, I wrote Rob a long letter. I told him he insulted Joan and owed her an apology. Also, he had insulted me by insulting her and I should have thrown him out of the house that night. I informed him that I would never again tolerate that tone and aggressive posturing and behavior toward her or me. Joan also wrote him a letter.

He replied to both of us with a feeble apology. He thanked Joan for cooking "him" good meals! I know Rob's craftiness: his way of letting her know she was no more than someone who cooked him good meals. Through his comments, he reaffirmed his rejection of our being family at Thanksgiving.

As things were coming to a head between Rachel and me, I was copying Rob with the e-mails from both of us, so he would be aware of what was being said: No Secrets! He also asked me to take him out of this loop and I did. The only exception was when I told him about Rachel's Mother's Day phone call and that I intended to honor her request and stay out of her life.

Remarkably, about seven months after Rachel's Mother's Day fiasco, Rob sent a blistering e-mail from of the blue. It was hateful. He listed my failures as a father and a man. (Apparently he had forgotten how he had extolled my virtues as a father and man in public at family meeting during Rachel's rebab.) He declared that my brother Joe and his family "that I admired so much," really did not like or respect me and that I should hear how they "talked about me behind my back." I had never heard such crap before from anyone.

That I was stunned by his unwarranted allegations and hostility is an understatement. I answered each charge Rob made in hopes of clearing up whatever was bugging him. His response was as derisive and dismissive as his original email. He then told me "... never to bother him again."

I replied that I would accommodate his request. I also explained that when he wanted to reestablish communication he would first have to truly apologize to both Joan and me. Unlike Rachel, Rob has never tried to weasel in the back door -- he's more like his father in that regard.

The Pain of Facing Dysfunction

It is disturbing that to get their way with me my children pronounced a conclusive ultimatum: "Get out of my life!" At the time I was in denial of a prevalent maladjusted attitude in my dysfunctional family: "shut-up and do it my way or there will be hell to pay!"

So, I sought to understand the irrational. Some of my thoughts were: Perhaps it is because I changed by setting boundaries and asking for respect for Joan and me and our marriage. Perhaps they just thought that by issuing such an ultimatum I would beg them to please let me be in their life and drop my request for respect, while they continued with their insults, lies, and manipulations aimed at sabotaging our marriage.

Regardless of their reasons, their removing themselves from our lives was a blessing. While the rejection was painful, they were not around to interfere with the early days of our marriage. Joan and I could focus on our relationship and each other without having to deal with their mean-spirited antics.

While I would like a mutually respectful adult relationship with my adult offspring, I know from years of studying psychology that they also need to sincerely want a mutually respectful adult relationship with me and they must make amends for their actions, words, and exclusions of Joan and me. My first approaching them would reinforce their dysfunctional behavior and my past dysfunctional tolerance of their insults, dismissals, and disrespect. Perpetuating and tolerating this dysfunctional pattern and relationship is not an acceptable outcome.

This "my way or the highway" attitude seems pervasive not only in the microcosm of my family, but in the macrocosm of the world. Bullies, it seems, are everywhere from American right wing political ideologues to Middle Eastern dictators and terrorist groups. I do not have the power to change these groups and their negative impact in the world. I can, however, refuse to tolerate bullying of my wife and me by members of my family. This is one way that I practice the motto of the Environmental Movement: Think globally; act locally.

So, I conclude this chapter as I began it, with a warning: My experience, observation, and research indicate that the more you change, even positive change, the more push-back you will receive from dysfunctional family members. I have many more examples but this book cannot hold all of them!

Self-awareness is required to recognize the dysfunctional behaviors we accept as normal. Strength and courage are needed to say "no more" and to set healthy boundaries. For those of us in recovery, failure to take these healthy measures keeps our recovery in constant jeopardy. I believe this failure is a reason that many in recovery merely survive or worst relapse back into addiction. Moving away from dysfunction is part of the psychospiritual growth that is necessary to eventually thrive.

Chapter 25

BEGINNING A NEW FAMILY – STRIVING TOWARD A FUNCTIONAL DYNAMIC

Opening to Love

Striving is not just working hard and overcoming challenges. It is also embracing blessings and exploring opportunities. It is about relaxing and moving into joy. It is about opening to love – and more.

I met Joan at the National Guild of Hypnotists (NGH) International Convention and Educational Conference in August, 2000. We did not know each other as we took a pre-convention course on ways to incorporate subtle energies into hypnosis practices. It was taught by the Dean of American Hypnotists, Ormand McGill.

A colleague, Judy, whom I met in a Neurolinguistic Programming (NLP) course the previous year knew Joan with whom she had taken the NGH Train the Trainers Course. She knew that we were both in McGill's course. She stopped by during the first break and told me that Joan wanted to meet me. She told me that Joan was on the mailing list for my weekly newsletter and that she really enjoyed it. At lunch break, she introduced us. It turned out that Joan had already attracted my attention as I thought she was the most alluring woman in the room.

Judy was meeting another mutual colleague and friend, Christine, after class and suggested we all meet after class for a glass of wine (coffee for me, of course). As the day progressed, I noted that not only was Joan physically attractive but also that she was exceptionally intelligent. She asked the most penetrating questions and accepted little on face value. (I later learned this was a by-product of her training as a lawyer.)

Judy, Christine, Joan, and I dined together that evening. Joan and I hit it off immediately. We enjoyed talking about hypnosis and our respective businesses. Later, Joan disclosed her interest in subjects like Numerology. She proceeded to "do my numbers," and I had to admit she nailed me quite accurately. There was one point where she was talking about my social aspects that she came out with what I refer to as her "naughty" laugh. It is like when a kid talks about a taboo subject to his friends. It was most endearing. Because we seemed to have a lot in common, it was at that point I cautioned myself not to come on to this woman and spoil a potentially dynamic collegial and business relationship.

Judy and Christine, however, decided to play matchmaker. The next night they arranged for us to go out to dinner again and for Joan to sit next to me in the car. Same thing at dinner: they made sure we were sitting side by side at the dinner table. At one point, when they were not around, I asked Joan if she was aware that they were playing Cupid, or was I imagining it. She laughed and said that not only were they doing it, there was no subtlety involved!

During the convention proper, we were both presenting seminars, ironically at the same time. We had agreed to meet after the presentations to compare notes. Both of us were flying high as our presentations were well received. I touched her shoulder and got a jolt of energy throughout my body that could best be described as libidinal. I jerked my hand away and noticed that she had slightly jumped when I touched her. I asked if she felt the energy. She said yes, but seemed to retreat if not physically, at least emotionally. (Much later I learned that she intentionally closed off this energy exchange because she was in the process of a divorce and had no intention of becoming involved with anyone.)

Over the next several days of the convention, we – quite literally – kept bumping into each other. It seemed like every time I took a break and headed across the lobby for a coffee or a bio-break, Joan would be coming the other way. We would always stop and chat, and never ran out of things to say. By the third day were both laughing at this recurring "coincidence" and agreed to meet for coffee and talk business before I left town.

What was supposed to be a 30-minute meeting turned into several hours. Regrettably I had to leave to catch the last ferry from Bridgeport. If I missed the ferry my drive time to Long Island would be increased by two hours. Joan and I hugged good-bye, and I got another shock of energy. I stepped back and looked at Joan. She felt it too. This time she smiled and told me to I should go so I could make the ferry.

On my drive and ferry ride to Long Island I could not get her out of my mind. Over the next several months we deepened the relationship over the phone and by e-mail. Both of us were moving slowly and trying (without much success on my part) to keep it strictly professional.

Later in the year, I invited Joan to New York for a week during the Christmas holiday season. I pulled out all the stops. I had a deal with a hotel manager in Manhattan: for a pair of Jets tickets he would comp me a room. I got a two-bedroom penthouse suite for three nights. (Joan and I had agreed there would be no pressure to have sex.) I also called a friend of hers and found out that she loved chocolate and roses, so I got plenty of both!

After three days in Manhattan we went to my little cottage overlooking Long Island Sound and I introduced her to some of the beauty of the Northport and Long Island. The weather was not too cold, so we were able to take some short walks on the beach. By that time, I had given up all pretense of "only a professional relationship." The week was incredible.

The Enneagram Excuse

Shortly after her New York visit I was looking for any excuse to visit Joan who was then living in Colorado. She suggested I might be interested in taking a weekend course on the Enneagram given by a Benedictine Nun, Sister Marion Belloti, the director of her Spiritual Direction program. She explained the concept of the Enneagram as a personality typing tool and its helpfulness for self-awareness. When I paused because of the Catholic Nun connections, Joan explained this was not the Catholic church of my childhood.

Not only did Joan and I have another wonderful time together but we were also beginning a journey that led each of us to become Enneagram Teachers certified by the Riso-Hudson Enneagram Institute. Over time the Enneagram proved to be the most useful self-awareness tool I have come across. It has been most beneficial to enhancing understanding of personal perceptions, behaviors, and reactions to circumstances. It has been an invaluable tool for personal psychospiritual development and for professional coaching. Hardly a day goes by when one of us does not bring up an Enneagram application. We have constantly experienced the accuracy of its descriptions of dominant perceptions, motivations, and behavioral patterns of individuals. For those in recovery it can be especially beneficial as it enhances the self-observation and self-awareness needed for psychospiritual growth. (*More on the Enneagram later.*)

Colorado: Moving to New Country

Not long after my trip to Colorado Springs, circumstances allowed me to move to there. I was doing some work for TPI at the Denver Community College, and there were multiple corporate executive coaching opportunities in that area. Joan organized a two-day peak performance seminar in Colorado Springs that went well. So, business-wise it made as much sense as staying in New York – where my corporate coaching gig had come to an abrupt end when the company was bought by another corporation.

Initially I had planned on renting my own apartment. As has become our custom, Joan and I openly discussed where we thought our relationship was heading. So, I moved in with her. We, however, made a pact that whatever happened to the romantic relationship – whether it lasted or not – we would remain professional colleagues and great friends. What a blessing this turned out to be.

It was a small apartment in a large complex located on Cheyenne Mountain. We discovered immediately that we could get along together and not get in each other's way – even in a small space. In hindsight we marvel at how well we did not get in each other's way.

We also took classes. I enrolled in the Spiritual Direction program at Benet Hill Center. Interestingly, Regis University, my master's alma mater, offered graduate credit for its courses. Joan was recruited by Sister Marion, the program director, to teach a few of its courses. This was a very invigorating time. We were getting to know each other on all levels: physical, emotional, intellectual, and spiritual. We were striving and flourishing.

England: Rejecting Old Country

In the early summer of 2001, Joan and I had the opportunity to go to England. Before moving to Colorado, I had met with an enthusiastic young entrepreneur from Great Britain, Jay (pseudonym). At the same time, a business associate (McD) and I were working on our third version of my online Virtual Coach business plan that I wanted to turn into a dot-com venture. The first two attempts had fallen apart. We needed an investor angel. Jay liked the idea and thought he could raise the capital in England. He seemed internet and computer savvy and initially came across as honorable. He took our business plan and my research back to England.

After a time lapse, he presented a proposal for me to conduct a three-day training utilizing my *5 Essential Mental Skills* program with an underperforming sales group in London. This was to be followed by executive coaching with the company's sales manager. The seminar would pay my expenses and then we could go up to Scotland and talk to a group of investors he had lined up. It all sounded great. His wife wanted Joan to come with me and invited us to stay in their home while in Scotland.

The seminar went extremely well. The weirdness began thereafter. On the first night that Joan and I met Jay's wife, she made some comments about his character that caused us concern. These comments were made when he was not in the room.

Things, however, seemed to progress smoothly. So Joan and I began to question if we had misinterpreted Jay's wife. We met several potential investors and checked out housing because the proposal included our relocating to Edinburgh for at least two years.

One of the investors wanted to run the day to day operation. I had questions as to his being the manager, but decided to hold them as he was not a key investor. After a fruitful meeting with the key investor, we all felt very positive.

Then my concerns were re-ignited. Jay was driving the car, the potential manager was next to him and Joan and I were in the back seat. Jay and the potential manager began to talk as if we were not there. They began discussing how, after a while, they could push me out and take over the venture – in essence just steal my research and my life's work. I was thinking about reminding them that we were in the back seat and could hear them, but Joan, sensing this, put her finger to her lips in the universal "Shhh" sign. They kept going on and on about how they could screw me over.

When we finally returned to Jay's house, he was all pumped up and telling his wife what a great meeting it was and that he felt the big investor was coming on board. I was confused and stressed. I excused myself and took long walk out into the country. I finally got tired and found a big rock to sit on and contemplate my next move. *Under stress I need solitude.*

After I returned, I sought Joan's counsel. We determined that forewarned was forearmed. Assuming the money came in, and since we knew what their overall plan was, we could cut out the rogue investor-manager and set it up legally where I could protect my interests. We decided to just be cool and ride it out, since it was our last night there.

At dinner Joan made some very positive affirmations about the future partnership. Jay's wife reacted in a bizarre fashion. Every time Joan said something positive, she took an opposite stance and declared it would not work. By the time we went to bed we realized that she was trying – for whatever reason – to sabotage the endeavor. Joan reminded me of the first night's conversation with her and then the bizarre conversation between Jay and the old guy in the car. We decided that the wife knew her husband was not to be trusted and was doing us a favor. We recalled the quote by Maya Angelo: "When they show you who they are, believe them." At that moment, I decided to pull the plug and have my business dream crash for the third time.

The next day, after we were safely back in London, I found internet access and e-mailed my web-master and my NY associate to inform them that the deal was off and to cut off Jay's access to the website. Shortly after this I came up with my *3 Head-Butt Rule*. (See Ch. 27.)

Back to the Future?

By the time we returned to Colorado Springs, I was in a deep funk. I was working hard putting on a positive face – faking it 'till I make it – but I was devastated. I was as low as I had been when I was initially fired from the Jets.

My work with TPI was sporadic at best. I gave up my position with American Airlines when I left NY, so I could not fly on the cheap any more. I had been turned down for several full-time executive coaching positions with corporations in Colorado. With my Master's in Psychology and training in distance education from National American University, I decided to look for adjunct online work to keep income coming in. I became certified by Colorado Community Colleges to teach online, but there were no courses available for fall 2001. Teaching on-ground was problematic because I would have to show up in class every week and would not be able to travel for TPI or anyone else.

These circumstances lead to another personal and professional review. I enjoyed teaching. To teach enough adjunct courses on-ground to make ends meet, I might as well teach full-time which also included insurance benefits. I began to search for full-time college jobs teaching psychology, but the school year was already starting. I also discovered that while my master's degree gave me some credibility in the corporate world, a PhD was needed to get a really good college position teaching psychology.

I had been doing all the right things from a positive thinking standpoint, yet I seemed to be going nowhere. I had learned a lot in the five years since leaving the Jets, but I was barely able make ends meet financially. I had not been able to pay Joan my 50% of the rent for several months. I was full of self-doubt and felt like a failure.

All this, of course, impacted my relationship with Joan. My divorce was not yet final. I had trusted SG to keep her word when she said she would sign the divorce papers. Later, I found out that she had told my cousin that she was never getting a divorce! She said this after the time she had promised me to sign the divorce papers and send them back to the lawyers.

Being a Nine on the Enneagram, I spent decades idealizing, defending, and making excuses for SG. It was a difficult habit to break, and Joan called me on it. I immediately got defensive. I projected SGs' manipulative and guilt inducing ways onto Joan who relied on my representation that I would complete my divorce shortly after I moved in with her. Even though I knew that Joan was trying to help me and wanted me to keep my promise, I could not stop my projections. Joan did not take it. Each of us realized that I needed to move out. I shut down completely.

The Lake

While living with Joan, she told me about her time in Durango after leaving her prior husband. She had spent six months on a mountaintop journaling, meditating, and reclaiming her self-respect and developing her spirituality. I knew that was what I needed: time on a mountaintop away from everything. Problem was, I was broke. I could not afford a week on a mountaintop, much less six months.

The closest retreat for me was my parent's cabin on Kentucky Lake, about 80 miles outside of Nashville. I reminded myself of some of the AA lessons about asking for help. Once again, I swallowed my pride and called my Dad. I told him I needed someplace without a lot of distractions to finish my book (*Develop the Winner's Mentality*). I told him I would pay him rent, but he said not to worry about that and we could work that out later. I could stay at the camp as long as I wanted.

It was a great relief. While I had some trepidation because SG had relocated from Dallas to Nashville, I knew the camp was out of the way for everyone since it was almost a two-hour drive on country roads.

Joan is *FOR* Me!

I hit another low point when I told Joan I was leaving. By that time, each of us wanted to be apart. I had totally shut down emotionally, like only a Nine on the Enneagram can do. However, I never want to hurt anyone, especially someone who had been loving, kind, and generous. She had also shown respect for my humanity and for me as a man even with my failings. The only other person I ever felt that level of respect from was my Dad.

One thing I learned about Joan is that she was – and is – *FOR* me. It was hard for me as she would "hold up the mirror" to have me reflect on things I said or how I was acting. When this occurred it was difficult to not suspect that she was not trying to manipulate me into doing something her way. I came to know that was not the case – but that was only in hindsight. It took courage on her part because she knew I might not be able to take it; but she also had the insight that I could not go on with the mistaken guilt about everything and everybody. As far as I had come – and I had come a long way – I still had miles to go before I got to positive health, well-being, and truly thriving.

Two days after 9/11/2001, I packed up a U-Haul, put my '88 BMW on a trailer, and headed cross-country to Nashville. Joan was in shock from 9/11; I had already been numb for weeks. Before I left, Joan stopped me at the door. I expected she was going to lash out and tell me what a rotten son of a bitch I was, that I should rot in hell, and so on. I thought I deserved that.

She did not do that. She suggested we pray together. I was shocked to say the least. My leaving had hurt her deeply, yet she wanted to pray with me rather than curse me or throttle me. While I may have been nonplussed, I will always remember her heartfelt good wishes. [Paraphrased] She prayed to God that I have a safe journey and that I soon find the peace I was looking for and deserved. She told me I was a good man and she appreciated her time with me. She said she would hold a space in her heart for my healing. I think she even said that we could be friends in the future. All I could say was Amen. And, thank you. (And I am not sure I said the thank you out loud.)

Charlie D Does It Again!

I was not out of Colorado before the full weight of that final encounter began to sink in. This woman, whom I had badly hurt and had projected SG's bullshit onto, had wished me well. She had actually prayed to God that I do well and be well. She promised that she would hold a space for my healing. This was a totally new paradigm for me. I never had that happen before. Hell, I had never even seen or heard that happen before. I may have read about it in some novel, but I never thought something like that could happen in real life. And, she meant it. I knew her well enough to know she meant every word of it.

"Wow, Charlie Dumbfuck, you really blew it this time! How in the world would I ever expect to find another woman with that kind of courage, compassion, integrity, and intelligence?" I had a debate with myself – some of it out loud since I was the only one in the truck – about whether or not I should turn around and go back. I could not reason out, however, why she would want me back. At this point I was an automaton. I was just going through the motions of living. I needed to find out who Bob Reese really is, or as I have come to call it: getting to *know who you am!**I felt I needed some solitude and simplicity to accomplish this.

*I recognize that "know who you am!" *Is not grammatically correct – that is on purpose. It makes it more memorable for my clients and students when I ask,* "Do you know who you am?"

Chapter 26

KNOW WHO YOU AM!

Who Is Bob?

When I arrived at my parents' house in Nashville my brothers, Tom and Joe, were there. After we said our hellos, they helped me unload my 54" projection TV from the U-Haul. I gave it to my Dad, who was suffering from macular degeneration, as rent for the camp. After the usual protests, he accepted it, and he really enjoyed being able to watch golf and football on the big screen.

Since I did not know the way, I followed my brothers to the camp. They helped me unload the truck and take it to a U-Haul franchise. After they left I began my "time on the mountaintop."

Time With Dad

The serenity at the lake was profound. It allowed me to get grounded and take a fearless self-inventory. The lake sojourn was also extremely valuable because I was able to spend some quality time with my Dad. About every other Sunday I would make the two-hour drive to Nashville and watch golf and/or football with him. There was no pressure about my work – or lack of it. He was just glad to have me there and I was glad to have time with him. We talked about football and golf. The only requirement was I was expected to fill him and my mom in on any "happenings" at the lake. They really missed living on the lake.

They had told me that the garden down the road from the camp was communal and I could help myself to anything growing there. Since it was fall there was little remaining. I was able to garner some bell peppers, squash, and tiny orange peppers. I told them that I assumed the tiny orange peppers were small bell peppers and that I got quite a shock when I cut into one and then absentmindedly licked the juice from my finger. I described thinking my head was going to explode it was so hot. They laughed until they had tears rolling down their cheeks, and I laughed with them. As they gasped for breath, they informed me that those were habaneras peppers – one of the hottest peppers in the world.

Spending quality time with my Dad turned out to be a very important component of learning *who I am*. I will always treasure those times I had with him. Later, when Joan and I went through Nashville after our wedding and on our way to our new home in Virginia, he gave us and our marriage his blessing. Before we headed out to Roanoke, he took me aside and confided that he thought I had "really married up." I agreed then and still do.

We visited again to celebrate his 80th birthday in October, 2004. He passed away that December. I still miss him. He was my first hero, and he remained so all my life. I have tried to model my life – especially my integrity – after him.

The Enneagram

Over the next few months at the lake I did not get much of my first book written, but I began to really come to terms with who I am. In a 5"x7" notebook I journaled daily using the 3-page method I learned during my executive coaching apprenticeship: I feel; I want; and whatever is on my mind. I also reviewed my old journals.

To deepen and broaden my personal examination, I looked to the Enneagram which I had begun to study in the Spiritual Direction program with Sister Marion Bellotti in Colorado. I read and reread Sister Marion's material that was primarily grounded in Richard Rohr's[44] work. I also purchased other books and attended seminars with other teachers of the Enneagram. All have their merits and were beneficial to my journey.

Analogous to AA's requirement that you acknowledge that you are an alcoholic, the beneficial and healthy use of the Enneagram requires that you identify your dominant worldview and acknowledge its hold on your thoughts, emotions, actions, and reactions. You identify your dominant worldview by honestly taking a self-assessment. (*You can take a free self-assessment, the RHETI, at enneagraminstitute.com*)

Concurrently, you must learn Enneagram basics. To begin, the Enneagram identifies nine distinct viewpoints or worldviews – nine dominant ways of being, feeling, thinking, and doing. Although they are numbered 1 through 9, the numbers *do not* denote any ranking or that one is more evolved than the others. Their most basic use is to illuminate how each of us defaults to dominant perceptual filters through which we interpret and approach issues, situations, and relations in our lives. From a psychological perspective the Enneagram also embraces the humanistic tenets of Carl Rogers and Abraham Maslow. That is, the goal is to integrate the healthy qualities of all the numbers to become a fully functioning person who is self-actualizing.

Fig. 1. The Enneagram

Figure 1 displays Riso and Hudson's[45] terms that summarize each dominant worldview. Brief descriptions of each worldview are provided in Appendix B. (More details on each worldview and levels of development are available at enneagraminstitute.com)

I often tell my students that the Enneagram is *simply complex*. That is, it begins as a simple personality typing tool and can progress to a very complex system for thorough self-examination and self-knowledge. Obviously I cannot explain all of the intricacies of the Enneagram in this book. If you are interested in exploring the Enneagram for healthy change, psychospiritual development, and moving towards self-actualizing, then the following three steps will get you started and the website at enneagraminstitute.com will provide plenty of needed initial material:

1. Identify your dominant worldview; observe its positive and negative influences on your thoughts, feelings, and actions, and ways to make healthy adjustments.
2. Identify your level of development and ways to move up the levels of development.
3. Learn about the positive and negative influences of the other dominant Enneagram worldviews and strive to integrate the positive qualities of each as required by the situations and relations of your life.

Identify Your Dominant Worldview

Each of us has a dominant worldview that has its particular perceptual filters which includes conscious and unconscious motivations, beliefs, fears, fixations, desires, patterns, weaknesses, and strengths. These constitute powerful conditions of understanding with roots in forces of influence (e.g., social and religious institutions, government, family, and community). They impact how we approach issues and challenges of our inner and outer worlds. Meaningful change requires understanding our dominant worldview and its influences.

From my self-assessment and study of the Enneagram, I learned that my dominant worldview is that of an Enneagram Nine. Nine's have a basic fear of loss and separation because they have a strong desire for unity – and thus strive for unity. In the Riso-Hudson typography the Nine is referred to as the Peacemaker (see Fig. 1). Riso and Hudson offer this description:

Nines are accepting, trusting, and stable. They are usually creative, optimistic, and supportive, but can also be too willing to go along with others to keep the peace. They want everything to go smoothly and be without conflict, but they can also tend to be complacent, simplifying problems and minimizing anything upsetting. They typically have problems with inertia and stubbornness. *At their Best*: indomitable and all-embracing, they are able to bring people together and heal conflicts.[46]

Identify Your Level of Development

After identifying your dominant worldview, the next step is to identify your level of development. Healthy change requires this step. The levels of development can be used to map how to progress to a higher level.

For each Enneagram type there are three broad levels of development: healthy, normally adjusted, and unhealthy or maladjusted. Each level reflects different characteristics and attributes of that dominant Enneagram worldview. That means a healthy Enneagram Nine functions differently than a normally adjusted Nine who functions differently from a maladjusted Nine.

As an active alcoholic I was functioning as a low level normally adjusted Nine. My first approach to looking at and dealing with situations was to go with the flow, deny problems and bad behaviors of others, suppress my related rage, tune-out, and/or mediate to keep peace and to hold situations and relationships together. I was blind to the fact that I was only encouraging further dysfunction and the worsening of the situations and bad behaviors of others – specifically my nuclear family.

As my alcoholism progressed I moved further down the scale into the unhealthy/maladjusted levels. Unhealthy Nines can be so disengaged that they appear indifferent. They can minimize problems (denial) and they often try to avoid conflict by engaging in addictive behaviors so they can "numb out." As I described earlier, when arriving home from work and realizing SG had been drinking, I would begin drinking to preemptively tune out her inevitable verbal abuse. Unhealthy Nines rarely have a strong sense of their own identity. They can stuff and stuff their resentments until they erupt – the eruption can be a volatile verbal rage.

Riso & Hudson Expand the Levels of Development

Over the years, Don Riso and Russ Hudson's[45] work proved to be the most helpful in my application of the Enneagram to mapping healthy development and psychospiritual growth. Most Enneagram teachers and coaches use only the broad descriptions of the three levels of development: healthy, normally adjusted, maladjusted. This delineation is sufficient to start the processes of self-examination and self-knowledge and to a general understanding of what is required to move up the levels of development.

Riso and Hudson, however, further delineate each of the above broad levels into three additional levels (Healthy: levels 1,2,3; Normally Adjusted: 4,5,6; Maladjusted: 7,8,9). This further delineation helped me understand more particularly what I needed to do to move up the levels of development.

The important point is that the Enneagram gave me insights into my own personality as I was experiencing more and more stress and disappointments in my life even though I was working harder and harder with good intentions. After working with the Enneagram and after much reflection, I finally admitted that I had been mainly operating at Level 6, a low level of normally adjusted, and steadily devolving to Level 7, a high level of maladjustment.

Level 6 (low normally adjusted) is the *Level of Overcompensation*. For a Nine this can result in downplaying of important problems leading to wishful thinking, minimizing problems becoming indifferent or even apathetic and increasingly stubborn, short-tempered and belligerent. As I was forced to face the reality that my hard work was not creating the success I envisioned, I moved further down to the unhealthy Level 7, the *Level of Violation*.

At Level 7, the Nine tries mightily to defend the illusion that everything is okay. I could be obstinate and willfully blind to my problems and at the same time felt powerless and inferior, which left me depressed and feeling like a doormat. If left unchecked, that could turn to hopelessness and potentially just giving up.

I recognized that I had been operating at these levels at the end of my drinking days. Now in 2001, after 10 years in recovery, I was there again. I knew that I could not afford to linger at these unhealthy maladjusted levels. I looked to the healthy levels (1, 2, 3) and to the highest level of normally adjusted (4) for individuals with a dominant Enneagram Nine viewpoint. I used these descriptions as a map for evolving my feelings, thinking, and acting: that is as a guide for my healthy development and psychospiritual growth.

Acknowledging that I had been operating at levels 6 and 7 was aided by the 12-Step program. My journaling was helping me be fearless in my continuing personal and spiritual inventory. At this time, it was less about who I may have wronged because of my drinking and more about learning who I really am and what I really wanted in life. I had to pull back the curtain on my "fake it 'til you make it" bravado; acknowledge my feelings of powerlessness and inferiority; and admit that I was in a depressive state. From there I claimed my right to be healthy and could begin climbing up the levels of development.

Building on my revelations from the Enneagram, I reviewed my main aspirational affirmations. I re-worded a few of them and made sure they were still realistic. That is, I could see myself achieving them. I read or created metaphorical stories that made them even more powerful. I created new hypnosis tapes/CDs to reinforce my affirmations, self-talk, and end-result visions. I edited them often as I learned more and more about who I am. I listened to them every night in bed and sometimes during my waking hours.

Honesty with yourself is mandatory for positive change. Honesty and change require courage. If you have been in recovery for more than a year, you have already demonstrated the requisite courage for these changes. So, begin where you are – you have more courage that you might think.

Identify and Integrate Other Worldviews

When looking at the Enneagram symbol (Fig. 1), notice the lines connecting specific numbers. These lines form a triangle and a hexagon, and they are referred to as the lines of integration and lines of stress or dis-integration.

Notice that the Nine, Three, and Six make up the points of the triangle. This connection is significant to these Enneagram types. As an Enneagram Nine I move toward the attributes of the Three for integration and toward the Six when under stress (dis-integration). So, in addition to looking at characteristics of a healthy Nine, I look to those of a healthy Three (The Achiever). Briefly, healthy Threes are self-assured, ambitious, competent, and energetic. They are diplomatic and poised and at their best they are self-accepting, authentic, and can be role models who inspire others.

Under stress, the Nine follows the line of dis-integration to the Six, taking on its negative attributes such as becoming more anxious and suspicious about pleasing others to keep the peace. At the unhealthy levels, I once again become sarcastic and self-punishing. (I can beat myself up worse than anyone else can.) Both the Nine and the Six share feelings of inferiority and helplessness and are depressed at these lower Levels of Development.

By knowing what to expect under stress, the Enneagram instructs me, the Nine, not to give up on my views and goals and not to default to those of others – for example, the family members who booted me out of their lives. By understanding the lines of dis-integration, being forewarned is forearmed. This is a very simplistic explanation of integration/dis-integration.

(To pursue further study of the Enneagram begin with the free materials available at enneagraminstitute.com.)

Tarot

Another tool that I use to get beyond my perceptual barriers is Tarot cards. Joan introduced me to meditating on Tarot cards for inspiring intuition and creativity. Before pulling a card from the deck, I choose a significant issue about which I want to expand my understanding. This issue is about something significant I need to know more about and need inspiration to go beyond my present understanding. I frame an open-ended question and release my preconceptions of my subject of inquiry. An example is: What more do I need to know to have a higher understanding of _____ (state the subject) so that I can proceed in a positive direction?

I then focus my attention on my open-ended question and my purpose as I shuffle the cards. As I shuffle, I enter into an attitude of being receptive and present to intuitive understandings and creative ideas and insights that emerge during my reading of the card that I pull. In this attitude I pull a card. I meditate on the card and my question. I then journal the intuitive understandings and creative ideas about my subject of inquiry.

Joan introduced me to noted Tarot scholars and books. We took a week-end course with cultural anthropologist Angeles Arrien, PhD[47], who greatly informed my appreciation for Tarot. Dr. Arrien made me feel as if she was speaking directly to me when she stated that our families often do not respect our humanity.

I also purchased James Wanless' *Voyager*[48] deck after hearing him speak at an NGH convention. To become familiar with the cards, Wanless suggests initially pulling a card for the day, reading about it in his book, and then journaling your insights. One thing I like about the *Voyager* approach is that it is mostly positive. I found it easy to identify with the different levels of meanings of the cards. As I read his book I realized how much I did not notice on the cards. For me this discovery was analogous to uncovering scotomas in actual life experiences.

After a while I interpreted my daily card through my own contemplation and then read the book's descriptions. I began letting my observations, circumstances, and intuition help me interpret the cards' meaning and application to my inquiry. In other words, why did this card show up in response to my inquiry. (This technique was encouraged by Joan when she introduced me to Tarot.)

In this way I began to appreciate the validity of my interpretations not mentioned in the book and their relevance to my inquiry. At the time I did not recognize that this Tarot practice was helping me to develop innate higher mental intuitive, creative, and intellectual skills. These mental skills are essential to observation – including exposing scotomas – and healthy decision making.

This Tarot practice taught me the importance of what Joan refers to as the Three Ss of Tarot: significance, sincerity, and synchronicity. When I sincerely ask a significant question synchronicity comes into play with my pulling the most relevant Tarot card. If I ask the same question in a different way or the same question on a different day I often pull the same card. This happens until I get the relevant message from the card. While it can be somewhat unsettling, even eerie, I learned that when the same card kept showing up, there is something more to learn from that card.

Each of us can develop higher mental, intuitive, creative, and intellectual skills. Tarot is one way to do so. When deciding to use Tarot, choose a deck that resonates with you. This can be a fascinating journey as there are many different Tarot decks.

Courage: Tangled and Dark

Journaling, the Enneagram, Tarot, and hypnosis were tools that I used to see beyond myself and to keep peeling back layers of the onion to learn who I am. Bonnie Raitt[49] has a song entitled *Tangled and Dark*. Quoting her lyrics:

> Gonna get into it
> Down where it's tangled and dark
> Way on into it, Baby
> Down where your fears are parked.
> Gonna tell the truth about it,
> Honey that's the hardest part.

While the song is about taking a chance and falling in love with a new person, it also sums up the difficulty of self-examination. Anyone in recovery for any length of time knows this difficulty. Building skills and the courage needed to "make a *searching* and *fearless* moral inventory" of yourself is challenging. Skills and courage are required to keep going down where it's tangled and dark – "where your fears are parked" – and to find the truth about yourself. That is, to know *who you am*!

The AA 4th Step – *Make a searching and fearless moral inventory of ourselves* – is so much more than the examination of conscience that I learned as a young Catholic boy. It requires going beyond identifying your wrongdoings (a great starting point though) and clarifying your values. You have to know your bottom line to healthily negotiate life. This requires both courage and stamina and is not a one-time effort. To be fearless, as Bonnie says, "… that's the hardest part."

The Reality of *Who I Am*! And Am NOT!

One of my first major self-realizations was that I am not a salesman; and I did not want to become one. When I reviewed my old 5x7 journals, a recurring theme emerged: I wanted structure, stability, and security. I actually craved structure, stability, and security. I also wanted the freedom to travel and teach anywhere in the world. I just did not want to sell myself or any products. My old journals were filled with pages regarding those themes. Now recent journaling with the benefits of insights provided by the Enneagram and other tools reiterated those themes.

Insight: while my vision of entrepreneurial achievement was a good one, it did not reflect who I really am. I now had a better understanding of me.

If You Can *SEE* It, You Can *BE* It!

Interestingly, these realizations brought other challenges, questions, and doubts. My questions included: Was I tamping down my original goals because they had not materialized? Was I intelligently adjusting and modifying my goals? Or – and this was a big one – was I quitting? I also re-examined the changes that I was not making. Once again, I was self-examining, and this time it included examining the efficacy of positive thinking and of concepts in cognitive-behavioral psychology and sport psychology.

Up until then, I made the mistake that so many people make: I saw success only as achieving the end-result goal. I did not appreciate what I had accomplished along the way. I had not acknowledged all my efforts, growth, and interim accomplishments as achievements and success. I had not celebrated that I had come a long way. With these realizations came insights for setting a new path. After I appreciated what I had accomplished, I could open up to even more! As the legendary basketball coach, John Wooden, said: "If you go as far as you can see, you will then see enough to go even farther."

Later, I concluded from my research that as long as you can visualize yourself achieving a goal that is from your beingness, it is realistic for you. From there I came up with the motto: *If you can see it, you can be it!*

I could see myself as a successful facilitator of a performance enhancement curricula that was relevant globally. (This vision was consistent with my facilitation of the Pacific Institute curricula.) My challenge with my own program, however, was with advertising and selling it. These are not my strengths and I had been expending an enormous amount of energy in that area. Also, while I love referrals, I do not enjoy much of the networking required to acquire them. My strengths are in designing programs, delivering them, and coaching those who want integrate those programs into their lives and enhance their special talents and strengths.

From these realizations I revisited an affirmation that summed up my way of being in life: "I am Progressive, Effective, and Authentic." I now created a story to accompany my P-E-A affirmation: People would be seeking me out like the tropical fish in Hanauma Bay did when I released peas into the water. People (like the fish) come in from all directions to benefit from what I have to offer. (See Appendix C).

My studies of energy and the energetic universe have also aided me. I have learned that when I am in harmony with who I *am* and what I truly want to do, the loving, intelligent universal life force energy supports my efforts. My reviews of my concept of the energetic universe, the Enneagram, and my journals helped me understand I needed to refocus my energy and my vision. I asked this very practical question: "What could I do that would use my love of teaching and coaching, that would give me some security and stability, and that would give me the freedom to step outside the organization to consult, facilitate, and educate anywhere I desired?"

I posed my question to Joe Pace while working with him on a large TPI contract with Denver Community College (DCC). He asked me if I had considered teaching at the college level. I had because I had enjoyed teaching at Katherine Gibbs in New York.

Joe came up with a plan that would benefit TPI's relationship with DCC and my career goals – a win/win/win. Because of my work with TPI and him, he was aware of both my teaching and administrative competencies. In fact, he had already appointed me as TPI's National Campus Coordinator for the Education Initiative. So, he suggested to the Dean of Academics at DCC that they create a full time position for me to coordinate the TPI roll-out, including teaching courses. It was to start with the main campus, but if successful in enhancing retention of students, they would roll it out to the other campuses. The Dean was all for the idea, but was not sure about budgeting the position. The energy, however, was now flowing.

I had worked with the strengths and weaknesses of the Enneagram Nine, improved on those by integrating the strengths of the Enneagram Three, and was now ready to integrate into an organization in a positive way as a healthy Six. I knew from my journaling and the Tarot that to be at my best I needed to adjust my vision of what I wanted to be in concert with who I am. When I brought my vision into focus with who I am, my life began to change in ways I desired and even better. I stopped working hard to *make* it happen. I began to *let it happen.*

On the personal side, I had kept contact with Joan. Each of us fulfilled the promise to remain good friends and great colleagues. I had occasionally e-mailed her with business questions and information; and she always responded professionally. While I still had a way to go to really discover all of *who I am*, I at least had pulled my head out of my ass and was able to apologize to her. I thanked her for her parting prayer and related how powerful and meaningful it was for me. We talked about the concept of "holding a space for my healing." I thought it was a profound act of compassion, yet did not really understand how it was achieved. I think this was the catalyst that allowed us to remain good friends, and eventually much more.

THE 13TH STEP
From Seeing to Being College Faculty

The concept of teaching at a college began to grow on me not only because I loved teaching but also because most colleges encourage pursuit of higher degrees, research, and even consulting. I began to explore and apply for faculty positions. I rapidly realized that most faculty positions in psychology required a PhD. With a master's degree my best shot might be an adjunct position teaching psychology. So I expanded my search to include faculty positions in athletic training education.

In late November 2001, I went on the National Athletic Trainers' Association website and came across a faculty position at a small college in Roanoke, Virginia: Jefferson College of Health Science (Jefferson). I applied a day after the application deadline.

Almost immediately I received a call from Mike Krackow, the Director of the Athletic Training Program. After he introduced himself, he asked me if I was the Bob Reese who used to be the Head AT with the Jets. While I was sure that my time with the Jets was the lead sentence in my cover letter, I said, "Yes."

Mike then informed me that, while I probably did not remember him, he had been a student AT at Hofstra (where the Jets training center was located) and that he had helped my assistant, Pepper, with player physicals a couple of times. He then asked, "Are you really interested in this job?" I asked him to tell me about it.

Mike explained that he was also Director for the Physical Therapist Assistant (PTA) program which was a two-year Associate degree program. He had created a 2+2 curriculum that would allow students to graduate as a PTA then spend two more years and earn a Bachelors' in Athletic Training.

I then asked him what teams I would be responsible for covering – every AT faculty position required 20 hours of work in the athletic training room. Apologetically, he informed me that Jefferson had no teams. He had arranged to farm his students out to Washington and Lee, Virginia Tech, and a local semi-pro hockey team. Upon realizing that I would not have to spend hours a day on a practice field or in the training room, I immediately informed him I was *very* interested in this job. I loved this guy's creativity.

I asked him if I would have time to pursue my PhD. He said "Absolutely!" He added that Jefferson would encourage me to do so; and, since he was the Director, he could arrange my teaching schedule around my graduate classes. In fact, he informed me he was in the final year of his doctorate in Education: Curriculum & Instruction at Virginia Tech, which was only 40 minutes away and which also offered some courses at the Roanoke Higher Education Center. When he asked if I could start in January it was an easy "Yes." We arranged for an interview about two weeks later.

When I arrived in Roanoke in mid-December the temperature was in the 70s. I knew that was unseasonable, but nevertheless it increased my positive feelings about the position. The downtown area of Roanoke reminded me of the Nashville of my youth. It "felt right" for me. I had come to appreciate this felt sense as a resonance that informs me when making decisions.

Because Mike had indicated that a decision might be made while I was in town, I anticipated an offer from Jefferson. Under these circumstances and because I had not heard back from Denver Community College, I called Joan. Trusting her objectivity, honesty, and ability to tap into the energetic realm, I asked her if she could discern which job would better serve my purpose in life. After describing what I was feeling and listening to me, she said she felt the Virginia position was most congruent with my needs and desires. It also felt right to me.

The interview was the next day, Friday. I was given a tour of the college and everybody I met seemed happy and engaged. I went through the formal interview process. We discussed my responsibilities and the salary. At the end of the day, Mike offered me the job. I accepted. I was to start the beginning of January.

I negotiated time to make several trips to Denver to complete the DCC project. More importantly I negotiated time to go to Salt Lake City for the 2002 Winter Olympics; I was still working with Adam Heidt[50], the luger. Everyone thought that would be great PR for Jefferson.

My goal of having a faculty position and being able to travel to coach and consult was being realized. Also, after taking the position at Jefferson, my life began to improve in all ways – to flow. I began to truly thrive!

Part 3

THE 13TH STEP – THRIVING

Chapter 27

FUNDAMENTALS FOR THRIVING

Flow

I have learned that when I use my strengths and am being my authentic self – who I am – things *generally* work well for me. That does not mean that everything is always positive or that nothing bad ever happens, it means the positives generally outweigh the negatives and things are relatively easy – they flow.[51]

The remainder of the book is about how I have incorporated and applied what I have learned in order to thrive and flourish in the world. While this book is geared toward those in recovery, these principles are ubiquitous. In fact, most of them are found in the relatively new field of psychology known as *positive psychology*[52].

Instead of diagnosing what is wrong with us and trying to fix us (bring us back to "a normal"), positive psychology looks at what is right and good about us and provides us with guidelines for improvement and well-being. Martin Seligman[53] introduced PERMA as a pathway to personal improvement and well-being. PERMA: P = Positive emotions; E = positive Engagement; R = positive Relationships; M = positive Meaning; and A = positive Accomplishments. A positive psychology approach to well-being strives to enhance each of these areas. Positive psychology also has three central concerns: positive experiences, positive individual traits, and positive institutions. Part 3: *Thriving in Recovery* focuses on positive experiences and positive individual traits.

Dark Night of the Soul

While it might seem odd to begin this section about thriving and positive experiences with the *dark night of the soul*, for me this experience was the beginning of my ability to thrive. I was introduced to the concept of the dark night as I listened to an audio tape by Carolyn Myss, *Spiritual Madness: The Necessity of Meeting God in Darkness*.[54] The dark night concept comes from St. John of the Cross. Myss describes the dark night:

> A dark night of the soul is when you feel lost, ungrounded and abandoned. Many people assume, and often mistake, the dark night for depression, or that it emerges into one's life following an emotional crisis, such as divorce. But a dark night will often enter a person's life in the midst of their most joyous time.

The dark night is also often referred to as the *Night Sea Journey*, here described by Thomas Moore:

> The night sea journey takes you back to your primordial self, not the heroic self that burns out and falls to judgment, but to your original self, yourself as a sea of possibility, your greater and deeper being. Night sea journey is a cosmic passage taken as a metaphor for our own dark nights, when we are trapped in a mood or by external circumstances and can do little but sit and wait for liberation. The darkness is natural, one of the life processes.

Myss declares that if you are leading a spiritual life, then experiencing the dark night is inescapable – INESCAPABLE! She states that "this deep and rich madness is an inescapable part of the contemporary mystical journey." Now, if your recovery is based in a 12-Step program, you know that the 12th Step refers to having a "spiritual awakening." To me, that presumes you will then lead a spiritual life. If you are leading a spiritual life and if the dark night is inescapable for those leading a spiritual life, then it is helpful to have some understanding of the dark night.

When I first heard about the dark night, I thought I had gone through it with going into rehab and becoming sober. That first year was hell, and so I naturally assumed that was my dark night. It was only after several years of slogging through my real dark night that I realized how dark – and long – the dark night of the soul could be.

In hindsight, my dark night began following an emotional crisis precipitated in part by the firing of Pete Carroll from the Jets. Notwithstanding the alcoholism and the attendant dysfunction, until then I believed I was leading a charmed life. My childhood was like the *Wonder Years*. Things I thought were terrible for me, like bad knees, turned out positive as they kept me out of Viet Nam. While I went to Purdue for Engineering, when I switched to Athletic Training I could not have been at a better place. Upon graduation, I became the youngest head AT in the country. Then I went to the NFL as an assistant with the Buffalo Bills and five years later became the head AT of the New York Jets at age 28. I had married my high school sweetheart and fathered two beautiful and healthy children. I had enjoyed working hard at my profession and promoting it. I was admired enough by my peers to be elected president of our professional organization, the Professional Football Athletic Trainers' Society (PFATS) and received the honor of *Most Distinguished Athletic Trainer* by the National Athletic Trainers' Association (NATA). I got to meet famous people and celebrities both in and out of football. I traveled to Europe three times because of my professional status. I had been a high functioning drunk! And while the first year of sobriety was the toughest thing I had ever encountered, it did not carry with it the depressive overwhelming weight of sadness of the dark night of the soul.

Myss describes the dark night as a "deep and rich madness." I went from that charmed life that protected me from my alcoholism and sustained me in all my dysfunctional relations, to one of constant difficulty. While the optimism I carried with me my prior 46 years stayed with me, life just became hard. Everything became a chore. It was truly maddening. Fortunately, I had my experience of recovery, the Pacific Institute curriculum, my apprenticeship as an executive coach, and my tools of hypnosis, the Enneagram, and Tarot to help me. I just kept putting one foot in front of the other – and that is a recommendation for anyone experiencing the dark night: keep moving forward.

Things had gone right for me for so long that the extended period of nothing seeming to go right wore me down to the core. There were times I pondered suicide, but I would not let myself dwell there. I told myself that only a selfish coward would take that way out and that suicide would also make me a world class hypocrite. By the time I moved into my parent's camp on the lake in 2001, I was just a shell of the successful person that I had always been prior to 1995. While I put on a brave and optimistic front, I was completely humbled and had tremendous self-doubt.

So, how do you navigate the dark night? Caroline Myss suggests you to examine your prayer life. She poses the following questions and premises to contemplate:

- Are you expecting God to solve problems that you should already have solutions to?
- Are you asking the Divine to take away the mysteries of your life, rather than trying to learn their lessons?
- The journey is not about controlling what you get, but embracing whatever comes.
- Realize that no matter which cards you are dealt you'll be guided to the lessons you need to experience.
- Your job is to master your responses to external events, not attempt to control them.

After contemplating the above, I incorporated two mantras as I navigated this night sea journey: 1) *Action relieves anxiety*; and 2) *What can I learn from this?* I repeated them often and followed their intent.

I also embraced Myss's advice about chaos:

- The moment you come to *trust chaos*, you see God clearly.
- Change is divine order, versus human order.
- When the chaos becomes safety to you, then you know you're seeing God clearly.

For me, Myss's advice about relating to *chaos* was in harmony with the Serenity Prayer which had also been guiding me: "God grant me the serenity to accept the things I cannot change; courage to change the things I can; and wisdom to know the difference." From this I learned to *let go* of the compulsion to expend energy on things I cannot control. The concept of letting go is incorporated into my *Winner's Mentality* curriculum (See Appendix D for a fuller explanation).

Also, I was familiar with chaos. The first experience everyone has being on the sideline during a NFL game describes it the same way: chaos. They are overwhelmed by the all the commotion, intensity, immediacy, pressure, and multiple levels of communication occurring simultaneously. The only way to navigate the chaos is to thoroughly know what the job requires and how to go about it in the most efficient way possible. After that, you can tune out the stimuli that are not critical for doing the job.

The great actor, Anthony Hopkins, said it best. When asked by James Lipton on *Inside the Actors Studio* about his is favorite curse word, he said it was actually a prayer. A Jesuit priest had once taught him the shortest prayer: "Fuck it!" That simple prayer embraces the concept of letting go and the overall message of the Serenity Prayer. That became another mantra as I encountered situations I could not control. *Fuck it!* Try it. It is quite liberating. It does not mean you do not care. It means that you recognize you cannot control the situation and that you have the wisdom to *let go* and not expend any energy trying to control it.

We also want to learn to let go of the need to be or feel comfortable. Todd Kashdan and Robert Biswas-Diener[55] drive home that point in their book, *The Upside of Your Dark Side*. We have to develop the ability to tolerate discomfort and dissonance. The Jets All-Pro running back, Freeman McNeil taught me much about the power of the mind to tolerate discomfort and dissonance. Several times in his career Freeman played with fractured ribs. Broken ribs are extremely painful. Not only do they deliver stabbing pain every time you are hit or tackled, but they hurt with every breath you take. Freeman never missed a practice or a game and never fumbled the ball when hit. He did so without taking shots or medication for the pain. When I queried him on how he was able to do this, Freeman told me simply, "It's my pain, Bob. I make it do what I want."

Now Freeman McNeil was talking about physical pain, but the same can be said of the psychic pain we experience from negative emotional states like the melancholy experienced during the dark night. Quitting addiction and maintaining recovery requires tolerating that pain, that discomfort, that dissonance. If you are in recovery then you can no longer drown, numb, or otherwise avoid that pain by drinking or drugging. In recovery you learn that you have the strength to overcome any obstacle life can throw at you. You not only have the strength; you also have the courage. So, just continue to put one foot in front of the other. Trust that it will get better – even if it feels like it never will.

Once you accept that you are in the dark night and are doing what you can to continue to move forward, how do you exit this madness? First, I had to come to understand that it was not my fault – it is no one's fault. It is not *your* fault, *BUT* it is your problem. Then, I learned patience: to patiently keep putting one foot in front of the other and to expect that, in the end, I would experience positive personal and spiritual growth. In this way I experienced the old adage: "if it doesn't kill you, it will make you stronger."

What is referred to in Tarot as a "tower experience" is often encountered during the dark night of the soul. For example, the Tower card in the Rider-Waite deck shows a medieval castle tower being struck by lightning and a man and woman hurtling head-first toward the ground. A common interpretation is that your world is going to be turned upside down and that things will not be the same – there will be chaos. Whether the entire dark night journey is a tower experience, or whether there are several specific events that qualify as tower experiences, there is a lack of control – and for me that was chaos. Caroline Myss insists that we must be able to trust the chaos. This requires the ability to let go – *Fuck it!* Those with control issues have a particularly difficult time at this point.

To understand how to profit and prosper from the dark night experience, you must discover *who you am*. Beyond being willing to perform a *fearless moral inventory* regularly, this discovery requires patience, setting firm boundaries, and practicing mindfulness. These tools will allow you to navigate through the chaos.

As soon as I agreed to take the position at Jefferson College, it was like the small dim light at the end of the tunnel became as bright as a cloudless sunny day. The malaise I had been experiencing seemed to lessen daily. While I knew nothing would be the same, I also knew I was on the right track. After almost seven years of trudging through the darkness, I began experiencing flow again.

Winner's Mentality: 5 Essential Skills for Enduring Success

In my professional and personal life as I went through the dark night, I also used the 5 Essential Mental Skills that I distilled in my master's project[56] and that make up the *Winner's Mentality Program*[57]. They are: Goal setting, visualization (and feelazation), energy management, effective thinking, and mental toughness.

Goal Setting

I am fond of the Yogi Berra quote, "If you don't know where you're going, you might end up someplace else." So, the first of the essential mental skills is goal setting – setting targets for achievement. In the *Winner's Mentality Program* goal setting is a six-step process: *identify* the goal, devise an *action plan*, *commit* to it, *act* on it, *monitor* your progress, and *attain* the goal. These are fully explained in *Develop The Winner's Mentality*.

Lou Tice tirelessly professed incorporating *end-result thinking* as you identify your goal[58]. Envision the end-result of your goal and then work backwards figuring out *HOW* the goal will be accomplished (that is you have to *see* it to *be* it). Tice stresses that you do not need to know the *HOW*, that it will become evident as your Reticular Activating System (RAS)[59] searches for the *How* once you have your sights set on the end-result. I have found that when you combine end-result thinking with the other essential mental skills you can actually *cause* your future.

Causing your future differs from *making* it happen. Using force of will and exercising control to make things happen may work occasionally – or in some cases like my own early life, quite often. But eventually you will run into that brick wall and all the force and control you can muster will not make it happen. In these situations, learning to *let* things happen instead of trying to *make* them happen becomes an imperative. From these experiences come the awareness that patiently doing what you need to do to move toward your end-result vision is how you can *cause* your future. It may not match up exactly with that end-result you originally envisioned, but hopefully it will be *Magis* – or even more.

When goal setting always employ Magis thinking. That is, leave room for the goal to be even better than you imagined. You can incorporate this into your goal setting by adding: "this, or even better/more" to your end-result goal. Do not limit yourself – be Magis!

For example, when I goal set for a life partner, I was initially satisfied with the concept of just being content. I surmised that if I could find contentment that would be relief of the misery I endured with SG. So I goal set for contentment – or even more (Magis). After Joan and I got back together, I realized a joy and happiness that was totally unimaginable when I initially set my end-result goal. My relationship with Joan is literally beyond my wildest dream of what a relationship could be. Hence, the need to leave room for Magis!

Visualization

Visualization is the second essential mental skill. To visualize is to create or recreate a picture in your mind. Visualization differs from daydreaming because it is purposeful.

Some people readily create an image in the theater of their mind.

Some people struggle with visualization because they do not actually "see" a picture in their mental theater. (I had this challenge.) For example, close your eyes and then count the number of windows in your bedroom. Could you actually see the room and the windows? For many years I could not. I just had a sense – a knowingness – there were three windows in the room. This knowingness, this perception, is visualization.

So, *everyone* can visualize. The exercise called *Go To Your Room* in Appendix E is one way to train yourself to visualize and create images. Practiced visualizers can also use this exercise for learning to take a third-person viewpoint as they actually see themselves performing an activity. This can be especially helpful for athletes to see themselves perform. Think about how valuable it would be to view your golf swing from any angle, and do it in your head.

Energy Management

Energy management encapsulates the maxim that we move toward and become like what we think about. Our thoughts have energy. I demonstrate this to my clients and students with the Paper Clip exercise. (Use Appendix F to experience moving a paper clip with your thoughts). We are energetic beings, our thoughts have energy, ergo, just as we can move a paper clip with our thoughts, we can use our thoughts to change and create (cause) our futures.

Energy management is also the basis of purposive goal setting espoused in cognitive and humanistic psychology and their offspring: the positive thinking and self-help movements. Purposive goal setting is a tool for creating or causing what we want.

Managing stress is also about managing energy. My experience, personally and professionally with clients, has been that managing energy is more effective than trying to manage stress. This makes sense because negative stress is the end-result of mismanaged energy.

I also found energy management more palatable terminology than stress management for sport coaches, especially team sport coaches. Most team sport coaches that have I encountered scoffed at the idea that their players might benefit from stress management techniques.

They often said, "If they can't handle the stress, they need to get out of the game!" These same coaches, however, would be enthused about teaching their team members how to conserve and better use their energy – techniques that some would call basic stress management techniques. (Over the years I witnessed a number of high round NFL draft picks wash-out because they could not handle the stress; no one was there to educate them in some simple techniques that may have allowed them to flourish.) Below are examples of some basic energy management techniques.

Shields Up!

The *Shields Up!* intervention helps to alleviate or prevent the stress felt when being demeaned or insulted. This technique is especially useful when you cannot get away from the perpetrator of insults (e.g., a boss, coach, spouse, parent, etc.), or when your immediate response is likely to inflame the perpetrator.

I devised *Shields U*p while working with a high school track star who was ready to quit track and forfeit a scholarship because the coach yelled at the athletes. First, I suggested she assume that the coach was trying to help the team improve, even though his method was counterproductive. Then, I introduced the concept of creating a semi-permeable energetic force field that would let in the positive information and repel the negative. Hence, *Shields Up*. She learned rapidly to activate her shield and to take in the coach's positive messages and ignore the negative ones. She taught the technique to her teammates, and they had a successful season in spite of the coach's yelling. She also started using it with her mother – whom she reasoned just wanted the best for her. She reported that their relationship improved dramatically.

I have also taught *Shields Up!* to numerous executives who have negative bosses, to clients in negative relationships, and to students struggling with authority figures in their lives. It works! While it is anecdotal, I also know it works because I used it with great success to protect myself from verbal assaults as I went through my divorce. So, if you know you are going to be in a situation where you are often put on the defensive, belittled, or made to feel guilty, just say "*Shields Up!*"

Practice the technique right now. Extend your arm with your palm facing out – like a policeman uses to stop traffic. Now, from your upward pointing finger tips imagine a force field emanating. This force field encases you in a protective bubble. Remember, it is semi-permeable; it lets in positive messages and repels negative messages. All you have to do to engage your shield is to hold your hand up and say "Shields Up!" (silently or aloud). The more often you engage it, the better it works. Since physically sticking out your hand can be off-putting, once you learn the technique you can engage your shield in ways that are imperceptible to others: e.g., simply lift a finger at your side and think *Shields Up!*"

Effective Thinking & Self-Talk

Effective thinking includes focus and concentration, breakthrough and creative thinking, the creation and use of affirmations, and positive-self talk. The most important component is *positive self-talk*. Lou Tice[56, 57], my mentor from The Pacific Institute, instructed: change your self-talk and you will change your behavior. This technique sounds so simple that many people do not believe it will work. But, as is often said in recovery: It may be simple, but it is not easy! Learning to monitor my self-talk and realizing the power of self-talk also helped me understand why AA sayings like "One day at a time" and "Take it easy" are effective.

Tice posits a *self-talk cycle* (see Fig. 2). In the self-talk cycle, self-talk creates a self-image, which, in turn, determines behavior or performance. The stronger the self-image, the more behavior reflects that self-image, which reinforces self-talk. So, changing self-image and behavior – e.g., improving performance – begins with changing self-talk. Use self-talk to strengthen a desired self-image. The self-talk cycle is a powerful feed-back loop.

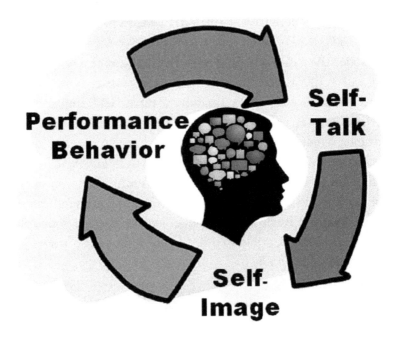

Fig. 2. Self-Talk Cycle

Self-images are stored attitudes, assumptions, expectations, and beliefs. Each of us have self-images for different roles in life – e.g., a self-image as a parent, spouse, sibling, offspring, student, etc. These self-images may be positive or negative and are constantly reinforced by our self-talk (thoughts and verbal statements) and by our behavior.

Self-images are tied to experiences and often to what we are told about ourselves. I use the example of the clumsy child to teach this concept. Imagine a toddler named Kevin tottering across the room and stumbling for no apparent reason. He falls unhurt. The father remarks, "Kevin sure is clumsy." That evening he reaches out and spills his milk, and mom says, "Wow, Kevin, you sure are clumsy!" Now, Kevin may be no clumsier than any other toddler, but if this opinion is repeated often enough, the child will internalize it. After enough repetitions, he will think, "I *am* clumsy." The opinion that he *am* clumsy becomes his self-image. His own self-image becomes a belief that he is clumsy. Consequently, the child will behave as his self-image—clumsy. Every time he trips or spills something, he reinforces his belief, "Gosh, I sure am clumsy!" This often spills over to others, even to friends, coaches, and teachers. So, Kevin grows up with reinforcing statements: "Boy, Kevin, you sure are clumsy, aren't you?"

Is Kevin doomed to be clumsy all his life? If nothing changes, the answer is "Yes."

Assume he is now a clumsy teen and everyone he knows thinks so. They even call him "Klutzy Kevin." I ask my students what Kevin can do to change. After several minutes they usually come up with some viable solutions like learning a martial art or dance as a means to overcome his clumsiness. Then I ask if that will "stick" if he does not change his self-talk? The answer is "No!"

Snap It!

The next question, of course, is what can Kevin can use to change his self-talk? A simple rubber-band around the wrist is one technique that can help.

Kevin, for example, needs to come up with an antonym for clumsy like graceful. If that is not macho enough for Kevin, he could use athletic or coordinated. The key is for Kevin to choose a word that creates and supports his end-result picture of being in control of his body, aware of his surroundings, and able to of adeptly navigate obstacles in his way.

Then every time Kevin does something clumsy – or even thinks about being clumsy – he snaps the rubber band on his wrist. As he does so, he replaces the negative thought with a positive image of himself by saying: "Stop it! That's not like me anymore. I am athletic, coordinated, and agile!" It is just that simple.

As mentioned earlier, it will not, however, be easy. The stronger the interfering self-talk and negative self-image, the more the creative subconscious will try to keep them as the primary self-image. Every time Kevin snaps his rubber-band and recites his positive statement about being athletic, coordinated, and agile, a little voice in his head will say, "No you're not. You are clumsy! You are Klutzy Kevin, remember?"

If, however, Kevin is diligent in his self-talk and augments a positive self-image with an activity that helps him improve his coordination, balance and spatial awareness, he will eventually replace his old self-image with the new positive one. Eventually, this new self-image becomes the dominant one and becomes habit.

The *Snap it!* exercise can be used for any change you need to make in your life. Positive self-talk has long been a staple as a sport psychology intervention for encouraging positive self-talk. Athletes in all sports use *Snap it!* NBA players have made it a fashion statement. I suspect the "cause bracelets" that have become so popular got their origin from the *Snap it!* intervention. So, *Snap it!* for a change!

I Am An Alcoholic!

Think about when you began your recovery. If you went through a 12-Step program, one of the first requirements was to admit you were an alcoholic (drug addict, etc.). When you shared at a meeting you introduced yourself as an alcoholic: "Hi. My name is Bob and I am an alcoholic." That "I am ..." statement is self-talk, which creates self-image, which, in turn, determines behavior.

It is not illogical to think that if I say I am an alcoholic, then I will want to drink. After all, that's what alcoholics do. With this admission, however, the alcoholic can realize a choice: I can drink or not drink. Remember earlier I talked about the compulsion to drink. When under the influence of this compulsion, there is no choice – I am going to drink. By admitting I am an alcoholic, I now have a choice.

Making this admission, however, leads to another challenge to those entering recovery: what is the picture of an alcoholic that they may have in their heads. If they picture a skid-row bum and they have not reached those depths of their alcoholism, this picture makes it hard to identify with being alcoholic and, thus, to admit: "I am an alcoholic." I know it was for me. I was a high-functioning drunk with a high-bottom; so I had to come to terms with what Bob the alcoholic really looked like. It took 10 days in rehab to recognize there were actually no skid-row bums in the unit. I had multiple conversations with several inmates I identified as high functioning alcoholics who were successful in middle and upper management positions. Two of them, a bank vice-president and a Lieutenant Commander in the Navy, had been given similar ultimatums from their organizations: get sober or get fired. As my image of an alcoholic changed, I was able to admit – and then say: "Hi, I am Bob and I am an alcoholic." Later, I used *Snap it* to create positive self-talk that supported my self-image of a sober Bob; and eventually as Bob who thrives in recovery.

If you are struggling with calling yourself an alcoholic, or if you have a problem with "slips," start referring to yourself as a "recovering alcoholic." Get a picture in your head of what being successful in recovery looks – and feels – like to you. Anytime you start thinking about a drink, then *Snap It!* and remind yourself who you now *am*: a recovering alcoholic.

The cognitive-humanistic theory that we move toward and become like what we think about helps explain the value of self-talk. Neuroscience with its modern imaging techniques also supports this concept. A basic neuroscience principal is Hebb's Law: Neurons that fire together wire together[60]. Each time we repeat and visualize the new self-image (positive end-result) we strengthen or reinforce neural pathways supporting the new self-images. On the flip side, the neural pathways to old self-images that fed your addiction begin to atrophy due to the lack of reinforcement. The new self-image results in desired changes in our actions and behaviors.

3 Head-Butt Rule

Another important intervention that came out of my struggling and striving years is the *3 Head-Butt Rule*. Simply stated: if on the way to a goal you bang your head into the same wall three times, you must back up and reassess the situation. This does not mean giving up on the goal. Reassessing includes determining how to go over, under, or around the wall instead of continuing to try and try to go through it. The 3 Head-Butt rule is the evolution of a popular definition of insanity: "Doing the same thing over and over and expecting different results." So ask and examine: What needs adjusting and modifying? My buzz-word question is: "What needs *adjustifying*?

I learned about the 3 Head-Butt Rule the hard way: by trying to *make* things happen. Sometimes I banged my head into the same wall so many times I lost count. The concept of the 3 Head-Butt Rule coalesced for me after the trip to Scotland where my business plan to create a virtual coach blew up for the third time. Some might call it an omen or a sign that I needed to change – and I suppose there is some accuracy to that viewpoint. I, however, came at it from an energetic perspective and decided I needed to either modify my goal or at least my approach to attaining the goal. As indicated earlier, the Scotland experience was among those that led me to consider going to graduate school and using the virtual coach as the basis of my dissertation.

I have found that employing the 3 Head-Butt Rule prevents the insanity of doing the same thing over and over while expecting different results. Invoking the 3 Head-Butt Rule in dysfunctional work or family situations – especially in families with alcoholism and/or drug addictions – is extremely difficult. The resistance and sabotage from others can be vicious. Hard choices may be required. Setting clear boundaries is a must. Enforcing them is essential.

Recall the incident with my daughter. I had ignored the 3 Head-Butt Rule as I constantly tried to coach her to overcome some of her negative patterns. After becoming aware that she was not changing and the insanity of going over and over the same problems, I put up a boundary that protected my time and served my personal needs. I told her not to call me on Friday afternoons and evenings as it intruded on my date night with Joan (the time Joan and I set aside from our work and pursuit of our PhDs). It was the only time during the week we could set aside for ourselves. Much like working in the NFL, the dysfunction in my nuclear family required that I be on call 24/7. When I held firm to the boundary of "no Friday intrusions" and would not answer her calls, she ostracized me. Eventually, she told me to get out of her life. She was in her thirties!

Recognizing these dynamics and having the courage and integrity to enforce boundaries can truly save your sanity. It is an essential step to being more efficient and effective and to thriving.

Feelazation.

Feelazation is the addition of powerful positive emotions to visualizations – including end-result goal setting visualizations. I came up with the term when I was working with players at the Jets for performance enhancement. Players would look at me quizzically when I used the popular sport psychology term of emotive imagery, even though I explained various ways to add emotion to their imagery. Finally, in frustration, I told one of them, "You know how to visualize, add some feeling to it: feel-a-zize it!" He got it and I've been using the term ever since.

When I first began to utilize feelazation, I had no concept of its true power. The more I included it in my hypnosis scripts and guided visualizations, the better the results. When I included it in the *Winner's Mentality* I said it rested somewhere between visualization and energy management. Later, as I had more experience and did more extensive research into feelazation for my dissertation, I realized that it is a stand-alone mental skill comprised of *positive emotive imagery, felt sense,* and *anchoring*.

Feelazation is more than the emotive imagery described by Shane Murphy[61] who had weight lifters lift their max, then get angry, and lift again. He showed that with the addition of the emotional component of anger they could lift more weight. For feelazation, the emotive imagery is always positive.

To positive emotive imagery I added the concept of "felt sense" described by Eugene Gendlin[62] in *Focusing*. Focusing involves identifying an emotion and finding it in your body; that constitutes developing a felt sense for the emotion. After my clients develop a felt sense for a positive emotion, they anchor that emotional felt sense with a key word or phrase and usually with a physical anchor like squeezing a fist or rubbing a thumb and forefinger together. (Anchoring is an NLP technique.) Anchoring a felt sense enables the recall of a mental-emotional state at will.

The more vividly you can visualize something, the more vividly you can feelazize it. In order to enhance the ability to feelazize I developed a *Feelazation Vividness Scale* (See Appendix G) to practice developing the felt sense in your body. Later I discuss the *Autogenic Training Meditation* (Appendix K), which is another tool to assist in feelazation. Learning to feelazize is a pivotal process that can provide a powerful assist in creating the change necessary to thrive. As with any mental skill, feelazation improves with practice. Moreover, feelazation dovetails nicely with one of the main theories of positive psychology, the broaden and build theory, which is discussed in the next chapter.

Mental Toughness (Grit)

Mental toughness is a common sports term. It is difficult to define, but everyone knows someone who is mentally tough – especially athletes like LeBron James and Serena Williams. People who demonstrate mental toughness possess persistence and resilience. They can keep going when the going gets tough and bounce back after a setback – or many setbacks.

Many sports coaches consider mental toughness innate, but, while it did not happen often, I witnessed several athletes learning how to become mentally tough. From my research and experience I have come to see mental toughness as a resultant from learning and integrating the other essential mental skills (goal setting, visualization, feelazation, energy management, and effective thinking) rather than as a stand-alone skill. Thus, mental toughness, persistence, and resilience can be learned and cultivated.

Grit is a positive psychology term analogous to mental toughness. Angela Duckworth, PhD, from the University of Pennsylvania is the best known psychological researcher of grit[63]. Her recently published the book: *Grit: The Power of Passion and Perseverance*[64], has in its title the word that is missing from earlier definitions of mental toughness: *passion*. It is the passion to be better than before that gives you grit. Without that passion, you cannot be mentally tough.

Duckworth agrees that, like mental toughness, grit can be learned. So do famed coaches like Pete Carroll who engaged Duckworth to consult with the Seattle Seahawks.

According to Duckworth, learning grit is a process. For example, when learning a new skill, first you try to do something that you can't yet do. Think about the first time you tried to dribble a basketball or hit a baseball. It was hard. Just like it was hard to learn to get through a day or a week without drinking or drugging.

Next, work at that new skill, using all your attention to master it as best you can. As you progress and in order to improve, you need feedback from a coach and your teammates to let you know that you are doing things correctly. In a 12-Step program, your sponsor is the coach. Or it can be your therapist, etc. Others in recovery are your teammates helping you along. Finally, you reflect, adjust, and modify to make the skill your own.

If you have been in recovery for more than a year, you have gone through Duckworth's steps whether or not you realized it at the time. If you have been in recovery for more than a year, you have the passion necessary to remain in recovery. You possess the mental toughness, the grit, the perseverance, the resilience, and the persistence necessary to change your life for the better. Just remember to learn from the past, and keep moving forward.

If you want to know more about grit and are curious regarding how much grit you possess, you can take the free Grit Scale at < http://angeladuckworth.com/grit-scale/>.

Chapter 28

POSITIVE EMOTIONS & THRIVING

Broaden & Build

The broaden and build theory was developed by Barbara Fredrickson who is the Kenan Distinguished Professor of Psychology and Principal Investigator of the Positive Emotions and Psychophysiology Lab at UNC Chapel Hill. The important role that positive emotions plays in helping us thrive and flourish cannot be understated. In a nutshell, the theory is that positive emotions appear to *broaden* peoples' momentary thought-action repertoires and *build* their enduring personal resources[65].

An easy way to understand this theory is to consider the linear nature of the thought-action repertoires of negative emotions like fear, anger, or disgust and their predictable behavioral outcomes. If we experience fear, we want to run. If we feel anger, we want to attack.

Positive emotions, on the other hand, do not have such linear and predictable thought-action results. For example, when feeling gratitude, we do what? When feeling joy, then we do what? There is not a linear thought-action or resulting behavior when feeling a positive emotion. Furthermore, Fredrickson posits that by becoming aware of and increasing the amount of positive emotions we experience we build up our positive energetic reserves; and, in turn, we become more resilient.

The importance of building up positive emotional reserves becomes more evident when comparing negative emotions to positive emotions in the context of focus, attention, and energy. During negative emotional experiences, focus and attention narrows, stress increases, and personal energy reserves are drained. This, in turn, weakens the immune system. During positive emotional experiences, the opposite occurs: focus and attention broaden and stress lessens. Energetic reserves are built up and enhance the immune systems which increases resilience and durability both emotionally and physically.

Even more importantly, in my opinion, is the ability of a reserve of positive emotions to *undo* the effect of the negative emotions. So, instead of experiencing the downward spiral toward sadness and depression that can accompany negative emotions, this *undo effect* can result in an upward spiral towards joy and happiness. It is like hitting the *undo* O button on your computer when you make a mistake.

The broaden and build theory explains why, in recovery, it is imperative to stay positive. It not only enhances resilience; it allows overcoming obstacles that may derail recovery.

How To Broaden & Build

Fredrickson's research has shown the science behind the old saying, "Stop and smell the roses." If we want to thrive in life, we need to stop and smell the roses – often. One of the simplest methods of broadening and building positive emotions is to savor something. The most common example of savoring is of food. Think of your absolute favorite food or non-alcoholic drink and then recall the last time you had it and relive that experience. I have my students savor a meal (or portion of a meal like dessert) and then they describe it in class in the most vivid language possible. Some of them close their eyes and drift into quite an ecstatic state. (See Appendix H; also refer to Appendix G).

Broaden and build research and savoring also provide support for feelazation and achieving goals. When visualizing a goal, find that felt sense of the positive emotion(s) associated with achieving it, and then anchor it so you can recall the positive emotion at will. In doing so you are building a positive thought-action repertoire from which you can reap all the positive results associated with it. To be effective over the long run savor, feelazize, and repeat often. This technique both broadens and builds resilience and overall emotional well-being; and it helps undo the effect of negative emotions.

Gratitude

The most important positive emotion for me is gratitude – in good and bad times. It is the default emotion that I go to whenever things are not going right. It enabled me to continue to put one foot in front of the other as I trudged through my dark night of the soul. Gratitude, quite frankly, is what has kept me sober over the years. It has taken me from just surviving in recovery, through striving to discern who I am, to thriving in life. Gratitude is the emotion I use most often to broaden and build my positive emotion storehouse.

Multiple exercises and interventions involving gratitude have been shown scientifically not only to broaden and build but also to increase enduring happiness[66, 67, 68]. One of the most powerful is the *Gratitude Letter*[66]. (Appendix I provides an example). It involves writing a letter to someone who had a major positive impact in your life, but whom you may not have thanked appropriately at the time – e.g., a teacher, a coach, parent, spouse, or significant other. The exercise requires you not only write the letter but also hand-deliver it and read it to the recipient. If you absolutely cannot do it in person, then you can phone or Skype the recipient. If the individual is deceased, you can go to the cemetery or mausoleum and read it aloud. My students always comment on what a great experience writing and delivering the *Gratitude Letter* was for them and how meaningful it was to the beneficiary of the letter. One student shared that his mother immediately grabbed the letter when he finished reading it, held it to her heart, and vowed to keep it forever.

Another popular gratitude intervention is the *Gratitude Journal*[67]. Reflect on the positive events (blessings) for which you are grateful and write them in your Gratitude Journal. Begin by listing three blessings a day. These may be as simple as being grateful for the food on your table, or witnessing a beautiful sunset. The idea is to realize the many people and things (blessings) deserving gratitude.

If you are utilizing the 5x7 Coaching Journal mentioned in Chapter 23, I strongly suggest adding a fourth page to the journal. That is: 1) I feel … ; 2) I want … ; 3) Anything that comes to mind; and 4) "I am grateful for …." Fill this page with blessings and those things for which you are grateful. By recording what you are grateful for you not only broaden and build positive emotion reserves you also get in the habit of paying attention to the positive blessings in your everyday life.

Be Present

Another key to thriving is the ability to *be present*. Experiencing serenity – a goal of 12-Step programs – requires being present. For me, "be present" was another concept that everyone talks about but no one tells you how to accomplish it.

In my second year of recovery I had the opportunity to scuba dive in the Florida Keys. I was on a very shallow dive, about 15-20 feet. Because it was a shallow dive, I was using less air which gave me more time under water so I did not feel the need to cover as much territory as possible (unlike my usual practice). I found myself hovering over a coral reef relaxingly watching the marine life. The longer I hovered, the more I noticed how much was actually going on. After a while I felt *true* serenity for the first time. There was nothing else going on. I was not thinking about the past or the future. I was consciously aware for the first time that I was *present* in the here and now. From that realization I then experienced an overwhelming sense of gratitude. Subsequently, anytime I want to feel serenity, I relive that experience in my mind.

Over time I realized that when I felt gratitude I also experienced serenity. I also began to consciously feel gratitude on a consistent basis, both spontaneously and intentionally. I have developed a discernible felt sense of it. I can now say that I live in a constant state of gratitude. I also naturally remind myself multiple times a day how grateful I am for my life. Sometimes, I close my eyes for a moment, take a deep breath, and center my thoughts and feelings on being grateful for something specific, someone, or on my life in general.

From a psychological standpoint I have learned that when I am in gratitude I am naturally present. So, if you are struggling to be present, be in gratitude. While in gratitude expand your awareness to how that feels mentally, physically, and emotionally – feelazize your gratitude.

Then, you will have experienced the feeling of being present and can return there often.

Mindfulness

Mindfulness helped answer my questions about being present: How can I reflect on a past experience and be present or in the moment? How can I practice end-result thinking, see myself achieving a future goal, and be present at the same time? Respectively, the answers are: by becoming aware that I am presently reflecting on a past experience and by being aware that I am presently looking toward a future goal.

Being present in the moment, or in reflection, or in planning for the future are often referred to as *mindfulness*. Jon Kabat-Zinn[69], one of the best known researchers on mindfulness states: "Mindfulness is paying attention in a particular way. On purpose. In the present moment, and nonjudgmentally."

Mindfulness is frequently associated with meditation; and meditation is a practice that enhances mindfulness. Meditation is not thinking about nothing; it is thinking about just one thing. Researchers have confirmed that individuals think more clearly after meditating [69, 70]. When you can still your mind and think about just one thing, it is like your brain says, "Whew! Thanks, I needed that!" And, we all need that.

(Audio files of several guided mindfulness meditations can be downloaded from my website: DrBobReese.com)

Compassion & Loving Kindness Meditation

Two meditations adapted from exercises developed by Lynn Johnson, PhD[71] are helpful to discern that *felt sense* in the body and feelazation. The first is an *Autogenic Training Meditation* (Appendix J) that I suggest using nightly for four weeks. Using this exercise, you learn to recognize the felt sense of feeling warmth and heaviness (or lightness) in your extremities.

Then, apply this learning to experiencing the felt sense of the emotion of compassion by using Johnson's exercise that he calls the *Compassion and Loving Kindness Meditation* (Appendix K). Compassion requires empathy with others coupled with a desire to help, especially to relieve suffering and pain. In this meditation spend a week feeling compassion and loving kindness for each of 5 categories: 1) yourself; 2) family members; 3) close friends; 4) acquaintances, that is people that you know but not well; and finally, 5) enemies. This is a 5-week exercise at a minimum.

I suggest writing weekly reflections on each category. My students' reflections are always positive. They report increases in happiness and overall well-being and a decrease in stress levels. More than two-thirds of them report that they continue the process even though they will not be graded or receive credit for their continuance of this practice. As a college professor you cannot ask for a more powerful endorsement!

Some people experience trouble finding compassion for themselves, even more than they do for their enemies. This is not unusual as most people, especially those of us in recovery, are so hard on ourselves that we can muster little compassion or even positive feelings for ourselves. If you find you are having a problem feeling compassion for yourself, begin with your spouse, child, or any friend for whom you find it easy to feel compassion. After experiencing the autogenic felt sense of compassion for those persons, then, you can more easily begin to feel compassion for yourself.

Compassion for self is essential! You cannot truly give to or care for others if you cannot give to or care for yourself. Your compassion for others must include compassion for yourself. Jack Kornfield[72], co-founder of the Insight Meditation Society and psychotherapist, stated: "If your compassion does not include yourself it is incomplete."

Emotion Differentiation & Regulation

Can you differentiate between joy and happiness? How about anger and rage? There is a difference between emotions but that difference can be very subtle. The levels within an emotional state can be complex. For example, what is the difference between pleased, glad, cheerful, and delighted? Or on the negative side: annoyed, irritated, cross, furious, and livid? Being able to differentiate the subtleties of emotions enhances the ability to regulate them and to broaden and build desirable emotions.

Studies examining emotion differentiation have been conducted mostly around negative emotions – especially anger. These studies show that the ability to differentiate the subtleties of complex emotional states improves the ability to regulate those emotions. That is individuals who can understand, clarify, and describe what they are feeling are more effective at managing aggressive tendencies associated with anger and channelling them into more positive directions.[73, 74, 75, 76]

A recent study by Kashdan, Barrett, and McKnight[77] suggests that, besides reducing psychological problems, enhancing emotion differentiation can increase various elements of well-being. The Compassion and Loving Kindness Mindfulness Meditation assists with discerning the subtle differences between positive emotions, for example love and compassion. Do you know the difference? Can you tell the difference in the felt sense of each?

Being aware of positive emotions *builds* them in your reserves. If you take the next step and work to discern the differences among discrete positive emotions, you naturally spend more and more time feeling those emotions. Discerning emotions is another way to broaden and build your storehouse of positive emotions.

So, if you practice autogenic mindfulness (see Appendix J & K) long enough, you will be able to differentiate the subtleties in the felt sense between emotions like love and compassion. Building a storehouse of positive emotions and the ability to undo the negative emotions associated with life's vagaries is a key component of thriving.

In *The Upside of Your Dark Side*[78] Todd Kashdan and Robert Biswas-Diener explain that being present or mindful requires a hyperaware state which is impossible to maintain 24/7. For this reason, a regular practice of mindfulness is needed in order to build our positive emotional reserves.

James Gross[79] tells us it is easier to regulate our emotions if, as we plan our day, we also plan how we will feel in advance about situations we are likely to encounter. Since most of us know what situations and individuals impact us positively and negatively we can use this information to prepare for those encounters. This is much easier than trying to suppress a negative emotional state once it has occurred. Barbara Fredrickson calls this *planning positivity*[80].

As someone in recovery you already do this in regard to your addiction as you avoid triggers – those circumstances, places, or people that make you want a drink or drug. Simply carry this practice over as you plan your day or create your to-do list. As you set your goals, add to that how you are going to feel during the pursuit and accomplishment of them. This practice will also give you a heads up on when you may need to activate *Shields Up!* Obviously stuff happens that can throw negativity your way, but you will be better able to adjust, modify, and persist as you build on your positive emotions.

The Value of Negative Emotions

Feeling negative emotions is neither good nor bad, right nor wrong. As humans we are going to experience negative emotions. For example, it is important to realize that feeling angry does not make you a bad person. In fact, negative emotions have value.

If you are in recovery, you know the value of negative emotions. How many of us would even be in recovery if we were happy all the time in our addiction? The sadness, the depression, the guilt and shame, the anxiety and fear that accompany not being in control of our behavior, the dread of losing a job, spouse, or family, such negatives moved us toward quitting our addiction. They can also help us stay in recovery.

Negative emotions cannot be avoided. To thrive in recovery, however, you need to understand why you feel down, angry, resentful, and/or fearful so that you can deal with them. Kashdan and Biswas-Diener liken the negative emotions to a GPS on the dashboard of your car giving you "metaphorical information about your location, the terrain in front of you and behind you, and your rate of progress." The negative emotions alert you when you are heading in the wrong direction and that you need to pay attention to the road you are travelling.

To thrive does not mean being happy all the time. Thriving means overcoming obstacles, learning from our mistakes, and, yes, enjoying life! Thriving is being a fully functioning person. This requires thinking, feeling, and acting congruently with a positive self-image that fosters realizing your potential.

Inside Out

Many alcoholics and addicts have a tendency toward perfectionism. For example, I vowed to be the best damn recovering alcoholic, ever! So, be careful not to judge yourself or beat up on yourself if you are not always being positive or the best. No one can be positive all the time – and it's okay not to be the best damn recovering alcoholic or best damn anything else.

Iris Mauss and her colleagues[81] demonstrate that overvaluing happiness, or pursuing happiness to an extreme, can actually increase loneliness. The 2015 Disney movie *Inside Out*[82] points out with its characters – Joy, Fear, Anger, Disgust and Sadness – that you need all your emotions. For example, to have Joy, you must also have Sadness. Some of our greatest moments of joy can follow a sad event. I cannot imagine anyone entering addiction rehab is happy about it. Yet, when we learn serenity and gratitude, we can experience the joy that comes with ongoing recovery. So, as they say in 12-Step programs: "Take it easy." There is nothing wrong with you if you are not wearing a happy face all the time. This harkens back to the necessity of including yourself in your compassion.

WIIFM?

Compassion for oneself leads to being selfless. Selfless is not selfish. Our culture sends mixed messages when it comes to thinking in positive terms about ourselves. While this is a problem in the culture-at-large, it was a larger problem in the alcoholic culture of my life from middle childhood into mature adulthood.

In general, as children grow and begin to do things on their own – like dress themselves – parents compliment them. They tell their children how smart they are and how proud they should be of themselves even if they have their shoes on the wrong feet and their pants on backwards. When children are complimented, their little chests well-up with pride in their accomplishments.

Somewhere in middle childhood, however, the tables get turned. In my case, if I was proud of getting an 'A' on an assignment and told someone about it, that became boasting or bragging – and that was unacceptable. Being raised Catholic I learned that if I took credit for anything – except my faults or sins – then I was selfish. That was compounded by the concept that if I did anything for myself without doing it for others first, then I was also being selfish.

I was introduced to the concept of *What's In It For Me?* (WIIFM?)[83] when I attended my first Lou Tice seminar as part of my peak performance expedition for Pete Carroll. I, of course, thought WIIFM was selfish. When I poll my students asking this question (What's in it for me?), 90% will always say it is selfish.

So, imagine a situation for which you have not made a decision. Now ask yourself, "What's in it for me?" Are you being selfish by asking this question?

By now you are probably guessing that the answer should be "No, it is not selfish." If you cannot quite wrap around that concept, then ask yourself, "If I help a little old lady across the street, what's in it for me?" The answer will probably be something like, "I did something to help someone, so I feel good."

What's in it for me? does not have to be about material things, like money or fame. WIIFM can just be about feeling good about yourself. It is good to feel good about yourself. Feeling good about yourself broadens and builds your reservoir of positive emotions.

Why are you reading this book? Hopefully there is something *in it* for you. Why did you stop drinking or drugging? Why do you stay in recovery? One of the first things I was told in rehab was that I had to do it for myself. I was told that if I wanted my recovery to be ongoing, I could not do it for someone else or because of someone else. It had to be for *me*!

In rehab the psychiatrist asked me about dynamics in my family and my profession. After I informed him, he told me it sounded like I took care of a lot of people. I did and I agreed. He then built on what the counsellors told me: I will not be able to care for others if I do not take care of myself first. I had to put my recovery first, and I did. But it was not until I heard about the WIIFM? concept that I was able to expand this into all areas of my life. It became another tool that I used often as I trudged through the dark night of the soul and into a life of thriving.

I come first: this is not selfish; it is actually selfless. It is selfless because when I ask that question, I am coming from a compassionate and altruistic place. I care about this person – Bob Reese. I want the best for him. I feel for him and with him.

This applies to all areas of life. Persons that care about themselves are not only healthier individuals, they are healthier friends, lovers, spouses, parents, employees, etc. In my thriving years, I have learned that when I am in my integrity, being congruent, and possess empathy for self, I can be that way in relationships. I have also experienced that healthy individuals want me to show up in ways that are nourishing for me. These individuals do not want me to "stuff it" and do for them without regard for my needs. In their wisdom, they know this is demeaning and likely leads to resentments and passive-aggressive or even aggressive behavior.

So, from my perspective, you should not do anything that has nothing in it for you. Why do you work? Why do you go to school? Why do you do any of the hundreds of things you do every day? If there is nothing in it for you, you need to then ask yourself, "Why am I doing this?" Understanding the WIIFM? concept allows you to set healthy boundaries. Recovering alcoholics and addicts know how necessary setting boundaries are to being sober and remaining in recovery. They are also necessary to thriving in life.

Now, there is a HUGE difference between asking "What's in it for me?" and saying "It's all about me." The latter *is* selfish and narcissistic. This attitude digs a dark hole in an individual's emotional soul that leads to misery and loneliness and that is a hole only the individual can fill. Filling the hole requires learning to properly ask and answer the WIIFM? question. With WIIFM? happiness and well-being are enhanced.

Focus on Strengths

Another basic tool utilized in positive psychology to foster thriving is focusing on your strengths. I did not formally learn about this technique until I was almost 15 years into my recovery. Upon learning about the concept, I recognized that I had been doing an analogous practice. I include the positive psychology format below because it has not only enhanced my thriving but I also believe that it would have been especially helpful early in my recovery.

The process begins with identifying your top five character strengths[84, 85] – your *signature strengths* – that can provide a pathway to thriving. You can identify your strengths by taking the free survey on the Values In Action (VIA) Institute on Character website: http://www.viacharacter.org/

After taking the VIA Survey and identifying your top five *signature character strengths*, reflect on each strength individually. You will probably notice your signature character strengths are the assets that you use most often to overcome challenges and navigate toward success. They are a huge component of *who you am.* While you may be surprised at the order, rarely is anyone shocked about their top five signature strengths.

Once identified, begin to work on improving and enhancing your signature strengths. This is a big shift for most of us because we have been schooled to focus on overcoming our weaknesses. While this has merit in many situations, many of us neglect to enhance what we are good at, our strengths. Focusing only on overcoming weaknesses and neglecting our strengths can be detrimental not only to our professional success but also to our ability to thrive and enjoy life.

Think about great athletes. They may spend a lot of time improving a weak part of their game, but they do not quit working on what makes them great. Basketball superstar LeBron James sought the help of Hakeem Olajuwon to improve his low-post game. While he may have spent hours a day working on new techniques, he did not neglect the skills that made him great – like his shooting. He continued to work on his shooting and has become more efficient and effective every year.

My five signature strengths are curiosity, gratitude, open-mindedness (which includes critical thinking), hope, and citizenship (which include teamwork and loyalty). Examining my signature strengths sheds additional light on why I was not keen on sales and why I thrived in graduate research, college teaching, and consulting. Sales is an endeavor that underutilizes my strengths. Effective teaching, on the other hand, draws on my signature strengths and on my intrinsic motivation to use them. They are who I am. I am best and feel authentic when I function in these ways. I work consciously to strengthen my signature strengths by paying attention to them and not taking them for granted. I enhance them by intentionally employing them in new and creative ways in the classroom, in my research, and in consulting – especially with groups.

Be-Do-Have

Another concept helpful for thriving is known popularly in the self-help movement as the *be-do-have paradigm shift*. Culturally, we are taught that if we work hard (*do*) then we will be able to *have* money, which will allow us to buy things, which, in turn, will allow us to *be* happy – eventually. That is, we *do*, in order to *have*, so that we can *be* (do-have-be). This is a deception.

When we learn to be present to build our positive emotional storehouse and to use our signature strengths not only is the deception revealed but a paradigm shift occurs: *be-do-have*. That is, we learn who we are (be), do from our beingness, and enjoy the fruits of our doing (have).

Studies in positive psychology have demonstrated that more money is not equated to more happiness[86]. They have shown that if you have no or little money, getting more money will increase your happiness but only to a point. After you reach a certain amount of money (currently about $75,000 annually in the U.S.), more money does not correlate with more happiness. The money can continue to rise, but the happiness levels out.

Gandhi is often quoted as saying, "Be the change you want to see in the world." Tolstoy said, "If you want to be happy, be." These quotes are both consistent with the be-do-have paradigm. So, be the happiness you want – now! Feelazize the happiness you want and find that felt sense in your body and anchor it. Revisit that feeling often and strengthen it. Make it a part of *who you am*. The best chance for thriving and happiness is being the person you want to be in the world. Then you will do things – even work – that you enjoy and that are meaningful. Be-do-have and you will thrive. When you shift to the be-do-have paradigm, you do not have to wait for happiness or serenity.

Chapter 29

FORGIVENESS

Forgiving is Important

One VIA Strength that I knew would not be high on my list of strengths is forgiveness. It came in as the 19th strength. Yet, forgiveness has been an important notion in my life. All the major religions proclaim that salvation requires love, compassion, *and* forgiveness.

The Abrahamic religions (Judaism, Christianity, and Islam) teach that we are born with Original Sin handed down from Adam and Eve. That is, we are born in sin. In psychology, Freud's concept of the Id builds off this creed. Indeed, much of Western psychology bowed to what Martin Seligman refers to as the "rotten-to-the-core" dogma[87].

Humanistic psychologists like Abraham Maslow and Carl Rogers and positive psychologists like Martin Seligman have disavowed the "rotten-to-the-core" dogma. I, too, reject this dogma. This position does not, however, disregard that there is evil in the world.

Alcoholics and addicts spend a lot of time on forgiveness, usually asking for forgiveness for transgressions due to behaviors while under the influence of alcohol or drugs. The 12-Steps provide a pretty good road map for asking for forgiveness for such transgressions (see Steps 4 through 9 in Appendix A). They, however, are not particularly helpful for forgiveness in other circumstances. Forgiveness becomes especially difficult for those in recovery as the person we often have the biggest challenges with forgiving is ourselves. No one can beat me up as thoroughly as I can for behaviors that I wish I had not engaged in – like yelling at my children.

Lou Tice was fond of saying, "We are taught 'Love thy neighbor as thyself'... we do – and that's the problem." Most people have a difficult time feeling compassion for and loving themselves. If you cannot forgive yourself, you cannot like – much less love – yourself.

Another problem of forgiveness for alcoholics is that we are likely from dysfunctional families and relationships. Many in our families or relationships do not understand what healthy forgiveness is. Many people say they forgive the alcoholic but then bludgeon them with reminders of what they did or have not done. The most obvious example in my family was my ex-wife constantly accusing me that I was never home, even after our divorce when she was living in another state! Even when she was living with another man! This allegation was also imposed by my daughter after she was an adult in her late twenties and living in another state.

Initially, I did not think I had a problem with forgiveness. I have always been a "live and let live" kind of guy and never actively sought revenge or retribution towards those who transgressed against me. That does not mean I did not find joy when someone who had slighted me got their comeuppance – I did. I also could harbor resentment for insults to me. I just never invested energy or industry in plotting or conniving to get back at someone.

I did not realize how much work I needed on forgiveness until I took Michael McCullough's Transgression Motivation scale[88]. I scored in the top 10% in both avoidance motivation and revenge motivation. I had never considered myself a vengeful person, but apparently I needed a lot of work in this area. Upon reflection, I began to realize that the art or act of forgiveness has always been a challenge for me.

Recognizing the necessity to examine this area, I turned to Joan. She had been on an extensive spiritual journey and is a spiritual director. She has a PhD in Human Science, has twenty-plus years' experience as a family law litigator, and was seasoned mediator whose work included high-conflict families. Additionally, she served on the Board of Directors for the Texas Association Against Sexual Assault (TAASA) and was trained as a rape crises counselor. Beyond this wealth of experience with people who might have challenges forgiving someone, she had also struggled with forgiveness for transgressions against her in her personal life. She had done her own research on the subject and given it much contemplation.

In one of our *morning conversations of marriage* (see Ch. 30 Relationships), Joan shared that in the rape crisis training at the University of Texas – Austin, she learned that sometimes *forgiveness is simply not seeking revenge.* This resonated with me. It is simple and to the point. In many cases, this may be all that is needed. In other cases, it provides a respite from the guilt of resentment or thinking about revenge until there is an ability to let go of any of the negative attachments associated with the transgression.

While I am still evolving on the subject, the following is where I am now. It is what works for me now. It is probably not the end of my evolution on the subject. If you are struggling with forgiveness, maybe it can help you.

Forgiveness Defined

There are numerous definitions for forgiveness. My concept of forgiveness requires letting go of the negative attachment to the source of the transgression and accepting that you cannot change the past. Laura Thompson and her colleagues[89] define forgiveness as a "freeing from a *negative attachment* [italics added] to the source of the transgression." This definition appeals to me because it allows the forgiver to include self, another person, or even a situation. It is one of the few definitions that include forgiving oneself. I also incorporate Oprah Winfrey's concept that that forgiveness is "to accept that the past can't change."

Understanding forgiveness also requires knowing what is *not* forgiveness. Forgiveness is not condoning; it is not reconciling; it is not giving in, excusing, or forgetting about; and finally, it is not a way to feel morally superior.

I expand on the above aspects of forgiveness below in the section entitled *Letting Go*. First though, why forgive?

Why Forgive?

Why do we need to forgive? Matthew 6:14-15 says: "For if you forgive others their trespasses, your heavenly Father will also forgive you, but if you do not forgive others their trespasses, neither will your Father forgive your trespasses." As mentioned earlier, forgiveness is required to go to heaven and for salvation by all major religions.

Scientific evidence also urges forgiveness. Studies reveal that forgiveness leads to improved physical and mental health and better relationships[90]. Studies show that the positive emotions of compassion and empathy are required for forgiveness[91]. So the act of forgiving itself, especially of forgiving oneself, becomes another example of utilizing the broaden and build theory to stockpile positive emotions and enhance personal resources.

Real Apology

Forgiveness often begins with an apology. A *real* apology requires an acknowledgment and understanding that an offense has been committed, an expression of remorse and regret, a sincere wish that the offense had not happened, a desire to make amends, and, if possible, making the amends. With a *real* apology the transgressor accepts not only responsibility for their action(s), but also accountability. With a *real* apology there is a transfer of power – of control – from the transgressor to the transgressed as the transgressor does not make demands on the transgressed. This gives the transgressed the space for the forgiveness to begin.

The transgressor accepting accountability seems to be the most difficult step in the process. The best demonstration of a transgressor's accountability that I have seen is described in a video of the Blue Angels precision flight team as they debriefed. Their standard is that when someone makes a mistake they need to "fess up and fix it." The "fessing up" is accepting the responsibility; the "fix it" part is the accountability and assures the other members of the team that the mistake will not happen again.

Transgressors almost universally fail to ask, "What can I do to make this right?" Without making it right, there is the suspicion that the transgressor mostly regrets getting called on the transgression and not on having done the deed. Without accountability there is no assurance it will not happen again.

In the world of addiction and recovery, accountability can be seen as the primary component of *tough love*. In tough love, firm boundaries are set and repeat offenses have real consequences. For example, in my intervention I was told to get evaluated for alcoholism and that I would have to do what the evaluators recommended or I would be fired.

Likewise, for self-forgiveness accountability must also be established. While others may forgive you for your past transgressions, only you can forgive yourself – and that requires holding yourself not only responsible but also accountable. That is, you must not only *fess up*, you have to *fix it*! You must do what is required to make it right, except, as it states in the 9th Step when doing so would injure the transgressed or others.

Non-Apology Apology

The non-apology apology goes like this: "Sorry *if* what I did/said offended you." What is left unsaid is that "I'm not sorry for saying or doing what I did. I am only sorry *IF* I offended you." The *IF* shifts the offensive conduct to the transgressed; the offensive conduct is now the transgressed being offended by what was said or done in the first place. So, the *IF* suggests that, by the way, it is your problem (perhaps even your fault) that you were offended!

I would like to say the non-apology apology is limited to politicians and celebrities, but it has become prevalent throughout our culture. Now, when people offer me one of these non-apologies, I point out to them that their "apology" contained none of the components of a *real* apology: I'm sorry. It's my fault (i.e., what I did was wrong). What can I do to make it right?

Be forewarned, however, if you choose this path it usually serves to really piss off the person offering the non-apology apology. They will aggressively and rapidly act to make you the "bad guy" for not accepting their non-apology. Some are emboldened to declare themselves the transgressed (victim), demand forgiveness from those whom they transgressed, and demand the original transgressed "fix" it!

They may threaten you in various ways and marshal other family members and friends against you. If you are in recovery, they may use language from the 12-Steps to try and manipulate you. If you have asked for a real apology, they may declare they are suffering and demand that you "fix it." You must be prepared to maintain your integrity, hold a healing space for them, and, if necessary, walk away from the relationship, even if it is familial. This is another reason it is imperative to know *who you am*!

Examination & Processing

Forgiveness requires examining the situation, whether you are asking for forgiveness or being asked to forgive another. You must look closely not only at the precipitating incident but also at its nature and the history of the incident and parties involved. This can get tricky. What is being forgiven? Is it an isolated event? Or is there a pattern of transgression or abuse? What is the nature and extent? If these are not ascertained, then how are the components of a real apology to be identified: that is what comprises accountability and responsibility?

For example, a close friend or family member can be very sarcastic. Her sarcasm can be funny, but the reality is that her comments are usually mean-spirited put-downs and slights. To keep the peace, nothing is said but resentments grow. Eventually the accumulated resentments combined with another transgression propel the victim to blow up and tell the perpetrator how awful her remarks are. Witnesses not familiar with the pattern will think the victim has overreacted to this one observed incident. The perpetrator will also try to isolate the insult to the observed incident so that the victim is blamed for losing his temper over a minor slight. Quite often the result of such an exchange has the victim getting blamed and apologizing to the transgressor.

This pattern is very common in all forms of abusive cycles from sarcasm to emotional, physical, and sexual abuse. This is why examining and processing the nature, pattern, and history of the incident(s) are important. It has to be broken down and examined thoroughly to understand the nature and extent of the transgression so that you can effectively respond and hopefully mitigate or stop the abusive cycle.

This flies in the face of those who tell us to forget it, let it slide, or just put it out of our mind and sweep it under the carpet. One problem is that people do not forget that easily. Another problem is that these suggestions only encourage more abuse by perpetrators and "preclude" forgetting. Moreover, not only do we not forget and put it out of our minds, we stuff it and resentments ferment. In this dynamic, when a victim blows up and apologizes for blowing up, the abuse cycle continues uninterrupted! If the victim happens to be an alcoholic, they may drink and this creates more problems and new reasons why *they* need to be forgiven.

As you consider the concept of stuffed resentments fermenting, it is important to recognize that the dark night of the soul is thought to occur due to a buildup of negative energy over a long period of time. All that negative energy that you have stuffed finally festers and negative events begin to manifest themselves due to this confluence of negative forces.

Whether you are in the dark night or not, you need to process your transgressions – small and large. You might say this processing is the crux of talk therapy. You share the experience and the emotions associated with the experience with someone who can listen, hear what you are saying, and feed it back to you so you can examine it further. Sharing at a 12-Step meeting can provide a setting for this dynamic.

I recommend that you not process with a close friend or relative because often they just want you to feel better in the moment and they likely hear you through their filters. They may listen, but they rarely hear you because they are so intent on formulating what they are going to say next. Quite often they can be dismissive and tell you that you are overreacting; that you should put up with it; or that you should just let it slide. This is especially true in a family where everyone is subjected to the same transgressor's offenses and has tolerated her over time. In fact, they will often minimize the transgressions and may even defend the transgressor. For example, if the mother of a family is extremely sarcastic and cuts down all the children equally, when you complain a sibling might say that you are just being too sensitive and "that's just mom."

So, while they think they have the best of intentions, they become invested in relieving the dissonance that you, and now they, are feeling. Then, they want to "fix" the situation by relieving dissonance, especially when family or a social circle are involved. Relieving dissonance is a band-aid approach that alone can never get to the core of the problem; it is temporary and only stops the immediate bleeding.

In the absence of a person you can trust to truly listen and hear you, journal about the incident and your feelings. When they come up again, record them again. Compare subsequent reflections with the original. This practice can open you up to a long-term view and approach to the problem. Be aware that if you provide the list to the transgressor they may accuse you of "keeping score" and put you down for that. Regardless, you need to process in order to respect your own humanity and alleviate resentments. Most likely the transgressor and other victims of the transgressor will be of little help to you and may act to deter your progress.

Processing vs. Rumination

Distinguishing processing and ruminating is important to the 13th Step. Processing is necessary as it leads to greater understanding of the situation, forgiving, and thriving. Rumination keeps you stuck in the same story and the status quo.

Rumination is repeated, aimless reliving the negative emotion and memories that further ingrains and imprints them. Rumination can impair critical and creative thinking needed to deal with problematic situations and people. It can drive away those who were initially compassionate and those who could help. Rumination can often lead to loss of confidence and even depression. Even when realizing a needed change, ruminators may not have the confidence to follow through. Ruminators get caught in a negative loop that, for example, keeps them in dysfunctional relations and exacerbates their self-blaming and belief that they must tolerate the situation or they are bad or unworthy.

Thus, it is important to develop practices to challenge and evaluate the negative events and relations that have been the subject of the rumination and that feed reliving negative emotions. These practices can include prayer, meditation, and self-talk improvement exercises discussed above. They can involve a personal coach, spiritual director, or healthy friend. The choices must be acceptable to the psyche of the individual seeking to change and thrive.

Processing is about changing how a situation is interpreted, experienced, and reacted to. This is also referred to as reframing. It requires critical thinking and creative thinking. Critical thinking, at a minimum, involves identifying limiting perceptions of the situation and uncovering, evaluating, and challenging assumptions of all parties to the situation, along with social constructs on which assumptions, statements and actions are based. Creative thinking is generating new ideas that have valuable and practical applications that help to change the situation and that further thriving.

Critical thinking and creative thinking take into account imagination and intuition. Together, these thinking skills strengthen the ability to identify and dis-identify from defensive mechanisms and fallacies that perpetuate rumination and psychological and emotional suffering. Defensive mechanisms and fallacies are common in our culture and, especially, in dysfunctional relationships. They are further described in Appendix L and Appendix M respectively.

Even armed with the above tools, processing a particularly painful event may evoke negative emotions. The good news is that processing helps to dissipate negative emotions which then serves to further elucidate the agitating event. So, when processing, acknowledge the anger, the fear, the embarrassment, the resentment, and even the hatred or rage that you may have previously suppressed, repressed, or subjected to one of the other defense mechanisms (see Appendix L).

Respect your right to have and feel emotions. Feel the emotion and recognize it for what it is: an emotion that you can heal and move beyond. Remember, emotions are neither good nor bad, nor right or wrong; they just are. It is what you do with the emotion – how you let it impact you and how you react – that is important.

Each time you process the situation, expect that the emotion will become less and less powerful. (If it does not, continue to journal!) When you no longer feel the negative emotion when reviewing the situation or incident, then you have probably processed it enough. Depending on the transgression, successful processing can take months, even years. So patience and courage are required.

Furthermore, it is not necessary to process in a linear fashion. That is, to process a particular transgression daily until it is powerless over you. That can actually be counterproductive. Process it, reflect on that process, then put it aside until it comes up again or a new or similar process requires you to revisit it. Also, if the negativity of the processing begins to bring you down, put it aside and feel gratitude for what you have accomplished.

Even after you think you have successfully processed a particular transgression, a reminder or similar circumstance may cause you to peel back another layer of the onion and understand the situation from an even deeper level. Once you have processed a transgression, you can then *let go* and move on. Remember, however, that you now have experience with healthy processing that can help you set and honor clear and firm boundaries.

Scientific studies and self-help literature support the above. From self-talk and neuroscience perspectives, rumination strengthens negative self-images and emotions and neural pathways that sustain them. Conversely, healthy processing builds new positive self-images and new positive neural correlates that sustain them. Processing is also a path to letting go.

Letting Go

Letting go of negative emotions is the core of forgiveness. Letting go is a process wherein the transgressed is free to make a realistic assessment of the harm done and feels safe enough to identify who is responsible for the transgression – i.e., the identity of the transgressor is relevant to identifying all negative emotions being felt and eventually letting go of them. This furthers overcoming feelings of resentment and anger associated with being a victim. If you are the victim in a dysfunctional relationship or situation it is critically important to remove yourself from the victim role and victim mentality because victims have no power[92].

So, letting go of negative emotions is a goal of processing the transgression. Interaction with the transgressor is not required for this process. In fact, it is usually not advisable as explained in the section entitled *Processing vs. Rumination*.

One practice for letting go is the Serenity Prayer:

> *God, grant me the serenity to accept the thing I cannot change,*
> *The courage to change the things I can,*
> *And, the wisdom to know the difference.*
> - Reinhold Niebuhr

Another effective practice for letting go is to give a negative emotion form and then throw it away. That is when you feel a negative emotion visually give it form and throw it away. You already know how to do this as you have learned the underlying techniques of the felt sense, visualization, and feelazation. This technique also helps you rid your body of negative emotions. Think about a situation which makes you angry – start with something that is just a mild irritant like the jerk that cut you off in traffic this morning. Recall and feel the emotion, for example anger. Then imagine a ball in your hand and infuse your ball with your anger (and any other accompanying negative emotions). That is transfer your anger and other negative emotions to the ball.

Some people actually see a stream of red anger flowing from their body into the ball. Others may see the ball change colors, size or weight. Still others may perceive this transference and change in the ball. Regardless of what you visualize and whatever way the transfer occurs, the aim is that the transfer of anger to the ball feels or is perceived as complete, then throw it away.

Physically go through the throwing motion and throw it away. The physicality of the movement facilitates reducing and even eliminating the anger. This technique helps individuals to let go of pain and tough negative emotions, including anger, fear, and resentments. Early on you may need to throw the ball with the negative emotions away multiple times during a processing session. Like any skill, the more often you practice it, the better you become at throwing away negative emotions.

So, if resentment, anger, or rage wells up inside you when processing a transgression, close your eyes, take a deep breath, and give it form. Visualize a ball and transfer the negative energy and emotion into the ball. Then, throw it away!

Sympathy, Empathy, and Compassion

Sympathy, empathy, and compassion are related, yet distinct, positive emotions. All three have a myriad of definitions. From my perspective, sympathy is feeling *for* someone. It is a feeling that carries wishes to see someone be better off or happier than they currently are. We feel sympathy for someone who has lost their job through no fault of their own or for someone who is grieving the death of a loved one.

Empathy is more complex. Empathy is feeling *with* someone. Empathy is perceiving, understanding, sensing, or feeling how the other is experiencing the loss of a job and its consequences[93]. It is altruistic in nature and differs from sympathy. It requires getting out of our own way to understand the personal experiencing (feelings, motives, and meaning) of another. A folk expression of empathy is "walking a mile in another's shoes." It can be feeling another's s pain. For example, young children are naturally empathetic. Recall a group of pre-K kids playing and one of them falls and skins his knee. The others gather around him and hurt with him – they feel his pain.

Compassion stems from the Latin for "co-suffering." Cognitively, compassion can be thought of as looking outside oneself and thinking about others as we interact with them and identify with their plight. In 12-Step rooms we are taught to identify with the speaker at a meeting and in that way relate what they are saying to ourselves. In this way compassion blends in sympathy and empathy.

Compassion is more active than sympathy and empathy. It makes you want to act on those feelings. This action may be simply caring about someone's well-being and respecting their humanity, but action is required for compassion.

Most forgiveness literature agrees that in addition to empathy, compassion is needed for forgiveness[94, 95, 96, 97]. Compassion for both the transgressor and the transgressed is necessary. Compassion clears the path to forgiveness. Transgressors who lack compassion for the transgressed bear responsibility for blocking forgiveness; their apologies lack empathy and are insincere. Remember also, your compassion is incomplete if you do not include compassion for yourself.

As transgressions occur we must choose: seek to understand the transgressor and identify reasons for the transgression, or let it slide and sweep it under the carpet or use other band-aid approaches (discussed in the above sections). The latter relieve dissonance and keeps us in denial of the transgression. If we default to "that is just who they are" or "it must be the culture they were raised in," they will likely repeat the transgression again and again. Or, more healthily we can elect to process the transgression to better understand the person or the situation. A benefit to seeking to understand is that we can experience some level of sympathy, empathy, and compassion for the person – even when they are not rational, logical, or possess any semblance of common sense. Once understood, we can let go of the pain, shame, or heartache that have resulted from the transgression. It is important to note that you should not let it go until you know what it is that you are letting go of and why you are letting it go.

Holding a Healing Space

Earlier, I mentioned that I did not fully understand Joan's statement about "holding a space for my healing." I first became aware of this concept when leaving Colorado. Joan wanted to pray with me. After wishing me well she said she would hold a space in her heart for my healing. I had no clue what this meant at the time. What I understand now is that she had profound compassion for me and *my* suffering. Through understanding compassion and by having compassion for myself, I came to understand holding a healing space and that led to a deeper experience of forgiveness for myself and others.

Holding a healing space for another is maintaining the feeling of compassion for someone. It is the ability to respect someone's humanity and wish them well without expecting anything from them. Holding a space does not require having continued contact with them and has nothing to do with the notion of reconciliation. It is heartfelt and means that you have no need for revenge. Holding a space for my healing is why Joan was able to keep her promise to remain good friends and great colleagues.

There are people in my life, some of them family, who are no longer close to me. Some have told me to get out of their life after I set healthy boundaries. Others have insulted me, attacked my integrity, or disregarded my humanity. As a teacher of psychology and a lifelong learner, I have sought to understand their motives. Rationality cannot explain such irrationality and hatefulness. Here is where compassion and forgiveness come to the rescue and allow for holding a healing space for them. I have compassion for them and I forgive them. I wish them well. I truly hope they have a wonderful life. And, my compassion is complete when I also have compassion for myself! In doing so I let go of any negative emotional attachments regarding them and my forgiveness is complete. I am also holding a healing space that includes me.

Reconcile? Forgive & Forget? Trust?

Reconciliation with the transgressor is *not* necessary for forgiveness. Many people erroneously think that they must "kiss and make up." There, however, is no requirement to reconcile with someone who has transgressed against you. The evidence of genuine forgiveness is personal freedom from a revengeful response.

Reconciliation and forgiveness are not interdependent. Reconciliation may only lead to more abuse by a transgressor. I agree with the Buddhist monk who said, "Tolerating abuse only invites more abuse." Moreover, God forgives our sins but does not eliminate all consequences created by our actions. After coming to these realizations, I began to readily see patterns of transgressions in my life.

I also do not buy into "forgive and forget." Forgive and let go, yes! But not forgive and forget. Forgetting is likely a recipe for disaster – it invites more abuse as neither the transgressor nor the transgressed have learned to think and act in ways that eliminate the transgressor's abuse of the transgressed. This conclusion is based on my personal experiences, those of others, and research. Some of these experiences are demonstrated by my personal stories in parts one and two of this book.

What about trust? Once trust is breached, it should not be readily re-established[98]. A renewed trust must be earned by actions over time. Here, Ronald Regan made a great point: "Trust, but verify." This principle is deeply understood by those in recovery or in any job that requires drug testing.

Virtues vs. Issues

No one can thrive in relationships where they constantly have to forgive another for repeated transgressions or where they have to seek forgiveness from another for their transgressions, whether alleged or actual. These are indicators of enmeshed, dysfunctional relationships. The lines between abused versus abuser become blurred. The responsibilities of enabler or co-dependent and addict are entwined in these dysfunctional relationships.

Who are the victims? Who are the perpetrators? Is the enabler of the addict a victim or perpetrator? What about the initial transgressor who abused alcohol or drugs in the past and who, being in recovery is psychologically and emotionally clubbed by others for their past drinking or drugging? Regardless, it is not a virtue to suffer these indignities.

Toby Rice Drews, author of the *Getting Them Sober*[99] series of books (GettingThemSober.com) likens suffering such indignities to a plastic garbage bag. Paraphrasing, she explains that we stretch and stretch to accommodate all the garbage that gets flung at us on a daily/weekly/yearly basis. The problem is we often 'pride ourselves' by thinking that it is a virtue that we can put up with *so* much. BUT, there is nothing virtuous about putting up with being harangued! It also invites more abuse.

This *putting up with*, however, is often a necessity to stay in a relationship. Because we are not willing to make the hard choice of leaving the relationship or because leaving does not seem to be the better choice at that time, we stretch and stretch to accommodate more junk. To avoid the toxicity of the garbage and to sidestep the build-up of resentments, we get into emotional trouble when we think (even a little bit) that it makes us "holy" or "virtuous" or "the nice guy" to have put up with harassment, abuse, or any degrading nonsense. Again, there is nothing virtuous about putting up with any form of degradation as it only invites more abuse – it will not get better.

We must ask ourselves: What is really going on? What issues – being insulted or abused – am I avoiding? Do I view my putting up with insulting and abusive behavior as virtuous? If so, then part of you subconsciously believes that you do not need to heal because we do not need to heal our virtues. Moreover, if we believe that our being virtuous is what maintains the relationship, we tend to strive to be more virtuous as our partner becomes more insulting and abusive.

There are serious concerns when leaving an abusive relationship. Those who perceive themselves as holding the power in the relationship – especially mental or physical abusers – do not accept changes without a fight. They do not allow the other to leave freely. In this case there are important concerns and questions, including safety. Are you emotionally prepared to make the changes needed? Are you able to safely make the changes? Are you able to do so in a way that serves your psychospiritual growth? These questions are important to consider and their answers will guide your preparations and actions. If you are staying in an abusive relationship, keep in mind that that the bag in which you are stuffing all those negative emotions will eventually overflow or burst.

Revenge

A chapter on forgiveness would seem incomplete without mentioning revenge. American culture supports the notion that if something offends us, then someone must pay for that hurt – whether real or imagined. The biblical concept of an "eye for an eye ..." is often used to validate this notion. Most people, however, want more than the "eye" of the transgressor. They want an eye and a tooth, or, both eyes! These individuals not only try to "get even" they want to "get ahead" of their perceived transgressors. A growing cultural trend is pre-emptive strikes by those who perceive that another will transgress against them.

Revenge is not necessary. Revenge does not foster positive emotions. It usually inflicts more emotional and mental damage on the revenge seeker. It is also said, that "the best revenge is a life well-lived." And, a life well-lived includes forgiveness, compassion, and respect for others and self.

In Sum

Taking in all the above, here are the main components of forgiveness

- Find out "Who You AM!"
- The first person you have to forgive is yourself
- You can't change the past
- For a *real* apology, accountability is as important as responsibility
- Learn to process – not ruminate
- Learn to 'Let Go!'
- Forgiving helps create positive emotions
- Cultivate empathy and compassion
- Hold a space for healing (especially for yourself)
- Tolerating abuse encourages more abuse
- Tolerating abuse is not virtuous
- Forgive – but don't forget
- Trust must be earned
- Forgiveness can simply be not seeking revenge
- Negative emotions can have value
- A life well-lived includes forgiveness, compassion, and respect for others and self
- Reinforce "Who You AM!"

With that in mind, here is how I handle forgiveness for those who have seriously transgressed against me:

- I develop unconditional acceptance for the transgressor to be who they *AM* – to follow their own path. I hold a space in my heart for their healing and I respect their humanity.

- I have unconditional acceptance of *me*. I hold a healing space for myself and I, too, can go my own way. I respect my humanity.
- With this concept: nothing is 'owed' to anyone; they don't owe me and I don't owe them. I let go.
- My message to them is: "Bless you. Go and have a happy and prosperous life."

Chapter 30

RELATIONSHIPS

Positive Relationships

Positive relationships make up the "R" in Seligman's PERMA[100]. While he is referring to all types of relationships – romantic, familial, friendships, social, and business – I want to primarily focus on romantic (love) relationships. Romantic relationships can give us the most joy and the most pain.

Unfortunately, many love relationships become tepid. With all the pressures of life, work, and raising children, the "love" portion of the relationship often becomes more of a duty or responsibility. Then, each partner in the relationships tends to emulate what was learned in their families of origins. The problem is, as mentioned earlier, 96% of all families are to some degree dysfunctional and the needs of individuals are ignored[101].

So, after recognizing dysfunctional patterns of interacting, going through a recovery program, identifying your Enneagram viewpoints, and doing other exercises suggested above, what can be done to create a healthy relationship that encourages the psychospiritual growth of both parties? To begin, Robert Sternberg[102] postulated that there are three primary components to a love relationship: passion, intimacy, and commitment.

Early in a romantic relationship passion rules. The partners cannot keep their hands off of each other and usually there is a lot of sex. The flame of passion of this falling in love stage, however, usually cannot burn at this intensity for extended periods.

In healthy relationships intimacy is the next stage. Intimacy involves the sharing of your feelings, hopes, dreams, and even secrets. Intimacy requires really getting to know one another and what each partner stands for. Breaking up after intimacy has been realized intensifies feelings of betrayal because of the sharing of those intimate feelings. Intimacy in the sexual sense becomes actually *making* love versus having sex. (I can't really describe this, but you will know it when it occurs!)

Assuming the partners are able to have a robust intimate relationship, they will most likely move into the commitment phase. This is where they express their dedication, devotion, and loyalty to one another – above all others. In our society, this generally takes the form of marriage, but can be any form of committed partnership.

The commitment stage is change not only for the couple, but also for their families of origin and close friends. This change becomes even more of a challenge for those from dysfunctional families where secrets, distrust, and quashing of feelings have held sway over family members. *Notice these are the same challenges facing ongoing recovery.*

If the marriage is a subsequent marriage, there can be even greater challenges involving children from the previous relationship. The dissonance extends beyond minor children living in the home to adult children. While children living at home, especially teens, can act out dramatically, adult children can also act out. Teen or adult children can undermine or outright sabotage a relationship where the partners do not possess a healthy knowledge of themselves and are unable to set firm boundaries.

Unsurprisingly, this acting out and sabotage in dysfunctional families can include members who have not been in close contact or close relationships with either of the parties – e.g., grandparents, aunts, uncles, and ex-spouses. It is analogous to the dog that buries a bone and forgets about it until another dog starts digging up the bone. The first dog rushes in to chase the second dog away from the bone. Said another way, this dynamic is like being pulled back into the preverbal barrel of crabs: that is where the crabs in the barrel attempt to pull down any crab trying to escape the barrel. At times of change, dysfunctional family members work mightily to protect "their bones" and to keep all the crabs in the barrel. Statistics show that many of us are up against dysfunctional families who lay claim to us as we change.

So the couple needs to establish healthy boundaries for their interactions with these people. As said before, each person must know *who they am* and they must design their relationship. The majority of time in a romantic relationship should be joyous; so this requires probing important questions like what promotes joy in this love relationship? For those from divorced and dysfunctional families this is a new question that must be answered by the partners. Then the couple needs to establish healthy bottom lines that will not allow those crabs or dogs to undermine their joy or define their relationship.

Respect

In my relationship classes students make a list of at least 10 positive qualities they want in their mate. I tell them to ignore physical traits because they will not be attracted to someone they find unattractive, so there is no sense spending time on listing height, color of hair or eyes, etc. Then I go around the class asking for the #1 most important quality on their list's. From semester to semester, the list is very similar. The #1 quality is usually one of the following: honesty, sense of humor, responsible (willing to work, hard-working), trust, love, and communication. One quality that is often left off the #1 list is *respect*. When I point out this missing component, everyone agrees it is important. I emphasize the point by moving it to the top of the list.

Why is respect the #1 quality? Without respect, none of the others on the list will work or make a difference. Without it, qualities like honesty, trust, and accountability for harmful actions and/or words will falter. Without respect, passion, intimacy and commitment cannot be sustained. Without mutual respect for each other, decision making is not shared. Without it, one seeks to dominant the other and unilaterally define the relationship. Without respect, the relationship collapses.

Respect is the key to intimacy. It requires both partners to value each other and their relationship; to accept each other for who they are; to appreciate what the other thinks, feels and does (empathy); to have compassion for the other; to be supportive and want the best for the other; to want the relationship to be mutually beneficial; to be able to talk openly and truthfully; and to be free to be vulnerable, honest, and trusting with each other. Respect is each partner being free to maintain their sense of self, beliefs, and goals. Respect is not isolating your partner and demanding that they change to satisfy your wants or demands.

Contempt

Lack of respect and inequality in relationship can rapidly lead to contempt: not only by the less dominant partner but also by the dominant partner. Contempt is indifference or disdain for others. It is a combination of anger and disgust. Its genesis lies in the perception that someone is inferior or just generally unworthy of respect or compassion. The philosopher Robert Solomon[103] says contempt degrades someone as subhuman.

Contempt is the polar opposite of empathy. Contempt is arrogant, even narcissistic. If you are held in contempt by someone, they disregard you, dismiss you, and often denigrate you – and anything you have to say. Contempt may be subtle or overt. For example, it can be as nonchalant as an eye roll or as obvious as a sneer where one side of the upper lip or one corner of the mouth is raised. It can begin with sarcasm and escalate to blatant put-downs, belittling, and guilt-tripping. Regardless of how contempt is displayed there is a break in the flow of conversation or dialog. You are rejected. You do not matter – only what you do for them matters. And, of course, you are not appreciated.

Like resentment, contempt is insidious. Samuel Johnson said, "Contempt is a kind of gangrene, which if it seizes one part of a character it corrupts all the rest by degrees." I look at it as a cancer in a relationship because, unlike gangrene, the toxic effects are not always seen as the cancer grows and grows until it metastasizes.

If you partner is contemptuous you need to recognize that they are not respecting your humanity and may even view you as subhuman. They are highly unlikely to ever truly forgive you for transgressions, even if they say they have. Their contemptuous attitudes must be healed before empathy, compassion, forgiveness is possible.

Being the recipient of another's contempt does not mean you did anything wrong. It is about them. It may have to do with their own lack of self-esteem, self-worth, or just their need to feel superior and in control. From my experience, if your partner is regularly contemptuous of you, the relationship is not worth salvaging. And this is true of all relationships, not only romantic ones.

Stereotypes & Nice-to-Nasty Ratio

Buying into stereotypes erodes respect and leads to contempt in a relationship. Healthy relationships require rejecting negative stereotypes that inundate our culture, especially those about men and women's roles in marriage. Reject notions like "the old ball and chain" (wives hold husbands back from what they really want) or "all men are pigs" (generalization that men treat women badly and are slobs). This is difficult because of the profundity of most sitcoms and TV ads portraying men as profoundly stupid beings only capable of drinking beer and watching sports. Similarly, many dramas still portray women as manipulative, helpless, and/or needy. The above stereotypes are good areas to practice your positive self-talk in order to disavow a negative stereotype.

Recently I walked in on small group of male colleagues who were sharing some of their negative stereotypical experiences regarding marriage with a young colleague who was just celebrating his first anniversary. After listening to several "this is what you can expect ..." examples, someone said, "Isn't that right, Reese?" I just shook my head and said, "No, that's not been my experience." (I had been happily married to Joan for more than 12 years at the time.)

These guys summarily dismissed me with some negative comment about "you psychology guys," but I did not allow myself to be drawn in to agreeing with the negative stereotype. Later the young professor came to my office and thanked me because he said he was beginning to think maybe all marriages were miserable. He said that he could not be happier in his marriage. I suggested that he not allow anyone to rain on his parade.

John Gottman[104], a psychologist specializing in relationships, says you need to maintain a 5:1 ratio of positive interactions to negative interactions to have a happy marriage. *Psychology Today* blogger J. Buri refers to this as the *Nice-to-Nasty Ratio*[105] and suggests modeling the Henry Roth (Adam Sandler) character in the movie *50 First Dates*[106]. Henry falls in love with Lucy (Drew Barrymore) who was in a car accident and suffers anterograde amnesia (no short-term memory). After a series of comedic missteps and challenges, Henry marries Lucy; and every day he has to remind her who he is. Every day he is patient, kind, and affectionate. Every day he must make his love clear. He essentially says, "You can trust me with your love because I will not take it for granted. I won't abuse it. I will not leave you with more scar tissue on your heart." Buri then asks the reader:

> "Can you imagine how our marriages (and our love relationships) would be thriving if each day we were intent upon elevating our nice-to-nasty ratio? If, every day, we were determined once again to show our partner just how much we love them and just how much we value them in our lives?"

Joan and I never miss an opportunity to express our love for each other: this can be a word, a simple touch, or expressing gratitude and appreciation out loud. Neither of us takes the simplest thing for granted. We recognize there are three entities involved in our relationship: there is me, there is her, and there is *US*. There is a constant re-affirmation of our love for each other and for *US* as a couple. This is not hard. It is not work for us. It is who we *am* and how we *be*. If this is missing in your relationship, incorporate it. Make it a habit. If it is mutual, your relationship will thrive and flourish.

Believe Them

The great poet Maya Angelou wrote: "When they tell you who

they are, believe them." This is great advice. Listen and observe what your potential partner, whether personal or professional, is saying and doing. Ask yourself: is this how I want to be treated? Individuals who make jokes at your expense do not respect you. Individuals who put you down, who make fun of your weight, your height, your religion, etc., etc., do not respect you. Believe that they are as they think, talk, and act! Anything else is your projection!

When in the throes of the passionate stage of a relationship, we often overlook negative conduct, especially if the person apologizes for their words and conduct. Are they apologizing because they make a mistake and truly did not mean what they said? Or, are they apologizing because you called them on it? Did they apologize "if they offended you"? If it is either of the latter two, beware. If the insult is repeated, be gone.

Why so strict? Observation over many years and my own experiences show that people do not change unless they have an awakening, like Paul on the road to Damascus. These are rare. Paul-like awakenings are deeply personal experiencing of a need and reason to change. For those in recovery, they may be analogous to hitting bottom and the concomitant awakening.

Do not wait for someone to get it. Remember life is precious. Remember tolerating abuse only encourages more abuse and does nothing positive for the abuser. So, when they tell you who they are, believe them and move on. This is tough love. This can be more helpful to the other person than can be imagined at the time. It may even provide them with an awakening.

Boundaries and Bottom Line

Clear boundaries are necessary in any relationship. Said another way, what is your bottom line? Knowing your boundaries is a large part of knowing *who you am*.

What are healthy bottom lines and boundaries for personal relationship? If you are having a hard time establishing them, start with the most egregious: cheating and physical, sexual and mental abuse are not tolerated. Period!

Young adults are often reluctant to discuss any hot button issues with their potential partner. They are either afraid of upsetting the relationship or they make the huge mistake of assuming their potential partner thinks like they do. If a relationship cannot survive a discussion of hot button issues, the potential partners are already displaying lack of respect and trust for each other and lack of commitment to building a healthy relationship.

Unfortunately, individuals often find themselves in a relationship or marriage before a problem comes up that challenges individual boundaries. For example, how to discipline children, in what faith they will be raised, and even how many kids they want to have. If there is mutual respect and an egalitarian relationship, these can be jointly resolved and boundaries established.

Commitment: Heaven on Earth?

During my time with Joan in Colorado, we became intimate. I shared thoughts and feelings with her that I had never shared with anyone. She did the same. While circumstances developed that resulted in my leaving Colorado, our honest intimacy created a bond that reinforced our commitment to remain friends and colleagues.

As I processed at the Tennessee lake house and thought about my relationship with Joan, I realized how much I loved her. I wanted to be with her in a relationship that was mutually respectful, loving, and beneficial. After I moved to Virginia, I knew it would be unfair of me to ask her to give up what she had built in Colorado and move across country to be with me in a committed relationship without providing her the legal protection of marriage. When I asked her to marry me, I was expecting a 'yes' or 'no' answer. Instead, she asked me, "Are you willing to make heaven on earth with me?"

When I tell this story in a relationship class, I always get a few, "Awwww's." To me, it sounds like when someone shows you a cute kitten, puppy, or an infant: "Awwww." People, especially young women, think this is a romantic question. Not so!

I had come to know Joan from our honest and intimate conversations. I also knew that her question was serious, not romantic or superficial. It was rooted in a deep belief that heaven begins in this life on earth and requires love, not fear of hell. I also knew that I was being asked a tough question from a seasoned litigator and that she expected a thoughtful, intelligent, and honest answer.

We spent the next hour or more discussing what "heaven on earth" meant to her – and then to me. We discussed many "bottom line" issues – both for her and for me. For example, we agreed that if anyone in our families acted in dysfunctional ways, I would handle those in my family and she would take care of hers. We promised each other that we would not let anyone sabotage our relationship. After this discussion, I asked her again to marry me. She asked me again if I would be willing to make heaven on earth with her. I said yes; then she said yes. We have been making heaven on earth ever since then.

Morning Conversations of Marriage

Communication is a necessity for a thriving relationship. One of the ways Joan and I keep our marriage strong is that every day, with very few exceptions, we have what we call our *Morning Conversation of Marriage*. While the title says it is a morning conversation, if we miss the morning, we have it in the evening. This conversation usually is over morning coffee and cereal and lasts at least 30 minutes. Depending on our schedules and the topic, our conversation may last two hours.

We discuss just about anything and everything from world events, politics, the economy, family matters, and areas of our psychological research and interests – we perceive these as personal. Joan often states that there is nothing more personal than the political. As part of the discussion, we share how certain incidents and situations make us feel and impact our thinking and acting. Our conversations are like our own 12-Step meeting, a therapy session, or a research seminar. Whatever the format, we are processing, not ruminating.

As a result, we have grown greatly in our understanding of ourselves and others. We are able to see patterns that impact us and others. For example, we discuss current situations in our extended families (usually dysfunctional) and how they are a microcosm of what is going on in the macrocosm of national politics and cultural attitudes. We often examine the impact of change on ourselves and others. Sometimes we discuss subtle meanings of a Tarot card. We use the Enneagram to understand others, including characters in a movies and TV shows. We discuss research that impacts our work and interests. We laugh at ourselves and at the possibility that others would find our conversations strange.

I know that most people's schedules do not allow for a daily conversation of marriage. If you cannot do it daily, work to set aside at least 30 minutes on the weekend where you can share what is going on in your life, regardless of how mundane it may seem. If you are or have been a member of a 12-Step program, you know how to initiate this type of conversation. Otherwise, remember, sharing is a skill we all learned as children. Once you get started, it's like riding a bicycle.

3 Essential Attitudes

Joan introduced me to Carl Rogers's three essential facilitative attitudes of a person-centered therapeutic relationship. Joan and I believe they are essential to healthy personal relationships because they provide the safety and encouragement which individuals need to thrive. The three essential attitudes are: unconditional positive regard, empathic listening and understanding, and congruency.

Unconditional positive regard is respect for each other's humanity and for the ability of each to develop in positive ways. It is appreciating each other as unique persons who are intelligent and who can evaluate their experiences. This includes the freedom and ability to make autonomous choices, along with accepting responsibility for them. Unconditional positive regard is not judgmental and is not contingent on acting, thinking, or feeling in certain ways. If you have unconditional positive regard for your partner, you cannot be contemptuous of him or her.

Although mutual respect is a precondition, unconditional positive regard does not mean there are no conditions on behaviors within the relationship – remember bottom lines. If you are treated with contempt, for example, there is no mutual respect. If a partner violates healthy boundaries, there is no respect. As discussed earlier, you must set clear boundaries and not go below your bottom line. Unconditional positive regard is grounded in mutual respect.

Empathic listening and understanding require a willingness to listen to your partner's feelings, emotions, and attitudes and to accurately understand the partner's lived experience, feelings and personal meanings from their perspective. Empathic listening requires focusing on your partner's inner worlds of subjective experiencing and being able to distinguish your own. You must know *who you am* so that you do not project your stuff onto to your partner and so that you do not allow your projections to influence your understanding. This also requires renouncing control over your partner and the outcome of a situation. It is not about winning, unless you are striving for a win-win. You must be present and pay attention. Without unconditional positive regard, empathic listening and understanding are not possible.

Congruency is being respectful of your partner as you truthfully and transparently share your experiencing in a way that upholds unconditional positive regard for them and that demonstrates having empathically listened and understood them. It requires being in your integrity which means not compromising your honest perceptions and strengths. Congruency is required to live with another in a climate of trust, respect, transparency, and authenticity.

Congruency requires not interpreting your partner's experiences from your projections of your *conditions of understanding* and *forces of influence*. Your conditions of understanding include your assumptions, beliefs, opinions, values, desires, emotions, fears, habits, memories, needs, past learned knowledge, personal myths, and habitual ways of understanding and interpreting. Your forces of influence include external circumstances that influence your awareness, perception, attitudes, thinking, and behavior – e.g. authority figures in one's family and communities; economic, educational, governmental, legal, political, religious, and social institutions and situations[107].

Create the Story of 'US'

For Joan and me, "US" is the archetypal partnership of love and respect that we have been creating and evolving, both singly and jointly.

While many people assume the cultural version of traditional marriage, we have mindfully sought to evolve the US archetype as a loving and powerful synergistic partnership that has all of the positive attributes of a thriving positive relationship (discussed above).

US is as important as either of us individually. US is not created and does not exist at the expense of either of us individually. US is a positive summation of Joan and me as individuals. We – as US – have accomplished so much more together than we ever could have individually.

One way we achieve this is by *resting in each other's strengths* as advocated by Hal and Sidra Stone[108]. So, while our very egalitarian partnership might appear rooted in traditional gender roles, it is based on mindful strategies to accomplish our goals that rest in our respective strengths. For example, I have a full-time position outside the home and do occasional minor household repairs typically done by men. Joan works from our home which gives her time to take responsibility for managing our personal affairs, and for writing, teaching online, and private consulting.

This arrangement capitalizes on each of our experiences, strengths, and preferences. I have already discussed mine. Joan has worked in the financial field and has been a lawyer. So, managing our financial affairs is no big job for her – and I really hate doing it. The fact that she handles this portion of our lives frees up many hours per month for me to put into my job as a professor and researcher. This is just one example of how we rest in each other's strengths.

Gratitude Dance

At the 2015 Fourth World Congress on Positive Psychology Suzann Pileggi Pawleski and James Pawelski presented a seminar on *Romance and Research: Connecting the Head and the Heart*. In it they introduced the concept of a *Gratitude Dance*. They also pointed out that many people have difficulty accepting thanks from their partner – or from anyone for that matter. Culturally we have been conditioned to downplay compliments by saying something like "Oh, it was nothing." This essentially negates the compliment and can make the person paying you the compliment feel dismissed or unimportant.

Like learning a new dance step, we have to learn to accept compliments. The next time someone says "Thank you," say, "You're welcome." If they pay you a compliment, say thank you and then to yourself reinforce your positive self-talk by saying "Yes, that's like me!" Imprint it even more by adding the compliment: "Yes, that's like me! I am kind and generous! (or thoughtful, etc.)"

Joan and I live in gratitude for US. We express our gratitude in the prayer we say before every meal, before going to bed, and as we end our conversation of marriage. Sometimes as we just feel a wave of gratitude wash over US, one of us begins with saying, "Thank you, God" and the other repeats it. Then, Joan will say, "Thank you, Bob." I reply with, "Thank you, Joan. Joan responds by thanking herself, "Thank you, Joan." Then I say, "Thank you, Bob." Then, individually, or together, we say, "Thank you, US!" This is usually followed by an "I love you" and an "I love US." Sometimes I emphasize it by saying, "I really, really, love US!"

While we have been saying this prayer for years, it is a great example of the *Gratitude Dance* because we always thank ourselves – which initially takes some getting used to. It is important that we can be grateful not only for what the other person means to us and to the relationship but also that we can appreciate what we mean and contribute. Once again you build that positivity storehouse by thanking yourself – and you should do it often!

Another thing that makes this a powerful experience is that Joan and I make sure we are present when we say the prayer. I work to never say it by rote, like I said the prayers of my youth. Even if I am running late for work, I will stop, set down my backpack, hold Joan's hands and look in her eyes. Then I take a deep breath and feel the gratitude within me and then pause. When I am present, we say our gratitude prayer. It is a dance we love to do.

Work vs. Support

In closing this section, I challenge a cultural stereotype that a lasting relationship or marriage requires hard work. Certainly my 30 years with SG was very hard work. Even the simplest decisions were difficult. The marriage "lasted" for 30 years because I worked hard at by being the "nice guy" by appeasing her complaints and fulfilling her demands. Also, because every little thing was a challenge, there was no time for growth and no way to thrive. But the question is: What is the purpose of a such a relationship?

One of the first things Joan and I noticed about our relationship: it was not hard work. We attended naturally to each other, to our relationship, and to ourselves. We dealt honestly, respectfully, and lovingly with challenges. In Colorado, we lived in a small apartment and shared an office. We rarely got in each other's way. We respected each other's need for privacy and solitude (for a Nine on the Enneagram, solitude is a way we recharge). When we went to dinner, to a movie, or just hung out – it was easy. It still is.

What is really going on when supporting each other and the relationship or marriage is hard work? What difficulties are being injected into the marriage? Is one or both partners having to alter negative past patterns? If so, can they support each other in these efforts? Early sections of this book offer suggestions for answering these questions. Professional therapy or spiritual direction may also be required. Bottom line questions include: Why is this relationship hard? Are destructive difficulties intentionally imposed? Or are the challenges natural to an evolving relationship?

The only hard work that Joan and I endured has been the destructive difficulties interjected by family, friends, and others who tried to sabotage our happiness and wreck our relationship. As indicated in the section on relationship commitment, the hard work was having to respond appropriately to dysfunctional family members. Joan and I are always about building a loving, joyous marriage (heaven on earth); and that is not hard work. Building a loving, joyous marriage should NOT be hard work.

Changing Relationships: Bad News & Good News

"When you change, I don't have good news for you." Carolyn Myss stated this conclusion unequivocally. She is referring to the impact your change can have on others.

Getting sober impacts how family and friends interact with you and relate to you. Some let you know they "liked you better when you were drinking!" Most, want you to be sober and remain in recovery. They may, however, consciously or subconsciously resent that your sobriety causes them to think about how much they may be drinking, even when not in your presence. The thought of curbing their drinking may anger them; and they may direct that anger toward you.

As a further reaction, they may consciously, or unconsciously, try to sabotage your recovery. Enablers and co-dependent family and friends may act out like "crabs in a barrel." This metaphor summarizes the dynamic that as you are climbing out of the dysfunction and persist in your recovery, they keep trying to pull you back into the barrel. Your challenge is to stay beyond the grasp of the crabs – to escape a dysfunctional families' relational enmeshments. This requires defining who you are, instead of being defined by others. Again, it is crucial that you know *who you am*.

Relationship enmeshments are grounded in manipulation and disempowering dependency. They are used as coping mechanisms. They are perpetuated by erroneous notions of love and loyalty and of ignorance of the nature of healthy relationships. Overcoming them requires setting firm boundaries to promote wellbeing along with a willingness to let go of those who threaten to leave you or have you ousted from the family or group.

When these saboteurs threaten you and turn their backs on you be in gratitude for their obviousness. Succumbing to such demands and tactics is never healthy or virtuous and will not ever be joyful or satisfactory to you or to them. A problem is that many of us do not know what healthy relationships entail and, therefore, have difficulty identifying the insidiousness of actions and patterns that keep us entangled in dysfunctional relationships. So, we have to learn to recognize dysfunctions; and for this reason I relate another experience below. You also have to look within yourself for what you are willing and ready to do in response.

Perhaps the first lesson is that the changes or impact of your recovery on other adults is about them – not you! It is their responsibility for handling what impacts them. You are not doing them harm when you become sober. Also, we do not change others – we can only change ourselves. Yet, if you are in recovery, you know that the changes in you – your attitudes, your responses, and your change in lifestyle – affected others and indirectly caused some to make changes. So, in the words of Don Miguel Ruiz, author of *The Four Agreements*[109]:

> Don't take anything personally. Nothing others do is because of you. What others say and do is a projection of their own reality, their own dream. When you are immune to the opinions and actions of others, you won't be the victim of needless suffering.

Thriving can also trigger attempts by dysfunctional family members to sabotage your wellbeing and to reestablish what they perceive as control over you – that is, your place in family pecking order. After I married Joan in 2002 and noticeably began rebuilding my life (personally, professionally, and financially), my adult offspring (then 27 and 32 years old) resurrected complaints about misdeeds that occurred before I became sober in 1991. Their complaints included their mother's chronic lament that I was never home. They added to their repertoire derogatory suggestions about how I changed since 2002 and inferred that Joan was the problem.

Around 2004-2005, they took turns closing me out of their lives. I had communicated to my son and daughter that I expected respect for me, Joan, and our marriage. From the time I married Joan, my daughter increased the frequency of her telephone calls and demanded my immediate availability at her whim. When I asked her to curtail her demands and refused to allow her to engage me for hours, she told me to get out of her life and that she was tired of my psychobabble (the coaching that she constantly had demanded). I was shocked when some months later my son also excluded me from his life. On hindsight, I realized that I had not consistently laid down and maintained healthy boundaries as they grew up in my household. The few firm boundaries

I did try to enforce were sabotaged by their mother – another indicator of family dysfunction.

As a parent who loves my children, I had to intentionally begin referring to them as *adult offspring* for whom active parenting to dissuade their exclusions of me was inappropriate. I also stopped making excuses for their behaviors. They are now 47 and 42 years old and, apparently, still living the stories of their choices and constructions.

My offspring were not alone in their dysfunctional reactions to my marriage and thriving. This is not surprising because my family at large is dysfunctional. In my family of origin three of four siblings are alcoholic and the fourth is an overeater who also drinks a lot. My mother freaked when I pointed this out. She became extremely defensive and told me I owed them all an apology for this mean-spirited insult. I reminded her of the context in which the statement was made (informative, not mean-spirited), that three of us had been through rehab, and our alcoholism has been openly discussed in the family. Still, she was intent on being insulted. (My sense is that she projected it as insulting her parenting and/or that she is ashamed of the above fact.)

Similarly, my siblings are in denial of her history of hurtful and mean-spirited conduct, which I will not detail in this book. Each of them has complained bitterly about her behind her back. One even exploded about her actions at a family wedding – embarrassing many. Yes, denial is alive and well in my family of origin; and so is ostracizing those who do not join in the denial by playing the game required by the dysfunction.

Generally, in dysfunctional families, members are not equally valued. They do not have comparable freedom of expression. For example, when a controlling member of the family acts out, others sacrifice their integrity and values to keep peace with the controller. Conflict with a controlling member is avoided. An objector will be ousted and criticized for protesting hurtful conduct and for asking for respect and an apology from the controlling member. The controlling member manipulates to become the victim of the situation and have other family members step up to get the objector in line. In the manipulation and dysfunction, the hateful and hurtful misdeeds of the controller are overlooked and, instead, focus is on the daringness of the objector in asking for respect and an apology. If the objector does not get in line, then focus is also on his spouse and marriage as the problem.

Specifically, I have many experiences with such dynamics. They are difficult to put in writing but I provide one to demonstrate the persistence of family dysfunction. The following situation which began in my sixties is consistent with my mother's conduct since my adolescence, throughout my first marriage and thereafter. Even in my sixties, I am not allowed to object to her hurtful actions and words. When she sent a hate-mongering, racist, and personally demeaning email to Joan, I objected. My objection was accompanied by an attempt to educate. I explained how the email was racist and hate-mongering on its face and how it created "the other" and reduced the other to something less than humans (picture of scroungy mutts). I pointed out how such emails incite overt discrimination.

She sent a non-apology ("I'm sorry if I offended you") that made Joan and me the problem for objecting to her disrespectful e-mail; and she elicited other family members to join her attack on Joan and me. She never apologized for the racist and hatemongering content of the email that reduced individuals to scroungy mutts – less that human. I objected and asked for a real apology. She was furious. She asked *how dare I* not accept her apology?

For over five years she actively elicited other members of the family to get me in line and to make Joan the "force" behind my objection. My siblings decried me for not letting it (her hate-mongering, racist email) slide. They objected to my asking for a real apology even though they initially acknowledged the offensiveness of the e-mail. They also blamed me for not "fixing" the situation. To perpetuate this farce, one sibling could not understand why I, the smartest person he knows, did not have the intelligence to "fix it." I replied that I had laid out the fix: a real apology that denounced racism and hatemongering would have put the situation behind us.

When my siblings failed to bring me in line, my mother's brother stepped up. He does not live near my mother or any of my siblings; so he was relying on her story. Among other errors, he insinuated that my deceased father would be in agreement with the dysfunctional conduct perpetrating the farce. He dismissed the hatemongering and racist email as obscure, although it had received national attention as being such on its face. Moreover, my father would not have responded to the situation as my mother's brother suggested. His suggestion was not consistent with my father's conduct and positions taken by him in analogous situations while he was living – one of which included my mother's acting out when I married my first wife (she also has a history of degrading her children's spouses). The point is that the way they treated Joan and me would not have been condoned by my father. As stated earlier, my father considered that I "married up" when I married Joan.

So, to this day, the family members who contacted me have not addressed my mother's initiating hateful actions or her failure to apologize for sending a hate-mongering, racist, and insulting email. She has never stated that she had no intention of furthering hate-mongering and racism that is so prevalent in the country or that she had no intention of demeaning Joan. So, when they show themselves as hate-mongers and racists, believe them!

The above dysfunctional conduct of family members caused me – and Joan – to do much processing. I considered and reconsidered my objections and requests for respect from my family and their responses. I prayed and meditated. I looked at each instance separately and also as part of the family pattern. I considered a sibling's suggestion to "let it slide." If I did that and just fell in line, I would be participating in spreading racism and hatemongering. I might as well throw away all the education, therapy, and self-improvement efforts that I have worked for since I began recovery. I would have to ignore my processing, praying, and meditating and my felt-sense of resonance on the matter that reinforces to me and confirms that that I am in my integrity and being congruent. In all these ways, I know that my conduct and my choices are moral and responsible ones based in conscience, not on enabling dysfunction, hate-mongering, and racism. I know who I *am*. To give up all of that would not be helpful to anyone. It would not create anything positive.

Again, be forewarned, as Carolyn Myss says: "I don't have good news for you when you change." She is referring to the negative reactions and demands of dysfunctional family and friends. But let us consider another perspective of this picture.

In this regard, I have reconsidered Myss's statement from my experiences. There has been good news for me! I have never been happier. I am no longer under the unnecessary stress and insults from dysfunctional family members. I am thriving and flourishing in many ways. My life is meaningful. My relationship with Joan is more loving and respectful than any that I have had or have witnessed throughout my life. She has given me more respect and love than any other person in my life – ever. So, there is good news! There can be good news for you, too. Once again contemplate the words of Don Miguel Ruiz[109]:

> If someone is not treating you with love and respect, it is a gift if they walk away from you. If that person doesn't walk away, you will surely endure many years of suffering with him or her. Walking away may hurt for a while, but your heart will eventually heal. Then you can choose what you really want. You will find that you don't need to trust others as much as you need to trust yourself to make the right choices.

Lastly, when examining your relationship with family, consider the following: Being genetically related doesn't make you family. Love, support, trust, sacrifice, honesty, protection, acceptance, security, compromise, gratitude, respect, and loyalty is what makes you family (Anonymous). If you know *who you am*, you will know who your family truly is.

Chapter 31

NEUROPLASTICITY

Self-Directed Neuroplasticity

Positive change is challenging to achieve and to sustain. Research shows that changing your brain is required for achieving and sustaining positive change. The information, exercises, and interventions presented in this book are aimed at contributing to you changing your brain to further the changes you desire.

Earlier when I described the self-talk cycle, I shared that when you change your self-talk you change your self-image which, in turn, changes your behavior. Neuroscience and scanning technology show that these changes occur in the brain: that is the actual structure of the brain – the neural pathways – also change. This ability for the brain to change is called neuroplasticity.

Neuroplasticity is important to thriving. Changes in our brain can change our mind. When you drink a caffeine drink or alcohol it changes your brain chemistry. That change in your brain has a resultant change in your mind. In a moderate dose, caffeine makes you more alert and aware; and it can increase awareness and enhance empathy and even happiness. Too much caffeine makes you jittery and unable to think efficiently. Similarly, while one drink of alcohol relaxes you, intoxication causes imbalances in the neurotransmitters, especially those involved in decision-making. For example, drug addicts are cautioned not to drink because after a few beers scoring some cocaine (or heroin, or meth, etc.) does not seem like a bad idea.

On the flip side, as your mind changes your brain changes. Without getting into the physiology, this is the premise behind bio-feedback. With visual or audio feedback you can learn to lower your heart rate and blood pressure by focusing your mind, usually on something relaxing like laying on a beach or watching a sunset. When I go to the doctor and my blood pressure is a little high, I ask them to re-take it. As they do I feelazize a beautiful sunset over Banderas Bay in Puerto Vallarta, Mexico. It brings my blood pressure right down to "normal" or better.

Neuropsychologist Donald Hebb[110] stated that "neurons that fire together, wire together." That means when we change our self-talk we excite new neurons to build new neural pathways that support the new self-image we want. Over time and with repetition the new synapses are strengthened and the neural cortex – or wiring – becomes thicker. Once the new wiring supplants the old wiring as the main circuit, the old wiring begins to atrophy and a process known as neuronal pruning occurs. Neuronal pruning means that if you do not use it you will lose it.

This very basic mini-lesson in neuroscience confirms that you can use your mind to change your brain to change your mind for the better. Psychiatrist Jeffery Schwartz from UCLA refers to this ability that we all have as *self-directed neuroplasticity*[111]. Self-directed neuroplasticity also helps explain the effectiveness of the self-talk cycle, the efficacy of the broaden and build theory, and other interventions discussed in this book.

Brain's Negative Bias

An ongoing challenge to self-directed neuroplasticity is the negative bias of the brain. Neuroscience shows us that negative stimuli get more attention and processing than positive stimuli. Evolutionary psychology tells us this is a survival mechanism that was used by humans for thousands of generations to save their lives. The cognitive psychology of learning and memory confirms we generally learn faster from pain than from pleasure; that negative interactions are more powerful than positive ones; and that negative experiences work their way into implicit memory. Both social and economic psychologies explain that people work harder to avoid a loss than to attain an equal gain; Richard Thaler refers to this as the *endowment effect*[112]. Martin Seligman in his early work[113] showed that learned helplessness is easy to create and is hard to undo.

In *Positivity*[114], Barbara Fredrickson describes her *positivity ratio* for broaden and build as needing three positive interactions to balance out one negative one (3:1). John Gottman[115] proposed that we need a 5:1 ratio of positive to negative interactions to have a happy marriage. One of my colleagues from the Pacific Institute, Joe Pace[116], was even more pessimistic. In his doctoral research on resilience and persistence, Joe determined an 11:1 ratio was needed. He describes it non-academically as you need 11 "Attaboys!" or pats on the back to overcome one "you suck!"

Wallowing in Positivity

Because of the negative bias of the brain, just having positive experiences or thoughts is not enough. Positive experiences pass through the brain like water through a sieve, while the negative experiences are caught in that sieve. How can we change this dynamic so that our brains become like Velcro for positive experiences and like Teflon for negative experiences – letting negativity just slide off? How can we overcome the brain's built-in negative bias? We need to actively imprint positive experiences into the brain to balance out negative experience.

How do we imprint positive experiences into the brain? First we become aware of our positive experiences and we do not shrug them off. A couple of techniques have already been discussed: emotion differentiation (explained with the *Compassion and Loving Kindness Mindfulness Meditation*) and practices of positive self-talk and positive thinking.

In addition, *wallow in positivity*: look for positive facts and let them become positive experiences that you *savor* for 10 to 30 seconds. Feelazize resulting positive emotions in your body; intensify them; then anchor them; and then sense them soaking into your brain so that a deep positive emotional memory is registered. For a positive image of wallowing in positivity think of a kid jumping into a pile of leaves and burrowing underneath. Or, even better, think about the delight of jumping under a large pile of covers on a cold night and wrapping them all around you like a cocoon. Joan likes to think of relaxing in a healing mud bath.

Regardless of the visual you choose, intensify and prolong your positive experiences and interactions and the resultant positive emotions as you wallow. Positive feelings and experiences that you take time to wallow in do not have to be anything extraordinary. They can be simply recognizing all is well in my life: I am alright; I feel safe; I feel love; I am grateful. Small pleasures, attainment of a goal, solving a problem, enjoying a cup of coffee qualify.

My default emotion to wallow in is gratitude. I do it as often as I can. Anytime you engage one of your signature strengths, wallow in that positivity. Wallowing in positivity enhances your positive resources and can provide resilience in painful and traumatic situations. It can boost your capacity to manage stress and negative experiences. It is self-nurturing. In short, wallowing in positivity enables you to thrive!

You can stop positive feelings from passing through the sieve by intentionally developing and using the above practices. As you practice wallowing in positivity, "stop and smell the roses" takes on a profound new purpose. Not only do you want to smell them, you want to appreciate the fact that you stopped to smell them and that you are amazed not only at their fragrance, but also the intricate beauty of the roses. Quoting one my favorite artists, Georgia O'Keeffe: "When you take a flower in your hand and really look at it, it's your world for the moment." So, recognize your positive emotions, be present with them, savor them, feelazize them, and then wallow in that positivity.

Chapter 32

WRAPPING UP

Striving to Thrive

I have shared my journey through alcoholism, my early years in recovery, and how I came to thrive in recovery. I hope my personal difficulties help you recognize not only the insidious nature of addiction but also how the relentless negativity of dysfunctional families and workplaces can infect well-being and prevent thriving. As important, I have offered practices that helped others and me to thrive. I encourage you to use them to help you thrive.

I am not trying to sell a program or start a church. Because I now thrive in recovery, I simply want to share what I've learned and what I practice. In early recovery I began to notice people in recovery that I thought served as good models, for example, my sponsor, Bobby, and SGs relative, Melanie. I would think: *I want some of what they have*, even though I wasn't sure what it was. I later learned that something was their confidence and associated courage in knowing *who they am.*

With respect to the practices discussed in this book, they are rooted not only in my observations and anecdotal experiences but also in research and much training and education including areas such as hypnosis, Tarot, the Enneagram, the cognitive-behavioral concepts utilized in sport and performance psychology, and the cognitive-humanistic interventions and theories of positive psychology. I have studied enough neuroscience to understand why these concepts and methods work.

Do not think you have to incorporate *all* the techniques and interventions contained in this book in order to thrive. Remember that recovery, like life, is a journey. It has taken me more than two decades to explore what works for me (and for US). Along the way I have discarded a number of techniques and interventions because they did not work for me or they lost their effectiveness for me. Remember that there is more to recovery than surviving. As long as you continue to strive – putting one foot in front of the other – you can thrive.

If you are relatively new to recovery, I suggest you focus initially on the following:

- Positive self-talk – its importance cannot be overstated.
- Your five signature strengths – they will enhance your striving ability.
- Empathy and compassion – reminder: your compassion is incomplete if it does not include you.
- Wallow in positivity – build up your positive storehouse to enhance your resilience and persistence.

To paraphrase my sponsor, Bobby M.: Take what you need – or can use – and leave the rest behind.

Bob's Prayer

In closing, I want to leave you with an example of how you can adjust, modify, and apply concepts or techniques to make them fit your needs. Dr. Bruce Wilkinson wrote a bestselling book called *The Prayer of Jabez*[117]. According to Wilkinson saying this prayer "of a little-known Bible hero, Jabez, can release God's favor, power and protection."

> Jabez called on the God of Israel saying, "Oh, that You would bless me indeed, and enlarge my territory, that Your hand would be with me, and that You would keep me from evil, that I may not cause pain." So God

granted him what he requested. (I Chronicles 4:10 NKJV)

This prayer is very open-ended. That is, there is a lot of room for "getting what you wish for" which may not be even close to what you really want. After I began using the prayer, I talked to my brother Tom who had introduced me to it. He shared that he had to stop using it because he was getting too much business and could not handle it. From my study and practice of psychology and hypnosis, I have learned that the subconscious needs specificity. With that in mind, I have adjusted and modified my *Prayer of Jabez*. I do not consider any version complete or the final version. My point to you is don't be afraid to adjust and modify other's techniques to make them best work for you. Below is my current version of the prayer:

Thank you, God, for all the blessings you have bestowed on me and 'US' in the past, in the present, and in the future.
Thank you especially for the blessing of Joan;
She is truly a beacon of light, love, and joy beaming into my heart and my life.

Thank you for my job and ancillary income.
They give me the flexibility and the security to pursue my dreams and goals so that I may best serve the Grail [*my purpose in life*].
Please continue to bless me by expanding, enhancing, and enabling my abundance; my health; and my well-being.
And, as you do so, please grace me with patience;
With presence;
With passion and purpose;
With courage;
With competence and confidence;
With diligence, determination, and discipline, especially regarding diet and exercise;
With intelligence, integrity, and intuition;
With sobriety;

And with plenty of serenity – again, so that I may best serve the Grail.

Be with me always;
Keep me away from evil;
Help me so that I never harm or injure anyone;
Also help me so that I can readily, rightly, and rapidly read and interpret your signs and symbols.

God bless our children: Rob, Rachel, and Byron.
Bless them so that they know their purpose [*in life*];
That they work in their passion;
And that they enjoy a long-term, mutually respectful love relationship with another.

Bless us all – including my family of origin
So that we may heal our family wounds,
And enjoy each other in mutually respectful adult relationships.
Until that time, help me hold a space in my heart for our healing.

Epilogue

HELP US HELP OTHERS

Quit & Recovery Registery

Beyond teaching psychology, another way I am giving back is my work on several of the research teams at the Addiction Recovery Research Center (ARRC) at the Virginia Tech-Carilion Research Institute (VTCRI) in Roanoke, VA. ARRC is under the direction of world renowned addiction researcher Warren Bickel, PhD.

One of the reasons I was drawn to Dr. Bickel's research is his view on addiction and recovery. He says, "Knowledge is not enough to change behavior. Addictive disorders are chronic, but they're treated as acute problems. We need to find creative ways to help people beyond their acute treatment episode."

The statistics regarding successful recovery have not significantly changed since I went into rehab in 1991. About one out of three people are successful in maintaining their recovery. While 33% is a great batting average in baseball, it is a pretty dismal percentage for overcoming addictions. Addictions have been referred to as *the* epidemic of the 21st century. While Ebola, Zika, and other viral diseases are frightening, addictions are more widespread and negatively impact more individuals, families, and economies worldwide.

An amazing fact is that with all the research that has been done on addictions, little has been done on the recovery process. Assumptions are made, but until recently no one has asked those of us in recovery how we stay in recovery. This is the mission of the International Quit & Recovery Registry (IQRR). The IQRR is a novel approach that employs crowd-sourcing technology to establish, maintain, and grow an unprecedented database on the process of recovery. The concept is to survey those in recovery from ANY addiction as to how they stay in recovery. An aim of this research is to help develop more effective strategies for recovery. If you would like to contribute to this important research and become a *Recovery Hero* by helping us help others in recovery, please go to the IQRR website < https://quitandrecovery.org> and register and take the surveys.

Early Data

The IQRR's first round of survey data was analyzed in November of 2012. There were over 3,063 respondents to the surveys. Some of demographics reported that 53.7% were female. Ethnicity of responders was 82.5% Caucasian; 5.3% African-American; and 3.3% preferred not to answer. The breakdown of the responders in recovery were: 51.7% alcoholics; 13% cocaine addicts; 8.8% opioid addicted; 7.9% stimulant abusers; and 5.4% prescription drug abusers. Of interest is that 96.3% reported having secondary addictions. 30.1% of those who did not report alcohol as the primary addiction, reported alcohol as their secondary addiction. 50% reported that in-patient therapy was the most effective therapy; and approximately 25% reported 12-Step programs as most effective.

Positive Psychology & IQRR

In 2012 the *Subjective Happiness Scale* (SHS) developed by Lyubomirsky and Lepper[118] was embedded in a much larger survey conducted by the IQRR. Amazon Mechanical Turk (mTurk) crowdsourcing service was used to poll hundreds of participants in recovery for more than one year. These findings indicated that those in recovery from an addiction were slightly less happy than those not reporting addictions. Men in recovery were slightly happier than women in recovery, who were also slightly more pessimistic. None of these findings were statistically significant[119].

In 2014 the SHS was again disseminated to a targeted group through the IQRR. Diener et al's *Satisfaction with Life Scale*[120] and Duckworth et al's *Grit Scale*[121] were also distributed to the same IQRR participants. A comparison of these findings to control populations were examined and discussed for a poster presentation at the 4th World Congress on Positive Psychology[122]. Comparisons for length of time in recovery were also available for the SHS and the GRIT. Findings as of May, 2015:

- SHS: Those in recovery scored significantly higher on SHS scale than the control[123].
- GRIT: No Significant Difference in GRIT score between groups[124].
- SHS & GRIT: Older people score higher in both groups.
- TREND: The longer one is in recovery the higher the score on SHS, SWLS, & GRIT.

A more recent look at accumulating data focused only on alcoholism and was presented in 2016 at the 39th Annual Research Society on Alcoholism (RSA)[125]. These results reveal that a greater length of time in recovery (1-5 years compared to 5-plus years) is associated with an increase in life satisfaction, grit, and happiness. They constitute the first results from the IQRR regarding length of recovery and personality characteristics.

A follow-up to that study was presented at the Fifth World Congress on Positive Psychology in 2017[126]. Again, using data from the IQRR, it sought to determine if there was a significant difference in the levels of happiness (SHS), life satisfaction (SWLS), and grit for those in recovery from alcoholism with less than 1 year in recovery compared to those with 2-5 years, and those with more than 5 years. While statistical significance is not present in every category, there is a definite trend toward more happiness, life satisfaction, and grit with more time in recovery.

These data can be used by clinicians to support individuals who are beginning the recovery process and can be presented as a prospect of hope and optimism that the road to recovery will become less difficult and ultimately result in an increased quality of life. These studies are just scratching the surface of how the internet and crowd-sourcing can be used to inform us how those in recovery are maintaining sobriety and even thriving. These projects are being refined and are on-going; and we need your input.

Social Interactome

Another research project that I am involved with at ARRC is a 3-year grant funded by the National Institutes of Health (NIH) National Institute on Drug Abuse (NIDA). In late 2015 this study began examining social networking as an addiction recovery tool. It will supplement information learned from the IQRR. While there are already social media sites to help people with addictions, this site has a more specific focus: to study the social physics of recovery using what is called the *social interactome* – an all-encompassing look at how social interactions influence specific behaviors.

This study takes advantage of the fact that humans are exquisitely social creatures and learn from each other. Also, social interactome is a low-cost method for providing additional help and encouragement during addiction recovery. If you are interested in participating in the Social Interactome study begin by registering at the IQRR site. Those who meet the criteria will receive an e-mail invitation to join the study (participants get paid).

Our goal at ARRC is to transform addiction treatment. Help us help others by participating. Also, if you are a researcher: we share data!

If you want to know more or participate in ongoing research, contact:

- ARRC (n.d.) Addiction Recovery Research Center. http://labs.vtc.vt.edu/arrc/
- IQRR (n.d.) International Quit & Recovery Registry. https://quitandrecovery.org/
- DrBobReese.com (n.d.) Magis Thinking to Thrive & Flourish. http://drbobreese.com
- VTCRI (n.d.) Virginia Tech-Carilion Research Institute. http://research.vtc.vt.edu

NOTES

Prologue
1. American Psychiatric Association. (2013). *Diagnostic and statistical manual of mental disorders* (5th ed.). Arlington, VA: American Psychiatric Association.

PART 1: THE DRINKING YEARS

Chapter 4: Teen Drinking
Senior Trip

2. Apparently I did a 1½ flip onto the asphalt. *That was the second of my mild traumatic brain injuries. The first occurred my freshman year when my cousin Jimmy Hatley, his buddy Sam, and I went to the store to get something for the grown-ups – probably cigarettes. When we got to the shopping center, everything was closed and the parking lot was empty; it was a Sunday. Jimmy decided we should play catch with a football. He kept sending me long and finally when I was about 30 yards from the car he and Sam jumped in the car and started driving off. I ran after them, and jumped on the rear bumper of my Aunt Gert's '53 Plymouth. When Jimmy hit second gear, I came off and landed on the back of my head. Out cold, they took me to the emergency room. I was out for about 12 hours. I suffered amnesia and to this day do not remember falling off the car. My amnesia was interesting in that I lost only the previous year.*

Trudy came over to help my Mom out while I was confined to bed rest. She had a lot of fun with my amnesia. She invited my girlfriend over and then, in front of her, asked me who my girlfriend was. With no hesitation, I named the girl I had been dating the year before. Fortunately, this only lasted a week. I remember Trudy constantly peppering me with questions and laughing heartily at my answers. I didn't get the joke.

Chapter 12: The Jets
Pre-Draft Physicals

3. *Several years earlier Jim Nicholas had published an article in an Orthopedic/Sports Medicine Journal about the propensity for loose-jointed athletes to suffer more minor ligament injuries – mild to moderate sprains – than tight-jointed individuals. Tight-jointed individuals, while on one hand having fewer minor injuries, had more severe or ruptured ligaments than their loose-jointed counterparts. He felt it was easier to surgically repair the ruptured ligaments than to deal with the loose-jointed individuals, so if you had a choice, choose the tight-jointed athlete. I was aware of the study and Dr. Godfrey, at Buffalo had thought it an interesting concept, but had believed an athletes' talent overruled any such theory. Unfortunately for me, I did not connect the theory to Dr. Nicholas until that moment. Over time his theory was discredited, but I had to contend with it head-on at that time. Dr. Nicholas had also helped invent the Lenox Hill De-rotation knee brace to stabilize Joe Namath's knees. It worked very well, but it was heavy, bulky, and slowed players down. This was the brace he was prescribing for Marvin Powell.*

Nicholas, J.A. (1970). Injuries to knee ligaments: Relationship to looseness and tightness in football players. *JAMA*. 1970;212(13):2236-2239. doi:10.1001/jama.1970.03170260032007

Chapter 14: The Beginning of an End
The Raiders & Walt's Meltdown

4. Nick then told me to do a drug inventory ...
   In the late 1970s and early 1980s keeping up with prescription drugs was becoming a priority in the NFL. Because of the drug culture of the 1970s, the ATs were more concerned than anyone else about players stockpiling pain pills and then taking them with alcohol to get high. With that in mind, we doled them out to the players in 24-48 hour dosages instead of just giving them a bottle of 30 pills as an ordinary person would receive. Prodding by the ATs led to the NFL instituting its first required prescription drug inventory of each team, about two years earlier. In 1982 we were being progressive at the Jets and were keeping the inventory on computer for the first time. This was before Windows and everything had to be coded and entered in D-base. The fact that I had not entered the most recent pharmacy order into the computer added to the challenge of coming up with an accurate inventory rapidly.

5. "You were disloyal to me with Henning ...
   After the 1978 season Dan Henning left to become Offensive Coordinator with the Miami Dolphins. Because the Jets had beaten the Dolphins twice in 1978,

Walt suspected that Don Shula had tampered with Henning before the hire so that he could figure out how we were beating them. I was called in for an informal testimony with Walt, Jim Kensil, and a NFL attorney. I told them I knew that Dan's contract was up, that he wanted a raise, and that was the extent of it. I had no knowledge that he was considering the Dolphins – or anyone else. It was common knowledge that I hated the Dolphins and Don Shula. During my five years in Buffalo, the Bills never beat Miami. There were several controversial games: one in particular that knocked the Bills out of the playoffs. Everyone was aware about my feelings toward Miami. The first time the Jets beat Miami in 1978, the Jets coaches awarded me a special game ball for my first victory over Miami. Buffalo players also called me; they wanted to know how it felt to beat Miami. Dan knew all this so he would have never told me about considering going to Miami. There were no tampering charges filed and Henning went to Miami.

6. … "Mud-Bowl" in Miami.
    When the Jets arrived in Miami for the AFC Championship game we were greeted with torrential rain. It had been raining for days and the field at the Orange Bowl had not been covered with a tarp as per NFL rules. The excuse the Dolphins gave was that the Orange Bowl was equipped with a pumping system to drain the field. The pumping system was overwhelmed so by game time there was standing water on much of the field. The Jets offense was built around two speedy receivers, Wesley Walker and Johnny "Lam" Jones, and in the mud and slop, their speed was negated. Our offense sputtered; and Miami won the game 14-0 and went to the Super Bowl. Of course, we all believed Don Shula had left the field uncovered on purpose to sabotage our offense – just another reason to hate Miami!

Chapter 15: Jets ~ Joe Walton Era (1983-89)
Big Changes

7. … Joe Walton took over as head coach.
    I always found it curious that after the Miami Mud-Bowl Walton "confessed" to the press that his inability to change the game plan from a passing game to a ground game had cost the Jets the game and a trip to the Super Bowl. While this was noble, I had not expected it to earn him the head coaching job.

PART 2: BEGINNINGS OF A SOBER LIFE

Chapter 19: The Coslet Years
Dennis Byrd

8. Reese, B. (2005a). *Develop the winner's mentality: 5 essential mental skills for enduring success.* Philadelphia: Xlibris.
9. Byrd, D., & D'Orso, M. (1993). *Rise and walk, The trial and triumph of Dennis Byrd.* NY: HarperCollins

Hypnosis

10. Rob Moore's case study …
    Reese, B. (1996). A case involving hypnosis/guided imagery as an adjunct treatment of a fractured wrist, *Athletic Therapy Today*, Vol. 1, No. 5, 18-20, September 1996

Chapter 20: The Pete Carroll Year (1994)
Ouch! My Back – Again!

11. … very careful about lifting and twisting.
    I was able to manage the herniated discs non-surgically until January 2015. At that time an insignificant mild twist resulted in nerve pain in my right groin area. After months of physical therapy, chiropractic, and osteopathic care, I finally had surgery in October 2015. Unfortunately, one thing seemed to exacerbate another and I had a second surgery in January 2016 and a third in April of that year. Currently I am asymptomatic from nerve pain stemming from these old back injuries.

1994 – The Season

12. Xs and 0s are the symbols coaches use to draw up football plays.

Are You Sitting Down?

13. *I should note that Dick Steinberg, the general manager, had been diagnosed with stomach cancer in the fall of 1994. I often wonder if that is why he did not fight for Pete Carroll to keep his job. Dick passed away in September, 1995.*

Chapter 22: Starting Over
Masters in Psychology: The Winner's Mentality

14. Anshel, M. H. (1994). *Sport psychology: From theory to practice* (2nd ed). Scottsdale, AZ: Gorsuch Scarisbrick.
15. Bunker, L., Williams, J. M., & Zinsser, N. (1993). Cognitive techniques for improving performance and building confidence. In J. M. Williams (Ed.), *Applied sport psychology: Personal growth to peak performance.* Mountain View, CA: Mayfield.
16. Loehr, J. E. (1994). *The new toughness training for sports.* New York: Dutton.
17. Martens, R. (1987). *Coaches guide to sport psychology.* Champaign, IL: Human Kinetics.
18. Murphy, S. M. (1995). Introduction to sport psychology interventions. In S. M. Murphy (Ed.), *Sport Psychology Interventions* (pp. 1-15). Champaign, IL: Human Kinetics.
19. Nideffer, R. M. (1992). *Psyched to win: How to master mental skills.* Champaign, IL: Leisure Press.
20. Orlick, T. (1990). *In pursuit of excellence: How to win in sport and life through mental training.* Champaign, IL: Leisure Press.
21. Ravizza, K., & Hanson, T. (1995). *Heads-up baseball: Playing the game one pitch at a time.* Indianapolis, IN: Masters Press.
22. Rotella, B. (1995). *Golf is not a game of perfect.* New York: Simon & Schuster.
23. Zinsser, N., Scott, B., & Camp, B. (1995). *Mental training for peak performance.* Unpublished Handbook. West Point, NY: USMA Center for Enhanced Performance.
24. Peale, N. V. (1952/1983). *The power of positive thinking.* New York: Fawcett Crest.
25. Robbins, A. (1992). *Awaken the giant within: How to take immediate control of your mental, emotional, physical & financial destiny.* New York: Simon & Schuster.
26. Covey, S. R. (1989). *The seven habits of highly effective people: Restoring the character ethic.* New York: Simon & Schuster.
27. Peck, M. S. (1978). *The road less traveled.* New York: Touchstone; Simon & Shuster.
28. Ziglar, Z. (1975/2000). *See you at the top.* Gretna, LA: Pelican Publishing
29. Tice, L. (1995). *Smart talk for achieving your potential: 5 steps to get you from here to there.* Seattle, WA: Pacific Institute.
30. Tice, L. (1992). *Investment in excellence for the 90's: Personal resource manual; Video phase 1 & 2; Audio phase 1 & 2.* Seattle, WA: Pacific Institute.
31. Tice, L. (1993). *Inventing your future.* Seattle, WA: Pacific Institute.

32. Gerber, R. (1955/2001). *Vibrational medicine: New choices for healing ourselves* (3rd ed). Santa Fe, NM: Bear.
33. Chopra, D. (1990). *Quantum healing: Exploring the frontiers of mind/body medicine.* New York: Bantam.
34. Chopra, D. (1994). *Magical mind, magical body.* New York: Crown.
35. Brennan, B. (1987). *Hands of light: A guide to healing through the human energy field.* New York: Pleiades Books.
36. Myss, C. (1996). *Anatomy of the spirit: The seven stages of power and healing.* New York: Harmony Books, Crown.
37. Millman, D. (1980). *Way of the peaceful warrior.* Novato, CA: H.J. Kramer/New World Library.
38. Reese, B. (1998). *Motivation for the millennium: Certification – mental skills trainer.* Unpublished Master's Project, Regis University, Denver, CO.
39. Reese, B. (2005a). *Develop the winner's mentality: 5 essential mental skills for enduring success.* Philadelphia: Xlibris.

Performance Enhancement Consultant

40. ... "rookie slump": *The rookie slump occurs after a rookie player survives the final cut and makes the team. Rookies rarely know how to pace themselves during training camp and approach every practice as if it were a college bowl game. By the time the pre-season is over and they make the team, they are exhausted mentally and physically. Now that they have made the team, they relax and they generally contribute little the first 4-6 weeks of the season.*
41. Reese, B. (2005b). *The impact of a mental skills training program for enhanced performance on a varsity intercollegiate volleyball team: A case study program evaluation of an educational intervention.* Ph.D. Dissertation, Virginia Polytechnic Institute & State University, Blacksburg, VA. http://nextstepfacilitations.com/wp-content/uploads/2010/02/Reese_PhD_Complete_120105.pdf

Chapter 24: Nuclear Family & Dysfunction
Dysfunction is the Norm

42. Bradshaw, J. (1988). *Bradshaw on: The family: A new way of creating solid self-esteem.* Deerfield Beach, FL, Health Communications.
43. Myss, C. (1996/2002). *Spiritual madness: The necessity of meeting God in darkness.* (audio CD) Louisville, CO: Sounds True.

Chapter 26: Know Who You AM!
The Enneagram

44. Rohr, R. (1992). *Discovering the Enneagram: An ancient tool a new spiritual journey.* New York: Crossroad Publishing
45. Riso, D., & Hudson, R. (1996). *Personality types: Using the Enneagram for self-discovery.* New York: Houghton Mifflin.

Identify Your Dominant Worldview
46. Riso, D. & Hudson, R. (n.d.). Enneagram type nine. Retrieved from: http://www.enneagraminstitute.com/TypeNine.asp#.U7w-ErG8OSE

Tarot
47. Arrien, A. (1997). The Tarot handbook: Practical applications of ancient visual symbols. NY: Jeremy P. Tarcher / Putnam
48. Wanless, J. (1998). *Voyager Tarot: Way of the great oracle* (3rd ed.). Carmel, CA Merrill-West Publishing.

Courage: Tangled and Dark
49. Raitt, B. (1991). Tangled and dark. Album: *Luck of the Draw.* NY: Capitol Records.

From Seeing to Being College Faculty
50. ... working with Adam Heidt. *One of my great thrills and successes in performance enhancement was working with Adam Heidt of the U.S. Luge team. Adam contacted me after a ninth-place finish in the 1998 Nagano Olympics. We worked together through the 2002 Salt Lake City Olympics. In Salt Lake he had a personal best each day and finished with a fourth-place finish, still the highest-ever singles finish for a U.S. luger.*

PART 3: THE 13th STEP – THRIVING

Chapter 27: Fundamentals For Thriving
Flow

51. Csikszentmihalyi, M. (1990). *Flow: The psychology of optimal experience.* NY: Harper & Row.

52. Seligman, M. E. P., & Csikszentmihalyi, M. (2000). Positive psychology: An introduction. *American Psychologist*, Vol 55(1), Jan 2000, 5-14. doi: 10.1037/0003-066X.55.1.5
53. Seligman, M. E. P., (2011). *Flourish: A visionary new understanding of happiness and well-being*. NY: Atria/Simon & Schuster

Dark Night of the Soul

54. Myss, C. (1996/2002). *Spiritual madness: The necessity of meeting God in darkness*. (audio CD) Louisville, CO: Sounds True.
55. Kashdan, T.B., & Biswas-Diener, R., (2014). *The upside of your dark side: Why being your whole self – not just your "good" self – drives success and fulfillment*. NY: Hudson Street Press.

Winner's Mentality: 5 Essential Skills for Enduring Success

56. Reese, B. (1998). *Motivation for the millennium: Certification – mental skills trainer*. Unpublished Master's Project, Regis University, Denver, CO.
57. Reese, B. (2005a). *Develop the winner's mentality: 5 essential mental skills for enduring success*. Philadelphia: Xlibris.

Goal Setting

58. Tice, L. (1993). *Inventing your future*. Seattle, WA: Pacific Institute.
59. Tice, L. (1992). *Investment in excellence for the 90's: Personal resource manual; Video phase 1 & 2; Audio phase 1 & 2*. Seattle, WA: Pacific Institute.

I Am An Alcoholic!

60. Hebb, D. O. (1949). *The organization of behavior*. NY: Wiley & Sons.

Feelazation

61. Murphy, S. M. (1986). *Emotional imagery and its effects on strength and fine motor skill performance*. Unpublished doctoral dissertation, Rutgers, New Brunswick, NJ.
62. Gendlin, E. T. (1981). *Focusing*. New York: Bantam.

Mental Toughness

63. Duckworth, A. L., Peterson, C., Matthews, M. D., & Kelly, D. K. (2007). Grit: Perseverance and passion for long-term goals. *Journal of Personality and Social Psychology*, 92 (6) 1087–110. DOI: 10.1037/0022-3514.92.6.1087
64. Duckworth, A. L. (2016). *Grit: The power of passion and perseverance*. NY: Scribner

Chapter 28: Positive Emotions & Thriving

Broaden & Build

65. Fredrickson, B. (March, 2001). The role of positive emotions in positive psychology: The broaden-and-built theory of positive emotions. *American Psychologist*. Vol. 56, 3, 218-226.

Gratitude

66. Seligman, M. E. P., (2002). *Authentic happiness*. NY: Free Press
67. Lyubormirsky, S. (2008). *The how of happiness*. NY: Penguin Books
68. Emmons, R. A. & McCullough, M. E. (2003) Counting blessings versus burdens: An experimental investigation of gratitude and subjective well-being in daily life. *Journal of Personality and Social Psychology*, Vol. 84, No. 2, 377–389. DOI: 10.1037/0022-3514.84.2.377

Mindfulness

69. Kabat-Zinn, J. (2011). *Mindfulness for beginners: Reclaiming the present moment – and your life*. Louisville, CO: Sounds True
70. Hanson, R., & Siegel, D. J., (2009). *Buddha's brain: The practical neuroscience of happiness, love, and wisdom*. Oakland, CA: New Harbinger Publications

Compassion & Loving Kindness Meditation

71. Johnson, L. (n.d.). *Autogenic training: Compassion and loving kindness meditation*. Retrieved from http://enjoylifebook.com/
72. Kornfield, J. (1994). *Buddha's little instruction book*. NY: Bantam (p. 28)

Emotion Differentiation & Regulation

73. Pond, R.S., Jr., Kashdan, T.B., DeWall, C.N., †Savostyanova, A.A. Lambert, N.M., & Fincham, F.D. (2012). Emotion differentiation buffers aggressive behavior in angered people: A daily diary analysis. *Emotion, 12*, 326-337.
74. Barrett, L. F., Gross, J., Christensen, T. C., & Benvenuto, M. (2001). Knowing what you're feeling and knowing what to do about it: Mapping the relation between emotion differentiation and emotion regulation. *Cognition and Emotion*, 15, 713–724. doi:10.1080/02699930143000239
75. Kashdan, T.B., Ferssizidis, P., Collins, R.L., & Muraven, M. (2010). Emotion differentiation as resilience against excessive alcohol use: An ecological momentary assessment in underage social drinkers. *Psychological Science, 21,* 1341-1347.
76. Tugade, M. M., Fredrickson, B. L., & Barrett, L. F. (2004). Psychological resilience and emotional granularity: Examining the benefits of positive

emotions on coping and health. *Journal of Personality*, 72, 1161–1190. doi:10.1111/j.1467-6494.2004.00294.x

77. Kashdan, T.B., Barrett, L. F., & Mcknight, P. E. (2015). Unpacking emotion differentiation: Transforming unpleasant experience by perceiving distinctions in negativity. *Current Directions in Psychological Science*. 24(1) 10–16. DOI: 10.1177/0963721414550708

78. Kashdan, T.B., & Biswas-Diener, R., (2014). *The upside of your dark side: Why being your whole self – not just your "good" self – drives success and fulfillment*. NY: Hudson Street Press.

79. Gross, J. J. (2001, Dec.). Emotion regulation in adulthood: Timing is everything. *Current Directions in Psychological Science December*. 10(6). 214-219. doi: 10.1111/1467-8721.00152

80. Fredrickson, B., (2009). *Positivity: Top-notch research reveals the 3 to 1 ratio that will change your life*. NY: Harmony

Inside Out

81. Mauss, I. B., Tamir, M., Anderson, C. L., & Savino, N. S. (2011, Aug.). Can seeking happiness make people happy? Paradoxical effects of valuing happiness. *Emotion*. 11(4): 807–815. doi: 10.1037/a0022010

82. Rivera, J., & Docter, P (2015). *Inside out* [Motion Picture]. USA: Pixar Studios/Disney

WIIFM?

83. Tice, L. (1992). *Investment in excellence for the 90's: Personal resource manual; Video phase 1 & 2; Audio phase 1 & 2*. Seattle, WA: Pacific Institute.

Focus on Strengths

84. The VIA survey and Signature Strengths are based upon Chris Peterson and Martin Seligman's Character Strengths and Virtues: A Handbook and Classification *(see below[83]). In this massive tome, they identify six broad and ubiquitous virtues found cross-culturally. They are: wisdom, courage, humanity, justice, temperance, and transcendence. There are 24 strengths that can be found as components of each of the virtues. These strengths are then defined and strategies are provided to cultivate each of them.*

85. Peterson, C., & Seligman, M. E. P. (2004). *Character strengths and virtues: A handbook and classification*. New York: Oxford University Press and Washington, DC: American Psychological Association. www.viacharacter.org

Be-Do-Have

86. Diener, E. & Biswas-Diener, R. (2008). *Happiness: Unlocking the mysteries of psychological wealth*. Indianapolis, IN: Wiley-Blackwell

Chapter 29: Forgiveness
Forgiving is Important

87. Seligman, M. E. P., (2002). *Authentic happiness.* NY: Free Press (p. x-xi)
88. McCullough, M.E., Rachal, K.C., Sandage, S.J., Worthington, E.L., Jr., Brown, S.W., & Hight, T.L. (1998). Interpersonal forgiving in close relationships: II. Theoretical elaboration and measurement. *Journal of Personality and Social Psychology,* 76, 1586-1603.

Forgiveness Defined

89. Thompson, L. Y., Snyder, C. R., Hoffman, L., Michael, S. T., Rasmussen, H. N., Billings, L. S., et al. (2005). Dispositional forgiveness of self, others, and situations: The Heartland Forgiveness Scale. *Journal of Personality.* 73, 313-359.

Why Forgive?

90. Enright, R. D., and the Human Development Study Group (1994). Piaget on the moral development of forgiveness: Reciprocity or identity? *Human Development,* 37, 63-80.
91. Tangney, J. P., Fee, R., Reinsmith, C., Boone, A. L., & Lee, N. (1999, August). *Assessing individual differenced in the propensity to forgive.* Paper presented at the American Psychological Association Convention, Boston.

Letting Go

92. Tangney, J. P., Fee, R., Reinsmith, C., Boone, A. L., & Lee, N. (1999, August). *Assessing individual differenced in the propensity to forgive.* Paper presented at the American Psychological Association Convention, Boston.

Sympathy, Empathy, and Compassion

93. Rogers, C. R., (1989). *The Carl Rogers reader.* NY: Mariner Books
94. McCullough, M.E., Rachal, K.C., Sandage, S.J., Worthington, E.L., Jr., Brown, S.W., & Hight, T.L. (1998). Interpersonal forgiving in close relationships: II. Theoretical elaboration and measurement. *Journal of Personality and Social Psychology,* 76, 1586-1603.
95. McCullough, Worthington, & Rachal, (1997). Interpersonal forgiving in close relationships. *Journal of Personality and Social Psychology,* 73 (2) 321-336
96. Wade, N. G., & Worthington, E. L. (2005). In search of a common core: A content analysis of interventions to promote forgiveness. *Psychotherapy: Theory, Research, Practice, Training.* 42 (2) 160-177

97. Worthington, E. L., Jr. (2005). *The power of forgiveness*. Philadelphia, PA: Templeton Foundation Press.

Reconcile? Forgive & Forget? Trust?
98. Enright, R. D., (2001). *Forgiveness is a choice*. Washington, DC: American Psychological Assoc.

Virtues vs. Issues
99. Drews, T. R., (na). *GettingThemSober.com Newsletter*. Received from GettingThemSober.com.

Chapter 30: Relationships
Positive Relationships

100. Seligman, M. E. P., (2011). *Flourish: A visionary new understanding of happiness and well-being*. NY: Atria/Simon & Schuster
101. Bradshaw, J. (1988). *Bradshaw on: The family: A new way of creating solid self-esteem*. Deerfield Beach, FL, Health Communications.
102. Sternberg, R. J. (1986). A triangular theory of love. *Psychological Review*, Vol 93(2), Apr 1986, 119-135. Retrieved from: http://dx.doi.org/10.1037/0033-295X.93.2.119

Contempt
103. Soloman, R. C., (1993). *The passions: Emotions and the meaning of life* (2nd Ed.) Indianapolis, IN: Hackett ISBN-13: 978-0872202269

Stereotypes & Nice-to-Nasty Ratio
104. Gottman, J.M. (1994). *Why marriages succeed or fail: And how you can make yours last*. NY: Fireside.
105. Buri, J. (2009). Psychology Today. *50 First dates and the nice-to-nasty ratio*. Retrieved from: http://www.psychologytoday.com/blog/love-bytes/200902/50-first-dates-and-the-nice-nasty-ratio
106. Segal, P. & Wing, G. (2004). 50 First dates. [Motion Picture]. USA: Sony

3 Essential Attitudes
107. Reese, J. (2010). *Examining intuitive-creativity via reading Tarot cards in a person-centered climate*. Ph.D. Dissertation, Saybrook University, San Francisco, CA. http://pqdtopen.proquest.com/doc/305239877.html?FMT=AI&pubnum=3396955

Create the Story of 'US'
108. Stone, H., Stone, S. (2000), *Partnering: A new kind of relationship*. Novoto, CA; New World Library

Changing Relationships: Bad News & Good News
109. Ruiz, D. M. (1997). *The four agreements: A practical guide to personal freedom (A Toltec wisdom book)*. Amber-Allen Publishing (November 7, 1997)

Chapter 31: Neuroplasticity
Self-Directed Neuroplasticity

110. Hebb, D. O. (1949). *The organization of behavior*. NY: Wiley & Sons.
111. Schwartz, J. M. & Gladding, R., (2012). *You are not your brain: The 4-step solution for changing bad habits, ending unhealthy thinking, and taking control of your life*. NY: Penguin/Avery Trade

Brain's Negative Bias
112. Thaler, R. (1980). Towards a positive theory of consumer choice. *Journal of Economic Behavior and Organization*, 1, 39-60.
113. Seligman, M.E.P.; Maier, S.F. (1967). Failure to escape traumatic shock. *Journal of Experimental Psychology* 74: 1–9. doi:10.1037/h0024514. PMID 6032570.
114. Fredrickson, B., (2009). *Positivity: Top-notch research reveals the 3 to 1 ratio that will change your life*. NY: Harmony
115. Gottman, J.M. (1994). *Why marriages succeed or fail: And how you can make yours last*. NY: Fireside.
116. Pace, J. (1985). *A measure of persistence in a group of proprietary college students*. PhD. Dissertation. Miami, FL, University of Miami.

Bob's Prayer
117. Wilkinson, B. (2000). *The prayer of Jabez: Breaking through to the blessed life*. Colorado Springs, CO: Multnomah Publishing.

EPILOGUE: Help Us Help Others
Positive Psychology & IQRR

118. Lyubomirsky, S., & Lepper, H. (1999). A measure of subjective happiness: Preliminary reliability and construct validation. *Social Indicators Research*, 46, 137-155. The original publication is available at www.springerlink.com.

119. Reese, B. (2013, June). *The 13th step: Thriving in recovery*. Workshop conducted at the Third World Congress on Positive Psychology, Westin Bonaventure, Los Angeles, CA.
120. Diener, E., Emons, R. A., Larsem, R. J., & Griffin, S. (1985). The satisfaction with life scale. *Journal of Personality Assessment.* 49 (1), 71-75.
121. Duckworth, A. L., Peterson, C., Matthews, M. D., & Kelly, D. K. (2007). Grit: Perseverance and passion for long-term goals. *Journal of Personality and Social Psychology*, 92 (6) 1087–110. DOI: 10.1037/0022-3514.92.6.1087
122. Reese, B., Koffarnus, M., Quisenberry, A., Bixel, K., Seymour, N., Bianco, A., Patterson, D., Bickel, W. (2015, June). *The 13th step: More on thriving in recovery.* Poster presented at the International Positive Psychology Association (IPPA) 4th World Congress on Positive Psychology, Orlando, FL.
123. Control: Lyke, J. A. (2008). Insight, but not self-reflection, is related to subjective well-being. *Personality and Individual Differences.* 46 (2009) 66–70 doi:10.1016/j.paid.2008.09.010. Elsevier Ltd.
124. Control: Eskreis-Winkler, L., Shulman, E. P., Beal, S. A., Duckworth, A. L. (2014). The grit effect: Predicting retention in the military, the workplace, school and marriage. *Frontiers in Psychology*. Doi: 10.3389/fpsyg.2014.00036
125. Quisenberry, A. J., Bixel, K. D., Poe, L., Reese, R., Bickel, W. K. (2016, June). The phenotype of happiness in recovery from alcohol: Length of recovery as a predictor. Poster presented at the 39th Annual Research Society on Alcoholism (RSA), New Orleans, LA.
126. Reese, B., Poe, L., Quisenberry, A. J., Bixel, K. D., Pope, D., Bickel, W. K. (2017, July). Length of Recovery as a Predictor of Happiness in Alcoholics. Poster presented at the International Positive Psychology Association (IPPA) 5th World Congress on Positive Psychology, Montreal, QC, Canada.

BIBLIOGRAPHY

Alcoholics Anonymous. (2001). *Alcoholics anonymous* (4th Ed). New York: A.A. World Services. ISBN 1-893007-16-2. OCLC 32014950

American Psychiatric Association. (2013). *Diagnostic and statistical manual of mental disorders* (5th ed.). Arlington, VA: American Psychiatric Association.

Anshel, M. H. (1994). *Sport psychology: From theory to practice* (2nd ed). Scottsdale, AZ: Gorsuch Scarisbrick.

Arrien, A. (1997). *The Tarot handbook: Practical applications of ancient visual symbols.* NY: Jeremy P. Tarcher / Putnam

Barrett, L. F., Gross, J., Christensen, T. C., & Benvenuto, M. (2001). Knowing what you're feeling and knowing what to do about it: Mapping the relation between emotion differentiation and emotion regulation. *Cognition and Emotion*, 15, 713–724. doi:10.1080/02699930143000239

Brennan, B. (1987). *Hands of light: A guide to healing through the human energy field.* New York: Pleiades Books.

Bradshaw, J. (1988). *Bradshaw on: The family: A new way of creating solid self-esteem.* Deerfield Beach, FL, Health Communications.

Bunker, L., Williams, J. M., & Zinsser, N. (1993). Cognitive techniques for improving performance and building confidence. In J. M.

Williams (Ed.), *Applied sport psychology: Personal growth to peak performance*. Mountain View, CA: Mayfield.

Buri, J. (2009). Psychology Today. *50 First Dates and the Nice-To-Nasty Ratio.* Retrieved from: http://www.psychologytoday.com/blog/love-bytes/200902/50-first-dates-and-the-nice-nasty-ratio

Byrd, D., & D'Orso, M. (1993). *Rise and walk, The trial and triumph of Dennis Byrd.* NY: HarperCollins

Chopra, D. (1990). *Quantum healing: Exploring the frontiers of mind/body medicine.* New York: Bantam.

Chopra, D. (1994). *Magical mind, magical body.* New York: Crown.

Covey, S. R. (1989). *The seven habits of highly effective people: Restoring the character ethic.* New York: Simon & Schuster.

Csikszentmihalyi, M. (1990). *Flow: The psychology of optimal experience.* NY: Harper & Row.

Diener, E., Emons, R. A., Larsem, R. J., & Griffin, S. (1985). The satisfaction with life scale. *Journal of Personality Assessment.* 49 (1), 71-75.

Diener, E. & Biswas-Diener, R. (2008). *Happiness: Unlocking the mysteries of psychological wealth.* Indianapolis, IN: Wiley-Blackwell

Duckworth, A. L., Peterson, C., Matthews, M. D., & Kelly, D. K. (2007). Grit: Perseverance and passion for long-term goals. *Journal of Personality and Social Psychology*, 92 (6) 1087–110. DOI: 10.1037/0022-3514.92.6.1087

Duckworth, A. L. (2016). *Grit: The power of passion and perseverance.* NY: Scribner

Drews, T. R., (na). *GettingThemSober.com Newsletter.* Received from GettingThemSober.com.

Emmons, R. A. & McCullough, M. E. (2003) Counting blessings versus burdens: An experimental investigation of gratitude and subjective well-being in daily life. *Journal of Personality and Social Psychology*, Vol. 84, No. 2, 377–389. DOI: 10.1037/0022-3514.84.2.377

Enright, R. D., and the Human Development Study Group (1994). Piaget on the moral development of forgiveness: Reciprocity or identity? *Human Development*, 37, 63-80.

Enright, R. D., (2001). *Forgiveness is a choice.* Washington, DC: American Psychological Assoc.

Eskreis-Winkler, L., Shulman, E. P., Beal, S. A., Duckworth, A. L. (2014). The grit effect: Predicting retention in the military, the workplace, school and marriage. *Frontiers in Psychology.* Doi: 10.3389/fpsyg.2014.00036

Fredrickson, B. (March, 2001). The role of positive emotions in positive psychology: The broaden-and-built theory of positive emotions. *American Psychologist.* Vol. 56, 3, 218-226.

Fredrickson, B., (2009). *Positivity: Top-notch research reveals the 3 to 1 ratio that will change your life.* NY: Harmony

Gendlin, E. T. (1981). *Focusing.* New York: Bantam.

Gerber, R. (1955/2001). *Vibrational medicine: New choices for healing ourselves* (3rd ed). Santa Fe, NM: Bear.

Gottman, J.M. (1994). *Why marriages succeed or fail: And how you can make yours last.* NY: Fireside.

Gross, J. J. (2001, Dec.). Emotion regulation in adulthood: Timing is everything. *Current Directions in Psychological Science December.* 10(6). 214-219. doi: 10.1111/1467-8721.00152

Hanson, R., & Siegel, D. J., (2009). *Buddha's brain: The practical neuroscience of happiness, love, and wisdom.* Oakland, CA: New Harbinger Publications

Hebb, D. O., (1949). *The organization of behavior.* NY: Wiley & Sons.

Kabat-Zinn, J. (2011). *Mindfulness for beginners: Reclaiming the present moment – and your life. Louisville,* CO: Sounds True

Kashdan, T.B., Barrett, L. F., & Mcknight, P. E. (2015). Unpacking emotion differentiation: Transforming unpleasant experience by perceiving distinctions in negativity. *Current Directions in Psychological Science.* 24(1) 10–16. DOI: 10.1177/0963721414550708

Kashdan, T.B., & Biswas-Diener, R., (2014). *The upside of your dark side: Why being your whole self – not just your "good" self – drives success and fulfillment.* NY: Hudson Street Press.

Kashdan, T.B., Ferssizidis, P., Collins, R.L., & Muraven, M. (2010). Emotion differentiation as resilience against excessive alcohol use: An ecological momentary assessment in underage social drinkers. *Psychological Science, 21,* 1341-1347.

Kornfield, J. (1994). *Buddha's little instruction book.* NY: Bantam

Johnson, L. (n.d.). *Autogenic training: Compassion and loving kindness meditation.* Retrieved from http://enjoylifebook.com/

Loehr, J. E. (1994). *The new toughness training for sports.* New York: Dutton.

Lyke, J. A. (2008). Insight, but not self-reflection, is related to subjective well-being. *Personality and Individual Differences.* 46 (2009) 66–70 doi:10.1016/j.paid.2008.09.010. Elsevier Ltd.

Lyubormirsky, S. (2008). *The how of happiness.* NY: Penguin Books

Lyubomirsky, S., & Lepper, H. (1999). A measure of subjective happiness: Preliminary reliability and construct validation. *Social Indicators Research*, 46, 137-155. The original publication is available at www.springerlink.com.

Martens, R. (1987). *Coaches guide to sport psychology.* Champaign, IL: Human Kinetics.

Mauss, I. B., Tamir, M., Anderson, C. L., & Savino, N. S. (2011, Aug.). Can seeking happiness make people happy? Paradoxical effects of valuing happiness. *Emotion.* 11(4): 807–815. doi: 10.1037/a0022010

McCullough, M.E., Rachal, K.C., Sandage, S.J., Worthington, E.L., Jr., Brown, S.W., & Hight, T.L. (1998). Interpersonal forgiving in close relationships: II. Theoretical elaboration and measurement. *Journal of Personality and Social Psychology*, 76, 1586-1603.

McCullough, Worthington, & Rachal, (1997). Interpersonal forgiving in close relationships. *Journal of Personality and Social Psychology*, 73 (2) 321-336

Millman, D. (1980). *Way of the peaceful warrior.* Novato, CA: H.J. Kramer/New World Library.

Murphy, S. M. (1986). *Emotional imagery and its effects on strength and fine motor skill performance.* Unpublished doctoral dissertation, Rutgers, New Brunswick, NJ.

Murphy, S. M. (1995). Introduction to sport psychology interventions. In S. M. Murphy (Ed.), *Sport Psychology Interventions* (pp. 1-15). Champaign, IL: Human Kinetics.

Myss, C. (1996). *Anatomy of the spirit: The seven stages of power and healing.* New York: Harmony Books, Crown.

Myss, C. (1996/2002). *Spiritual madness: The necessity of meeting God in darkness.* (audio CD) Louisville, CO: Sounds True.

Nicholas, J.A. (1970). Injuries to knee ligaments: Relationship to looseness and tightness in football players. *JAMA.* 1970;212(13):2236-2239. doi:10.1001/jama.1970.03170260032007

Nideffer, R. M. (1992). *Psyched to win: How to master mental skills.* Champaign, IL: Leisure Press.

Orlick, T. (1990). *In pursuit of excellence: How to win in sport and life through mental training.* Champaign, IL: Leisure Press.

Pace, J. (1985). *A measure of persistence in a group of proprietary college students.* PhD. Dissertation. Miami, FL, University of Miami.

Peale, N. V. (1952/1983). *The power of positive thinking.* New York: Fawcett Crest.

Peck, M. S. (1978). *The road less traveled.* New York: Touchstone; Simon & Shuster.

Peterson, C., (2006). *A primer in positive psychology.* NY: Oxford.

Peterson, C., & Seligman, M. E. P. (2004). *Character strengths and virtues: A handbook and classification.* New York: Oxford University Press and Washington, DC: American Psychological Association. www.viacharacter.org

Pond, R.S., Jr., Kashdan, T.B., DeWall, C.N., Savostyanova, A.A. Lambert, N.M., & Fincham, F.D. (2012). Emotion differentiation buffers aggressive behavior in angered people: A daily diary analysis. *Emotion, 12,* 326-337.

Quisenberry, A. J., Bixel, K. D., Poe, L., Reese, R., Bickel, W. K. (2016, June). *The phenotype of happiness in recovery from alcohol: Length of recovery as a predictor.* Poster presented at the 39th Annual Research Society on Alcoholism (RSA), New Orleans, LA.

Raitt, B. (1991). Tangled and dark. Album: *Luck of the Draw.* NY: Capitol Records.

Ravizza, K., & Hanson, T. (1995). *Heads-up baseball: Playing the game one pitch at a time.* Indianapolis, IN: Masters Press.

Reese, B. (1996). A case involving hypnosis/guided imagery as an adjunct treatment of a fractured wrist, *Athletic Therapy Today*, Vol. 1, No. 5, 18-20, September 1996

Reese, B. (1998). *Motivation for the millennium: Certification – mental skills trainer.* Unpublished Master's Project, Regis University, Denver, CO.

Reese, B. (2005a). *Develop the winner's mentality: 5 essential mental skills for enduring success.* Philadelphia: Xlibris.

Reese, B. (2005b). *The impact of a mental skills training program for enhanced performance on a varsity intercollegiate volleyball team: A case study program evaluation of an educational intervention.* Ph.D. Dissertation, Virginia Polytechnic Institute & State University, Blacksburg, VA. http://nextstepfacilitations.com/wp-content/uploads/2010/02/Reese_PhD_Complete_120105.pdf

Reese, B. (2013, June). *The 13th step: Thriving in recovery.* Workshop conducted at the Third World Congress on Positive Psychology, Westin Bonaventure, Los Angeles, CA.

Reese, B., Koffarnus, M., Quisenberry, A., Bixel, K., Seymour, N., Bianco, A., Patterson, D., Bickel, W. (2015, June). *The 13th step: More on thriving in recovery.* Poster presented at the International

Positive Psychology Association (IPPA) 4th World Congress on Positive Psychology, Orlando, FL.

Reese, J. (2010). *Examining intuitive-creativity via reading Tarot cards in a person-centered climate.* Ph.D. Dissertation, Saybrook University, San Francisco, CA. http://pqdtopen.proquest.com/doc/305239877.html?FMT=AI&pubnum=3396955

Riso, D. & Hudson, R. (n.d.). *Enneagram type nine.* Retrieved from:

http://www.enneagraminstitute.com/TypeNine.asp#.U7w-ErG8OSE

Riso, D., & Hudson, R. (1996). *Personality types: Using the Enneagram for self-discovery.* New York: Houghton Mifflin.

Rivera, J., & Docter, P (2015). *Inside out* [Motion Picture]. USA: Pixar Studios/Disney

Robbins, A. (1992). *Awaken the giant within: How to take immediate control of your mental, emotional, physical & financial destiny.* New York: Simon & Schuster.

Rogers, C. R., (1989). *The Carl Rogers reader.* NY: Mariner Books

Rohr, R. (1992). *Discovering the Enneagram: An ancient tool a new spiritual journey.* New York: Crossroad Publishing

Rotella, B. (1995). *Golf is not a game of perfect.* New York: Simon & Schuster.

Ruiz, D. M. (1997). *The four agreements: A practical guide to personal freedom (A Toltec wisdom book).* San Rafael, CA: Amber-Allen Publishing

Seligman, M. E. P., (2002). *Authentic happiness.* NY: Free Press

Seligman, M. E. P., (2011). *Flourish: A visionary new understanding of happiness and well-being.* NY: Atria/Simon & Schuster

Seligman, M.E.P.; Maier, S.F. (1967). Failure to escape traumatic shock. Journal of *Experimental Psychology* 74: 1–9. doi:10.1037/h0024514. PMID 6032570.

Seligman, M. E. P., & Csikszentmihalyi, M. (2000). Positive psychology: An introduction. *American Psychologist*, Vol 55(1), Jan 2000, 5-14. doi: 10.1037/0003-066X.55.1.5

Schwartz, J. M. & Gladding, R., (2012). *You are not your brain: The 4-step solution for changing bad habits, ending unhealthy thinking, and taking control of your life.* NY: Penguin/Avery Trade

Soloman, R. C., (1993). *The passions: Emotions and the meaning of life* (2nd Ed.) Indianapolis, IN: Hackett ISBN-13: 978-0872202269

Sternberg, R. J. (1986). A triangular theory of love. *Psychological Review*, Vol 93(2), Apr 1986, 119-135. Retrieved from: http://dx.doi.org/10.1037/0033-295X.93.2.119

Stone, H., Stone, S. (2000), *Partnering: A new kind of relationship.* Novoto, CA; New World Library

Tangney, J. P., Fee, R., Reinsmith, C., Boone, A. L., & Lee, N. (1999, August). *Assessing individual differenced in the propensity to forgive.* Paper presented at the American Psychological Association Convention, Boston.

Thaler, R. (1980). Towards a positive theory of consumer choice. *Journal of Economic Behavior and Organization*, 1, 39-60.

Thompson, L. Y., Snyder, C. R., Hoffman, L., Michael, S. T., Rasmussen, H. N., Billings, L. S., et al. (2005). Dispositional forgiveness of self, others, and situations: The Heartland Forgiveness Scale. *Journal of Personality.* 73, 313-359.

Tice, L. (1992). *Investment in excellence for the 90's: Personal resource manual; Video phase 1 & 2; Audio phase 1 & 2*. Seattle, WA: Pacific Institute.

Tice, L. (1993). *Inventing your future*. Seattle, WA: Pacific Institute.

Tice, L. (1995). *Smart talk for achieving your potential: 5 steps to get you from here to there*. Seattle, WA: Pacific Institute.

Tugade, M. M., Fredrickson, B. L., & Barrett, L. F. (2004). Psychological resilience and emotional granularity: Examining the benefits of positive emotions on coping and health. *Journal of Personality, 72*, 1161–1190. doi:10.1111/j.1467-6494.2004.00294.x

Wade, N. G., & Worthington, E. L. (2005). In search of a common core: A content analysis of interventions to promote forgiveness. *Psychotherapy: Theory, Research, Practice, Training.* 42 (2) 160-177

Wanless, J. (1998). *Voyager Tarot: Way of the great oracle* (3rd ed.). Carmel, CA Merrill-West Publishing

Wilkinson, B. (2000). *The prayer of Jabez: Breaking through to the blessed life*. Colorado Springs, CO: Multnomah Publishing

Worthington, E. L., Jr. (2005). *The power of forgiveness*. Philadelphia, PA: Templeton Foundation Press.

Ziglar, Z. (1975/2000). *See you at the top*. Gretna, LA: Pelican Publishing

Zinsser, N., Scott, B., & Camp, B. (1995). *Mental training for peak performance*. Unpublished Handbook. West Point, NY: USMA Center for Enhanced Performance.

APPENDIXES

Appendix A

THE 12 STEPS OF ALCOHOLICS ANONYMOUS

These are the original twelve steps as published by Alcoholics Anonymous:

1. We admitted we were powerless over alcohol—that our lives had become unmanageable.
2. Came to believe that a power greater than ourselves could restore us to sanity.
3. Made a decision to turn our will and our lives over to the care of God *as we understood Him.*
4. Made a searching and fearless moral inventory of ourselves.
5. Admitted to God, to ourselves, and to another human being the exact nature of our wrongs.
6. Were entirely ready to have God remove all these defects of character.
7. Humbly asked Him to remove our shortcomings.
8. Made a list of all persons we had harmed, and became willing to make amends to them all.
9. Made direct amends to such people wherever possible, except when to do so would injure them or others.
10. Continued to take personal inventory, and when we were wrong promptly admitted it.

11. Sought through prayer and meditation to improve our conscious contact with God *as we understood Him*, praying only for knowledge of His will for us and the power to carry that out.
12. Having had a spiritual awakening as the result of these steps, we tried to carry this message to alcoholics, and to practice these principles in all our affairs.

Alcoholics Anonymous (4th ed.). Alcoholics Anonymous World Services. ISBN 1-893007-16-2. OCLC 32014950

Appendix B

THE ENNEAGRAM

The following one-word descriptors can be expanded into four-word sets of traits. Keep in mind that these are merely highlights and do not represent the full spectrum of each type. For further explanation, please visit the Enneagram Institute < https://www.enneagraminstitute.com >

Type **One** – The Reformer – is principled, purposeful, self-controlled, and perfectionistic.

Type **Two** – The Helper – is demonstrative, generous, people-pleasing, and possessive.

Type **Three** – The Achiever – is adaptive, excelling, driven, and image-conscious.

Type **Four** – The Individualist – is expressive, dramatic, self-absorbed, and temperamental.

Type **Five** – The Investigator – is perceptive, innovative, secretive, and isolated.

Type **Six** – The Loyalist – is engaging, responsible, anxious, and suspicious.

Type **Seven** – The Enthusiast – is spontaneous, versatile, distractible, and scattered.

Type **Eight** – The Challenger – is self-confident, decisive, willful, and confrontational.

Type **Nine** – The Peacemaker – is receptive, reassuring, agreeable, and complacent.

Enneagram Levels of Development

Healthy Person
(Seeker: self-actualizing in important areas of life)

- Strives to transcend status quos
- Ego strength not domination of ego needs and ego defensive mechanisms
- Seeks knowledge beyond horizons of current understanding
- Works on transforming personality
- Creatively constructs and negotiates internal and external worlds
- Desires to actualize unique potentialities and realize "calling"
- Appreciates other viewpoints
- Concern beyond self
- Win-win orientation

Normally Adjusted
(Statistically average person: Majority of people. NOTE: *Normal does NOT mean healthy*)

- Short-term, ego-centric success and resolutions
- Frustrated by patterns, conditions of understanding, forces of influence
- Determined to maintain status quo (does not strive to significantly change)
- Identified with ego needs

- Distortion of perceptions
- Defensive mechanisms (see Appendix L)
- Misuse of logical fallacies (see Appendix M)
- Inadequate consideration of rights, needs, and humanity of others
- Need to identify, develop, and trust their strengths
- Win-lose orientation

Unhealthy / Maladjusted
(Reactor: Growing population)

- Pursues immediate gratification
- Polarization (black & white thinking) Delusions
- Compulsive
- Manipulative
- Abusive of self and others
- Extremely destructive; destructive immoderation (overindulgence)
- Psychopathologies
- Lose-lose orientation

The above Enneagram Levels of Development were compiled in a course workbook by Joan Reese, PhD, for her Triune Approach to Positive Aspirations: Compatible Methods for Self-Directed Healthy Decision Making. *They are reprinted with permission. For more about Joan's* Triune Approach to Positive Aspirations *visit: DrJoanReese.com.*

Appendix C

P-E-A AFFIRMATION

The first formal affirmation I created while taking the TPI curriculum was: I am Progressive, Effective, and Authentic. While I was working on the Affirmation section of the *Develop the Winner's Mentality*, Joan and I were discussing what made affirmations work for us.

Joan and I wanted people to seek us out for our talents and skills. (We are not into advertising and marketing our services. Joan was a lawyer before lawyers could advertise. At that time, lawyers attracted clients via word of mouth and networking.) We needed an affirmation and a story for attracting clients. I vividly remember my first-time snorkeling in Hanauma Bay in Hawaii. At that time, we could buy a pack of frozen peas and as we released them in the water beautiful tropical fish would come up to us to eat the peas. So, I combined my affirmation P-E-A – Progressive, Effective, and Authentic – with the story of my Hanauma Bay experience. My affirmation and vivid image was people being naturally attracted to me and coming steadily in large numbers for my services.

So, now my question was, since coming to this realization that I was not an effective salesperson, what type organization could I work in where my affirmation would still work? Judging from the positive events I have manifested (*caused*) in my life, I'd say I found the right organization in Jefferson College!

Appendix D
LETTING GO

Letting go is about releasing negatives such as resentments and anger, so that you do not burn valuable energy that could be utilized to accomplish your goals. *Letting go* of resentments and anger also prevents a build-up of stress.

Letting go is about *control*. You are *in control* in situations where you are responsible and accountable for your performance or behavior. If your performance goes awry, it is natural to get upset with yourself, but you must *let it go*! Correct your performance in your mind, or take notes if appropriate, and then LET – IT – GO! Commit to take corrective actions at the appropriate time, and then do those actions.

You are *not in control* of a situation where the outcome is influenced by the actions of others because you have no control over their actions. If you are not in control of a situation, you must certainly *let it go*! For example, when I lived in New York, no matter how much I planned to be somewhere on time, I could not control the traffic on the Long Island's Northern State Parkway. I can know the standard traffic patterns and project how long I need to arrive on time at my destination. I can check the news for traffic jams on the parkway and even leave a little early to give myself a cushion. At that point I have done all I can do. If I find myself in heavy traffic, I must *let go* of the anger and frustration because I have no control if someone has had an accident or their car broke down. *Letting go* does not mean I don't care about not arriving on time.

By *letting go*, you achieve control: control of your emotions, control of your attitude, and control of your life. *Letting go* is achieved by integrating the 5 Essential Mental Skills.

I also use the Serenity Prayer for *letting go*. It is a great way to remind yourself about *letting go:* "Grant me the serenity to accept the things I cannot change, the courage to change the things I can, and the wisdom to know the difference."

Letting go is not an intellectual exercise. Some self-help gurus make *letting go* seem like an intellectual exercise that is easy to accomplish. "Oh sure, my boss yelled at me today for something completely out of my control, but I just let it go! I'm not harboring a resentment, and I'm not angry." *NOT!*

Letting go is difficult for many reasons. You may work in one of those dysfunctional environments where insecurity reigns and appearance of caring is actually more important than caring itself. If you don't show that you are upset when your boss yells, you may be perceived by the boss and others – and even sometimes by yourself – as not caring about the business. If that's the case, be careful of how you *appear* to others as you learn and practice the technique of *letting go*.

When needing to *let go* remember the following:

- If you are not in control, you can't change it. So *LET IT GO!*
- If you are in control, and it needs to be changed – change it! Then *LET IT GO!*
- Knowing the difference and *letting go* is wisdom!

The above is modified from *Chapter 12: Mental Toughness* in *Develop The Winner's Mentality* (Reese, 2005).

Appendix E

VISUALIZATION – GO TO YOUR ROOM EXERCISE

Imagine yourself in your favorite room. It could be your living room, family room, your den, whatever it is – your favorite room. Now, imagine sitting in your favorite place in that room. It could be a chair, sofa, or even your bed, whatever is your favorite place to relax. As you sit in your favorite place, close your eyes and count the number of windows in the room. Remember, you don't have to literally *see* them; you may just get a sense of how many windows are in the room. Once counted, open your eyes and think about what that "looked" like.

After counting the windows and reflecting on the process, once again close your eyes and "look" at the wall in front of you there in your favorite room. Is it painted, paneled, or papered? What color is it?

Now imagine what is on that wall. What do you see, sense, or perceive on that wall? Maybe it is a TV or maybe pictures or bookshelves or a window. See what is on that wall. Get a feel for what is on that wall. You *know* what is on that wall.

After you get that image, shift your attention and your view to wall to the left of the wall you are now observing. Now, imagine what is on the wall on the left-hand side – the left hand wall. Is there a fireplace? Is there a door? Maybe there are sliding glass doors. What does it look like? What is on the left wall? Get a sense of what that wall is looks like?

After you get that image, then imagine the wall on your right side. What does it look like? Is there a door, windows, pictures, a painting, artwork? If there is a window, what kind of window treatment is there? If there is a picture, what are the details? Spend more time on the right wall than you did on the left wall. Where are the electrical sockets? What does the baseboard look like? Do this until you *know* everything that's on that wall.

When you've accomplished that, imagine the wall behind you and what is on that wall. After you get this image, and you have successfully examined the entire wall behind you, take a deep breath and open your eyes again. Reflect on the process.

SEE, I knew you could visualize.

The "Go To Your Room" visualization exercise was adapted with permission from *Disidentification for Stress Reduction Handbook* by Paul Haber, Ph.D. 1988; http://www.stress-institute.com

Appendix F

PART 1 ENERGY MANAGEMENT – THE PAPER CLIP EXPERIMENT

- **Take an ordinary paper clip and a piece of string about 6" long.**
- Tie one end of the string around the paper clip, so that it becomes a pendulum.
- Hold the free end of the string between the thumb and index finger of your dominant hand so that the paper clip is dangling freely.
- Rest your elbow of the arm holding the string on your knee or the top of a table or desk so it will be stabilized.
- With the elbow resting on something stable, your arm should be in the shape of a "V" with the paper clip dangling down from your thumb and index finger.
- With your free hand "still" the clip so it becomes motionless.
- Now, cup the palm of your free hand and place it about ½" beneath the paper clip.
- Be still and watch what happens!

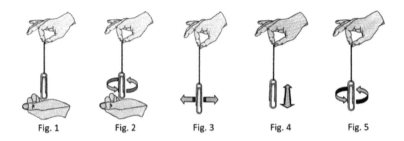

Fig. 1 Fig. 2 Fig. 3 Fig. 4 Fig. 5

What should be happening is that the clip will begin to swing in a circular motion without you doing anything! Pretty Freaky, huh? (Figs.1 & 2). This is natural: your energetic field is moving the clip. If the clip is not moving, close your eyes and think of something else – a pleasant visualization, or even what you have to do tomorrow. Then open your eyes and take a look. If it's still not moving, check out what you were thinking. You may be thinking, "be still", or, "this can't move." You're probably fighting it with some thought. Don't be afraid, it's just your energetic field moving the clip.

Even if your paper clip doesn't seem to be moving, proceed to the next part of the exercise anyway.

Part 2: Putting Energetic Thought to Work (Fig. 3)
Now for the real fun!

- Once again, still the clip.
- This time just let the clip dangle without your other hand beneath it.
- Using only your thoughts – don't move your arm or hand – make the clip swing toward you, and away from you.
- Just focus your attention on the clip as you think, "come toward me and move away from me."

Ah-Ah, don't move that arm. That's not necessary. The clip will move at the direction of your thoughts!

Is it moving toward you and away from you? What did you think about when it started happening? Some people are shocked or scared. While teaching a seminar in England, the Director of Sales for the company I was working with was so startled he let out a yelp and threw the clip across the room.

When you get the clip to move toward you and away from you, go directly to the Exercise #3.

Need Help?

Having a problem getting the clip to move? First of all, remember this is a *skill* – not magic. And, like any skill, it can be learned and improved with practice. Read through the following and then try it again and this time adding the visualization.

- First, still the clip.
- Now, using your imagination, close your eyes and imagine the following:
- Imagine the sun. Get a sense of the power of the sun – the energy of the sun.
- The sun is the most powerful source of energy in our solar system, so just imagine the sun and its energy.
- Not the heat of the sun, just the energy.
- Imagine that the energy of the sun is focused in a beam going right into the middle of your forehead.
- This energy then travels around your head and down through your neck. It continues down through the arm holding the clip all the way to your fingertips.
- There it moves into the string causing the clip to move toward you and away from you.
- See it moving in your minds' eye, feel it moving.
- Now, open your eyes and see that it is moving.
- Repeat this exercise until you get it to move.

If that doesn't work, get a child to help you. Preferably someone who has not reached their teens. Children have less preconceived notions about what can and cannot be done. If you still can't do it – don't give up. All it means is that you are resisting it. Come back and try it again later as you learn to *let go* of your resistance.

Wrong Way?

If you are able to make the clip move, but it's going in the wrong direction (side to side as opposed to toward you and away from you), you may have experienced what is commonly referred to as a *grasshopper mind*. That means that your thoughts jumped around, and you are not controlling them. With practice, you will gain control of your thoughts and of the direction.

Even if you are not successful with the directional component, continue with the exercise doing the best you can. If you still have problems, read Chapter 10, "Thinking Deliberately" in *Develop the Winner's Mentality* and come back and try the Paper Clip Exercise again.

Part 3: Side to Side (Fig. 4)
- **Again, still the clip.**
- Now, using the energy of your thoughts, make the clip move from side to side. Think "move left, then right; left – right."
It's getting easier now, isn't it?

Part 4: Round & Round (Fig. 5)
- **OK, still the clip again. This time try making it stop just with your thoughts.**
- Once it is still – make it go in a circle (without holding your palm beneath it).
- Think, "Circle – move in a circle" (Envision a clockwise or counterclockwise motion.)

Got it? Now, can you make it reverse direction without "stilling" it by hand? If so, the Star Wars *Force* is strong within you.

Practice, Practice, Practice!

Remember, this exercise is a skill. As such, it can be enhanced and improved by practice. The more often you do it, the more proficient you will become and the easier it will be.

BONUS: Take a Paper Clip Break

Whenever you're having trouble concentrating or focusing, take out your paper clip and practice the above exercises for 2-3 minutes. When you stop, you'll find that you've just performed a mini-meditation. Your brain and your mind will work better.

I often tell my teenage clients and my students that when they can make the clip move in figure 8 patterns, then it's time to call Yoda, the Jedi Master from *Star Wars*, because they are now ready to begin training as a Jedi Knight! May the *Force* be with you.

Magic?

This is not magic. By focusing your attention on thinking about the direction you want the paper clip to move, your mind tells your brain to send kinetic energy down through your arm and fingertips and into the string. If you were hooked up to extremely sensitive measurement device, you would see that there is actually some "microscopic" movement in your fingertips. This movement – energy – is then amplified as it travels down the string (pendulum), resulting in movement of the paper clip.

It's neither magic nor some woo-woo, New Age incantation or witch's spell. It is just physics at work. The *ah-hah* realization is that you *cause* it to go the direction you want it to go by simply thinking about it. You can change the direction of the pendulum by changing your mind. Now that's power! If you can cause the pendulum to change directions by merely changing your mind, what else can you cause to happen?

Do you think you can cause a change in direction of your life? I hope so. *Causing* your success should no longer be in doubt! This is the basis of becoming self-efficacious – an agent for *change*!

This above paper-clip exercise was taught to me at a graduate level sport psychology course at the University of Virginia by Professor Linda Bunker, PhD. She was demonstrating the power of visualization. For me, it goes beyond visualization and demonstrates graphically the first two statements in Maxim #2 of the *Winner's Mentality System*:

- We are energetic beings.
- Our thoughts have energy.

These statements explain why the third statement is true.

- We move toward and become like what we think!

With this in mind, from now on think of your thoughts as *things*. Choose carefully which thoughts you will entertain and put energy into. That is, pay attention to your self-talk!

The above is modified from *Chapter 7: Energy Management* in *Develop The Winner's Mentality* (Reese, 2005).

Appendix G

FEELAZATION

Perform this exercise by first visualizing an event and then by feelazizing the emotion associated with the event. If your felt image is "very clear" give it a 3; a "fairly clear" felt image rates a 2; and an "unclear" felt image rates a 1. If you cannot form a felt image, or if it's very "unclear" or "indiscernible", give it 0.

After reading each item, close your eyes, picture it as clearly as you can, feelazize it as intently as possible, spend some time – at least one or two minutes in that felt emotion – and record your rating. Revisit the *Feelazation Vividness Scale* periodically until you can make each feelazized image a 3.

1. Visualize someone you are/were in a very close relationship with.
    a. See him/her standing in front of you. _____
    b. Imagine him/her laughing. _____
    c. Picture his/her eyes. _____
    d. Picture his/her smile. _____
    e. Hear his/her laugh. _____
    f. Imagine you are in an embrace _____
    g. How do they make you feel? _____
    h. Where in your body do you feel this feeling? _____
    i. Enjoy it! Name it! Anchor it! Hold it! _____

2. Imagine your 8th birthday (you may substitute any year in which you had a wonderful party). _____
   a. Visualize the surroundings. _____
   b. Where did it take place? Can you see the surroundings? _____
   c. See what you were wearing. _____
   d. See how many people you can identify. _____
   e. Can you see what they were wearing? _____
   f. Imagine:
      - You are ready to blow out the candles and make a wish.
      - There is a huge pile of presents at the end of the table.
      - All of your friends are singing *Happy Birthday* to you. _____
   g. How do you feel? _____
   h. Where in your body do you feel this feeling? _____
   i. Enjoy it! Name it! Anchor it! Hold it! _____
3. Imagine your best ever performance (it can be a sport, theater, presentation, spelling bee, etc.). _____
   a. Visualize the surroundings. Make them as vivid as possible. _____
   b. Place yourself back in the event – near the end. _____
   c. The event is over, and you have excelled! _____
   d. Everyone is congratulating you – they may even be cheering. _____
   e. How does that make you feel? _____
   f. Where in your body do you feel this feeling? _____
   g. Enjoy it! Name it! Anchor it! Hold it! _____

Once you have become competent with feelazizing past events, you can begin to feelazize your future. The above *Feelazation Vividness Scale* exercise is from *Develop the Winner's Mentality* (Reese, 2005, p. 278)

Appendix H

SAVORING: EXERCISE & REFLECTION

Savoring refers to our awareness of pleasure and our deliberate attempt to make it last. Think of it as the opposite of coping. (*The following is adapted from an assignment given in my Positive Psychology Course.*)

Exercise: Between now and the assignment due date pick a meal that you plan to enjoy (you don't have to "go out," but that will make it even more special). Instead of choosing a wonderful appetizer, a wonderful entree, a wonderful wine or beer, and a wonderful dessert, choose one – and only one – to be the focus of your meal and *savor it* without flooding your taste buds with all the others.

After savoring one part of the meal – savor the event. Use the following '**Savoring Strategies**' as a guideline and incorporate as many as are appropriate:

- **Sharing with Others:** Share your experience of the meal with someone (in other words, relive the experience).
- **Memory Building:** Take mental (or actual) photographs or even a physical souvenir of the event to reminisce about later with others.
- **Sharpening Perceptions:** Focus on certain elements of the experience – and block out others.

- **Absorption:** Let yourself get totally immersed in the pleasure and try not to think about other matters – Wallow in the positivity.
- **Self-Congratulation:** If the meal (or part of the meal) is a reward for some accomplishment, do not be afraid of pride – enjoy it. Tell yourself how impressed others are and remember how long you have waited for this moment or event to happen.

Reflection: At some point after the experience reflect not only on the experience of the meal, but also on savoring the experience of the meal and the impact of the 'Savoring Strategies'.

Appendix I

GRATITUDE LETTER

Pick a person in your life whom you would like to thank, someone who has meant a lot to you. Rather than picking your roommate, boyfriend, or girlfriend, you should pick some special person in your life that has made a big impact, perhaps a bigger impact than they were aware of, and whom *you never adequately thanked* (e.g. a teacher, a parent, a coach, a mentor, etc.). Also, for this initial exercise, do not pick a person who is too easy for you to thank.

Write this person a letter. After you've written it, contact the person and ask to visit in person. **Read the letter aloud when you are face to face**. If a face-to-face visit is not possible, then read it aloud to them over the phone (or on Skype, etc.) and then send them the letter. [Should the person be deceased, seriously consider a trip to the cemetery, etc.) REMINDER: bring tissues to the reading.

Sometime soon after reading the letter to the person, reflect on the total experience: how it was to write the letter, and then what emotions you experienced as you read it to them (and how they reacted), and then finally how you felt after the exercise. This reflective portion is necessary for you to begin to discriminate the subtle differences in your emotions.

This exercise was adapted from *A Primer in Positive Psychology* by Christopher Peterson (2006, NY: Oxford) & *Authentic Happiness* by Martin Seligman (2002, NY: Free Press). It appears in multiple publications, blogs, etc. without attribution.

Appendix J

AUTOGENIC TRAINING MEDITATION

Practice the Autogenic Training as prescribed below a minimum of one time per day for one month. (I suggest at bedtime). Reflect briefly (150-200 words) yet substantively on the process at the end of each week for four (4) weeks. After 4 weeks also write a summary reflection of your experience.

Many students and clients create an audio file of the above and download it into their media player for listening.

NOTE: The successful practice of Autogenic training will be necessary for the Compassion & Loving Kindness Exercise.

AUTOGENIC TRAINING

The autogenic training exercises below can help you recover from anxiety, stress, and tension. Persons who practice autogenic training twice a day fall asleep better and sleep more deeply. They think more clearly and are less prone to anxiety or depression. People who meditate each day for fifteen to twenty minutes, once or twice a day, age more slowly. They are less likely to become ill.

Repeat every phrase, silently, in your mind, <u>three times</u>. Say the phrase in a quiet, thoughtful way. Pause after and notice how you feel. Focus on your feelings for two or three breaths. Practice each set of exercises until you are quite comfortable with them.

Set 1:
  I feel quite quiet... I am easily relaxed...
  My right arm feels heavy... My left arm feels heavy... My arms feel heavy and relaxed...
  My right leg feels heavy... My left leg feels heavy... My arms and legs feel heavy and relaxed... My hips and stomach are quiet and relaxed... My breathing is calm and regular... My heartbeat is calm and regular... My shoulders are heavy... My face is smooth and quiet... I am beginning to feel quite relaxed...

Set 2:
  My right hand is warm... Warmth flows into my right hand... My left hand is warm... Warmth flows into my left hand... Warmth flows into my hands... My hands are warm... My right foot is warm... My left foot is warm... My hands and feet are warm... Warmth flows into my hands and feet... My eyes are comfortably warm and peaceful... My forehead is cool and my eyes are warm... I am warm and peaceful...

Set 3:
  I am beginning to feel quite relaxed... I feel calm and confident... I appreciate myself and others... My life has many blessings... I see my own blessings... I appreciate life more and more...

Set 4:
  Just for today, I anger not, I worry not... I am grateful and humble... I do my work with appreciation... I am kind to all...

This exercise was adapted from Lynn D. Johnson, PhD with permission. http://enjoylifebook.com/

Appendix K

COMPASSION AND LOVING KINDNESS MEDITATIONS

The Autogenic Training Exercise (Appendix J) should be conducted prior to beginning the Compassion & Loving Kindness Meditation.

This exercise should be performed daily over a 6-week period. There are five categories for the compassionate meditation explained below. At the end of every week you will write a brief reflection on the appropriate category of compassionate meditation After 5 weeks, write a substantive reflection on the entire process and any changes that may have occurred in your attitudes or your life.

Compassion and Loving Kindness Meditations Exercise

Do you want to be much more joyful than you could have imagined? Developing the skill of *compassion* may be the most powerful way you can do that. Let's talk about this skill and you can decide if it is something you want to cultivate.

Compassion means to be able to understand how someone is feeling and to want to relieve suffering. You see there are two parts. First, you have to be able to *empathize* with another person. Second, you *cultivate the wish to help*.

This meditation tool to enhance compassion requires the incorporation of autogenic training (see Appendix J). With autogenic training the idea is to repeat a phrase in your mind three times, notice the result, and then repeat another phrase. For example, I might repeat "My right arm feels heavy." Then I notice a relaxed, heavy feeling coming into my arm.

For this meditation you should think of five categories of people you will develop compassion towards.

1. Yourself
2. Family members
3. Close friends
4. Acquaintances – people you know but not well
5. Finally: enemies

Work on the first three for several weeks before working on the last two.

Oddly enough, some people balk at focusing first on themselves. I understand that, depending on how you were raised, you may have discomfort with that idea. But consider, you cannot give to another what you yourself do not have. If you don't feel deep kindness and appreciation towards yourself, how can you feel it with another? The Buddhists taught this concept as a key foundation. So, did Jesus with the directive: "You must love your neighbor as yourself." (Mark 12:31, New International Version)

If you struggle with number one – please continue working on it throughout the exercise, as it is a major component of knowing 'Who you AM!' You may want to start with family and then close friends, and then return to yourself when you master the feeling. Remember: **To thrive and flourish in life you must be able to love, respect, and have compassion for yourself!)**

Phrases you can use (Remember to repeat 3 times): "I feel kind and tender toward (say and think of a *target person*, such as myself, my spouse, my child) . . . I feel warm and sensitive toward (target) . . . I feel love and warmth toward (target) . . . I wish all good for (target) . . . I feel patient and helpful toward (target) . . ." You can write your own phrases; make sure they illustrate the feelings you want to cultivate.

Felt Sense & Feelazation: As with the Autogenic Training you did prior to this exercise, practice feeling the positive emotions – love, compassion, gratitude, kindness, etc. – in your body. This also enhances your ability to discern the discreet differences in these emotions. When you can feel the positive emotion – anchor it and name it so you can recall it.

Practice this exercise every day. Dr. Johnson suggests during the lunch hour; I prefer bed-time. Regardless of the time, set aside fifteen to twenty minutes to practice this. Be sure to not go to sleep, but stay reasonably alert and focused. (*Feel free to make an audio file for each of the five categories. Some of my students just add each new category to the one they have been working on. They say it helps them deepen their compassion. Consider this also if you are having a problem with a particular category; just keep it in the meditation.*)

NOTE for Enemies Meditation: Many people struggle with how to frame compassion for their enemies. Try saying this: "I have been practicing a compassionate release for those that have wronged me." Then pronounce the person's name and the pain they caused, e.g.: "John lied about me to my boss. Now as I wipe my hand over my heart, head and shoulders, I declare that I am breaking the bonds the bind us. I do not have the desire to hold this hurt, sorrow, anger or pain any longer. As I wipe my hand across myself my heart, head, and shoulders, I cancel any bonds that may be holding us together. I am free. I am not to judge John for the actions that he did. I am free and peaceful. Every time I do say this I feel more free and more peaceful." [This exercise is also compassion to yourself as it allows you to release feelings of ill will. You may also want to "hold a space" for their healing and yours.]

Other ways to actually practice compassion are to perform acts of service and kindness towards others. You might consider reading to children in the hospital, fixing up the home of a widow or single mother, finding employment for those out of work, and so forth. There are many opportunities to volunteer. Turn your intent into acts.

This exercise was adapted from Lynn D. Johnson, PhD with permission.

Appendix L

DEFENSE MECHANISMS

Defense Mechanism	Definition	Example
Denial	Not accepting reality because it is too painful.	You are arrested for drunk driving several times but don't believe you have a problem with alcohol.
Displacement	Channeling a feeling or thought from its actual source to something or someone else.	When you get mad at your brother, you break a plate.
Projection	Attributing unacceptable thoughts or feelings to someone or something else	You get really mad at your husband but scream that he's the one mad at you.
Rationalization	Justifying behaviors & real motivations by substituting "good", acceptable reasons for them.	You justify cheating on your taxes but insist that everyone does it & that you work really hard and love your country.
Reaction Formation	Adopting beliefs, attitudes, & feelings contrary to what you really believe.	You say you love the refugee children but demand their immediate deportation.
Suppression	The effort to hide & control unacceptable thoughts or feelings.	You are attracted to someone but say that you really do not like that person at all.

Sublimation	Redirecting unacceptable, instinctual drives into personally & socially acceptable channels.	Intense rage redirected in the form of participation in sports such as boxing, football, punching bag.
Repression	Burying a painful feeling or thought from your awareness though it may resurface in symbolic form.	You forgot the time of your father's funeral.
Undoing	Trying to reverse or undo a thought or feeling by performing an action that signifies an opposite feeling than your original thought or feeling.	You have disdain for poor people so you volunteer at a soup kitchen. You support racist policies, but adopt a black child.
Isolation of affection	Attempting to avoid a painful thought or feeling by objectifying & emotionally detaching from the feeling.	Acting aloof & indifferent toward someone when you really dislike that person.
Splitting	Everything in the world is seen as all good or all bad with nothing in between.	You think your best friend is absolutely worthless when she forgot a lunch date with you.
Regression	Reverting to a past less mature way of handling stresses & feelings.	You & your spouse get into an argument so you stomp off into another room & pout.
Altruism	Handling your own pain by helping others.	After your spouse dies, you keep busy by volunteering at your church.
Humor	Focusing on funny aspects of a painful situation.	A person jokes about losing hair during treatments for cancer.

The above Defense Mechanisms were compiled in a course workbook by Joan Reese, PhD, for her Triune Approach to Positive Aspirations: Compatible Methods for Self-Directed Healthy Decision Making. *They are reprinted with permission.*

For more on Joan's Triune Approach to Positive Aspirations *visit DrJoanReese.com*

Appendix M

FALLACIES

Fallacies are errors in reasoning. They include irrelevant or illicit statements. They lack supportive, valid evidence. They include the following:

- **Ad hominem:** An attack on the character or background of a person rather than his or her opinions or arguments. You only support racial equality because your sister married a _____.
- **Ad populum:** An emotional appeal that speaks to positive (such as patriotism, religion, democracy) or negative (such as terrorism or fascism) concepts rather than the real issue at hand. E.g., if you believe in democracy you would object to registration of guns and background checks. If you are a true American you do not buy foreign cars.
- **Begging the Claim:** A conclusion that requires proof and validation is assumed within the stated claim. E.g., dirty, polluting coal should be banned. I.e., the need to logically explain coal as dirty and pollution is not explained. Instead, all that is offered is a blanket statement.
- **Circular Argument:** A restatement of an argument rather than actually proving it. E.g., Neil deGrasse Tyson is a good communicator because he speaks effectively. I.e., here the evidence is the same as the argument (the point that is being made). Need additional information (not repetitive statements) to explain why Tyson is a good communicator.

- **Either/or:** A conclusion that oversimplifies the argument by reducing it to two sides or choices. E.g., We can either ban guns or become a killing society. Here, the multiple choices between the extremes are ignored.
- **Genetic Fallacy:** A conclusion based on an argument that the origins of a person, idea, thing, or theory determine its character, nature, or worth, even when not inherently related. E.g., individuals of mixed races are just mutts who drain our society. The Volkswagen Beetle is an evil car because it was originally designed by Hitler's army.
- **Hasty Generalization:** Rushing to a conclusion before you have all the relevant facts. E.g., even though I only heard the overview of the course, I can tell it will be informative.
- **Moral Equivalence:** Minor misdeeds equated with major atrocities. E.g., the policeman gave me a ticket. He is a Hitler.
- **Post hoc ergo propter hoc:** Assumption that if 'A' occurred after 'B' then 'B' must have caused 'A.' E.g., I ate shrimp. Now I am sick. The shrimp made me sick.
- **Red Herring:** A diversionary tactic that avoids key issues by avoiding opposing arguments rather than addressing them. E.g., The fish in the Gulf may now be unsafe but what about the need for oil for our economy. Here, the discussions switches from safe food to economic issues. Must we really ignore food safety for economic consequences?
- **Slippery Slope:** Conclusion based on the premise that if A happens, then eventually through a series of events from B through Y will happen and end in Z happening, too. This is basically equating A and Z. So, if we don't want Z to occur, A must not be allowed to occur either. E.g., if there are background checks, the government will take our guns.
- **Straw Man:** Oversimplification of an opponent's viewpoint followed by attacking the opponent. People who don't support increasing the minimum wage hate the poor.

The above Fallacies were compiled in a course workbook by Joan Reese, PhD, for her Triune Approach to Positive Aspirations: Compatible

Methods for Self-Directed Healthy Decision Making. *They are reprinted with permission.*

For more on Joan's Triune Approach to Positive Aspirations *visit DrJoanReese.com*

INDEX

3 Essential Attitudes, 334, 368
3 Head-Butt Rule, 254, 289-290
5x7 Journal (Notebook), 228, 268
12-Step(s) [of Alcoholics Anonymous], xvii, 383

AA, Alcoholics Anonymous, xvii, 3, 10-11
Abramoski, Ed (Abe), 56, 72
Accountability [& Responsibility], 310, 312
Addiction Recovery Research Center (ARRC), xi, xiii, xv, xx, 353
Adjustifying, 289
Anchor / Anchoring, 291, 295, 306, 347, 408
Anderson, George, 134
Anderson, Kenny, 102
Angelou, Maya, 330
Anshel, Mark, 217
Archer, Dr., 212, 214-216
Autogenic Training Meditation, 291, 298, 404

Barrymore, Drew, 330
Bauer, Joe, 38
Bauer, Ma-Maw, 36-38
Bauer, Tom Jr., 38-39
Belloti, Sr. Marion, 250, 252, 259
Bethard, Bobby, 207
Bickel, Warren, xiii, xv, 353

Biswas-Diener, Robert, 279, 300
Bradshaw, John, 229
Brennan, Barbara, 218
Broaden & Build Theory, 292, 294-295, 310, 346
Brown, Willie, 21
Bunker, Linda, 217, 397
Brummagen, Arthur [Maj.-General], 212-215
Bruno, John, 211-212
Buri, J., 330
Buffett, Jimmy, 78
Burruss, Pepper, 89-90, 92, 106, 111, 125, 129, 136, 143, 176-77, 180-182
Byrd, Dennis, 178-180, 183

Cahill, Bob, 162, 165
Carroll, Pete, 185, 198, 212, 220, 277, 292, 303
CG [SG's sister], 87, 231
Chopra, Deepak, 217-218
Coach University, 223
Compassion, 156-157, 243, 257, 270, 298-300, 302, 307-308, 310, 318-320, 323, 328-329, 347, 350
Compassion and Loving Kindness Meditation, 298, 406-408
Congruency, xxi, 334-335
Conway, Darryl, 181, 202

Coslet, Bruce, 4, 130, 194, 220
Covey, Stephen, 217
Csoka, Louis [Col.], 186

Daly, Chuck, 62
Dark Night of the Soul, xxi-xxii, 276-277, 280, 296, 303, 313
Davey, Tim, 89, 100
Davis, Al, 102-103
Davis, Colle, 223-224, 228
Davis, Otho, 192-193, 198-199, 206
Defense Mechanisms, 315, 409-410
Drews, Toby Rice, 321
Duckworth, Angela, 292-293, 355
Dyer, Pat, 34, 61, 67

Effective Thinking, 217, 281, 285, 292
Empathic Listening and Understanding, 334-335
Empathy, 19, 155, 157, 299, 304, 310, 318-319, 323, 327-329, 345, 350
Emotive Imagery, 291
Endowment Effect, 347
End-result Thinking, 227, 281-282, 298
Energy Management, 281, 283-284, 291-292, 393-398
Enneagram, 259-265, 385-387
Eriksonian Hypnosis, 182
Esiason, Boomer, 184, 212-213

Fallacies, 315, 411-413
Feelazation, 281, 290-292, 295, 298, 317, 399-400
Felt Sense, 233, 272, 291, 295, 297-300, 306, 317, 343, 408
Flow, 275, 281
Flynn, Bill, 62
Foley, Tim, 34

Forgive & Forget, 320
Fredrickson, Barbara, 294-295, 300, 347
Freud, Sigmund, 307
Fry, Bob, 109

Gandhi, Mahatma, 306
Gastineau, Mark, 95, 97, 131
Gerber, Richard, 217
Glenn, Aaron, 183
Go To Your Room [Visualization Exercise], 391-392
Goal Setting, 133, 180, 208, 217, 219, 222, 226, 242, 281-283, 290, 292
Godfrey, Joe [Dr. G], 72, 74, 81
Gottman, John, 330, 347
Griese, Bob, 35
Grit, 355
Gratitude Dance, 336-337
Gratitude Letter, 296, 403
Gross, James, 300
Gutman, Steve, 129, 160, 182, 196, 202, 206, 119

Haber, Paul, 192, 217, 392
Hatley, Gert, 13, 31, 33, 37, 50
Hatley, J. B., 13, 18, 31, 33, 38-39, 50
Hatley, Jimmy, 20, 23, 28, 35, 94, 122
Hatley, Tiffany, 122-123
Hatley, Trudy, 13-14, 24-26
Hampton, Bill, 79-80, 91
Hanratty, Terry, 35
Hanson, Tom, 217
Heidt, Adam, 272
Hebb, Donald, 346
Henning, Dan [Sandy], 88-89, 92-94, 109
Hershman, Elliott, 117, 125, 173, 200

Hess, Leon, 10, 83-85, 99, 101-102, 105, 109, 124, 126-127, 161, 168, 183, 191, 195-197, 202-203
Hickey, Mike [Jets], 86, 112, 129
Hickey, Michael [Lexicor], 213, 216
Hudson, Russ, 263
Holding a Healing Space, 319-320
Holovak, Mike, 84-85
Holtz, Lou, 79, 88
Hopkins, Anthony, 279
Horton, William, xi

Ingram, Mark, 195
International Quit & Recovery Registry (IQRR), xiii, xxii, 354, 356
Issues [vs. Virtues], 321-322
Izzo, Lenny, 217

James, LeBron, 292, 305
Johnson, Johnny, 184
Johnson, Lynn, 298

Kabat-Zinn, Jon, 298
Kashdan, Todd, 279, 300-301
Kensil, Jim, 89, 98-100, 104-107, 114, 119
Keyes, Leroy, 47, 56
Kirwan, Pat [PK], 218
Klecko, Joe, 83, 97-98, 100, 102
Kleinschmidt, Dean, 48, 143
Koffarnus, Mikhail, xi,
Kotite, Rich, 195-206, 231
Krackow, Mike, 271

Lanahan, Jude, 31
Law of Attraction, 222
Ledbetter, Bob [Lois], 93, 96, 107, 109
Leonard, Thomas, 223

Letting Go, 279, 309, 316-317, 319, 389-390
Lexicor, 212-214, 216, 221
Lipton, James, 279
Loehr, Jim, 217
Lott, Ronnie, 183-184
Lyons, Marty, 95, 98

M., Bobby, 161-165
Magis, xxii, 282
Marchetti, Tony, 58, 72-73, 79
Marino, Dan, 194-195
Martens, Rainer, 217
Marshall, Leonard, 184
Maslow, Abraham, 260, 307
Massman, Fritz, 62, 64
Matthew [6:14-15], 310
Mauss, Iris, 302
McCullough, Michael, 308
McDermott, John [McD], 224
McGill, Ormand, 248
McNab, Diana, 187, 190-191
McNeil, Freeman, 97, 102, 279-280
Meditation
    Autogenic Training Meditation, 291, 298, 404-405
    Compassion and Loving Kindness Meditation, 298, 406-408
    Mindfulness, 298
Melanie [SGs relative], 154-157, 161, 349
Mental Toughness, 217, 219, 223, 281, 292-293
Mersereau, Scott, 178
MG [SG's sister], 234
Michaels, Walt, 79-80, 84, 91, 97, 109, 118, 194, 196, 215
Millman, Dan, 218
Mindfulness, 298, 300

Morning Conversation of Marriage, 333
Moore, Rob, 183
Moore, Thomas, 276
Mount, Rick, 39, 47
Munoz, Anthony, 102
Murphy, Shane, 217, 291
Murry, Joe [Joe Murder], 74, 79
Myss, Carolyn, 276-280, 338, 343-344

Newell, Pinky, 33, 48, 66, 90
Neurolinguistic Programming [NLP], 182, 248
Neuroplasticity [Self-directed], 345-346
Niebuhr, Reinhold, 317
Nice-to-Nasty Ratio, 329-330
Nicholas, Jim [Nick the Knife], 81, 83, 85, 98, 100, 106, 126, 152, 173, 199-200, 215-216
Nideffer, Bob, 217
Night Sea Journey, 276, 278
Nine [Enneagram Type], 241, 265

O'Keeffe, Georgia, 348
Olajuwon, Hakeem, 305
Orlick, Terry, 217

Pace, Joe, 225-226, 270, 347
Paper Clip Experiment [Energy Exercise], 393-398
Patten, Joe [Joe P], 7-8, 202, 129
Pawleski, Suzann Pileggi & James, 336
P-E-A Affirmation, 388
Peale, Norman Vincent, 217
Peck, M. Scott, 217
Pellman, Elliot, 136, 143, 153, 173, 178, 199, 206, 214
PERMA, 275, 325

Phipps, Mike, 34, 47
Pickel, Bill, 134, 184
Positivity Ratio, 347
Powell, Marvin, 83, 85
Prayer of Jabez, 350-351
Price, David, 198, 202-203, 206
Processing [vs. Ruminating], 314-318

Raitt, Bonnie, 267
Ramos, Frank, 92, 99, 103-105
Rauch, John, 58, 68
Ravizza, Ken, 132-133, 183, 186, 217
Real Apology, 310-312, 323, 342
Reese & Sons, C. H., 13-14, 18, 27, 29, 44, 48, 61
Reese, Bobby [Dad], 12-19, 23, 25, 29-30, 32-33, 38, 44, 49-51, 127-128, 167, 255, 258
Reese, Delia, 14, 26
Reese, Franny [mom], 13, 23, 44, 49-51
Reese, Jane, 18
Reese, Jimmy, 13-14, 17
Reese, Joan, xiii, 237-241, 244-256, 259, 265-267, 270, 272, 282, 290, 308-309, 319-320, 329-330, 332-338, 340, 342-344, 348, 351
Reese, Joe [Margie], 17-18, 44, 240, 258
Reese, Rachel, 71-72, 114-115, 121, 128, 147, 152, 154, 156-159
Reese, Rob, 70-73, 107, 114-115, 120, 128, 152, 154, 158-159, 166-167, 170, 174-176, 183, 230, 242-246, 352
Reese, Tom, 17-18, 44, 46, 258
Responsibility [& Accountability], 312, 323
Ringo, Jim, 77, 80, 82
Riso, Don, 263

Robbins, Anthony, 217
Robinson, Greg, 194
Rogers, Carl, 260, 307, 334
Ross, Bobby, 207
Rotella, Bob, 217
Royer, Jim, 84-85, 107, 127, 129, 195, 199
Rozelle, Pete, 89
Ryan, [Father Ryan H.S.], 15, 19-21, 26, 28, 31-32, 43, 235-236
Ruiz, Don Miguel, 340, 344
Ruminating [vs. Processing], 314

Saban, Lou, 68-69, 72, 77, 194
Sandler, Adam, 330
Savoring, 295, 401-402
Schwartz, Jeffery, 346
Scott, Brad, 186, 191, 211, 217
Scotoma, 222, 266-267
Sekanovich, Dan, 109
Self-Talk [Cycle], 227, 285-286, 345-346
Seligman, Martin, 275, 307, 325
Serenity Prayer, 279, 317, 390
Seymour, Jim, 35
SG [Bob's ex], 5, 10, 19, 25, 28-29, 38-39, 41, 43-62, 68-72, 76-77, 82, 86-87, 91, 93-96, 98, 100, 113-117, 119-125, 129, 137, 142, 146-147, 151-159, 161-163, 168-170, 173-176, 195, 202, 204, 206, 215, 230-238, 241, 243, 254-256, 263, 282, 338, 349
Sherman, Ray, 194
Shield's Up [Intervention], xxi
Shula, Don, 103
Simpson, O. J., 56-57, 77
Skinner, Bob, 39-41, 46
Social Interactome, xiii, 356
Snap It! [Intervention], 287-289

St. John of the Cross, 276
Steinberg, Dick, 4, 9, 126-127, 129-130, 132-133, 135-136, 152, 160, 173, 180, 183, 185, 191, 196, 199, 207
Sternberg, Robert, 325
Sunderland, Marv, 188
Sweek, Bill, 47
Sweeny, Jim, 183
Sympathy, 27, 155, 318-319

Tarot, 265-267, 270, 278, 280, 334, 349
Thaler, Richard, 347
Thomas, Waunda, 226
Tice, Lou, 188, 190, 217, 221-223, 225, 227, 281, 285, 303, 308
Tolstoy, Leo, 306
Toon, Al, 176-178, 183, 212

Unconditional Positive Regard, 334-335
Undo Effect, 295
'US' [The Story of], 335

Vaske, Dennis, 214
VIA Character Strengths, 305
Virtues [vs. Issues], 321
Visualization, 133, 181, 187, 217, 219, 281-283, 290-292, 317, 391-392, 394-395, 397

Young, Lonnie, 184
Yukica, Joe, 62

Walker, Wesley, 83-84, 97
Wallowing in Positivity, 347-348
Walton, Joe [J-Dub], 109, 113, 124-125, 131, 152
Ward, Al, 81, 84, 89
White, Reggie, 184

WIIFIM? [What's In It For Me?], 303-304
Wilkinson, Bruce, 350
Williams, Jim, 4, 198-199
Williams, Perry, 193
Williams, Serena, 292
Winner's Mentality Program, 219, 221, 281
Who You Am!, 257-258, 268, 312, 323
Wolf, Ron, 180, 184
Wooden, John, 47, 269

Zigglar, Zig, 217
Zinsser, Nate, 186-187, 191, 211, 217

CPSIA information can be obtained
at www.ICGtesting.com
Printed in the USA
FSHW011643051218
54260FS